Not so bad

Vol. 1

E.Hae

NETCOMICS

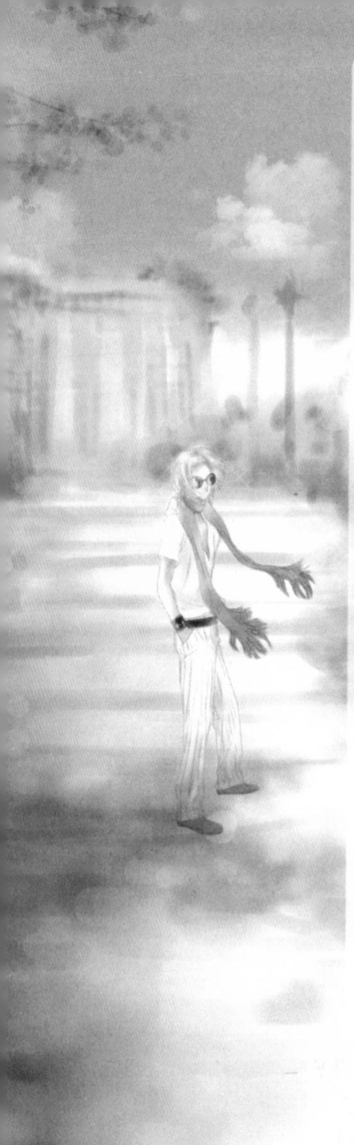

Not So Bad Vol. 1

Story and Art by E.Hae

English translation rights in USA, Canada, UK, NZ, Australia arranged by
Ecomix Media Company
395-21 Seogyo-dong, Mapo-gu, Seoul, Korea 121-840
info@ecomixmedia.com

- Produced by **Ecomix Media Company**
- Translator Jeffrey Yi
- Pre-Press Manager Yesook Ahn
- Graphic Designer Eunsoon Cheon
- Editor Wanda Albano
- Managing Editor Soyoung Jung
- President & Publisher Heewoon Chung

NETCOMICS

P.O. Box 3036, Jersey City, NJ 07303-3036
info@netcomics.com
www.NETCOMICS.com

This is a fictional work.
Any resemblance to actual events or locales or persons, living or dead, is entirely coincidental.

ISBN: 1-60009-055-9

Second printing: August 2007
10 9 8 7 6 5 4 3 2
Printed in Korea

Hello! My name is E.Hae.

My heart is pounding at the thought of having my work published
in a foreign language. I hope many will read my book.

My interests as a writer are more geared towards the characters' emotions
and mental states rather than certain incidents or stories.
I look at the kind of relationship that a person creates when he meets
another person. My hope and task is for that relationship, whether it's
between soul mates, families, or temporary lovers who are merely passing by,
to continue being sweet and constructive kind of human love,
and as much as possible, not destructive to humanity.

Of course, when it comes to the art, the real issue is do I draw as well as
I wish? What I draw really is quite different from what I have in my mind.
I pluck the hairs from my face every time I have to work between
what's inside my head and what my hand actually creates.
So, my conclusion is, well... I pat myself on the back and tell myself that skills aren't
something that you can accumulate in a day, and just live my daily life fleeing from the
problem. (But then there will be no artistic progress!) (Laughing)
I may be something of a dull-witted artist,
but please give me lots of love all the same.
I will appreciate your steady interest and criticism.

Constellation: Virgo
Blood type: AB

Contents

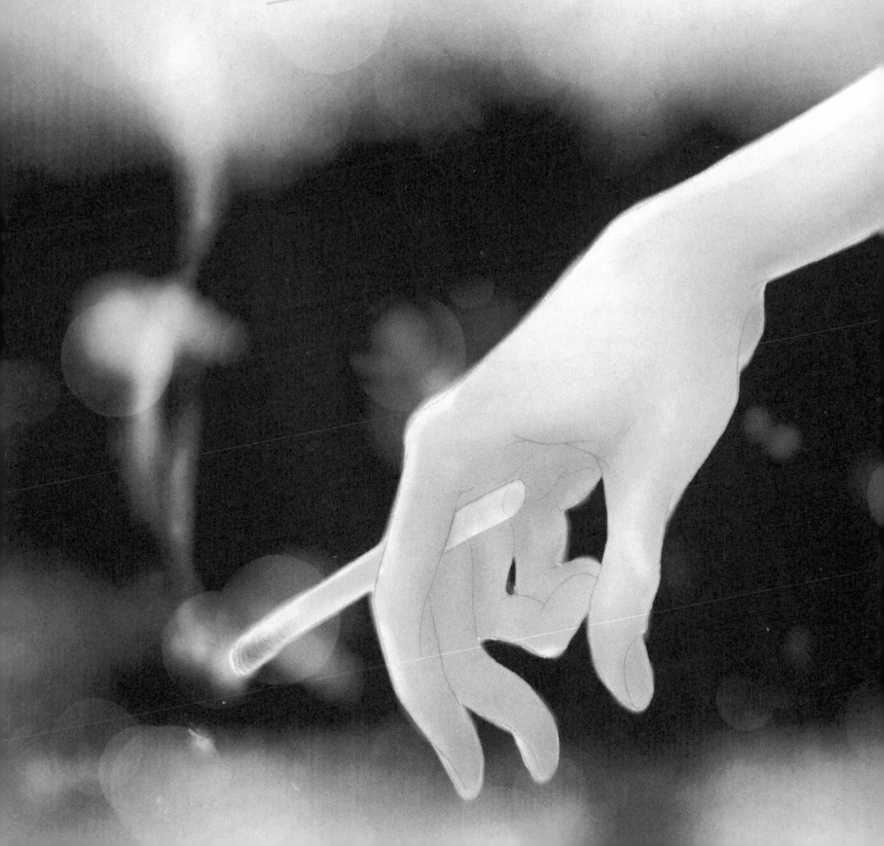

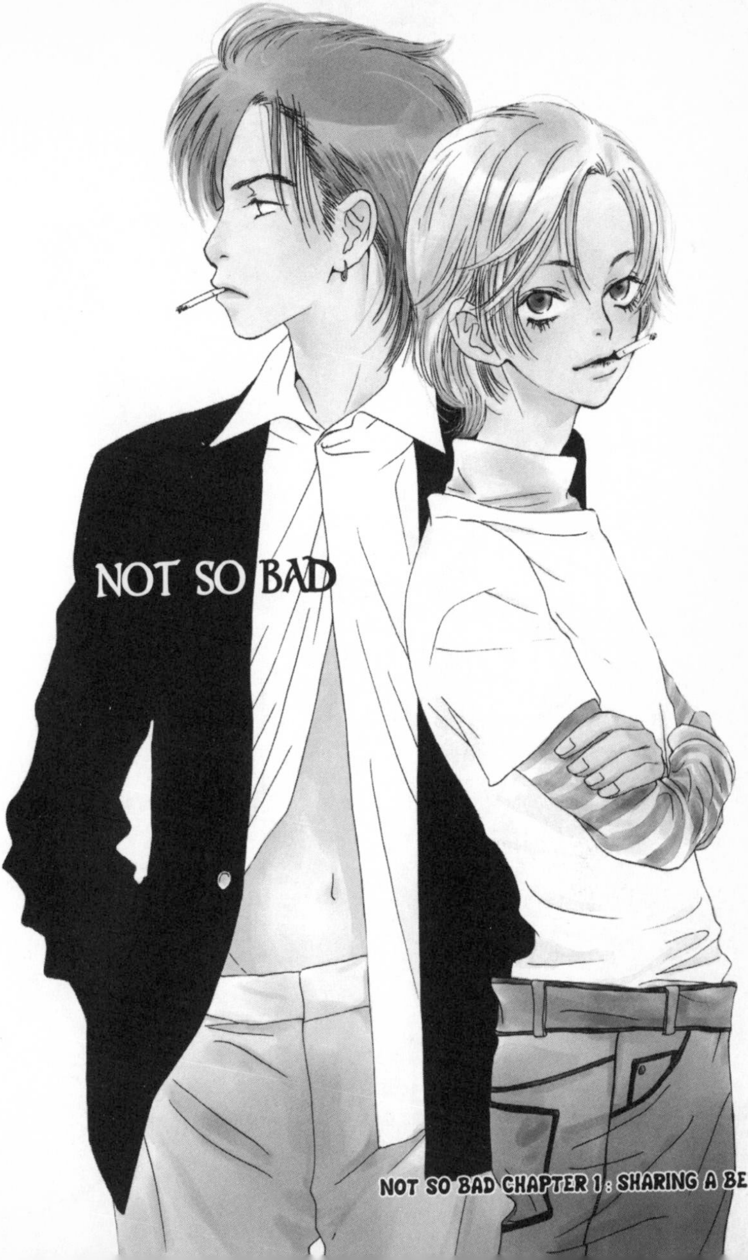
NOT SO BAD
NOT SO BAD CHAPTER 1 : SHARING A BED

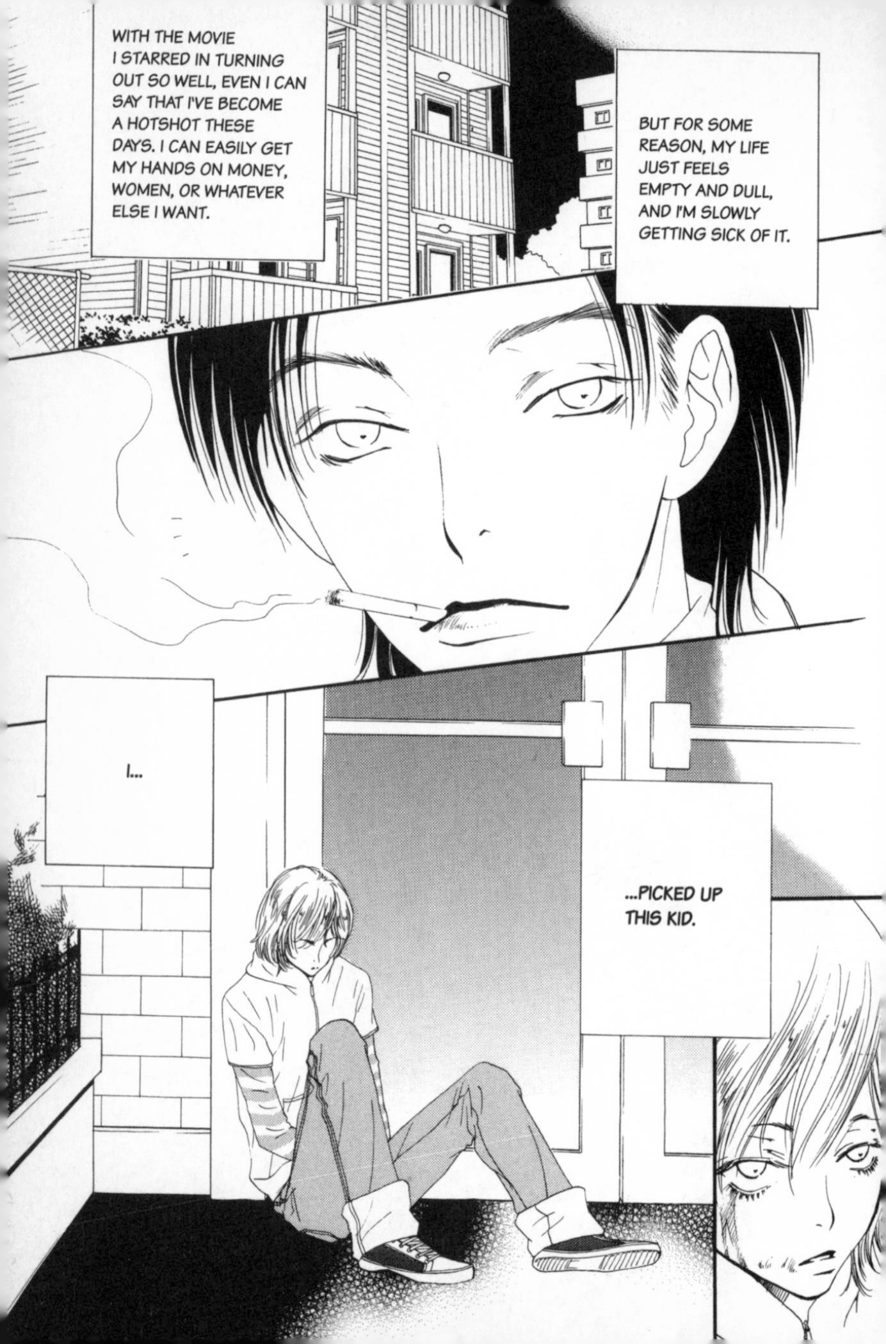
WITH THE MOVIE I STARRED IN TURNING OUT SO WELL, EVEN I CAN SAY THAT I'VE BECOME A HOTSHOT THESE DAYS. I CAN EASILY GET MY HANDS ON MONEY, WOMEN, OR WHATEVER ELSE I WANT.
BUT FOR SOME REASON, MY LIFE JUST FEELS EMPTY AND DULL, AND I'M SLOWLY GETTING SICK OF IT.
I...
...PICKED UP THIS KID.

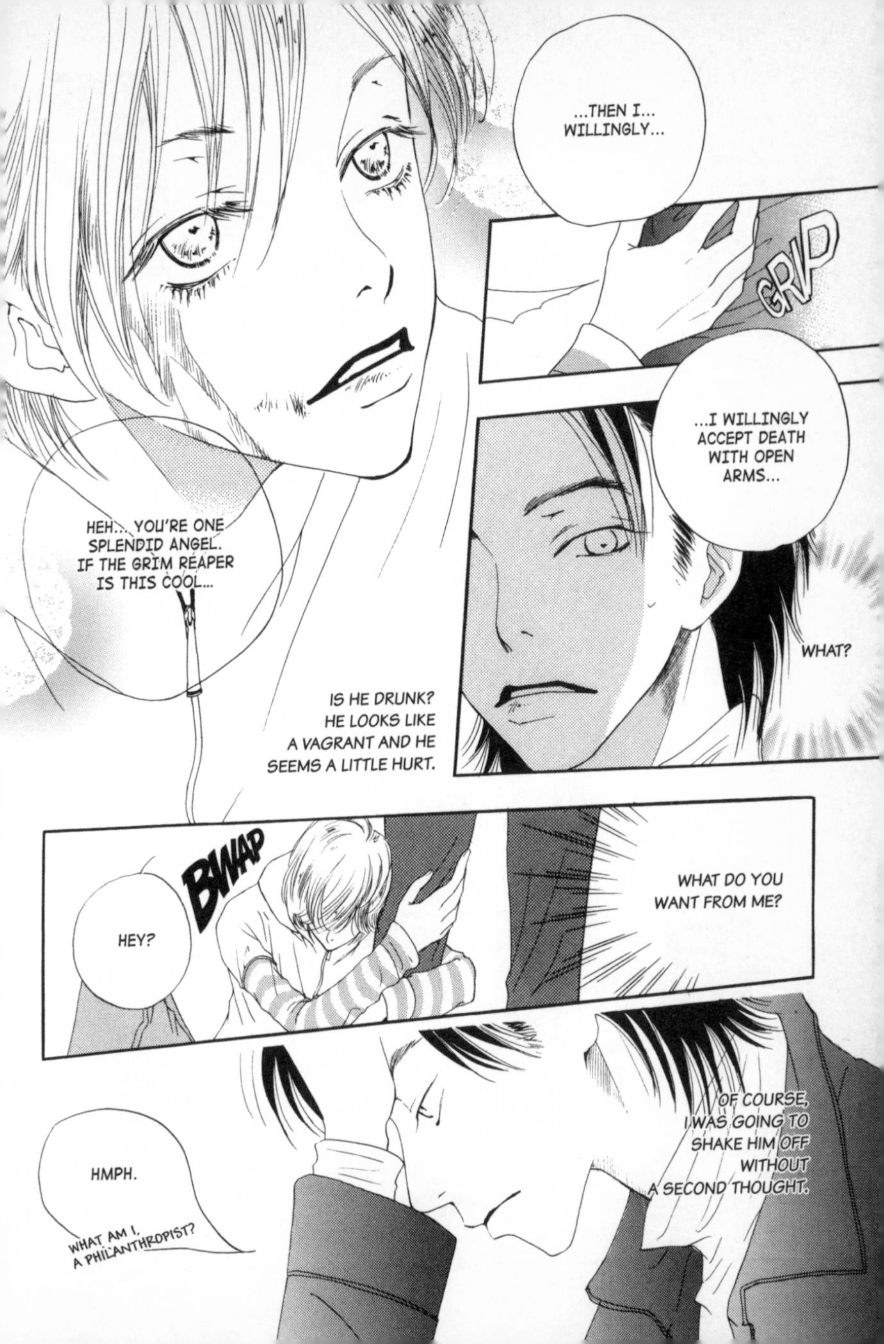
HEH... YOU'RE ONE SPLENDID ANGEL. IF THE GRIM REAPER IS THIS COOL...
...THEN I... WILLINGLY...
GRIP
...I WILLINGLY ACCEPT DEATH WITH OPEN ARMS...
WHAT?
IS HE DRUNK? HE LOOKS LIKE A VAGRANT AND HE SEEMS A LITTLE HURT.
BWAP
WHAT DO YOU WANT FROM ME?
HEY?
OF COURSE, I WAS GOING TO SHAKE HIM OFF WITHOUT A SECOND THOUGHT.
HMPH.
WHAT AM I, A PHILANTHROPIST?

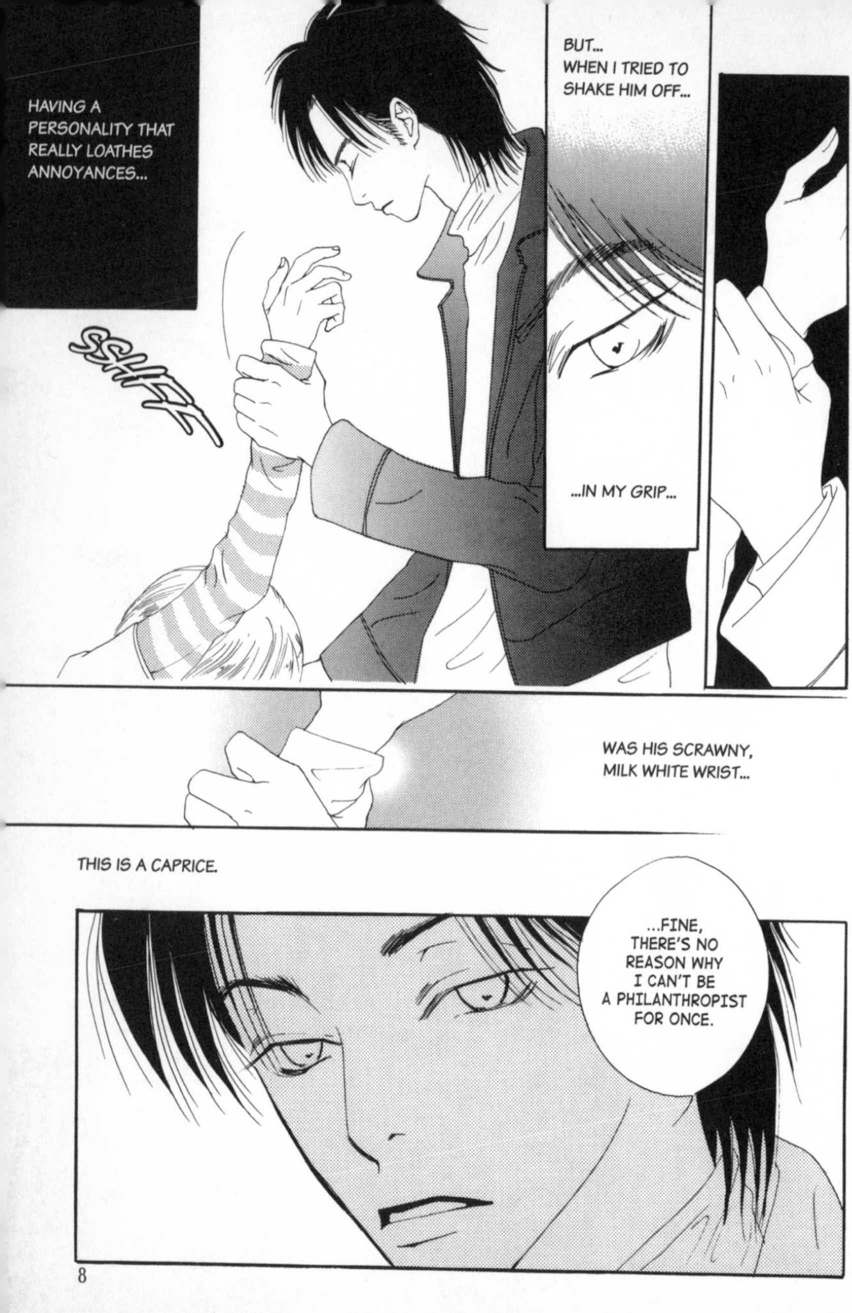
HAVING A PERSONALITY THAT REALLY LOATHES ANNOYANCES...
SSHFF
BUT... WHEN I TRIED TO SHAKE HIM OFF...
...IN MY GRIP...
WAS HIS SCRAWNY, MILK WHITE WRIST...
THIS IS A CAPRICE.
...FINE, THERE'S NO REASON WHY I CAN'T BE A PHILANTHROPIST FOR ONCE.

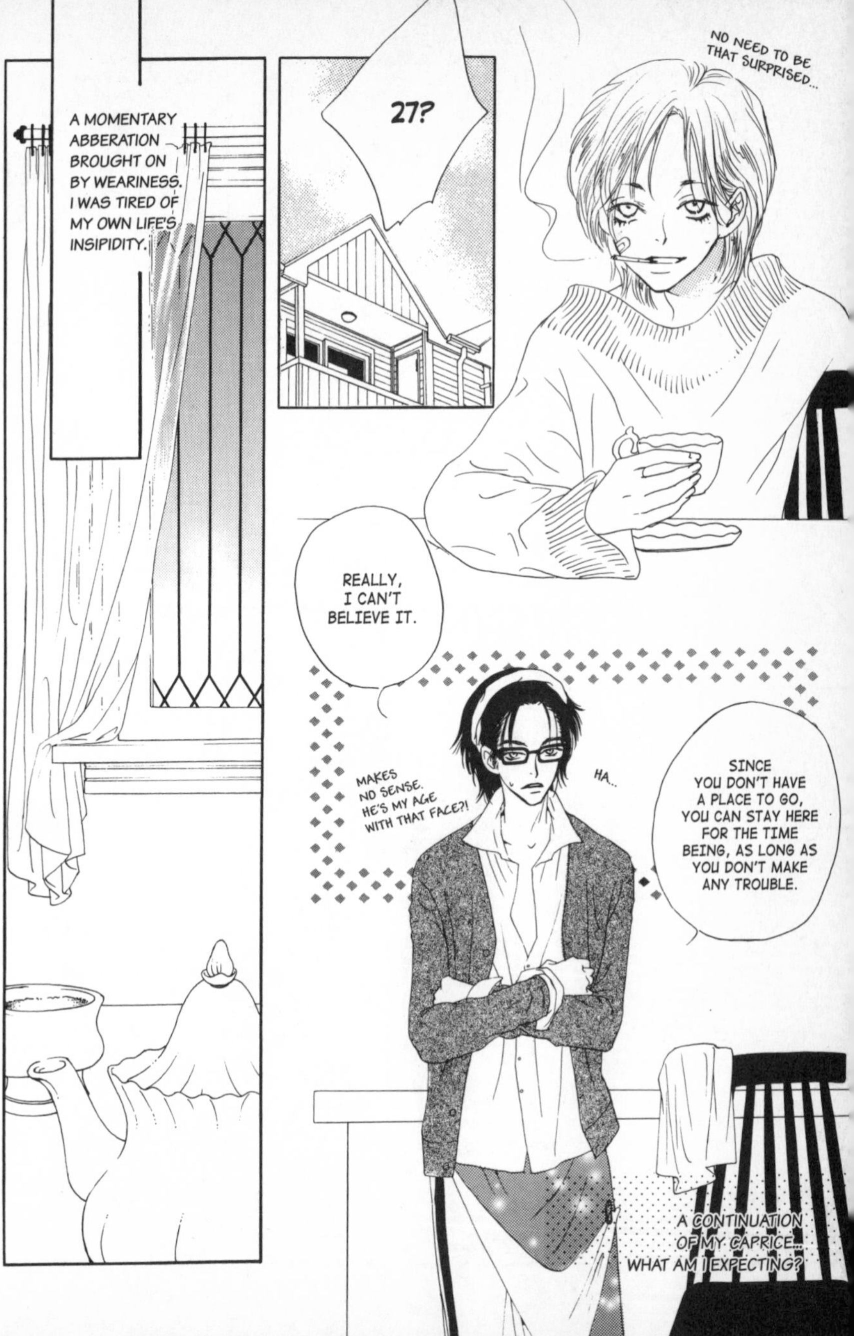
NO NEED TO BE THAT SURPRISED...
27?
A MOMENTARY ABBERATION BROUGHT ON BY WEARINESS. I WAS TIRED OF MY OWN LIFE'S INSIPIDITY.
REALLY, I CAN'T BELIEVE IT.
SINCE YOU DON'T HAVE A PLACE TO GO, YOU CAN STAY HERE FOR THE TIME BEING, AS LONG AS YOU DON'T MAKE ANY TROUBLE.
HA..
MAKES NO SENSE. HE'S MY AGE WITH THAT FACE?!
A CONTINUATION OF MY CAPRICE... WHAT AM I EXPECTING?

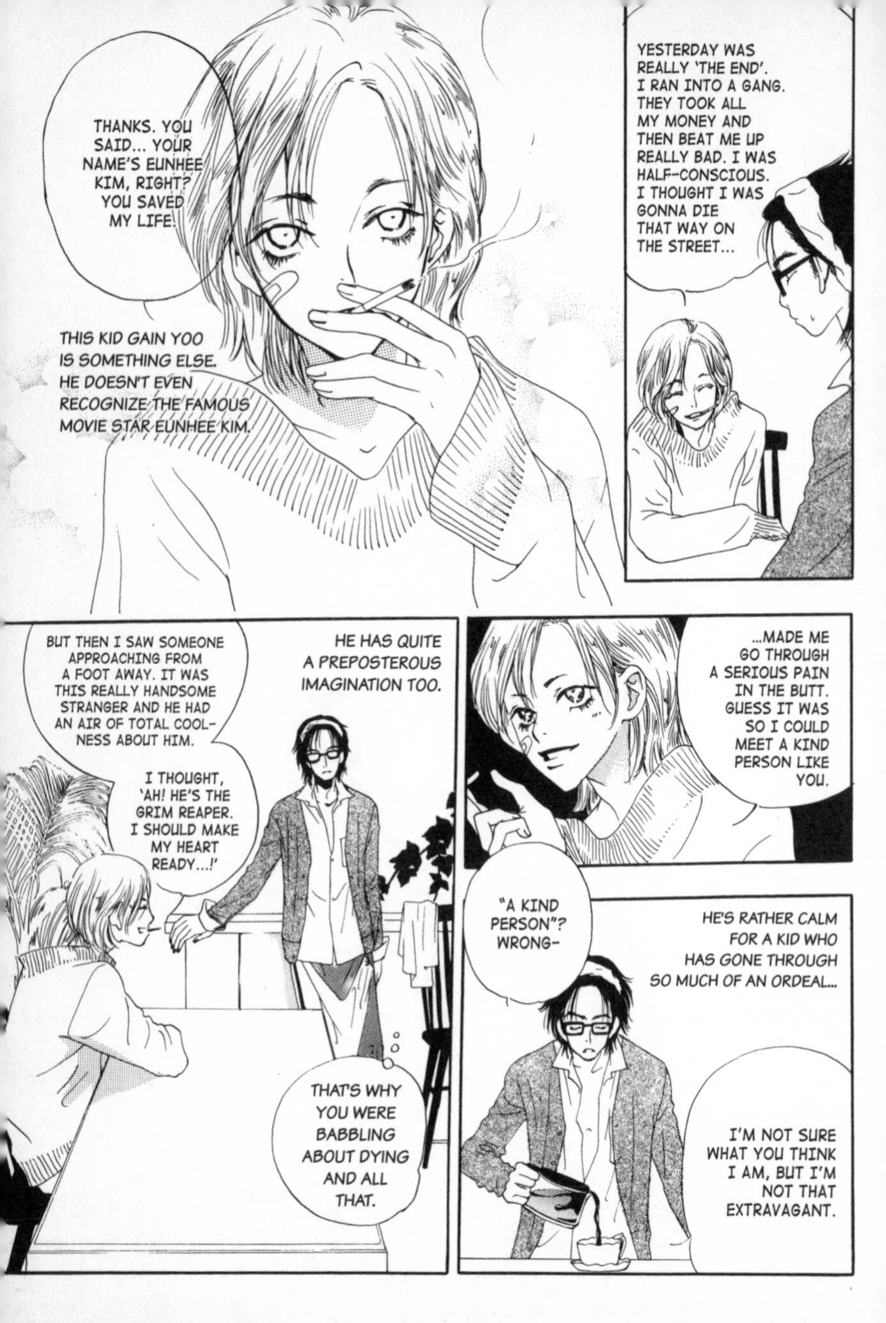
THANKS. YOU SAID... YOUR NAME'S EUNHEE KIM, RIGHT? YOU SAVED MY LIFE.
THIS KID GAIN YOO IS SOMETHING ELSE. HE DOESN'T EVEN RECOGNIZE THE FAMOUS MOVIE STAR EUNHEE KIM.
YESTERDAY WAS REALLY 'THE END'. I RAN INTO A GANG. THEY TOOK ALL MY MONEY AND THEN BEAT ME UP REALLY BAD. I WAS HALF-CONSCIOUS. I THOUGHT I WAS GONNA DIE THAT WAY ON THE STREET...
BUT THEN I SAW SOMEONE APPROACHING FROM A FOOT AWAY. IT WAS THIS REALLY HANDSOME STRANGER AND HE HAD AN AIR OF TOTAL COOL-NESS ABOUT HIM.
I THOUGHT, 'AH! HE'S THE GRIM REAPER. I SHOULD MAKE MY HEART READY...!'
HE HAS QUITE A PREPOSTEROUS IMAGINATION TOO.
THAT'S WHY YOU WERE BABBLING ABOUT DYING AND ALL THAT.
...MADE ME GO THROUGH A SERIOUS PAIN IN THE BUTT. GUESS IT WAS SO I COULD MEET A KIND PERSON LIKE YOU.
"A KIND PERSON"? WRONG-
HE'S RATHER CALM FOR A KID WHO HAS GONE THROUGH SO MUCH OF AN ORDEAL...
I'M NOT SURE WHAT YOU THINK I AM, BUT I'M NOT THAT EXTRAVAGANT.

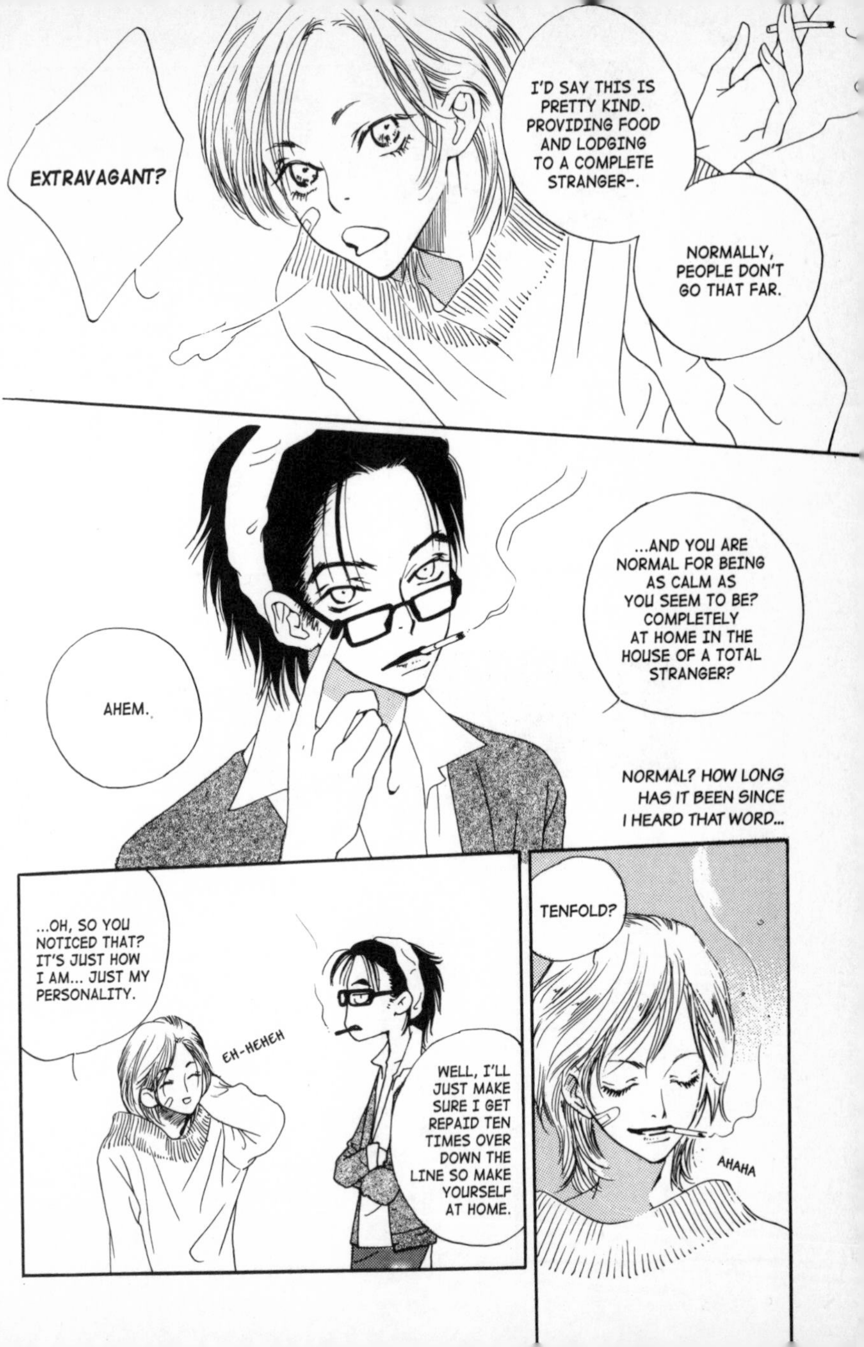
EXTRAVAGANT?
I'D SAY THIS IS PRETTY KIND. PROVIDING FOOD AND LODGING TO A COMPLETE STRANGER-.
NORMALLY, PEOPLE DON'T GO THAT FAR.
AHEM.
...AND YOU ARE NORMAL FOR BEING AS CALM AS YOU SEEM TO BE? COMPLETELY AT HOME IN THE HOUSE OF A TOTAL STRANGER?
NORMAL? HOW LONG HAS IT BEEN SINCE I HEARD THAT WORD...
...OH, SO YOU NOTICED THAT? IT'S JUST HOW I AM... JUST MY PERSONALITY.
EH-HEHEH
WELL, I'LL JUST MAKE SURE I GET REPAID TEN TIMES OVER DOWN THE LINE SO MAKE YOURSELF AT HOME.
TENFOLD?
AHAHA

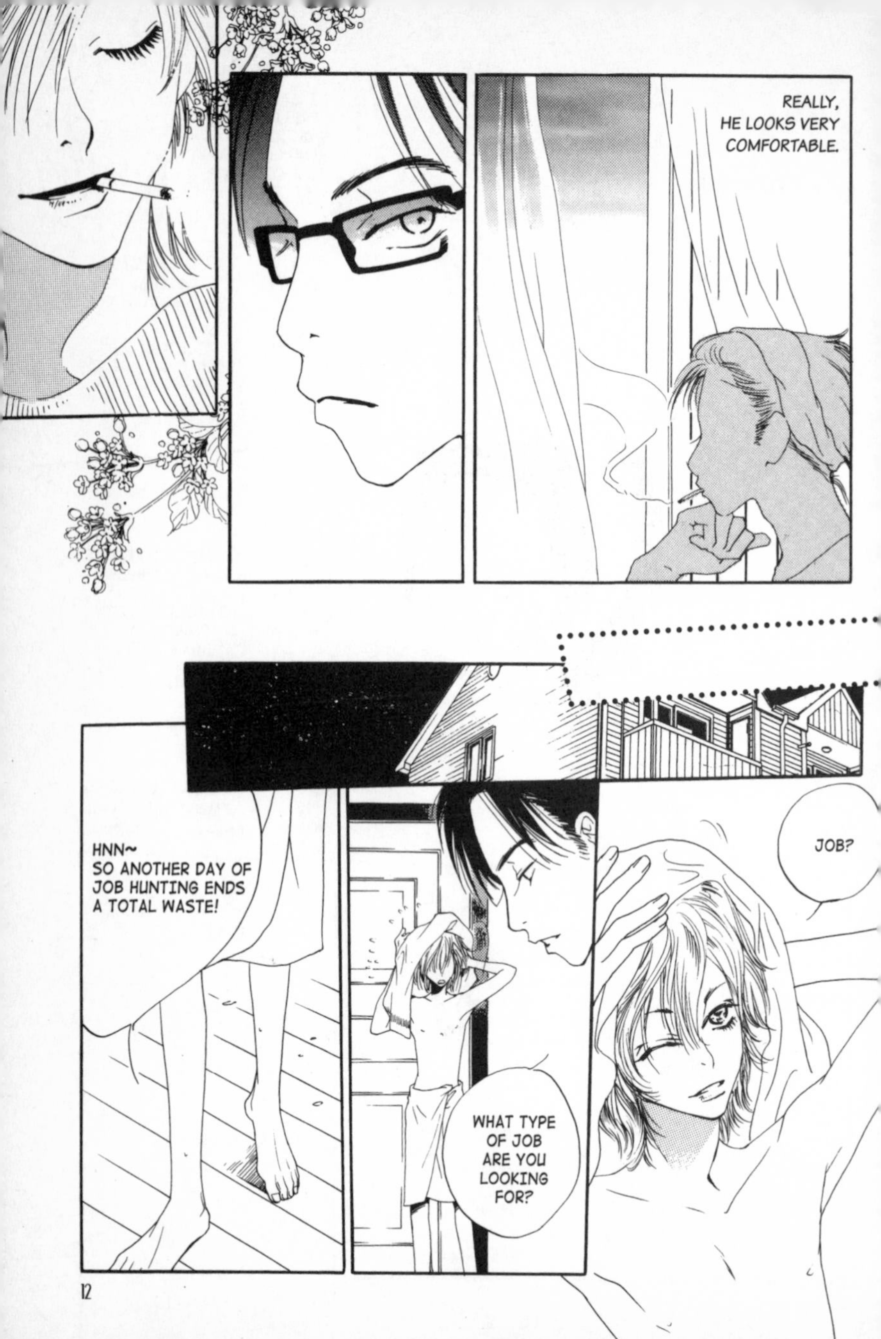
REALLY, HE LOOKS VERY COMFORTABLE.
HNN~ SO ANOTHER DAY OF JOB HUNTING ENDS A TOTAL WASTE!
JOB?
WHAT TYPE OF JOB ARE YOU LOOKING FOR?

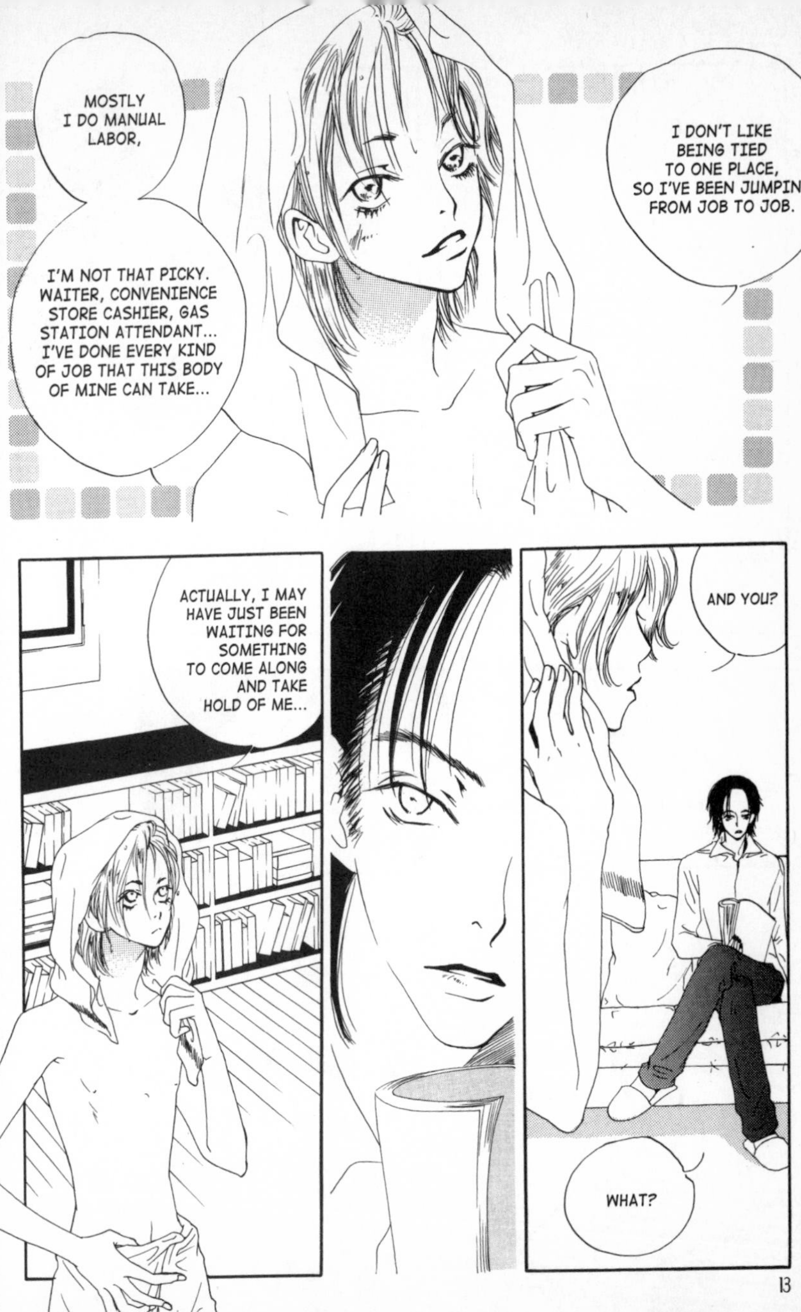
I DON'T LIKE BEING TIED TO ONE PLACE, SO I'VE BEEN JUMPING FROM JOB TO JOB.
MOSTLY I DO MANUAL LABOR,
I'M NOT THAT PICKY. WAITER, CONVENIENCE STORE CASHIER, GAS STATION ATTENDANT... I'VE DONE EVERY KIND OF JOB THAT THIS BODY OF MINE CAN TAKE...
AND YOU?
WHAT?
ACTUALLY, I MAY HAVE JUST BEEN WAITING FOR SOMETHING TO COME ALONG AND TAKE HOLD OF ME...

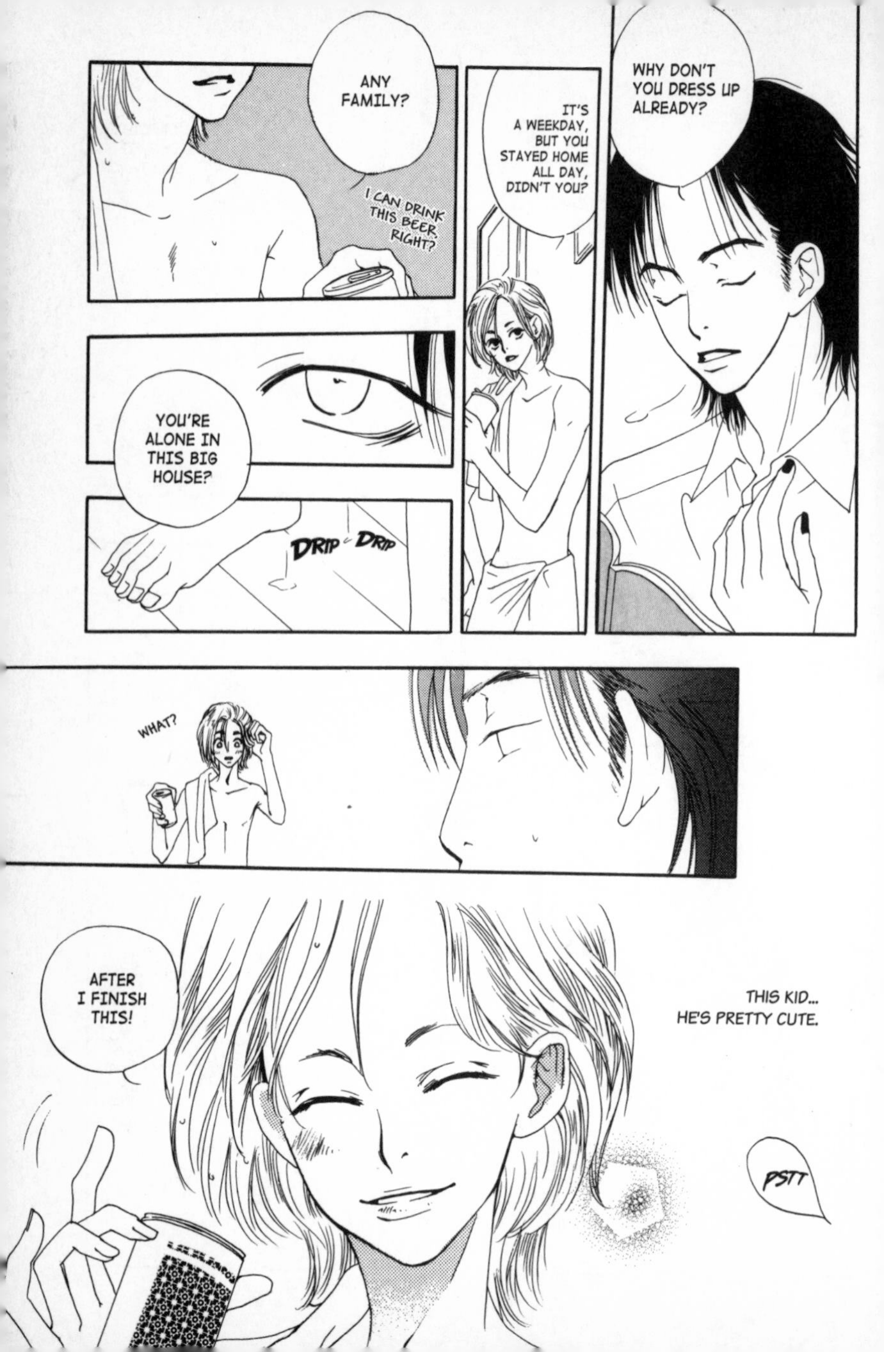
WHY DON'T YOU DRESS UP ALREADY?
IT'S A WEEKDAY, BUT YOU STAYED HOME ALL DAY, DIDN'T YOU?
ANY FAMILY?
I CAN DRINK THIS BEER, RIGHT?
YOU'RE ALONE IN THIS BIG HOUSE?
DRIP DRIP
WHAT?
THIS KID... HE'S PRETTY CUTE.
AFTER I FINISH THIS!
PSTT

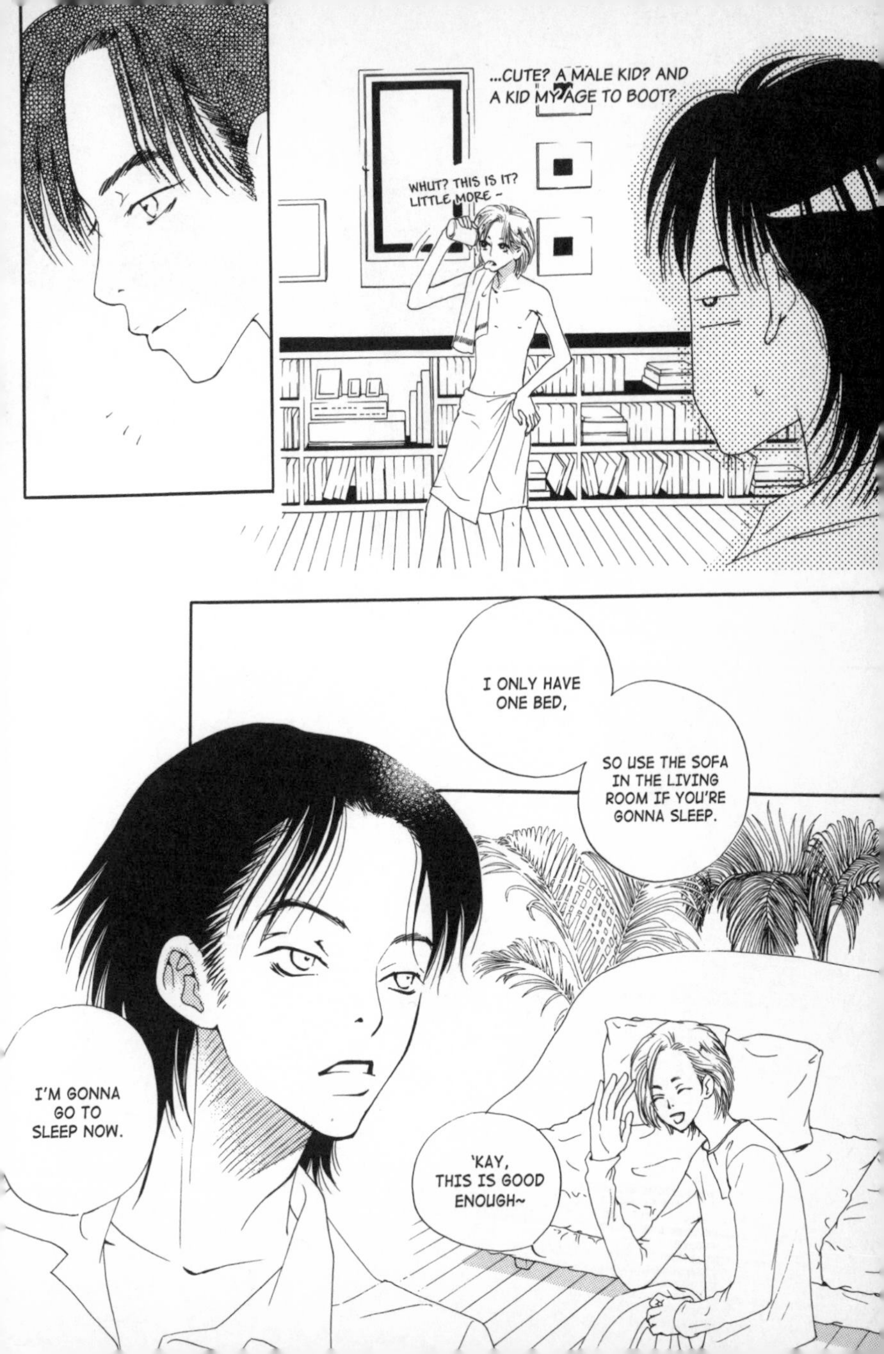
...CUTE? A MALE KID? AND A KID MY AGE TO BOOT?
WHUT? THIS IS IT? LITTLE MORE ~
I ONLY HAVE ONE BED,
SO USE THE SOFA IN THE LIVING ROOM IF YOU'RE GONNA SLEEP.
'KAY, THIS IS GOOD ENOUGH~
I'M GONNA GO TO SLEEP NOW.

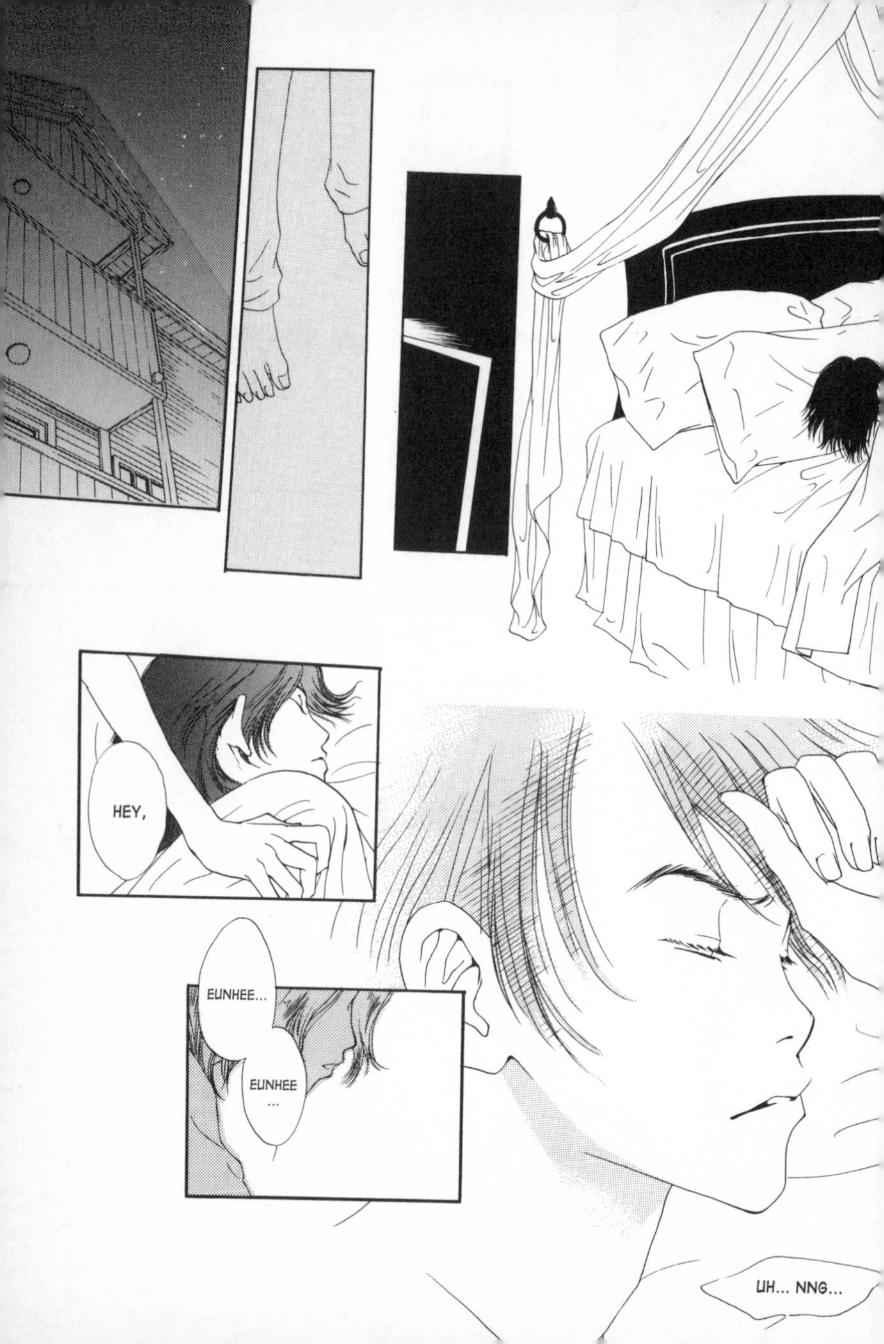
HEY,
EUNHEE...
EUNHEE
...
UH... NNG...

...

WHAT?

EHH...

SORRY
FOR WAKING
YOU UP, BUT...

THE LIVING
ROOM'S COLDER
THAN I EXPECTED.
SORRY, BUT CAN
WE SLEEP
TOGETHER?

...

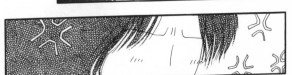

......

...TOGETHER?

......

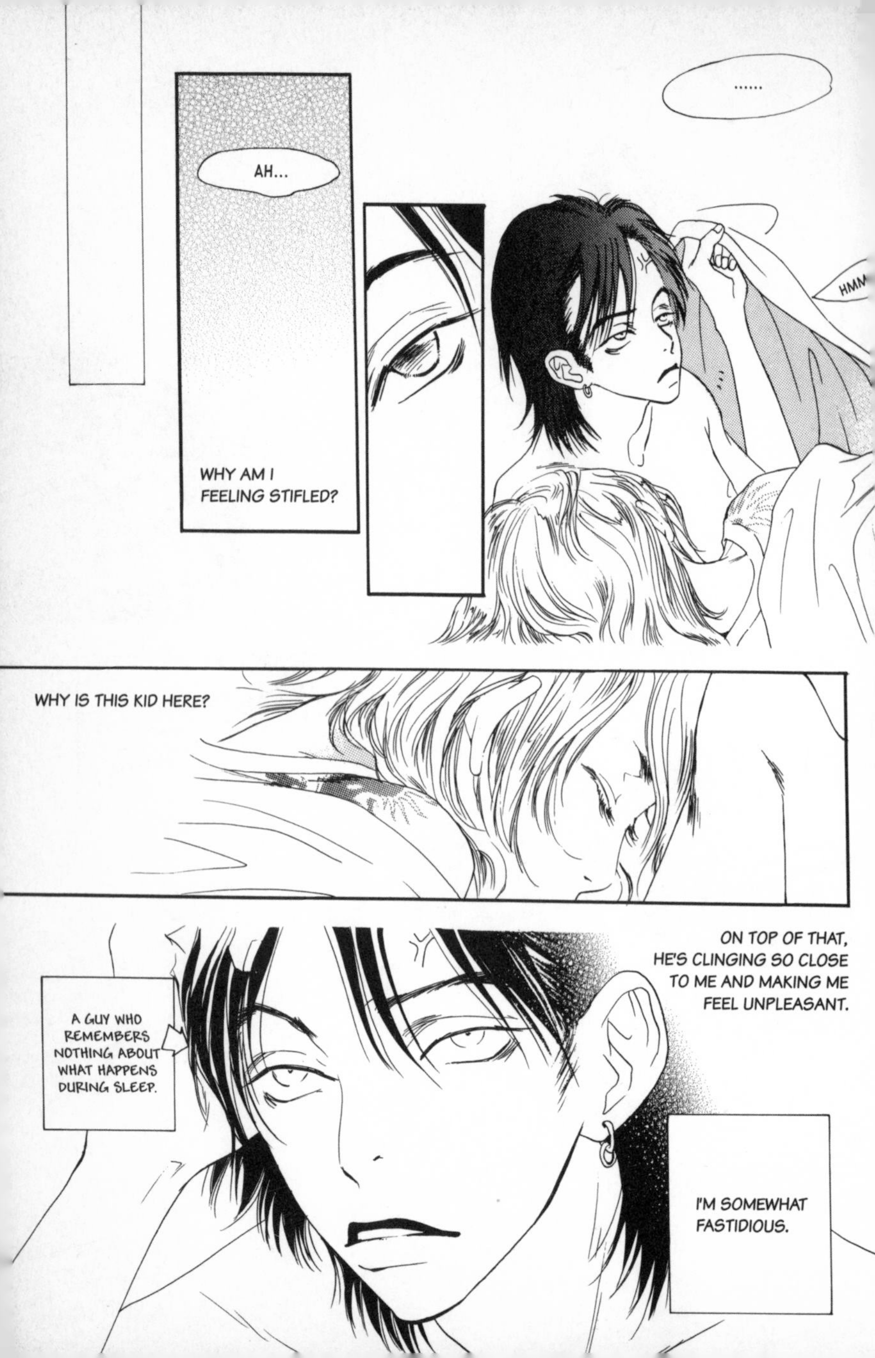
......
AH...
WHY AM I FEELING STIFLED?
HMM
WHY IS THIS KID HERE?
ON TOP OF THAT, HE'S CLINGING SO CLOSE TO ME AND MAKING ME FEEL UNPLEASANT.
I'M SOMEWHAT FASTIDIOUS.
A GUY WHO REMEMBERS NOTHING ABOUT WHAT HAPPENS DURING SLEEP.

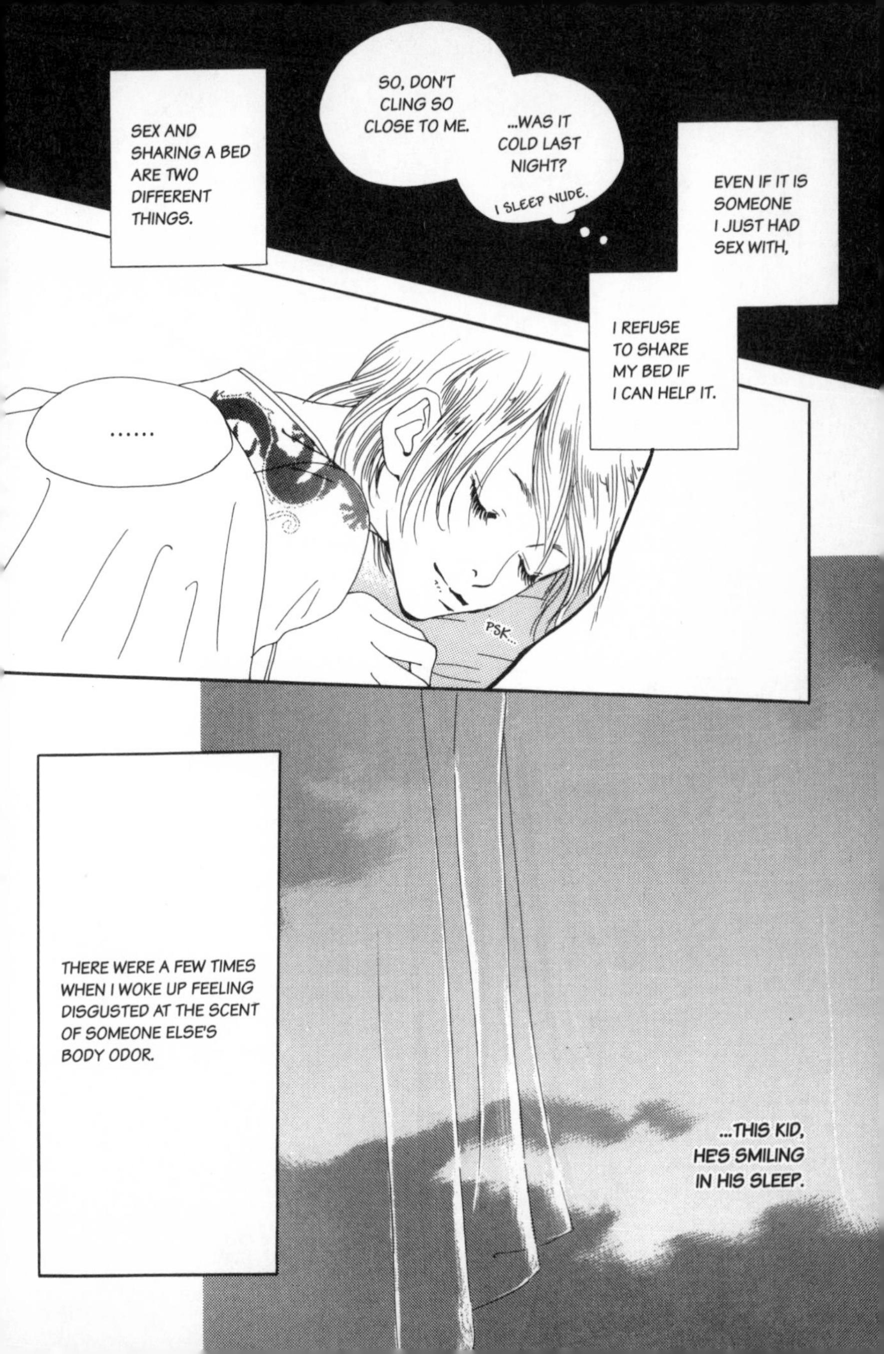
EVEN IF IT IS SOMEONE I JUST HAD SEX WITH,
I REFUSE TO SHARE MY BED IF I CAN HELP IT.
SO, DON'T CLING SO CLOSE TO ME.
...WAS IT COLD LAST NIGHT?
I SLEEP NUDE.
SEX AND SHARING A BED ARE TWO DIFFERENT THINGS.
......
PSK...
...THIS KID, HE'S SMILING IN HIS SLEEP.
THERE WERE A FEW TIMES WHEN I WOKE UP FEELING DISGUSTED AT THE SCENT OF SOMEONE ELSE'S BODY ODOR.

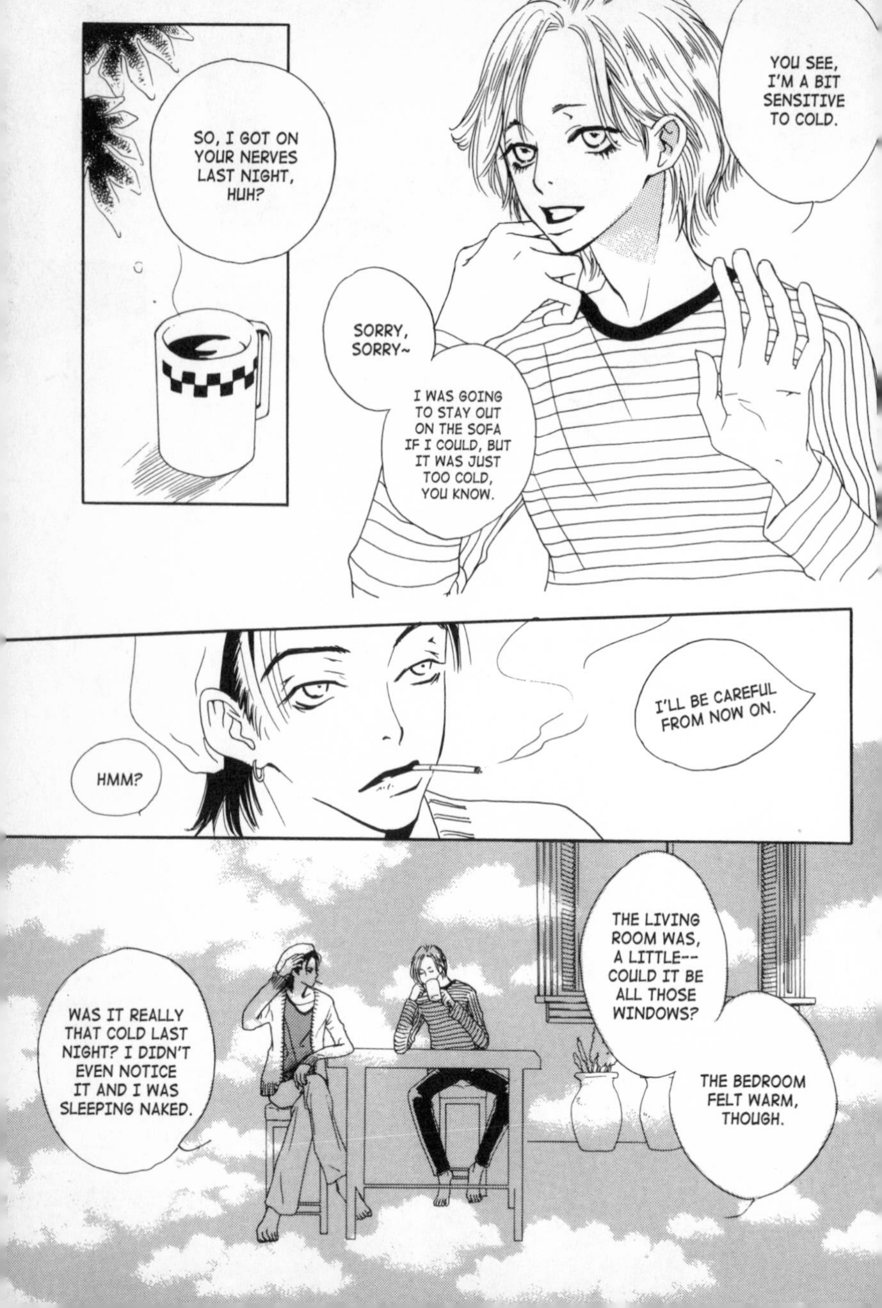
SO, I GOT ON YOUR NERVES LAST NIGHT, HUH?
SORRY, SORRY~
I WAS GOING TO STAY OUT ON THE SOFA IF I COULD, BUT IT WAS JUST TOO COLD, YOU KNOW.
YOU SEE, I'M A BIT SENSITIVE TO COLD.
HMM?
I'LL BE CAREFUL FROM NOW ON.
WAS IT REALLY THAT COLD LAST NIGHT? I DIDN'T EVEN NOTICE IT AND I WAS SLEEPING NAKED.
THE LIVING ROOM WAS, A LITTLE-- COULD IT BE ALL THOSE WINDOWS?
THE BEDROOM FELT WARM, THOUGH.

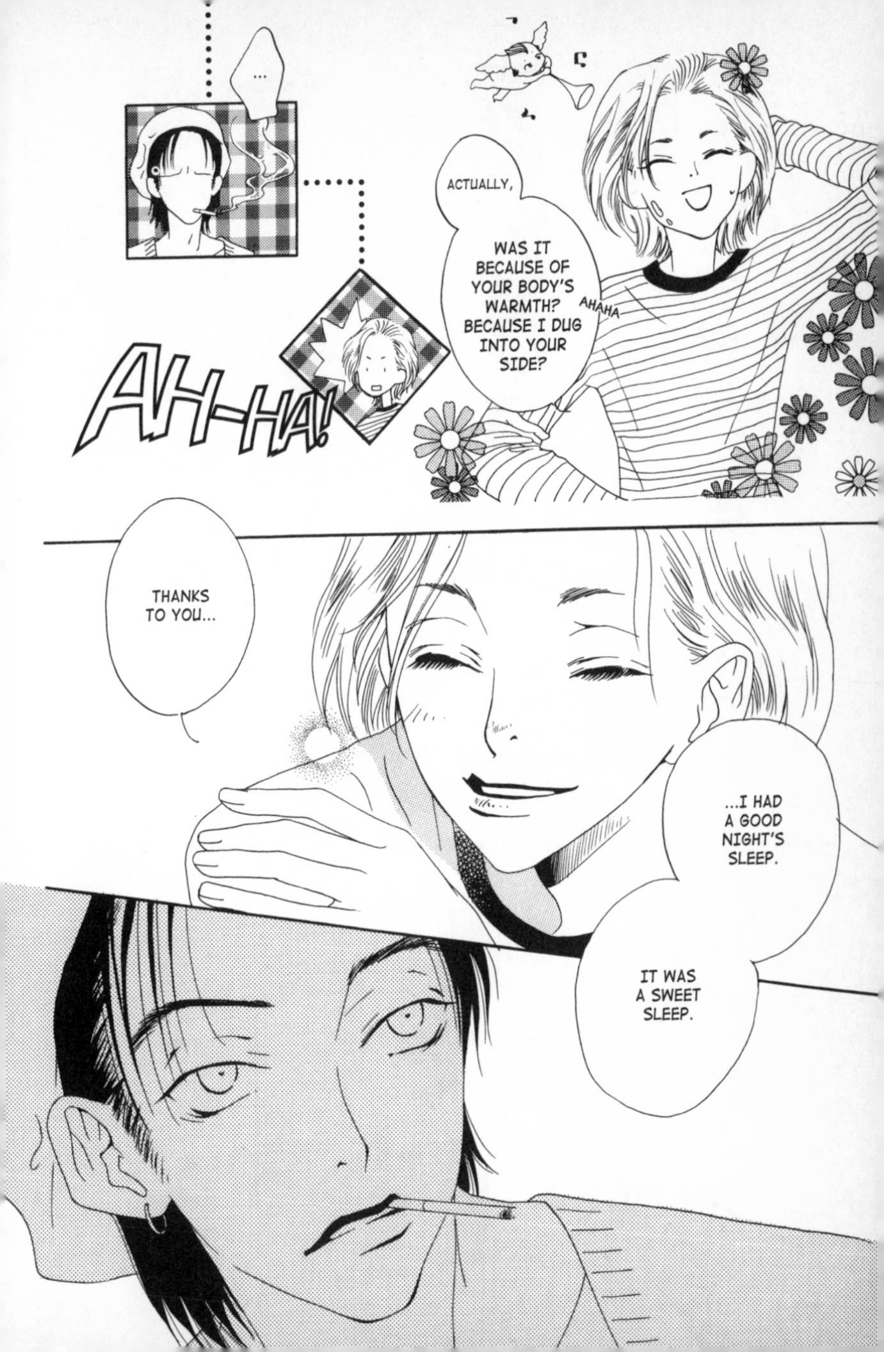

...
ACTUALLY,
WAS IT BECAUSE OF YOUR BODY'S WARMTH? BECAUSE I DUG INTO YOUR SIDE?
AHAHA
AH-HA!
THANKS TO YOU...
...I HAD A GOOD NIGHT'S SLEEP.
IT WAS A SWEET SLEEP.

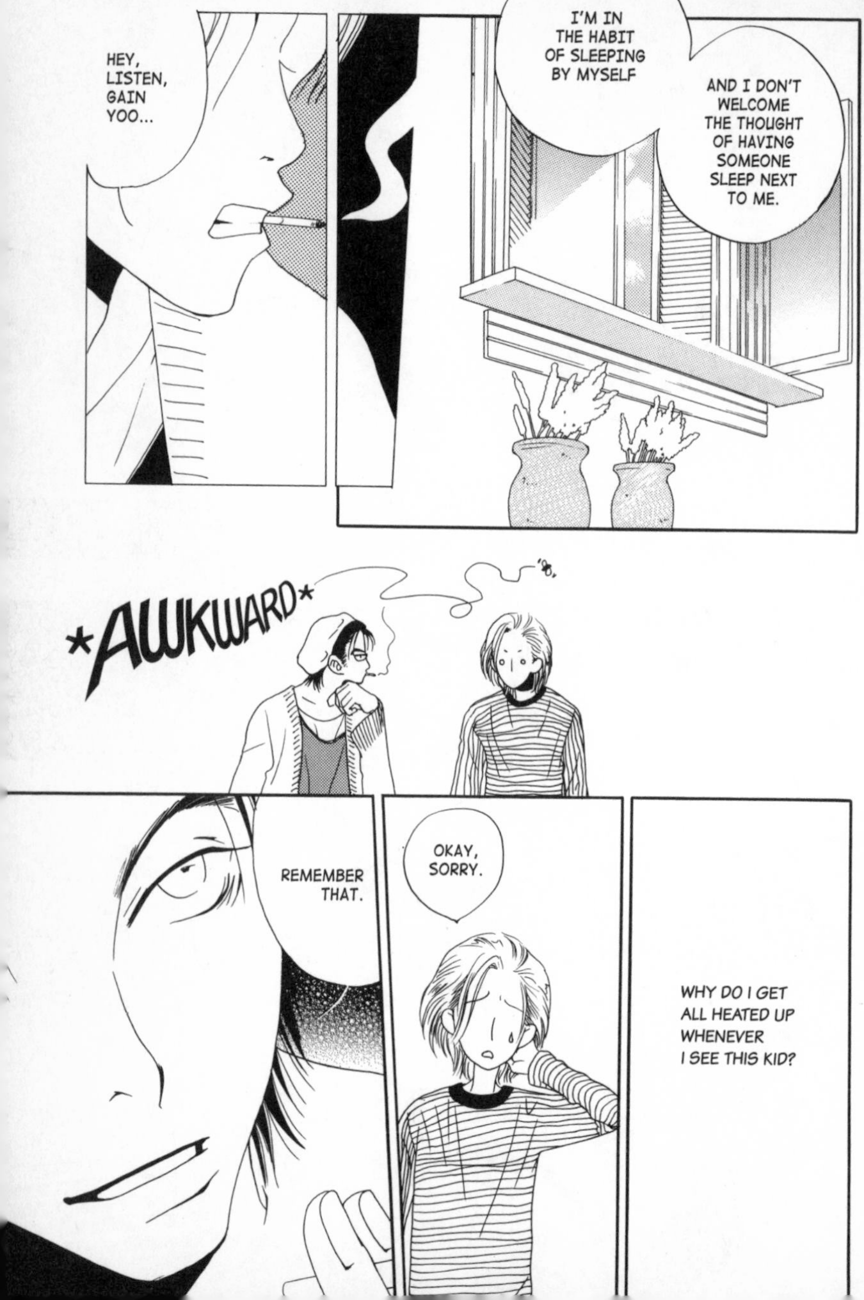
HEY, LISTEN, GAIN YOO...
I'M IN THE HABIT OF SLEEPING BY MYSELF
AND I DON'T WELCOME THE THOUGHT OF HAVING SOMEONE SLEEP NEXT TO ME.
AWKWARD
REMEMBER THAT.
OKAY, SORRY.
WHY DO I GET ALL HEATED UP WHENEVER I SEE THIS KID?

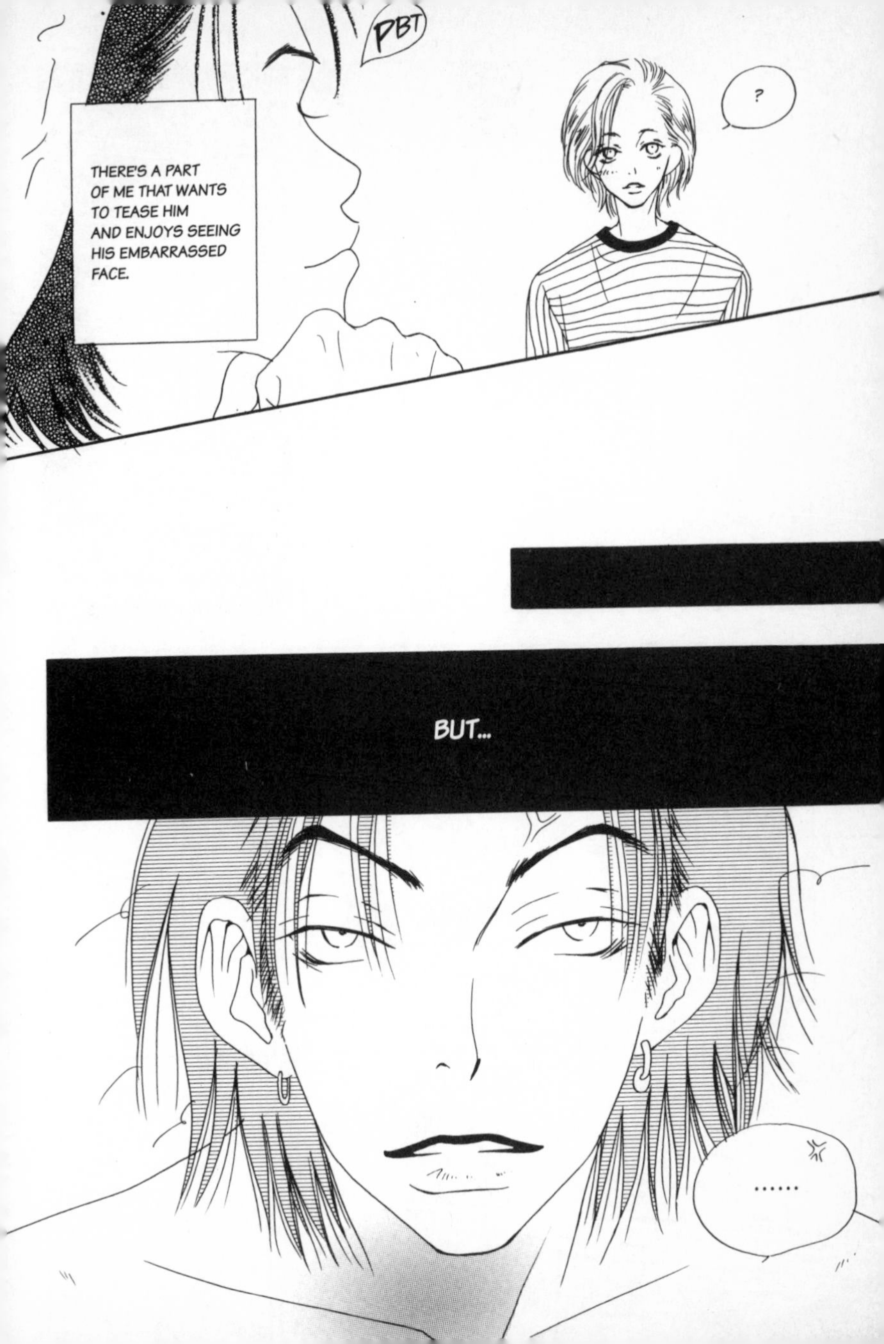
PBT
?
THERE'S A PART OF ME THAT WANTS TO TEASE HIM AND ENJOYS SEEING HIS EMBARRASSED FACE.
BUT...
......

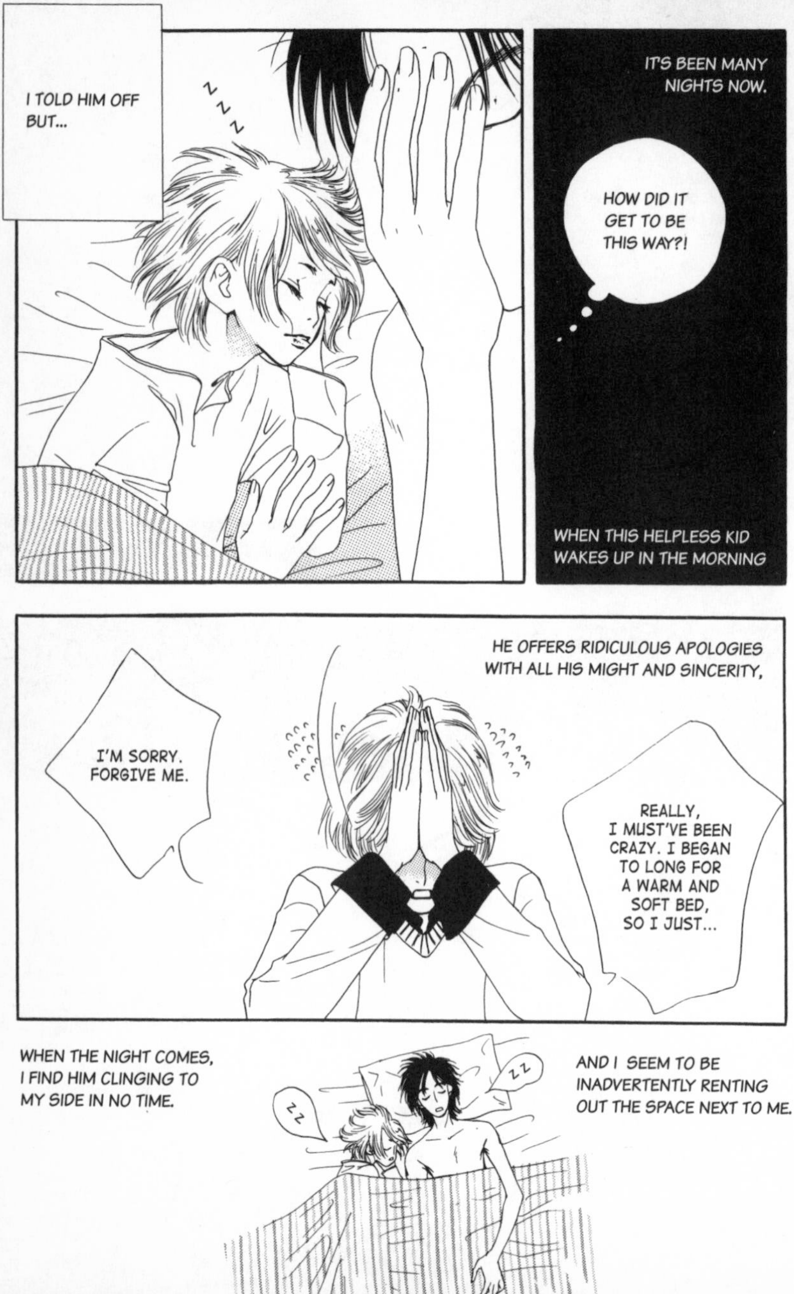
IT'S BEEN MANY NIGHTS NOW.
HOW DID IT GET TO BE THIS WAY?!
WHEN THIS HELPLESS KID WAKES UP IN THE MORNING
I TOLD HIM OFF BUT...
ZZZ
HE OFFERS RIDICULOUS APOLOGIES WITH ALL HIS MIGHT AND SINCERITY,
REALLY, I MUST'VE BEEN CRAZY. I BEGAN TO LONG FOR A WARM AND SOFT BED, SO I JUST...
I'M SORRY. FORGIVE ME.
WHEN THE NIGHT COMES, I FIND HIM CLINGING TO MY SIDE IN NO TIME.
AND I SEEM TO BE INADVERTENTLY RENTING OUT THE SPACE NEXT TO ME.
ZZ
ZZ

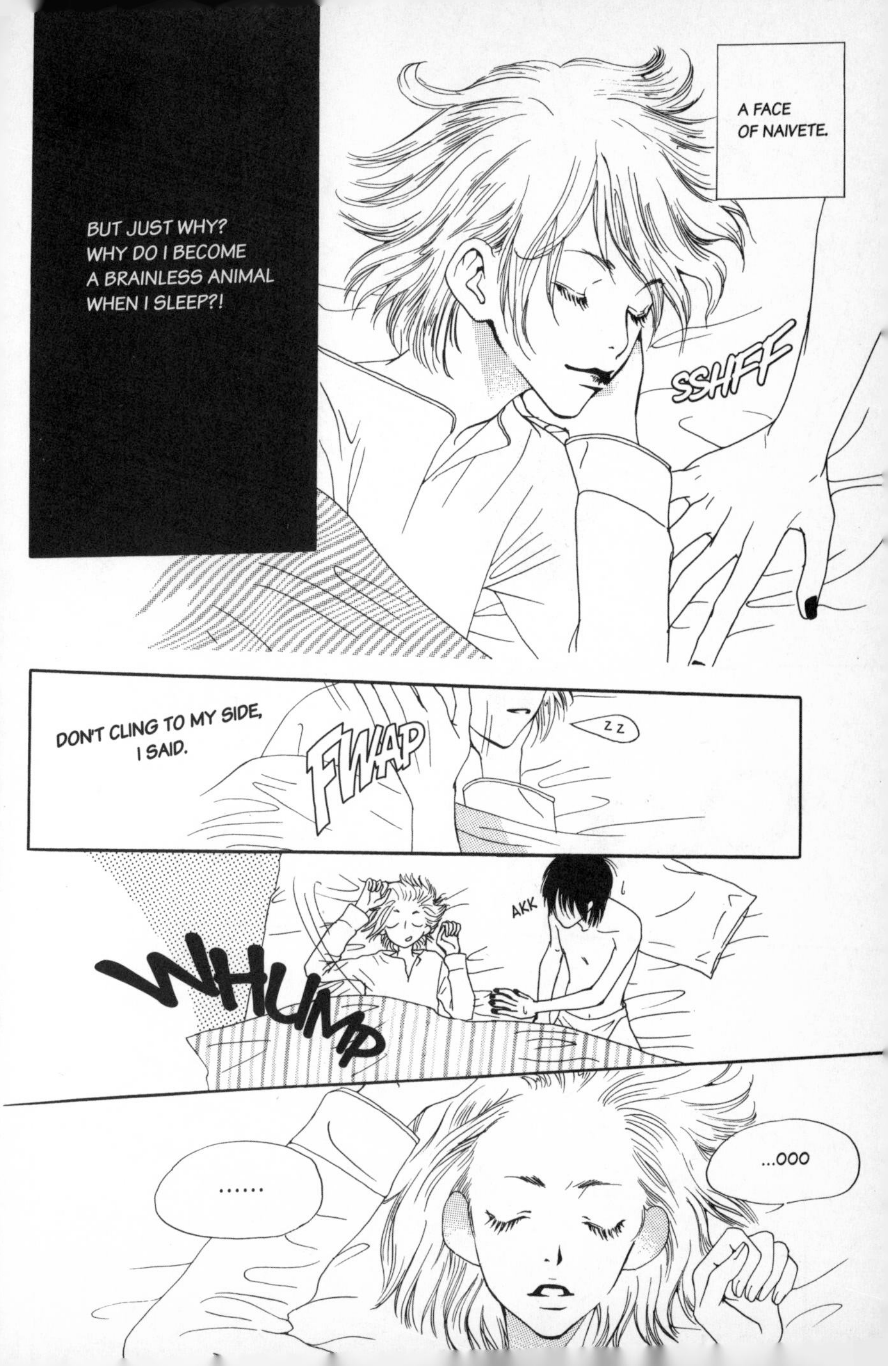
A FACE OF NAIVETE.
BUT JUST WHY? WHY DO I BECOME A BRAINLESS ANIMAL WHEN I SLEEP?!
SSHFF
DON'T CLING TO MY SIDE, I SAID.
FWAP
Z Z
AKK
WHUMP
...OOO
......

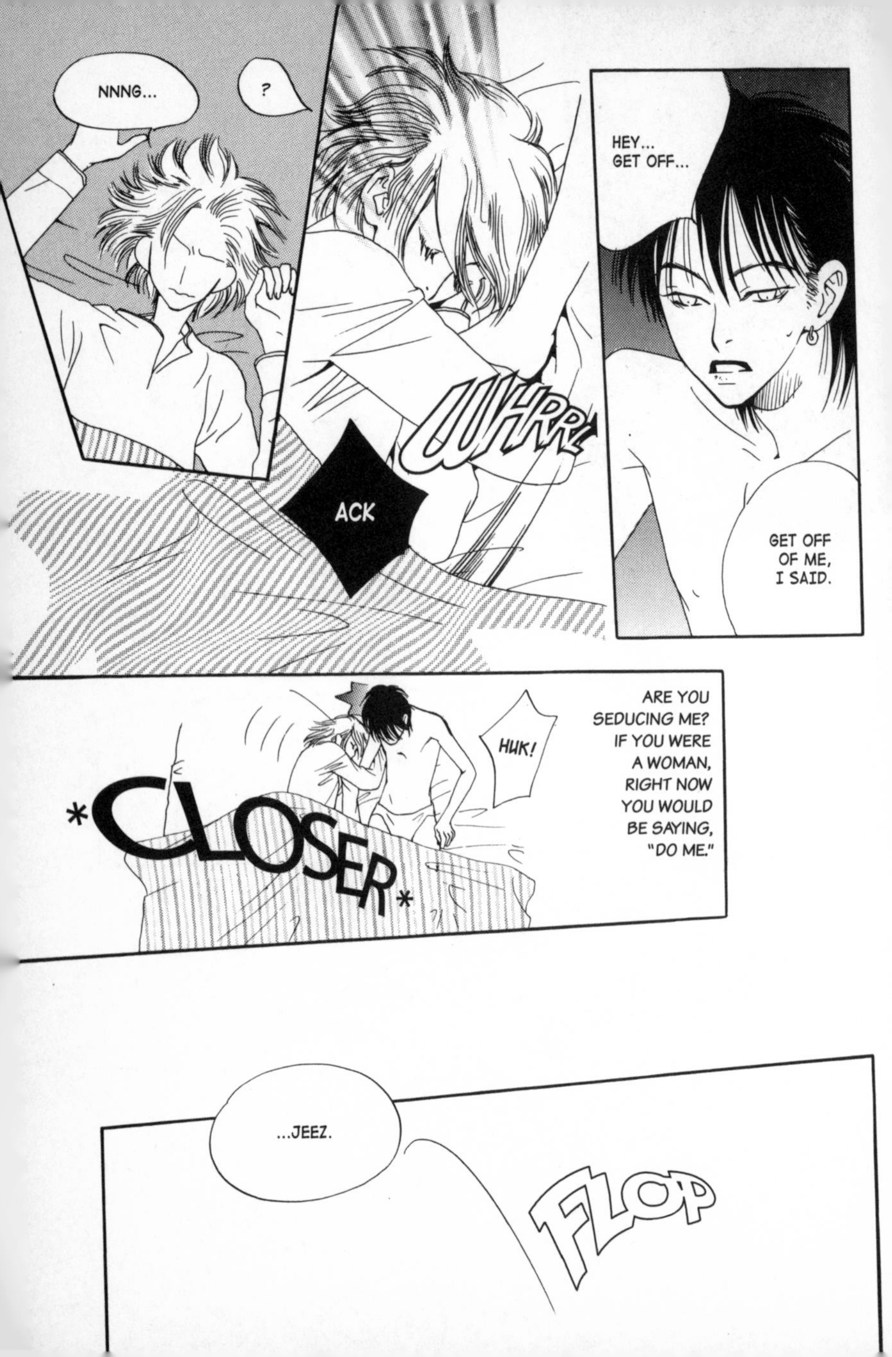
HEY... GET OFF...
GET OFF OF ME, I SAID.
WHRRL
?
NNNG...
ACK
ARE YOU SEDUCING ME? IF YOU WERE A WOMAN, RIGHT NOW YOU WOULD BE SAYING, "DO ME."
HUK!
CLOSER
...JEEZ.
FLOP

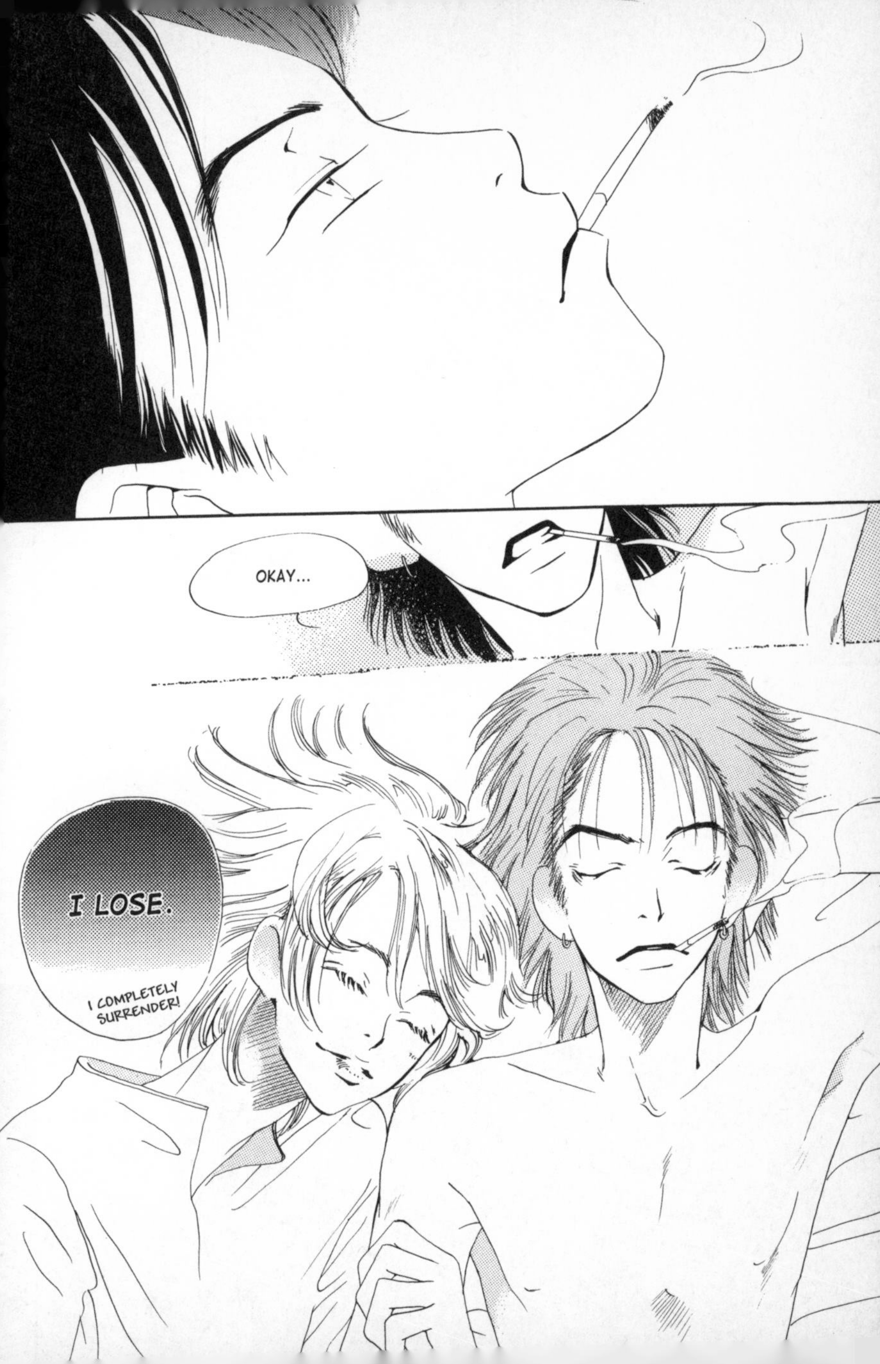
OKAY...
I LOSE.
I COMPLETELY SURRENDER!

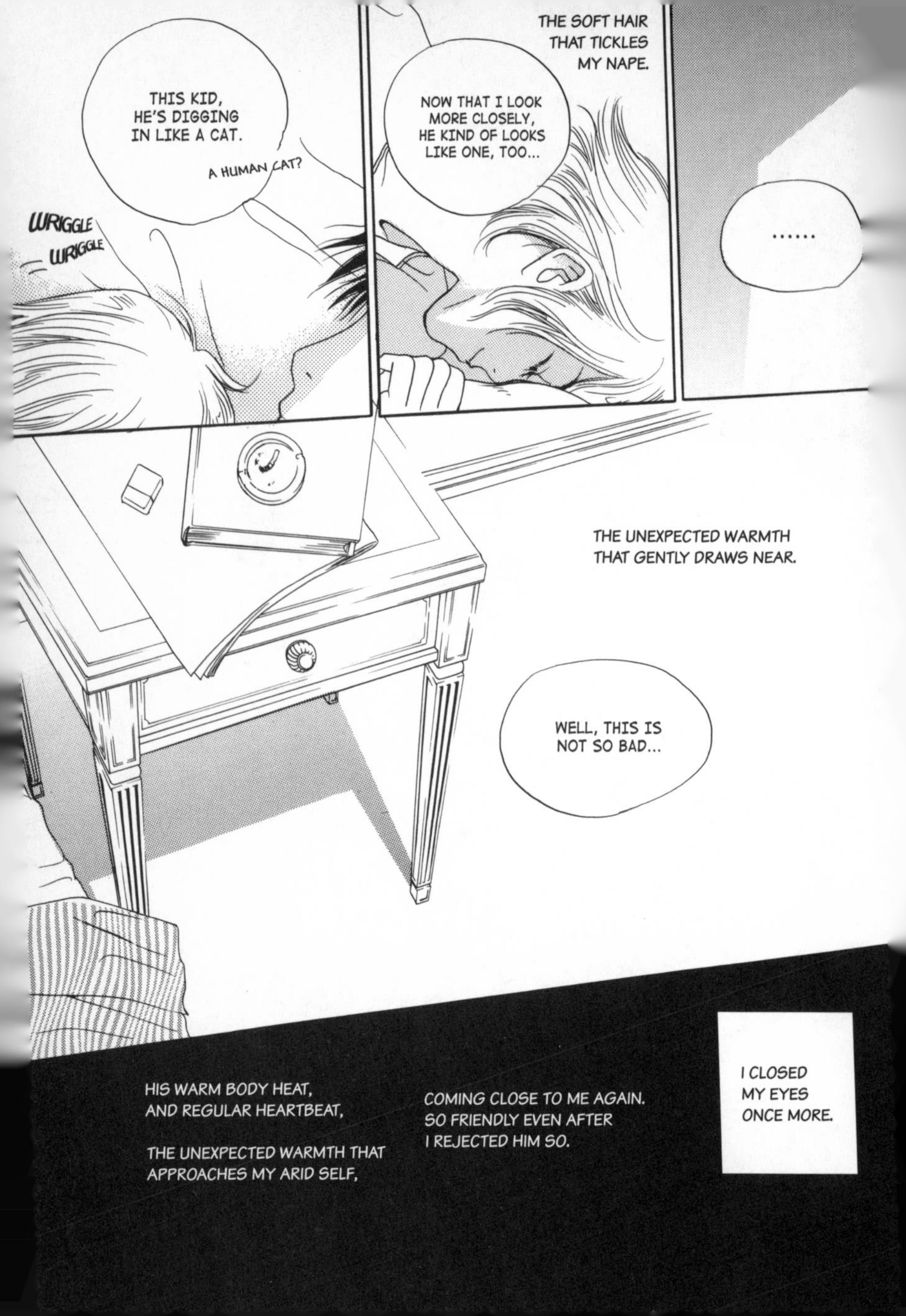
THE SOFT HAIR THAT TICKLES MY NAPE.
......
NOW THAT I LOOK MORE CLOSELY, HE KIND OF LOOKS LIKE ONE, TOO...
THIS KID, HE'S DIGGING IN LIKE A CAT.
A HUMAN CAT?
WRIGGLE WRIGGLE
THE UNEXPECTED WARMTH THAT GENTLY DRAWS NEAR.
WELL, THIS IS NOT SO BAD...
HIS WARM BODY HEAT, AND REGULAR HEARTBEAT,
THE UNEXPECTED WARMTH THAT APPROACHES MY ARID SELF,
COMING CLOSE TO ME AGAIN. SO FRIENDLY EVEN AFTER I REJECTED HIM SO.
I CLOSED MY EYES ONCE MORE.

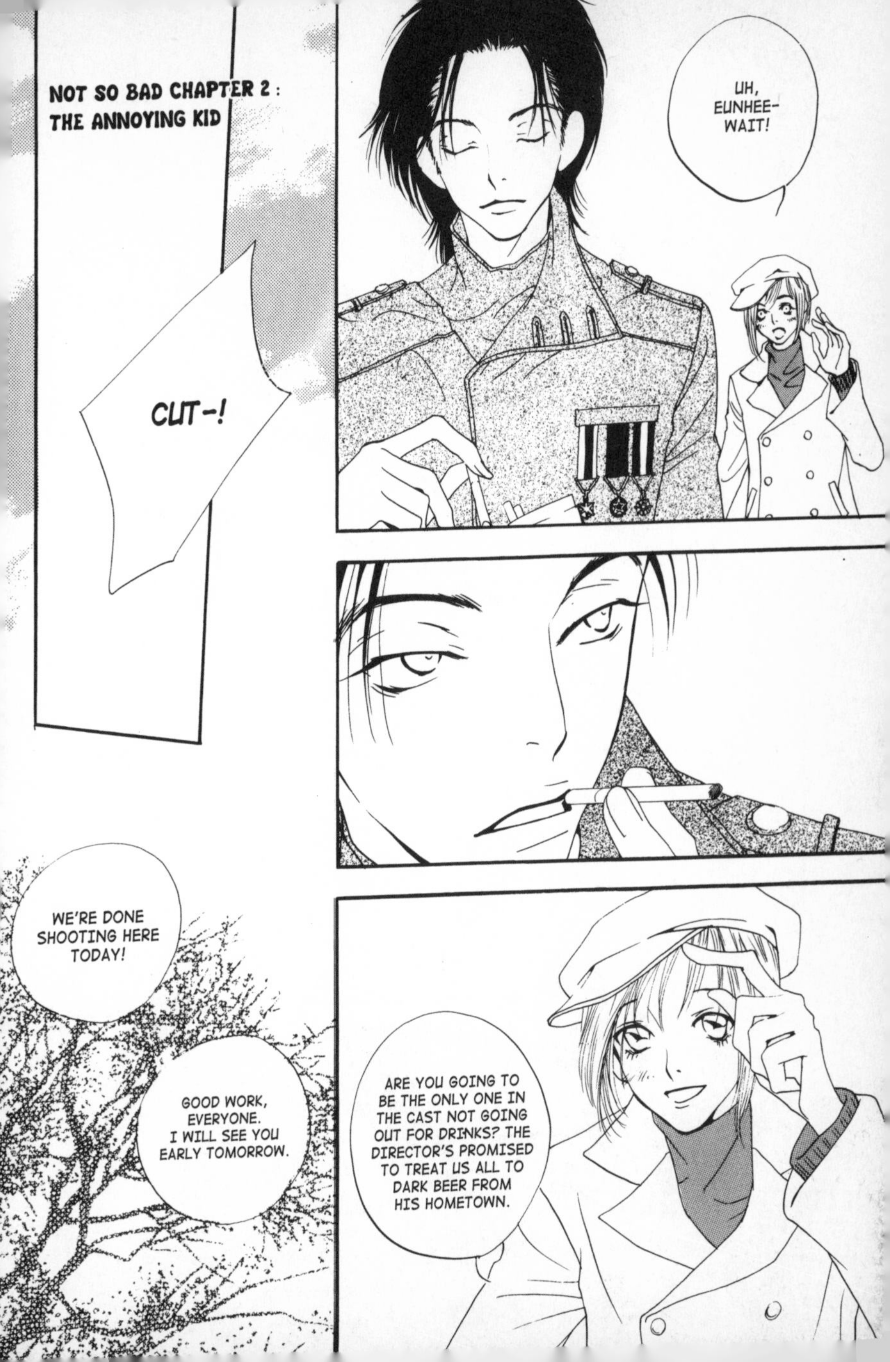
NOT SO BAD CHAPTER 2 : THE ANNOYING KID
CUT-!
UH, EUNHEE-WAIT!
WE'RE DONE SHOOTING HERE TODAY!
GOOD WORK, EVERYONE. I WILL SEE YOU EARLY TOMORROW.
ARE YOU GOING TO BE THE ONLY ONE IN THE CAST NOT GOING OUT FOR DRINKS? THE DIRECTOR'S PROMISED TO TREAT US ALL TO DARK BEER FROM HIS HOMETOWN.

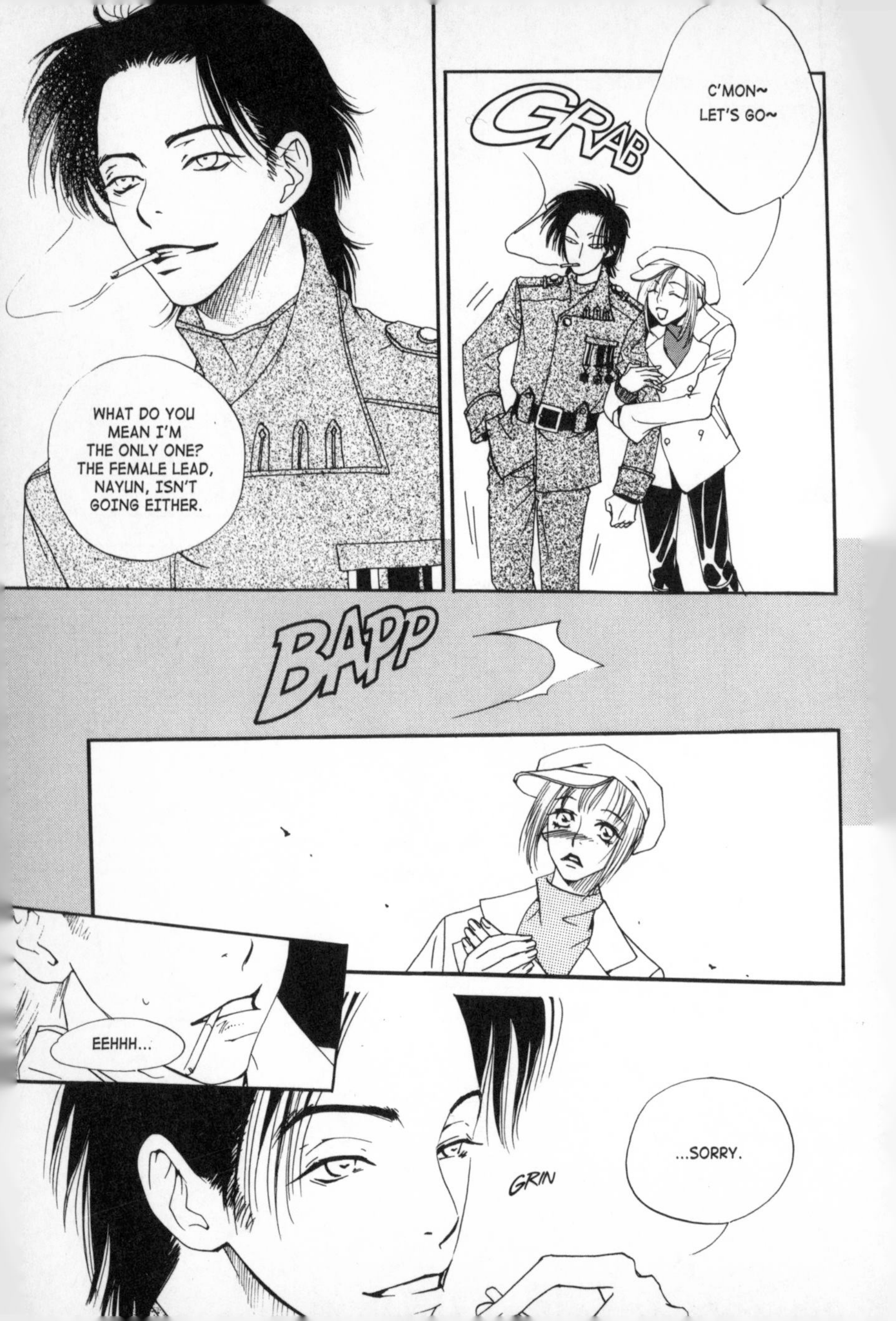
WHAT DO YOU MEAN I'M THE ONLY ONE? THE FEMALE LEAD, NAYUN, ISN'T GOING EITHER.
GRAB
C'MON~ LET'S GO~
BAPP
EEHHH...
GRIN
...SORRY.

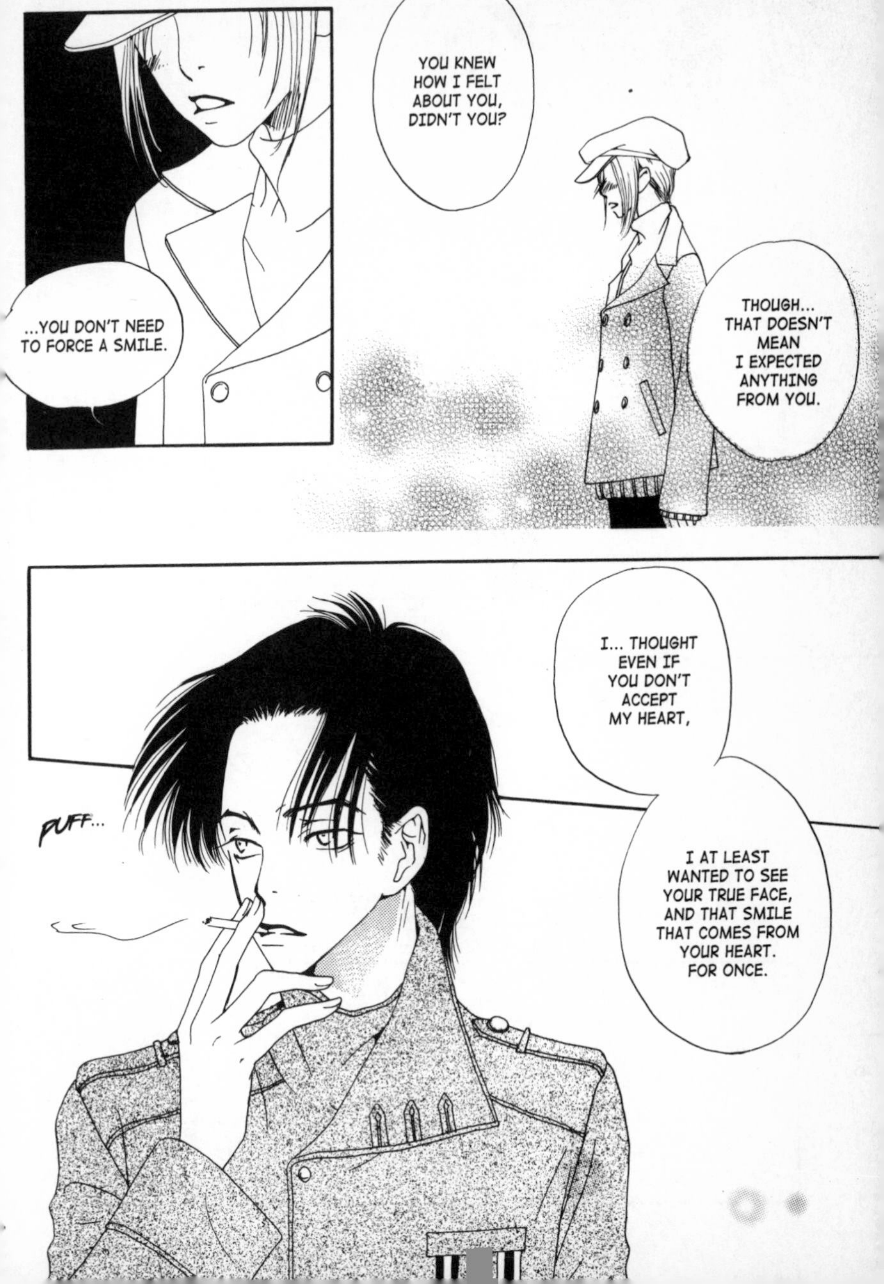
YOU KNEW HOW I FELT ABOUT YOU, DIDN'T YOU?
THOUGH... THAT DOESN'T MEAN I EXPECTED ANYTHING FROM YOU.
...YOU DON'T NEED TO FORCE A SMILE.
I... THOUGHT EVEN IF YOU DON'T ACCEPT MY HEART,
I AT LEAST WANTED TO SEE YOUR TRUE FACE, AND THAT SMILE THAT COMES FROM YOUR HEART. FOR ONCE.
PUFF...

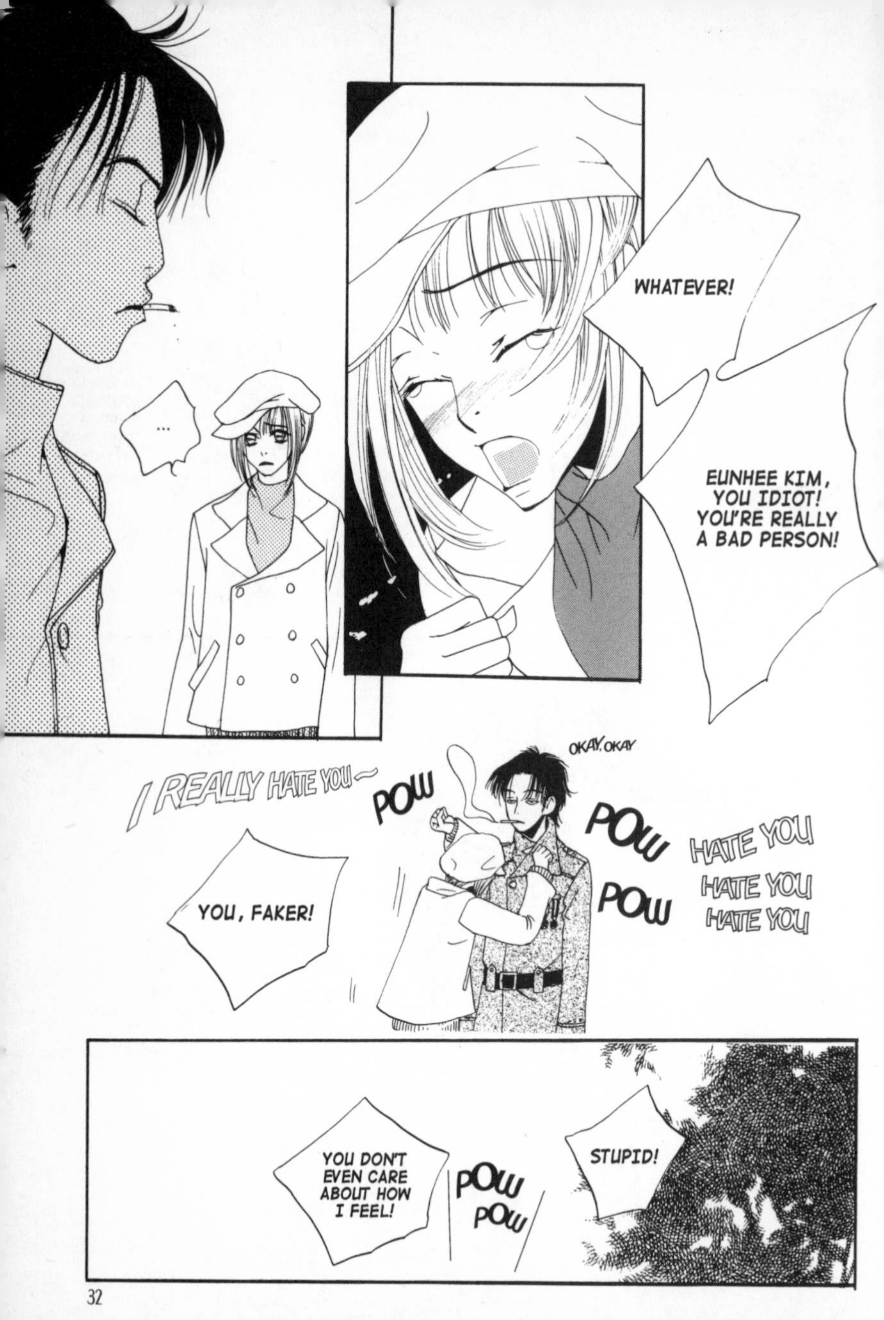
...
WHATEVER!
EUNHEE KIM, YOU IDIOT! YOU'RE REALLY A BAD PERSON!
I REALLY HATE YOU~
POW
OKAY, OKAY
POW
POW
HATE YOU
HATE YOU
HATE YOU
YOU, FAKER!
YOU DON'T EVEN CARE ABOUT HOW I FEEL!
POW
POW
STUPID!

......

DON'T ASK ME TO SHOW... ...ANY FACE OTHER THAN MY ACTING FACE.

I MYSELF DON'T EVEN REMEMBER–

SUCH A THING.

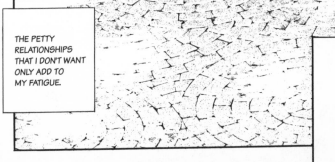

THE PETTY RELATIONSHIPS THAT I DON'T WANT ONLY ADD TO MY FATIGUE.

COLD WIND CUTS THROUGH ME– IT'S LIKE HAVING A BIG HOLE IN MY HEART.

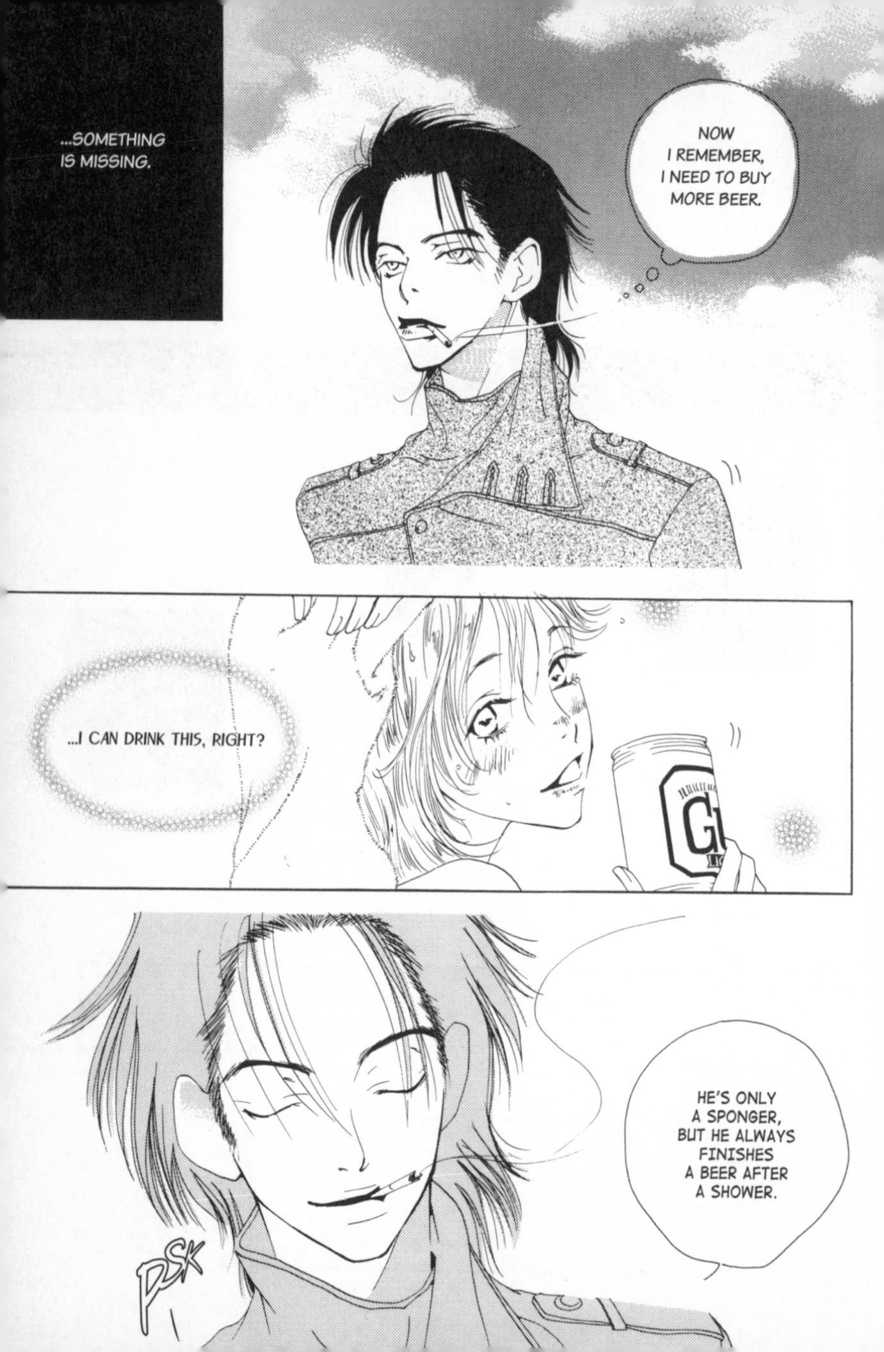
...SOMETHING IS MISSING.
NOW I REMEMBER, I NEED TO BUY MORE BEER.
...I CAN DRINK THIS, RIGHT?
HE'S ONLY A SPONGER, BUT HE ALWAYS FINISHES A BEER AFTER A SHOWER.
PSK

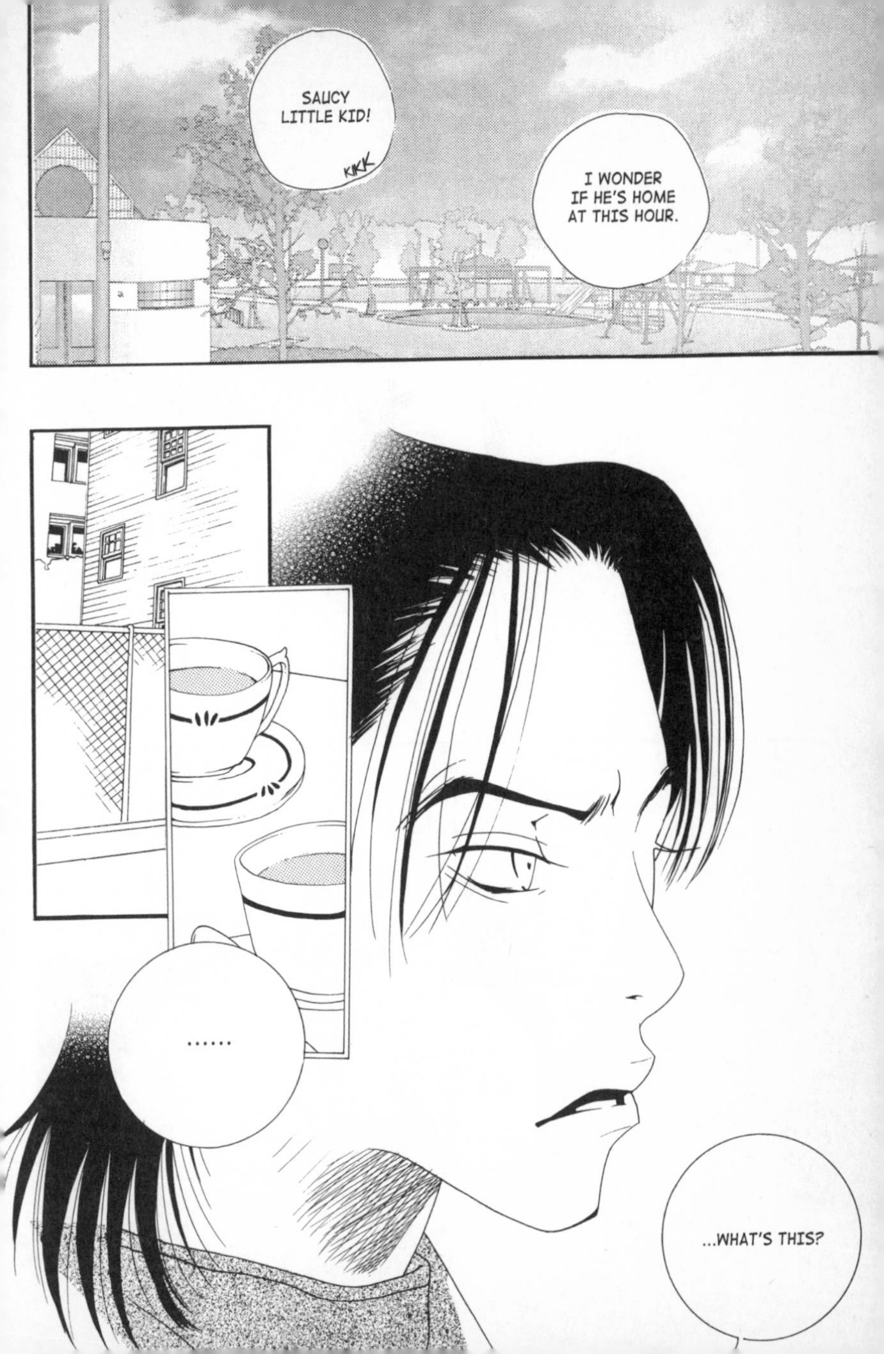

SAUCY LITTLE KID!
KIKK
I WONDER IF HE'S HOME AT THIS HOUR.
......
...WHAT'S THIS?

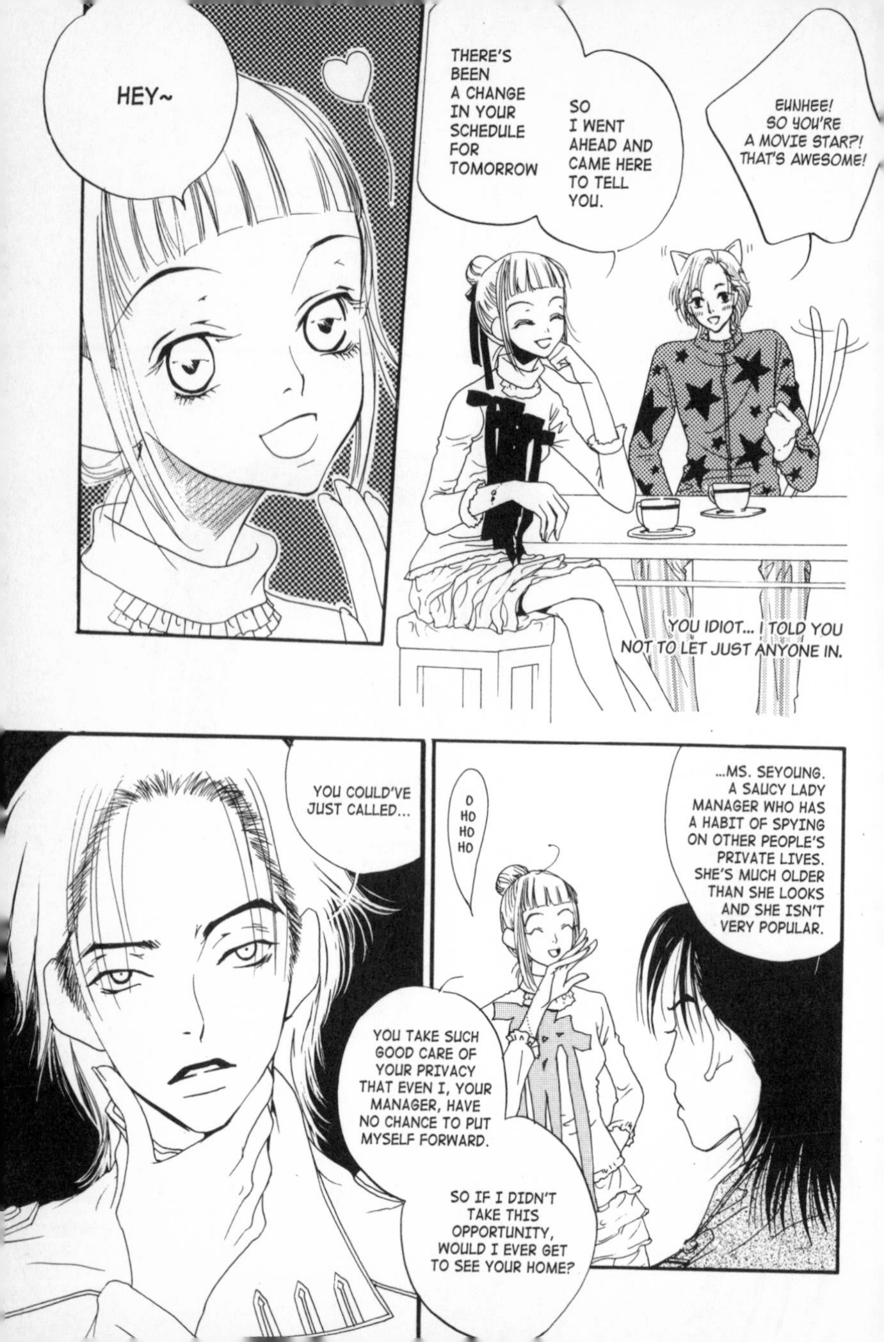
HEY~
THERE'S BEEN A CHANGE IN YOUR SCHEDULE FOR TOMORROW
SO I WENT AHEAD AND CAME HERE TO TELL YOU.
EUNHEE! SO YOU'RE A MOVIE STAR?! THAT'S AWESOME!
YOU IDIOT... I TOLD YOU NOT TO LET JUST ANYONE IN.
YOU COULD'VE JUST CALLED...
O HO HO HO
...MS. SEYOUNG. A SAUCY LADY MANAGER WHO HAS A HABIT OF SPYING ON OTHER PEOPLE'S PRIVATE LIVES. SHE'S MUCH OLDER THAN SHE LOOKS AND SHE ISN'T VERY POPULAR.
YOU TAKE SUCH GOOD CARE OF YOUR PRIVACY THAT EVEN I, YOUR MANAGER, HAVE NO CHANCE TO PUT MYSELF FORWARD.
SO IF I DIDN'T TAKE THIS OPPORTUNITY, WOULD I EVER GET TO SEE YOUR HOME?

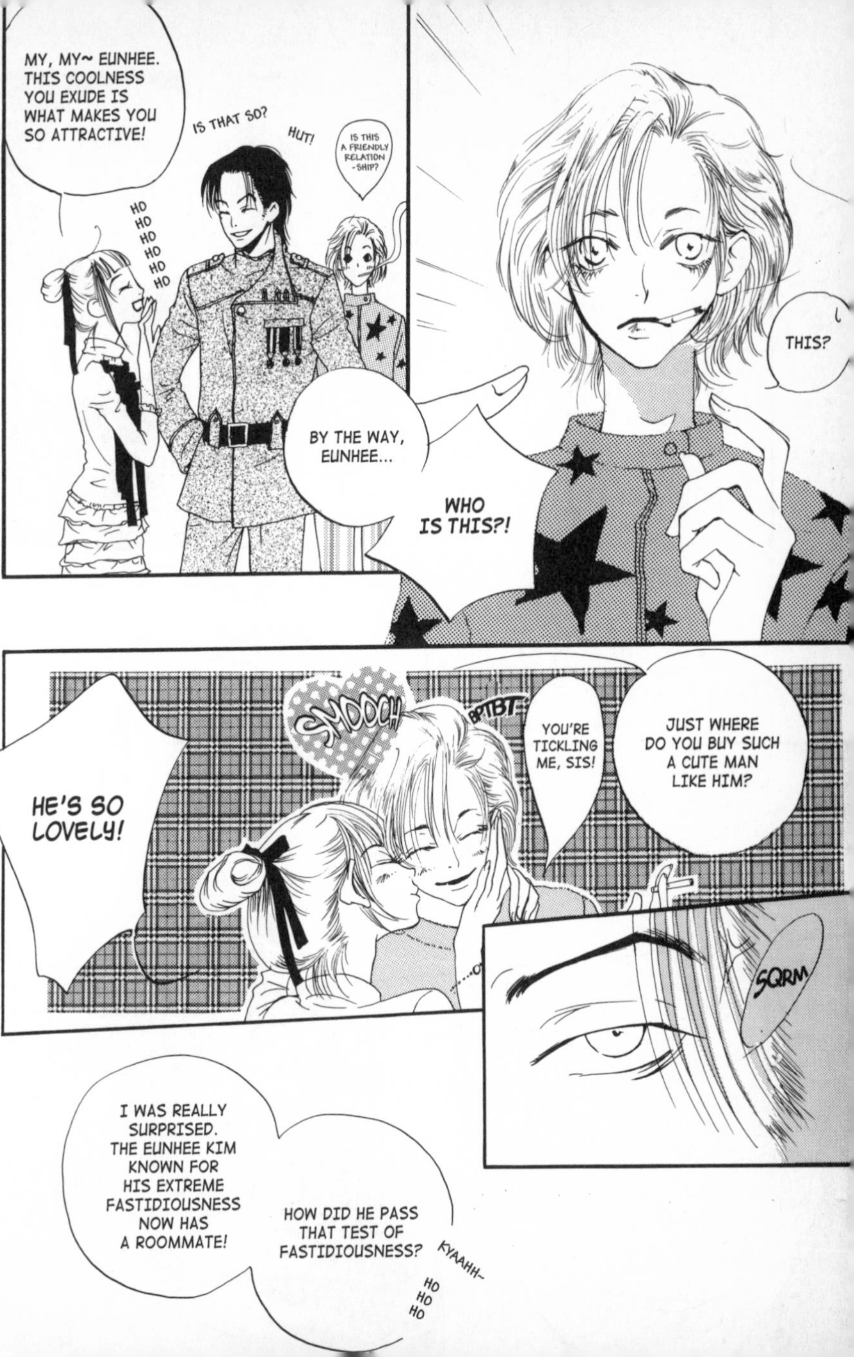
MY, MY~ EUNHEE. THIS COOLNESS YOU EXUDE IS WHAT MAKES YOU SO ATTRACTIVE!
HO HO HO HO HO HO
IS THAT SO?
HUT!
IS THIS A FRIENDLY RELATION -SHIP?
BY THE WAY, EUNHEE...
WHO IS THIS?!
THIS?
HE'S SO LOVELY!
SMOOCH
BPTBT
YOU'RE TICKLING ME, SIS!
JUST WHERE DO YOU BUY SUCH A CUTE MAN LIKE HIM?
SQRM
I WAS REALLY SURPRISED. THE EUNHEE KIM KNOWN FOR HIS EXTREME FASTIDIOUSNESS NOW HAS A ROOMMATE!
HOW DID HE PASS THAT TEST OF FASTIDIOUSNESS?
KYAAHH-
HO HO HO

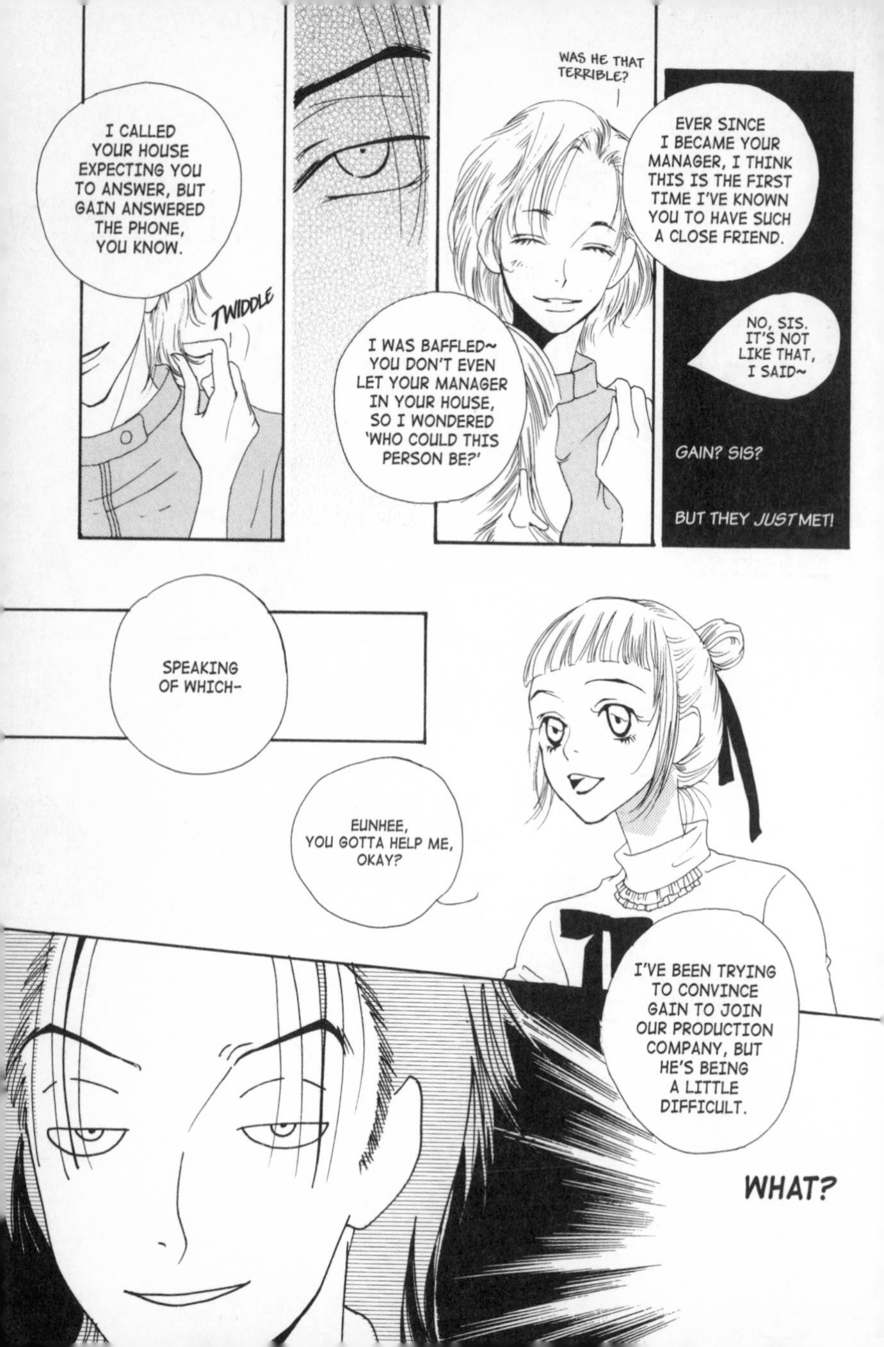
I CALLED YOUR HOUSE EXPECTING YOU TO ANSWER, BUT GAIN ANSWERED THE PHONE, YOU KNOW.
TWIDDLE
WAS HE THAT TERRIBLE?
EVER SINCE I BECAME YOUR MANAGER, I THINK THIS IS THE FIRST TIME I'VE KNOWN YOU TO HAVE SUCH A CLOSE FRIEND.
I WAS BAFFLED~ YOU DON'T EVEN LET YOUR MANAGER IN YOUR HOUSE, SO I WONDERED 'WHO COULD THIS PERSON BE?'
NO, SIS. IT'S NOT LIKE THAT, I SAID~
GAIN? SIS?
BUT THEY *JUST* MET!
SPEAKING OF WHICH-
EUNHEE, YOU GOTTA HELP ME, OKAY?
I'VE BEEN TRYING TO CONVINCE GAIN TO JOIN OUR PRODUCTION COMPANY, BUT HE'S BEING A LITTLE DIFFICULT.
WHAT?

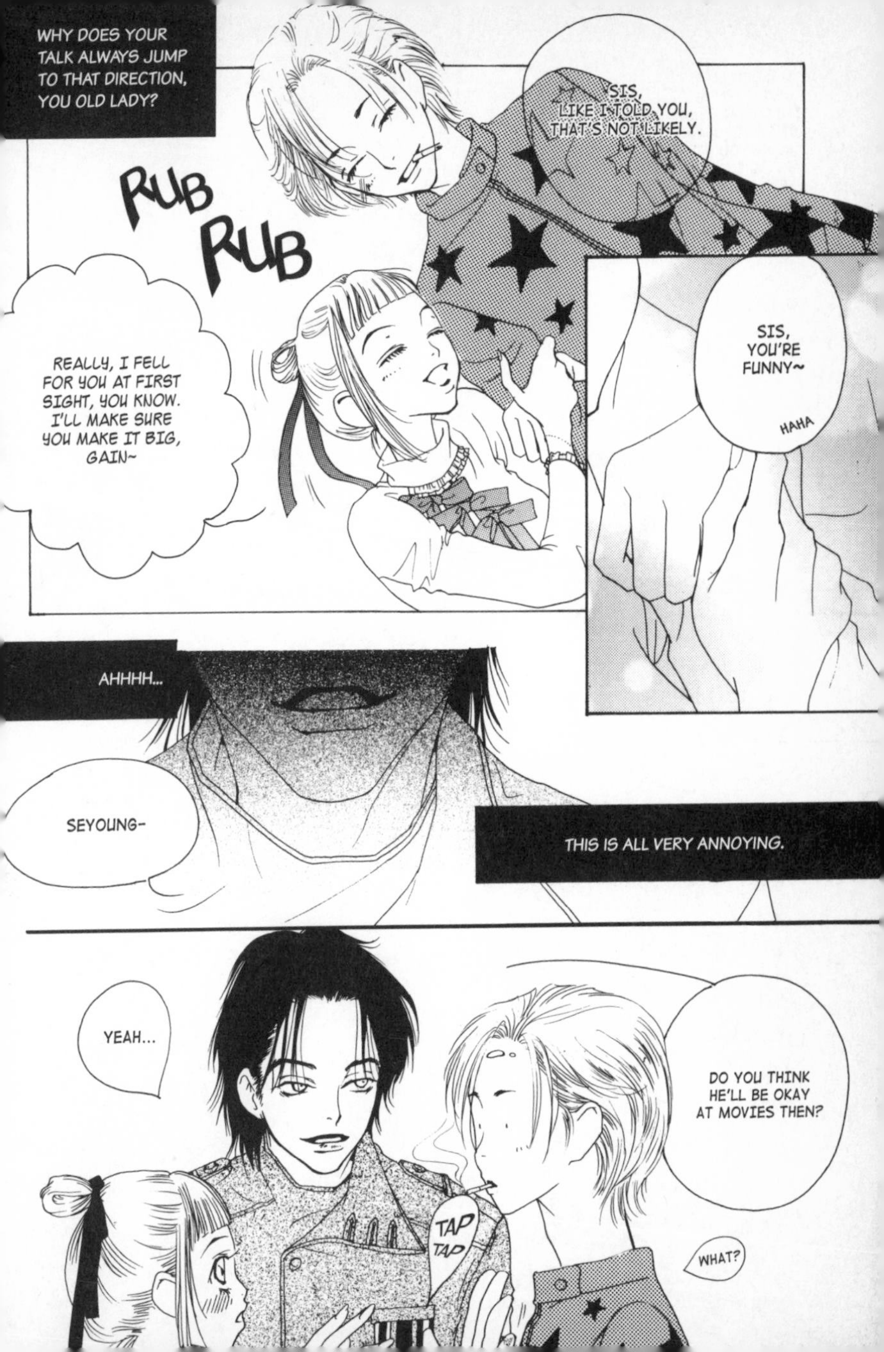

WHY DOES YOUR TALK ALWAYS JUMP TO THAT DIRECTION, YOU OLD LADY?
SIS, LIKE I TOLD YOU, THAT'S NOT LIKELY.
RUB RUB
REALLY, I FELL FOR YOU AT FIRST SIGHT, YOU KNOW. I'LL MAKE SURE YOU MAKE IT BIG, GAIN~
SIS, YOU'RE FUNNY~
HAHA
AHHHH...
SEYOUNG-
THIS IS ALL VERY ANNOYING.
YEAH...
DO YOU THINK HE'LL BE OKAY AT MOVIES THEN?
TAP TAP
WHAT?

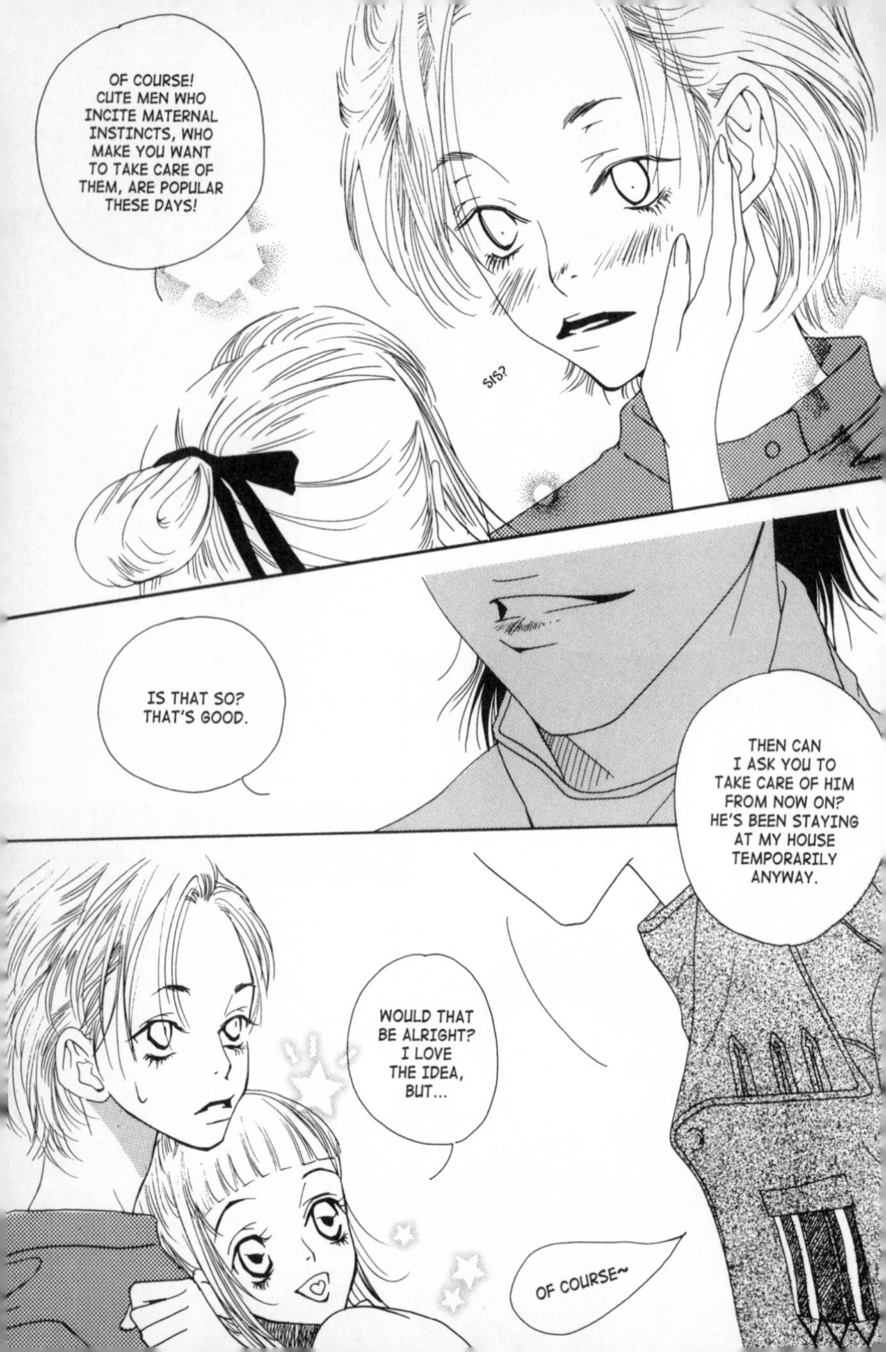
OF COURSE! CUTE MEN WHO INCITE MATERNAL INSTINCTS, WHO MAKE YOU WANT TO TAKE CARE OF THEM, ARE POPULAR THESE DAYS!
SIS?
IS THAT SO? THAT'S GOOD.
THEN CAN I ASK YOU TO TAKE CARE OF HIM FROM NOW ON? HE'S BEEN STAYING AT MY HOUSE TEMPORARILY ANYWAY.
WOULD THAT BE ALRIGHT? I LOVE THE IDEA, BUT...
OF COURSE~

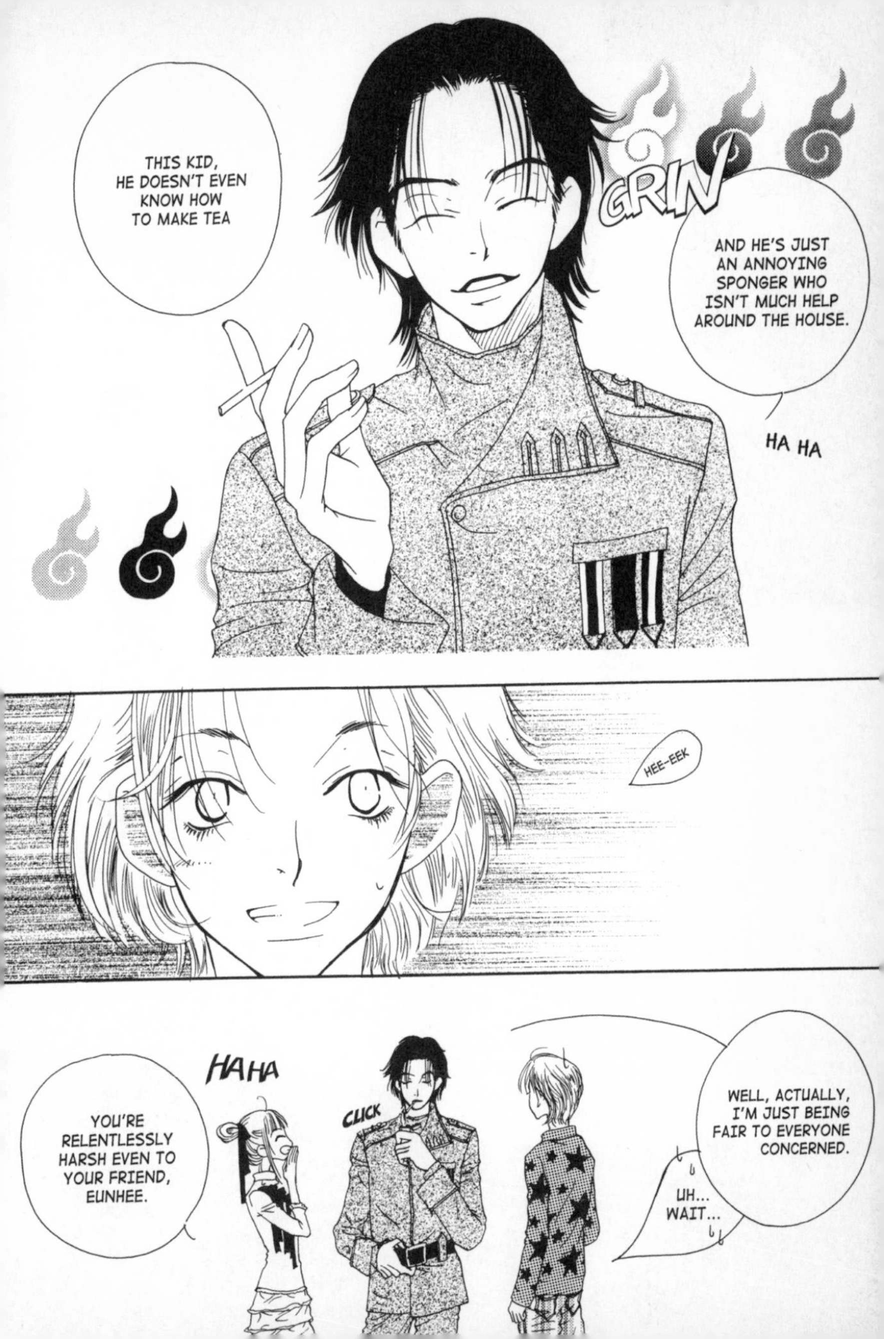
THIS KID, HE DOESN'T EVEN KNOW HOW TO MAKE TEA
GRIN
AND HE'S JUST AN ANNOYING SPONGER WHO ISN'T MUCH HELP AROUND THE HOUSE.
HA HA
HEE-EEK
HAHA
YOU'RE RELENTLESSLY HARSH EVEN TO YOUR FRIEND, EUNHEE.
CLICK
WELL, ACTUALLY, I'M JUST BEING FAIR TO EVERYONE CONCERNED.
UH... WAIT...

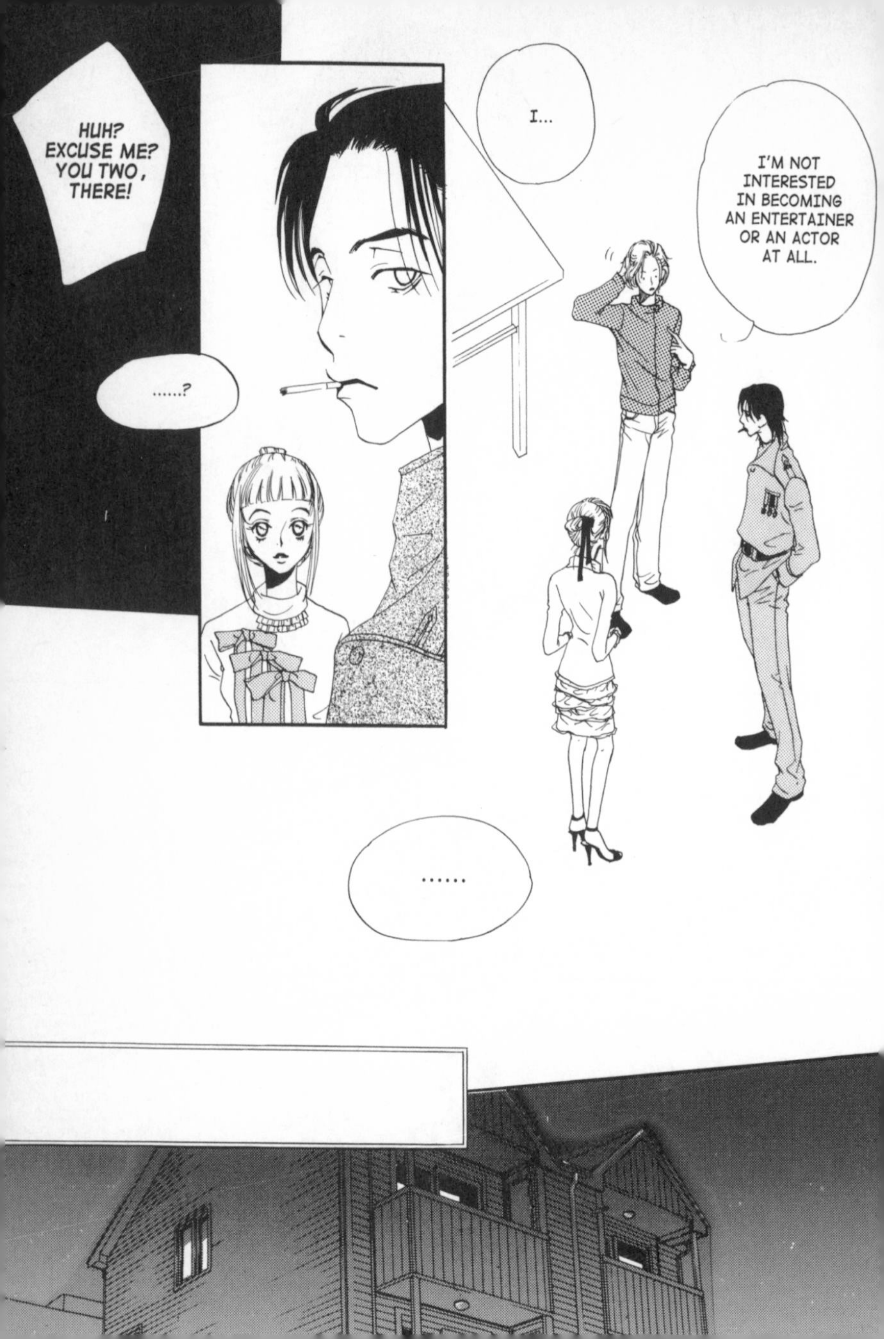
I'M NOT INTERESTED IN BECOMING AN ENTERTAINER OR AN ACTOR AT ALL.
I...
HUH? EXCUSE ME? YOU TWO, THERE!
......?
......

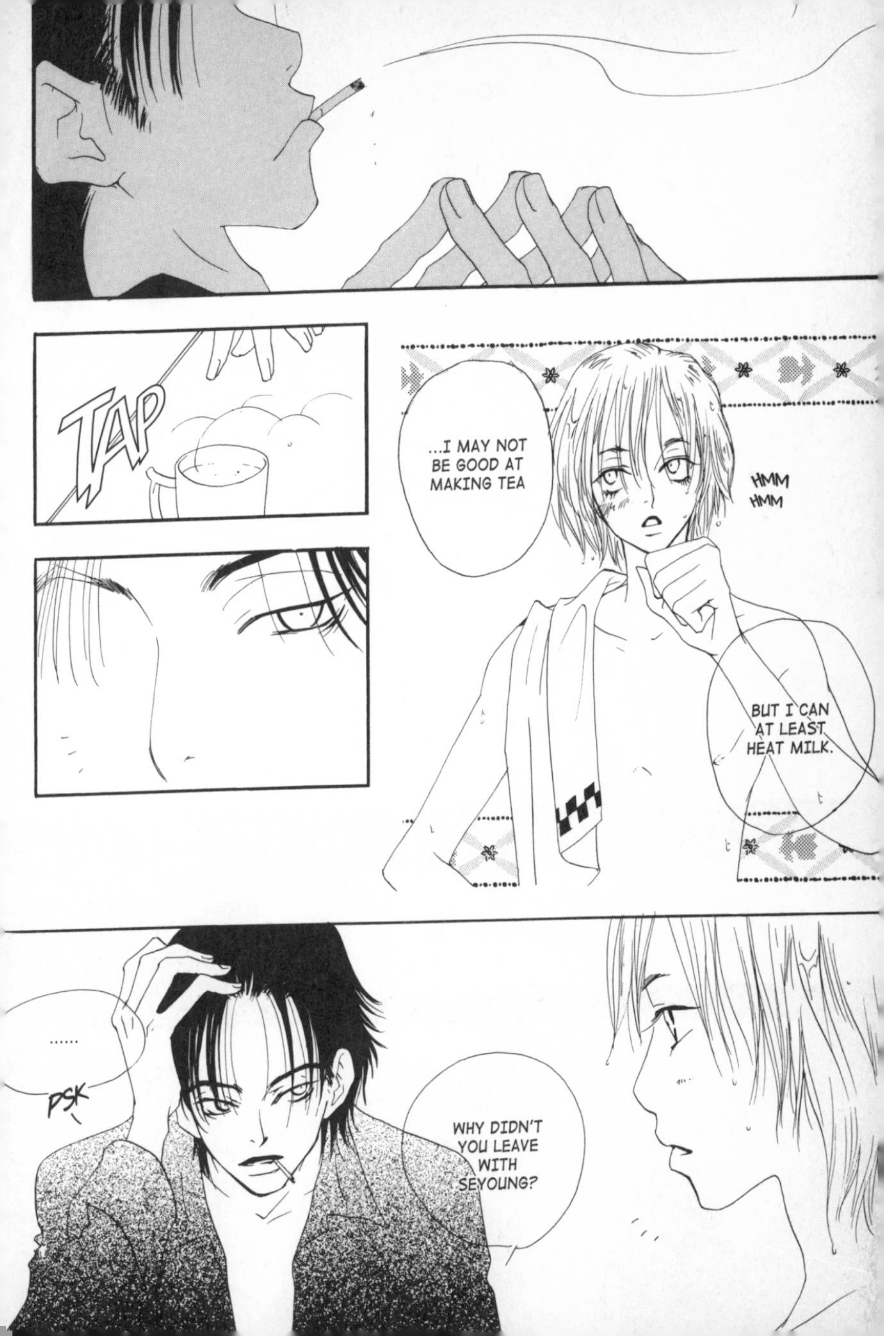
TAP
...I MAY NOT BE GOOD AT MAKING TEA
HMM HMM
BUT I CAN AT LEAST HEAT MILK.
......
PSK
WHY DIDN'T YOU LEAVE WITH SEYOUNG?

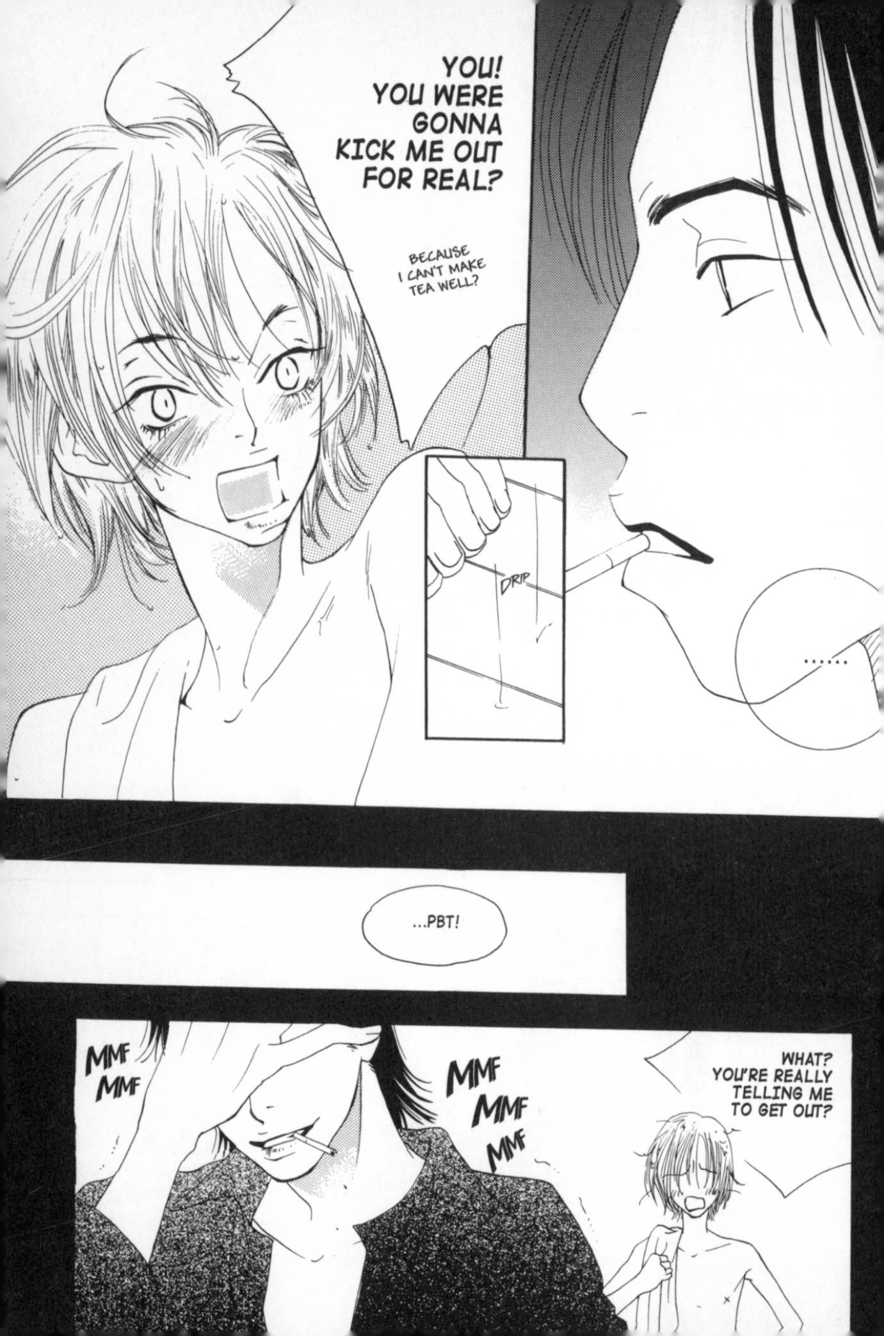
YOU! YOU WERE GONNA KICK ME OUT FOR REAL?
BECAUSE I CAN'T MAKE TEA WELL?
DRIP
......
...PBT!
WHAT? YOU'RE REALLY TELLING ME TO GET OUT?
MMF MMF MMF
MMF MMF

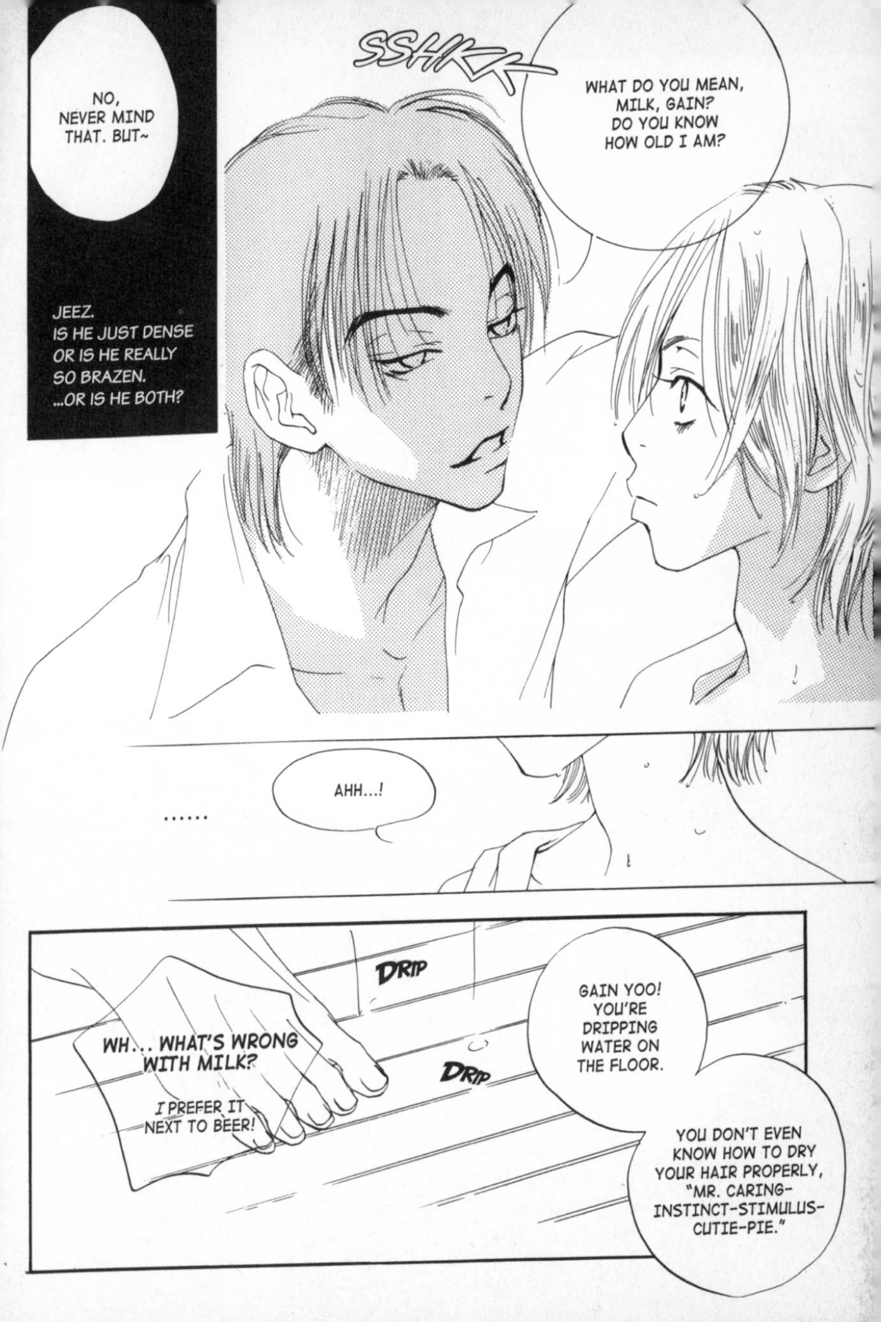
SSHKK
WHAT DO YOU MEAN, MILK, GAIN? DO YOU KNOW HOW OLD I AM?
NO, NEVER MIND THAT. BUT~
JEEZ. IS HE JUST DENSE OR IS HE REALLY SO BRAZEN. ...OR IS HE BOTH?
AHH...!
......
GAIN YOO! YOU'RE DRIPPING WATER ON THE FLOOR.
YOU DON'T EVEN KNOW HOW TO DRY YOUR HAIR PROPERLY, "MR. CARING-INSTINCT-STIMULUS-CUTIE-PIE."
DRIP
DRIP
WH... WHAT'S WRONG WITH MILK?
I PREFER IT NEXT TO BEER!

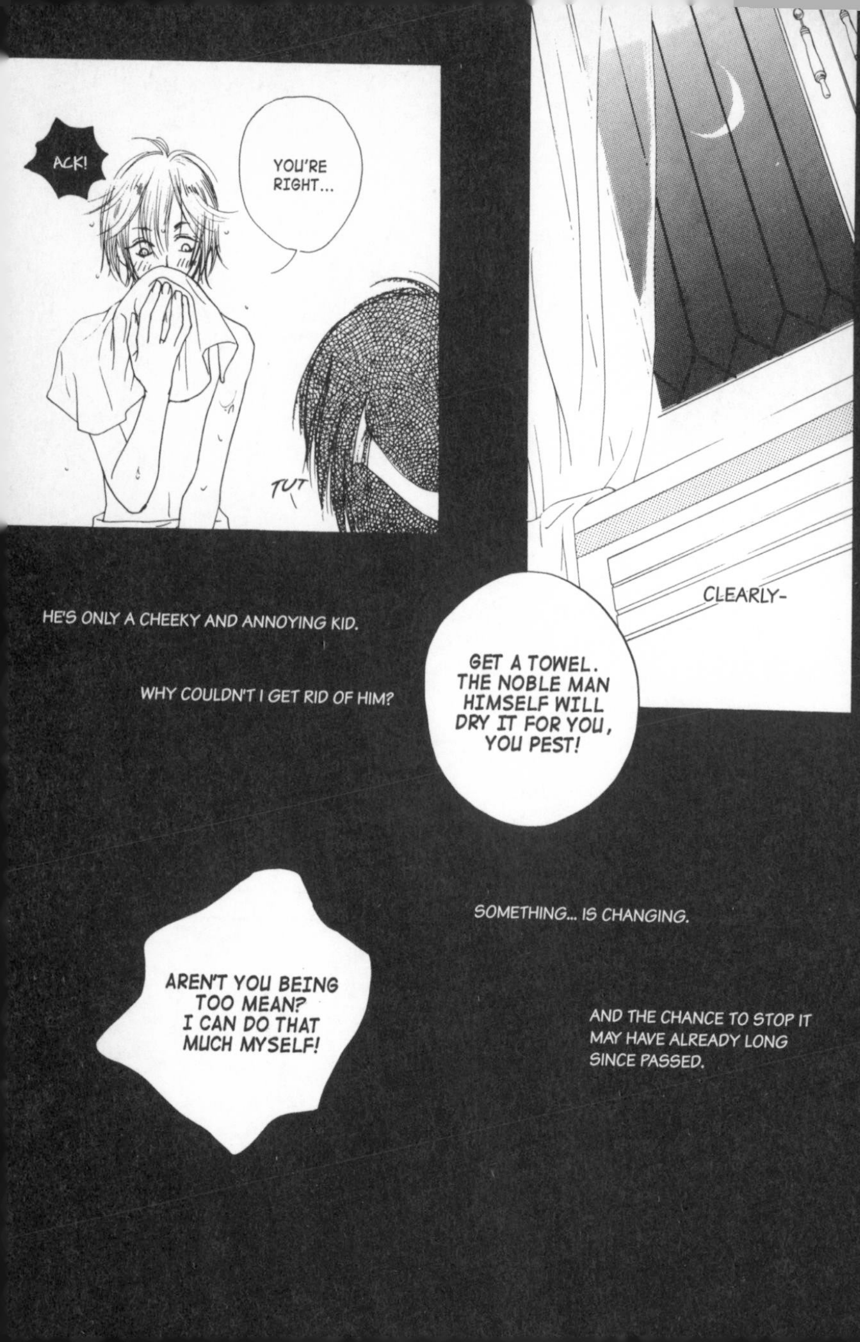
CLEARLY-
ACK!
YOU'RE RIGHT...
TUT
GET A TOWEL. THE NOBLE MAN HIMSELF WILL DRY IT FOR YOU, YOU PEST!
HE'S ONLY A CHEEKY AND ANNOYING KID.
WHY COULDN'T I GET RID OF HIM?
SOMETHING... IS CHANGING.
AND THE CHANCE TO STOP IT MAY HAVE ALREADY LONG SINCE PASSED.
AREN'T YOU BEING TOO MEAN? I CAN DO THAT MUCH MYSELF!

NOT SO BAD CHAPTER 3 : A TOUCH OF COLD

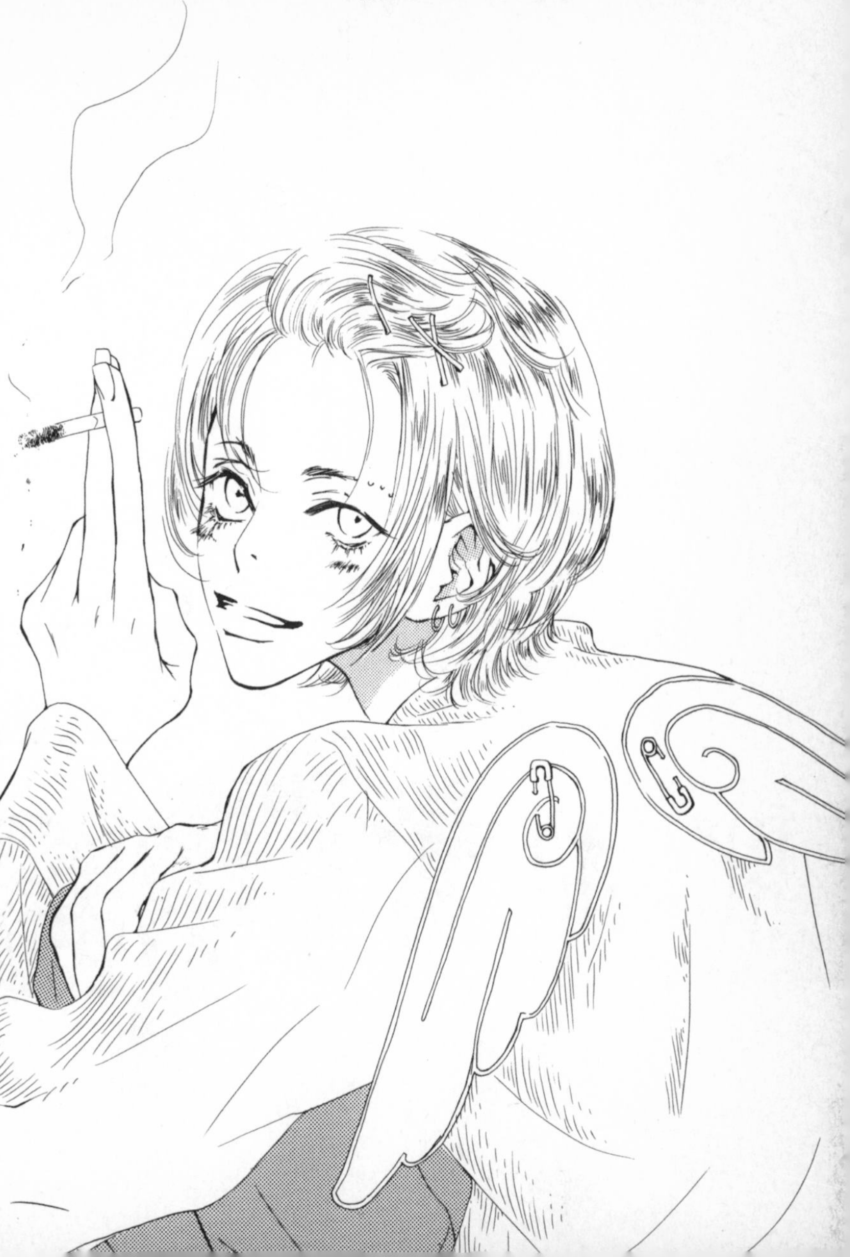

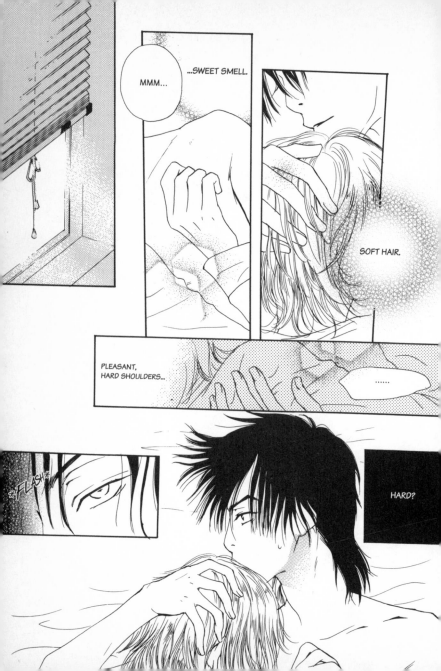

...SWEET SMELL.

MMM...

SOFT HAIR.

PLEASANT, HARD SHOULDERS...

......

FLASH

HARD?

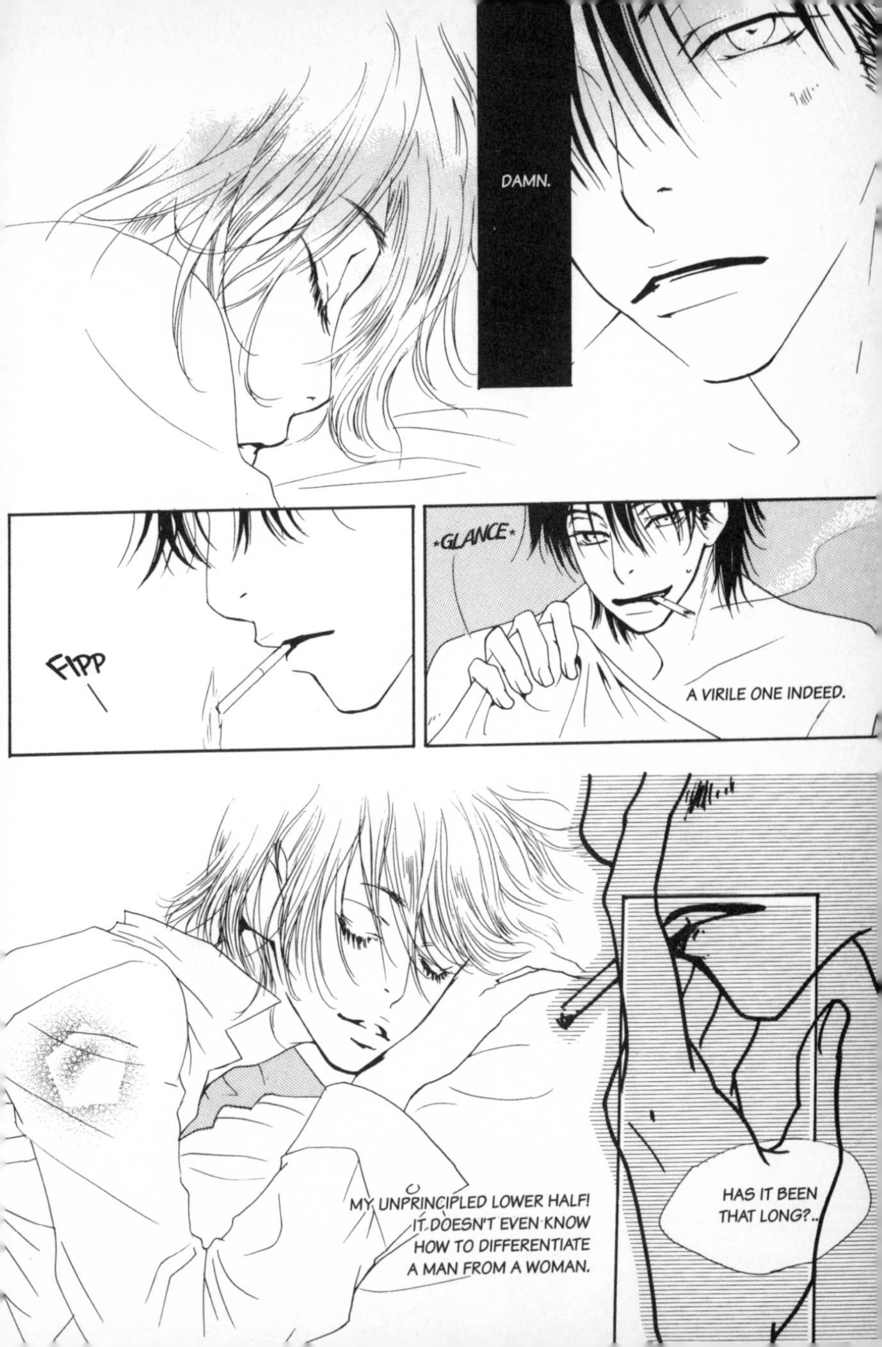
DAMN.
GLANCE
A VIRILE ONE INDEED.
FIPP
HAS IT BEEN THAT LONG?..
MY UNPRINCIPLED LOWER HALF! IT DOESN'T EVEN KNOW HOW TO DIFFERENTIATE A MAN FROM A WOMAN.

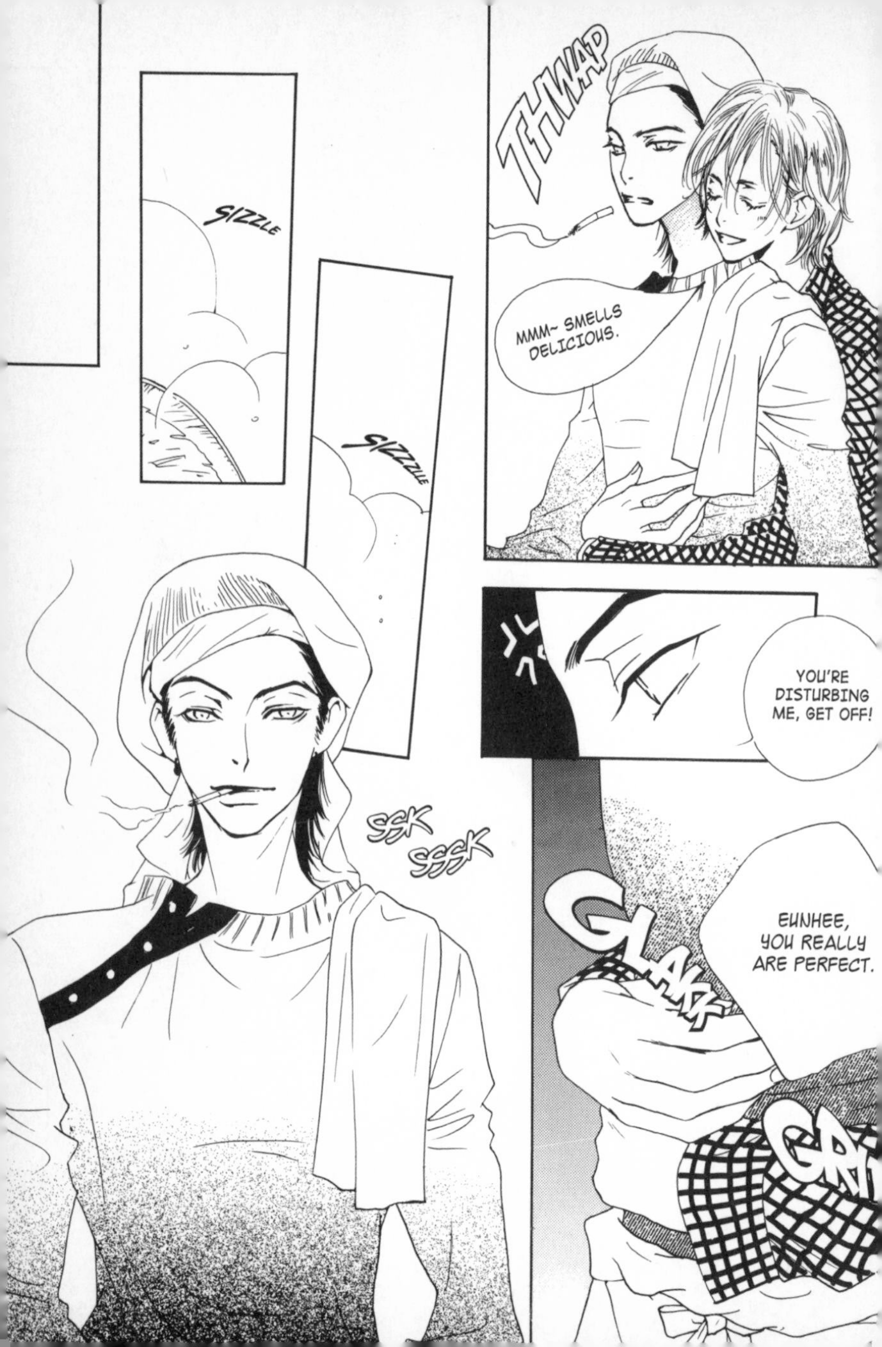
SIZZLE
SIZZZLE
SSK SSSK
THWAP
MMM~ SMELLS DELICIOUS.
YOU'RE DISTURBING ME, GET OFF!
GLAKK
EUNHEE, YOU REALLY ARE PERFECT.

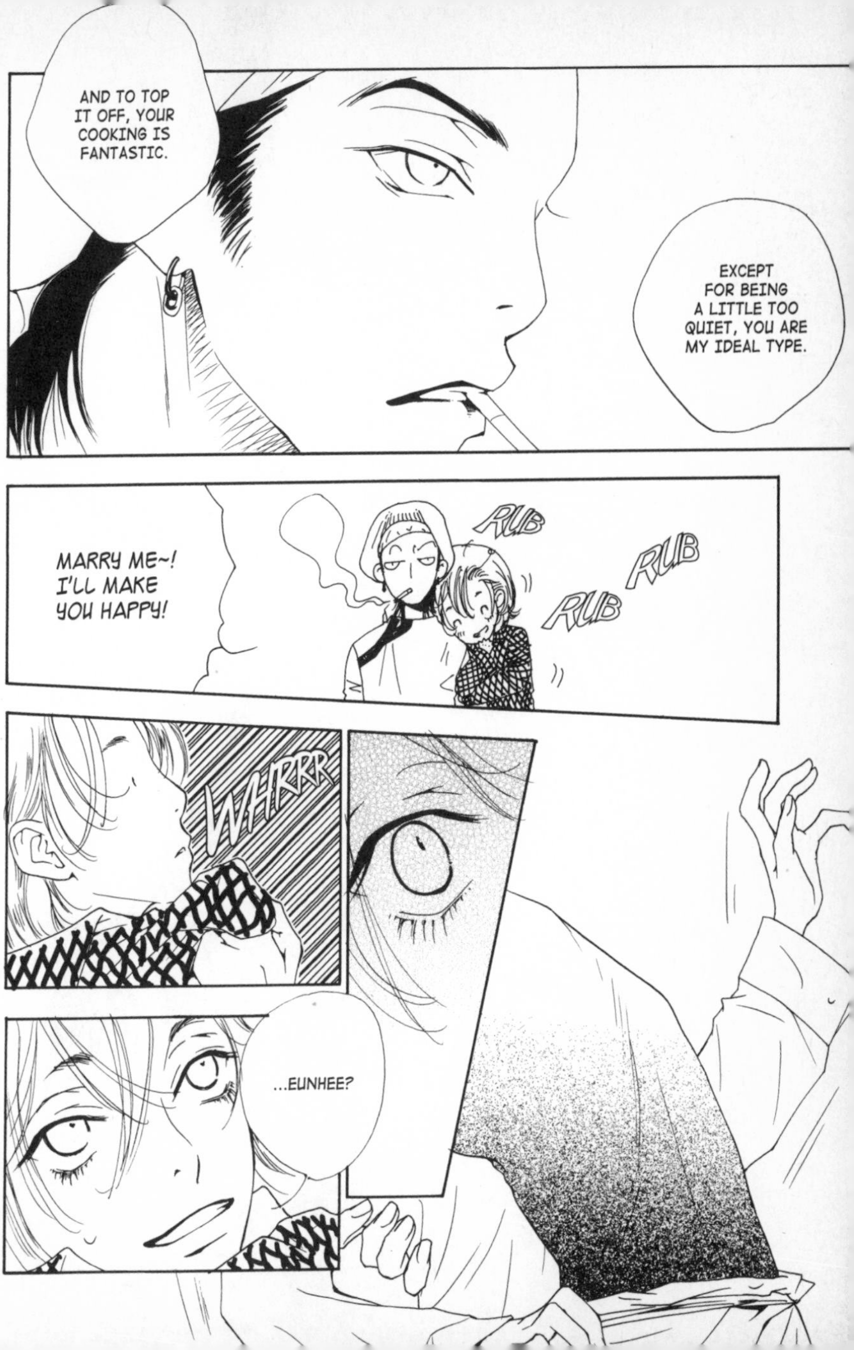
AND TO TOP IT OFF, YOUR COOKING IS FANTASTIC.
EXCEPT FOR BEING A LITTLE TOO QUIET, YOU ARE MY IDEAL TYPE.
MARRY ME~! I'LL MAKE YOU HAPPY!
RUB
RUB
RUB
WHRRR
...EUNHEE?

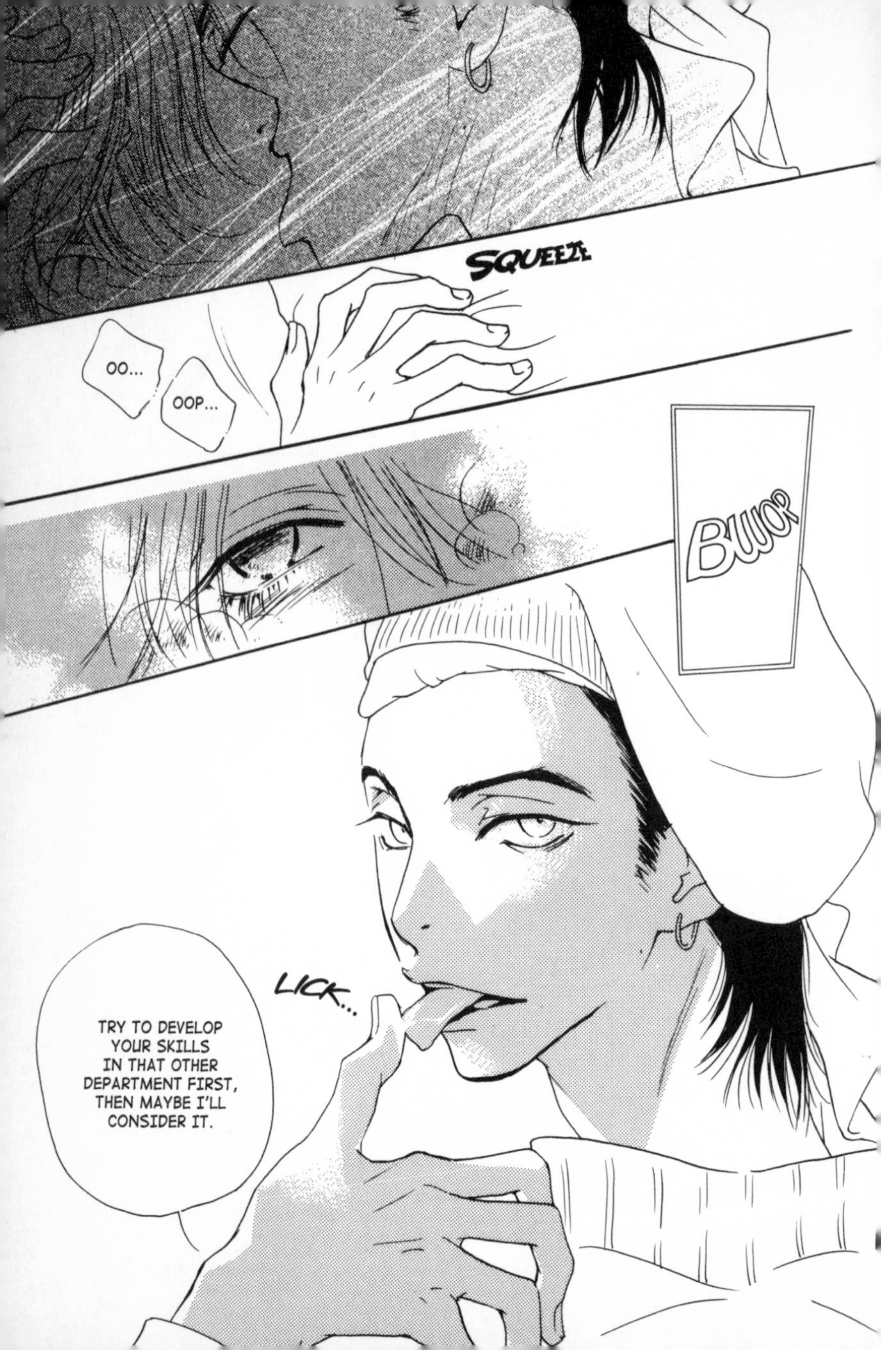
SQUEEZE
OO...
OOP...
BWOP
LICK...
TRY TO DEVELOP YOUR SKILLS IN THAT OTHER DEPARTMENT FIRST, THEN MAYBE I'LL CONSIDER IT.

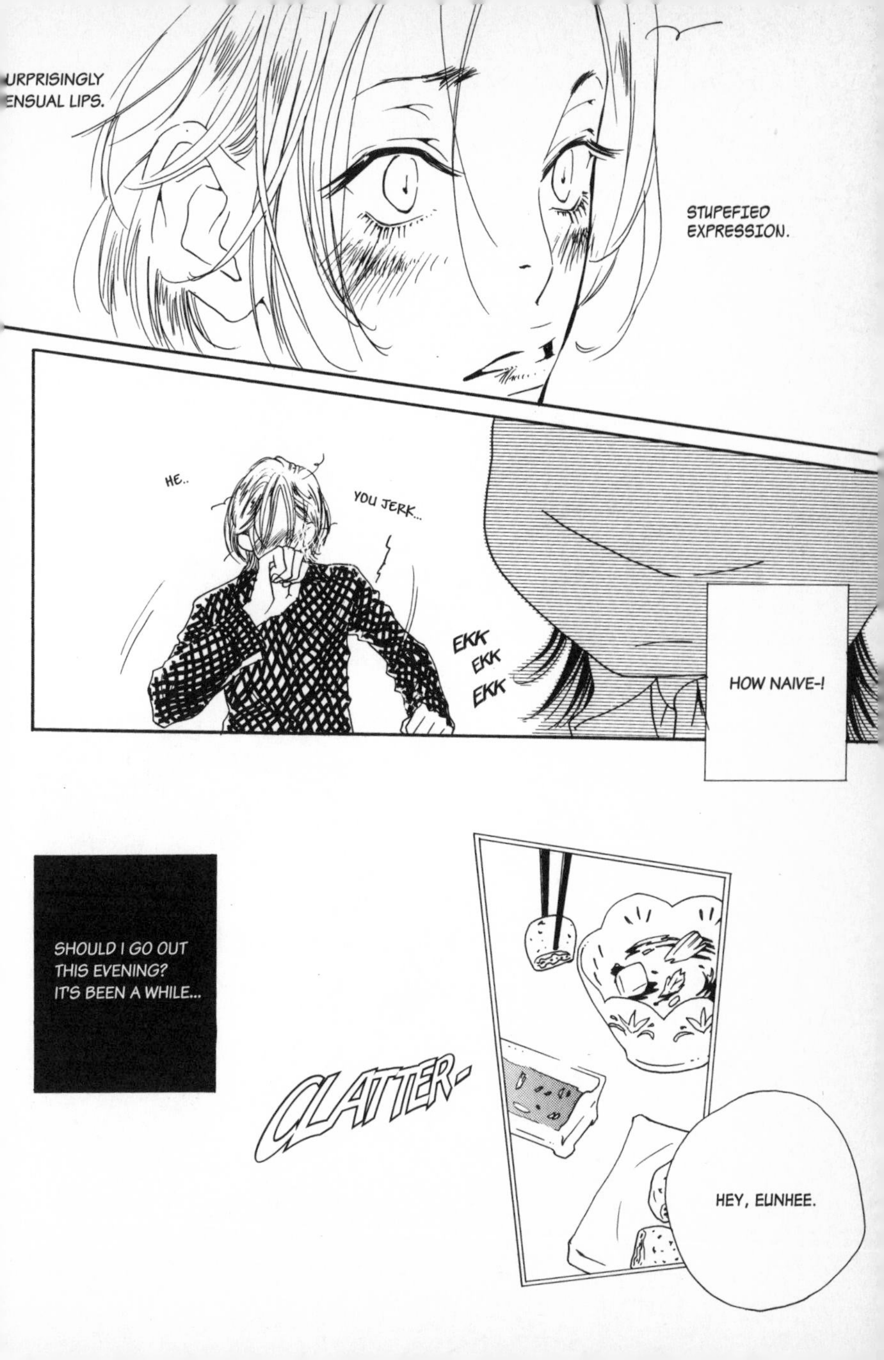
URPRISINGLY
ENSUAL LIPS.
STUPEFIED
EXPRESSION.
HE..
YOU JERK...
EKK
EKK
EKK
HOW NAIVE-!
SHOULD I GO OUT
THIS EVENING?
IT'S BEEN A WHILE...
CLATTER-
HEY, EUNHEE.

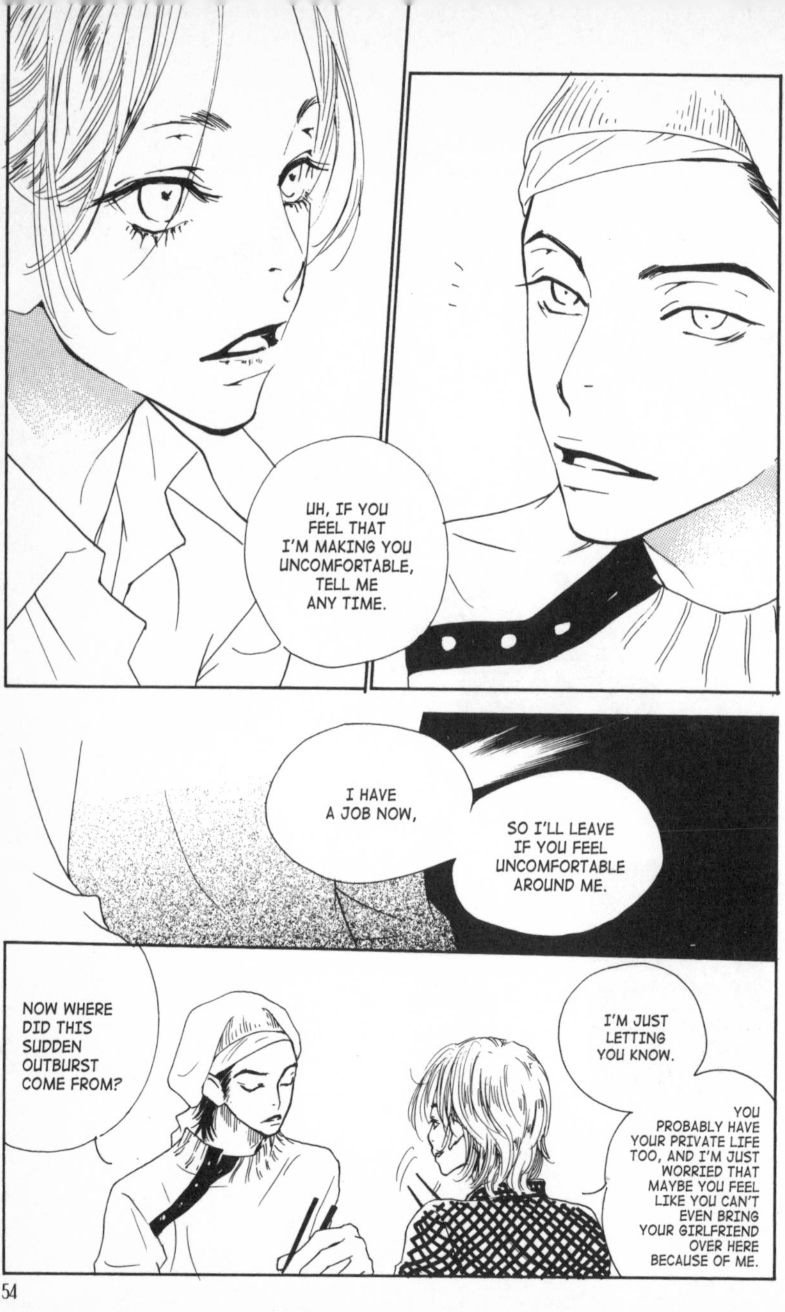
UH, IF YOU FEEL THAT I'M MAKING YOU UNCOMFORTABLE, TELL ME ANY TIME.
I HAVE A JOB NOW,
SO I'LL LEAVE IF YOU FEEL UNCOMFORTABLE AROUND ME.
NOW WHERE DID THIS SUDDEN OUTBURST COME FROM?
I'M JUST LETTING YOU KNOW.
YOU PROBABLY HAVE YOUR PRIVATE LIFE TOO, AND I'M JUST WORRIED THAT MAYBE YOU FEEL LIKE YOU CAN'T EVEN BRING YOUR GIRLFRIEND OVER HERE BECAUSE OF ME.

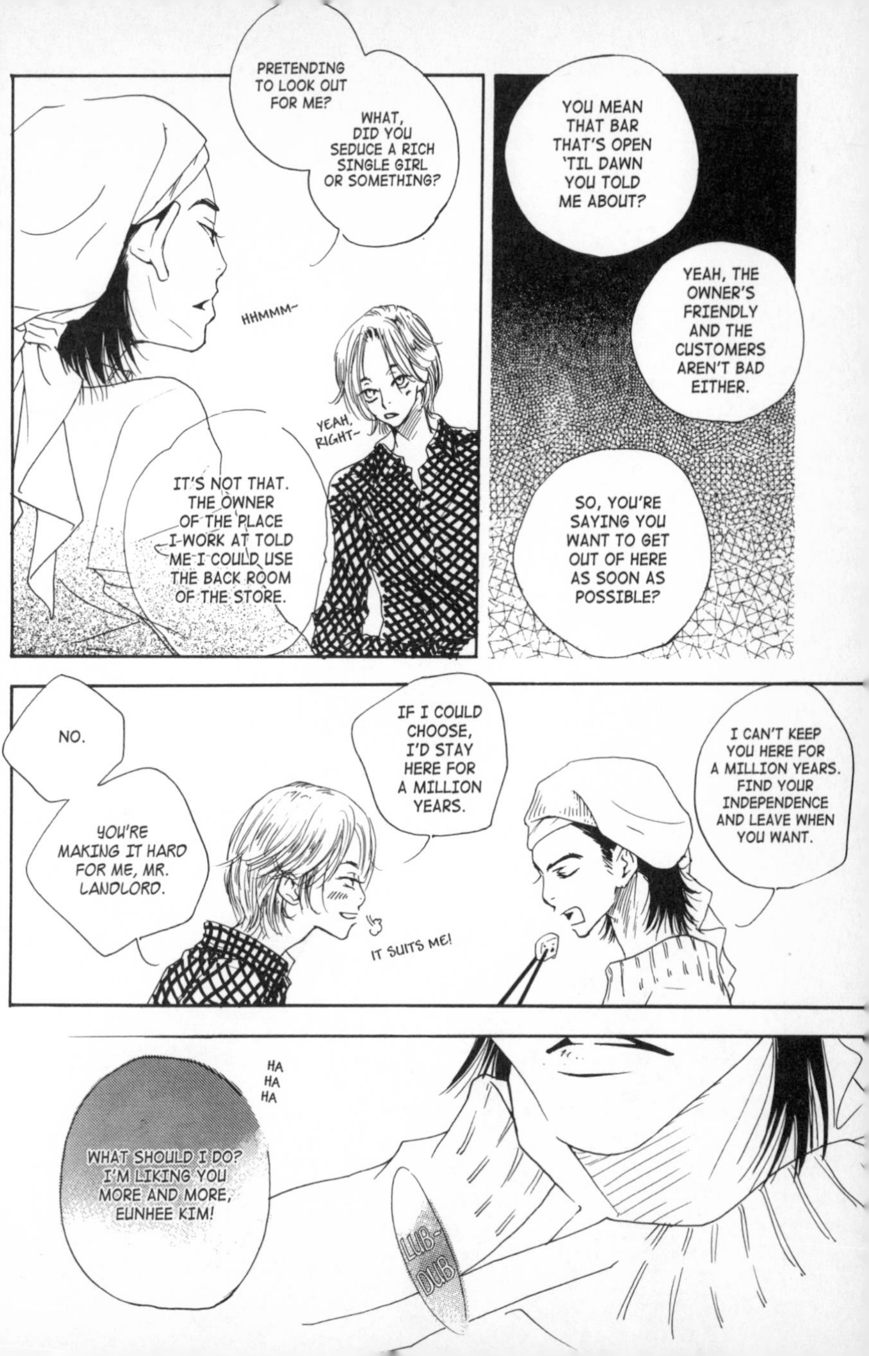
PRETENDING TO LOOK OUT FOR ME?
WHAT, DID YOU SEDUCE A RICH SINGLE GIRL OR SOMETHING?
HHMMM~
YEAH, RIGHT~
IT'S NOT THAT. THE OWNER OF THE PLACE I WORK AT TOLD ME I COULD USE THE BACK ROOM OF THE STORE.
YOU MEAN THAT BAR THAT'S OPEN 'TIL DAWN YOU TOLD ME ABOUT?
YEAH, THE OWNER'S FRIENDLY AND THE CUSTOMERS AREN'T BAD EITHER.
SO, YOU'RE SAYING YOU WANT TO GET OUT OF HERE AS SOON AS POSSIBLE?
NO.
YOU'RE MAKING IT HARD FOR ME, MR. LANDLORD.
IF I COULD CHOOSE, I'D STAY HERE FOR A MILLION YEARS.
I CAN'T KEEP YOU HERE FOR A MILLION YEARS. FIND YOUR INDEPENDENCE AND LEAVE WHEN YOU WANT.
IT SUITS ME!
HA HA HA
WHAT SHOULD I DO? I'M LIKING YOU MORE AND MORE, EUNHEE KIM!
LUB-DUB

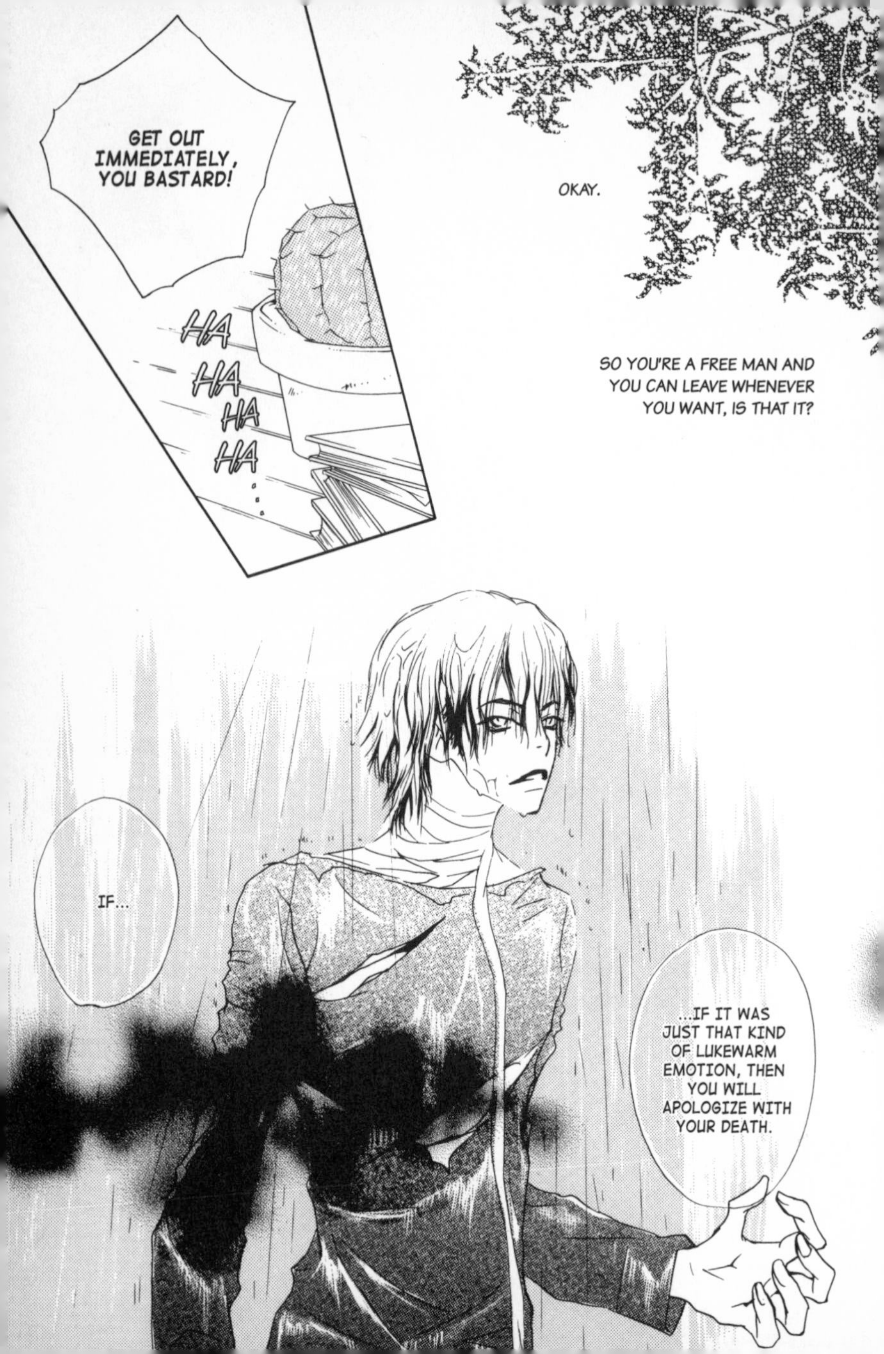
GET OUT IMMEDIATELY, YOU BASTARD!
HA HA HA HA...
OKAY.
SO YOU'RE A FREE MAN AND YOU CAN LEAVE WHENEVER YOU WANT, IS THAT IT?
IF...
...IF IT WAS JUST THAT KIND OF LUKEWARM EMOTION, THEN YOU WILL APOLOGIZE WITH YOUR DEATH.

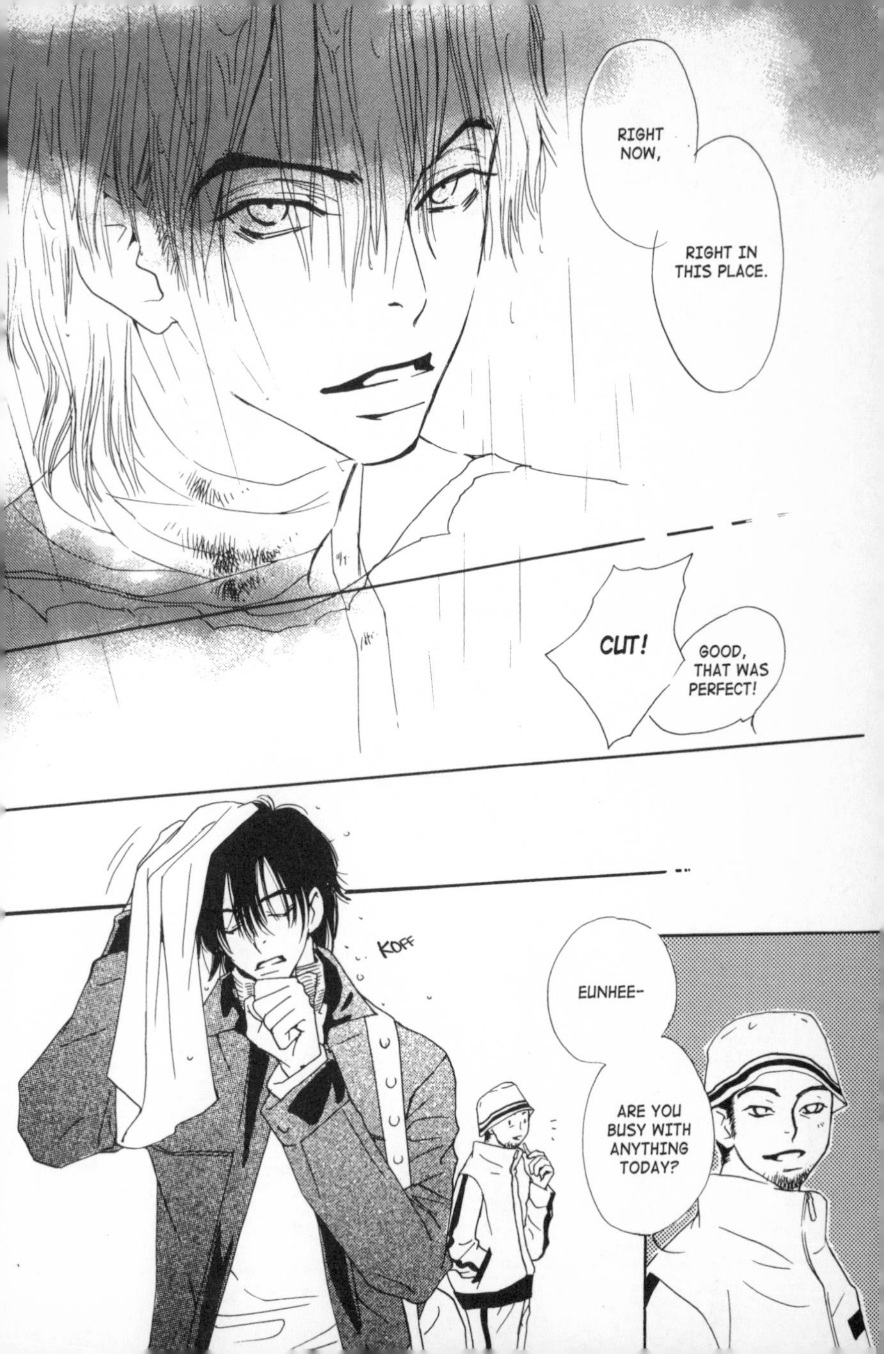
RIGHT NOW,
RIGHT IN THIS PLACE.
CUT!
GOOD, THAT WAS PERFECT!
KOFF
EUNHEE-
ARE YOU BUSY WITH ANYTHING TODAY?

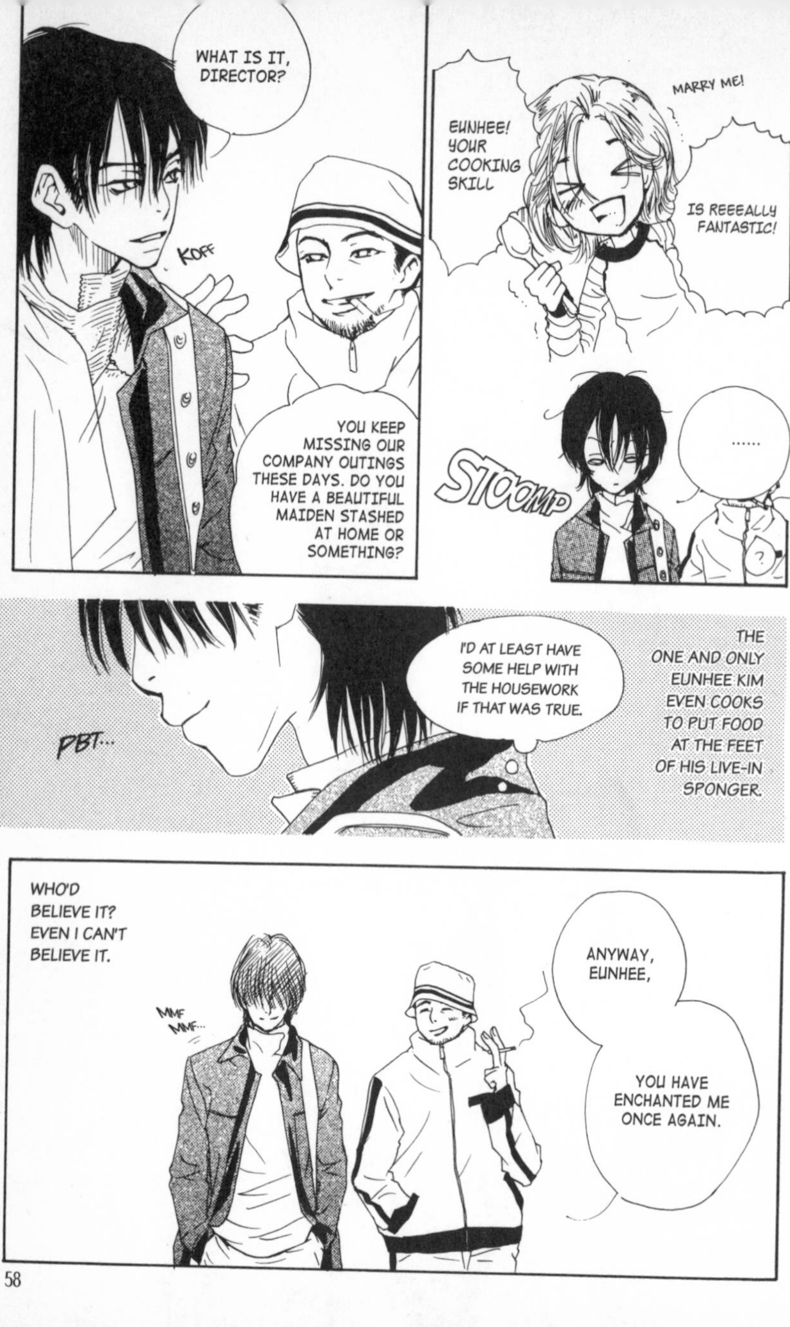
WHAT IS IT, DIRECTOR?
KOFF
YOU KEEP MISSING OUR COMPANY OUTINGS THESE DAYS. DO YOU HAVE A BEAUTIFUL MAIDEN STASHED AT HOME OR SOMETHING?
EUNHEE! YOUR COOKING SKILL
MARRY ME!
IS REEEALLY FANTASTIC!
STOOMP
......
?
PBT...
I'D AT LEAST HAVE SOME HELP WITH THE HOUSEWORK IF THAT WAS TRUE.
THE ONE AND ONLY EUNHEE KIM EVEN COOKS TO PUT FOOD AT THE FEET OF HIS LIVE-IN SPONGER.
WHO'D BELIEVE IT? EVEN I CAN'T BELIEVE IT.
MMF MMF...
ANYWAY, EUNHEE,
YOU HAVE ENCHANTED ME ONCE AGAIN.

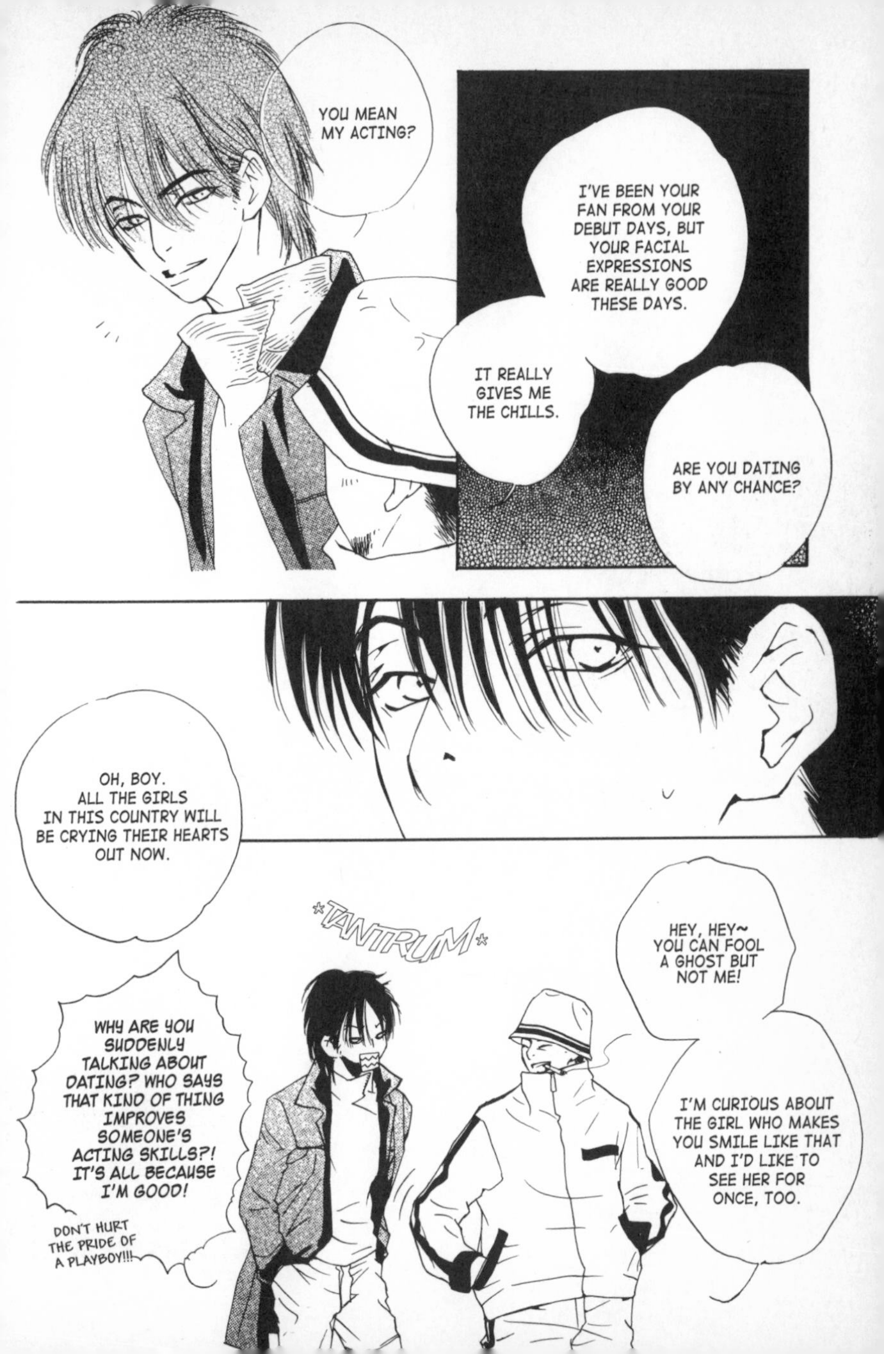
YOU MEAN MY ACTING?
I'VE BEEN YOUR FAN FROM YOUR DEBUT DAYS, BUT YOUR FACIAL EXPRESSIONS ARE REALLY GOOD THESE DAYS.
IT REALLY GIVES ME THE CHILLS.
ARE YOU DATING BY ANY CHANCE?
OH, BOY. ALL THE GIRLS IN THIS COUNTRY WILL BE CRYING THEIR HEARTS OUT NOW.
TANTRUM
WHY ARE YOU SUDDENLY TALKING ABOUT DATING? WHO SAYS THAT KIND OF THING IMPROVES SOMEONE'S ACTING SKILLS?! IT'S ALL BECAUSE I'M GOOD!
DON'T HURT THE PRIDE OF A PLAYBOY!!!
HEY, HEY~ YOU CAN FOOL A GHOST BUT NOT ME!
I'M CURIOUS ABOUT THE GIRL WHO MAKES YOU SMILE LIKE THAT AND I'D LIKE TO SEE HER FOR ONCE, TOO.

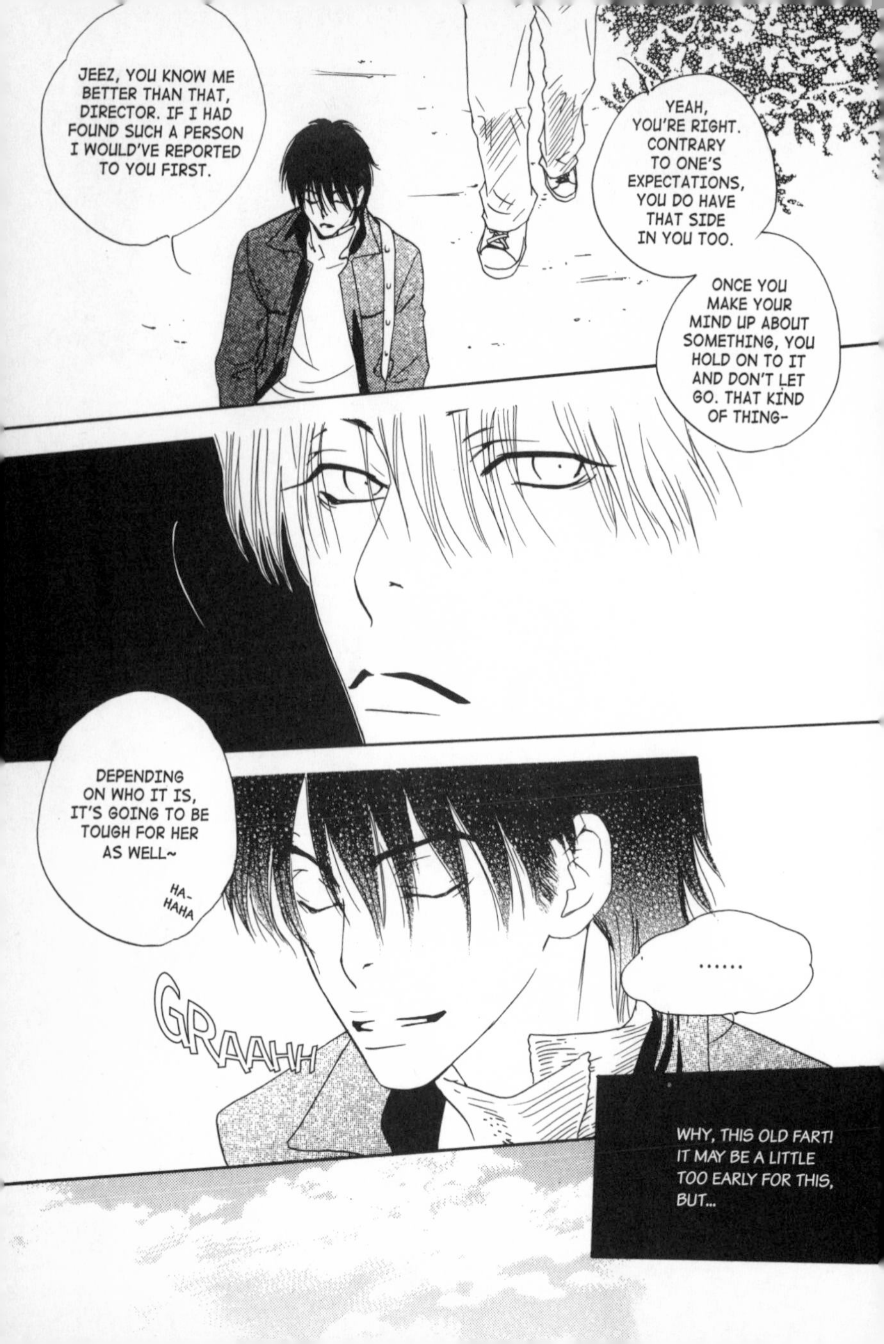
YEAH, YOU'RE RIGHT. CONTRARY TO ONE'S EXPECTATIONS, YOU DO HAVE THAT SIDE IN YOU TOO.
JEEZ, YOU KNOW ME BETTER THAN THAT, DIRECTOR. IF I HAD FOUND SUCH A PERSON I WOULD'VE REPORTED TO YOU FIRST.
ONCE YOU MAKE YOUR MIND UP ABOUT SOMETHING, YOU HOLD ON TO IT AND DON'T LET GO. THAT KIND OF THING-
DEPENDING ON WHO IT IS, IT'S GOING TO BE TOUGH FOR HER AS WELL~
HA-HAHA
......
GRAAHH
WHY, THIS OLD FART! IT MAY BE A LITTLE TOO EARLY FOR THIS, BUT...

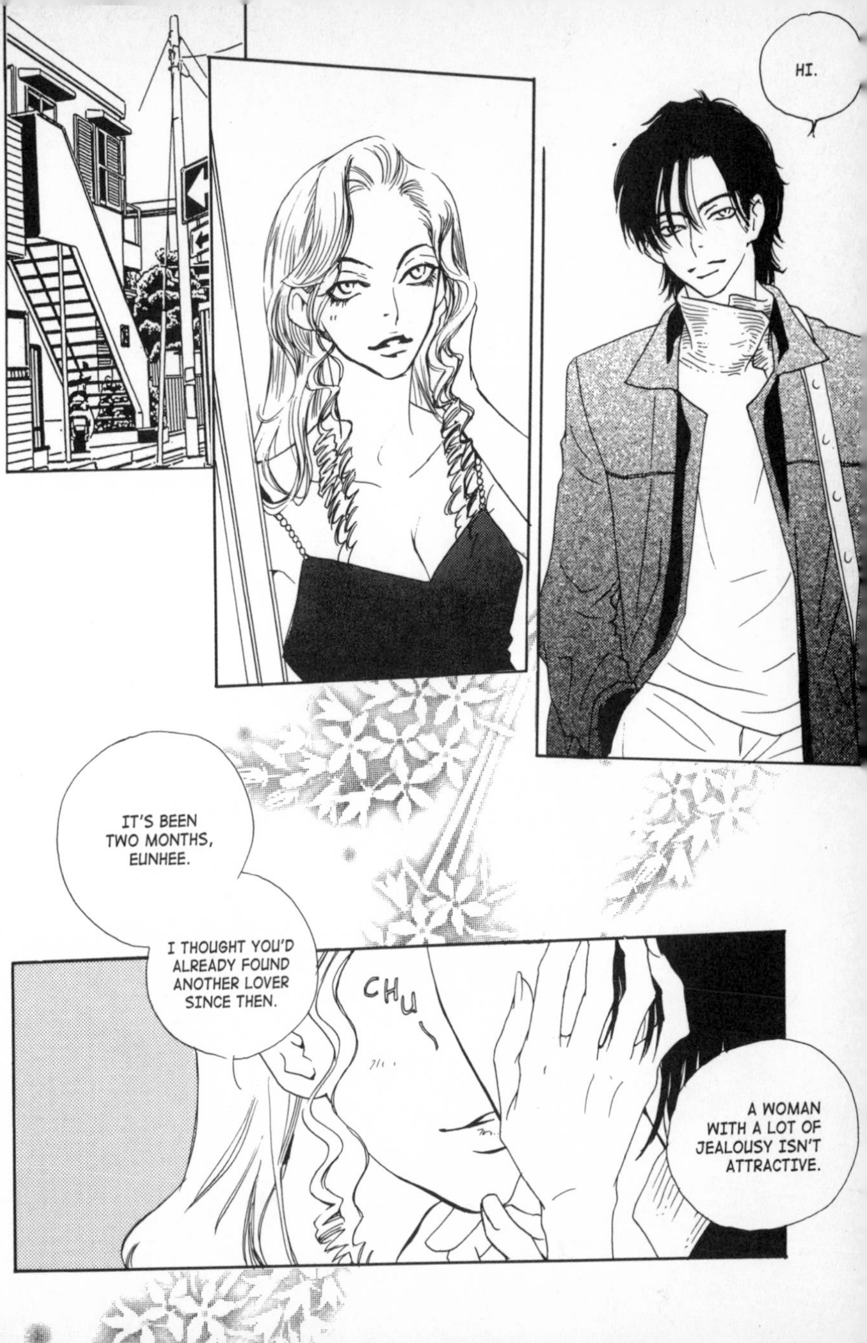
HI.
IT'S BEEN TWO MONTHS, EUNHEE.
I THOUGHT YOU'D ALREADY FOUND ANOTHER LOVER SINCE THEN.
CHU
A WOMAN WITH A LOT OF JEALOUSY ISN'T ATTRACTIVE.

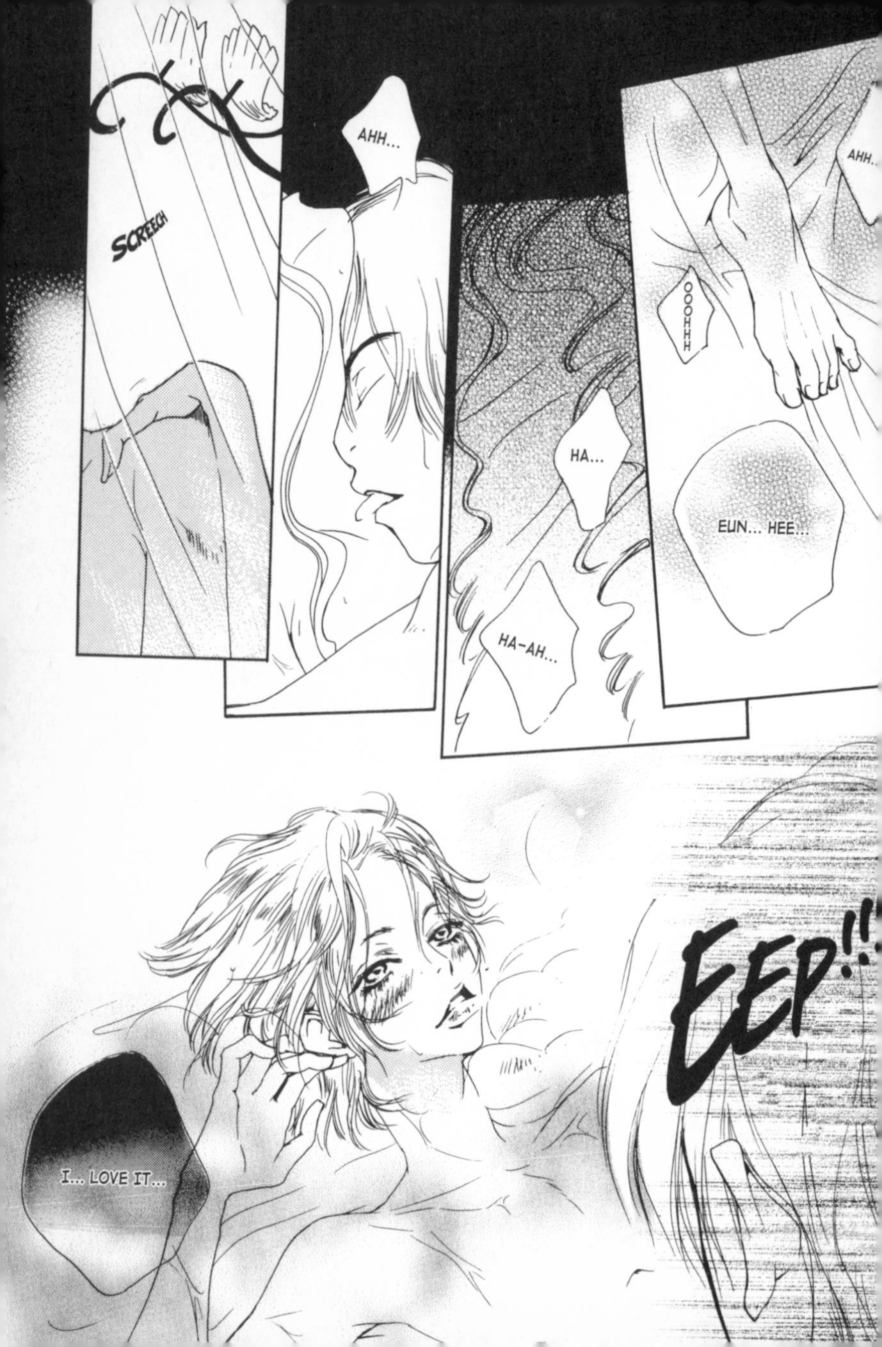
SCREECH
AHH...
HA...
HA-AH...
AHH...
OOOHH
EUN... HEE...
I... LOVE IT...
EEP!!

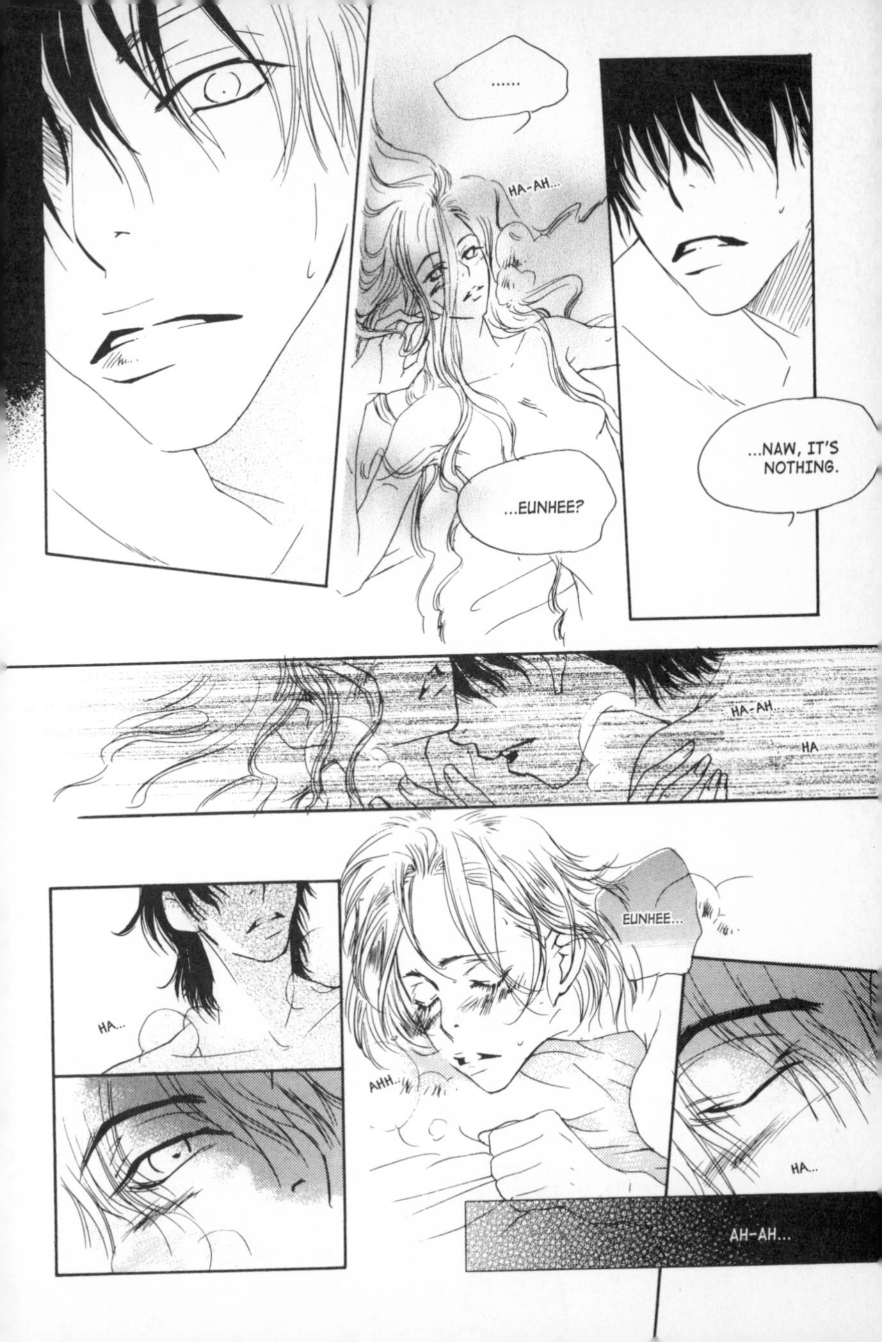
......
HA-AH...
...NAW, IT'S NOTHING.
...EUNHEE?
HA-AH..
HA
EUNHEE...
HA...
AHH..
HA...
AH-AH...

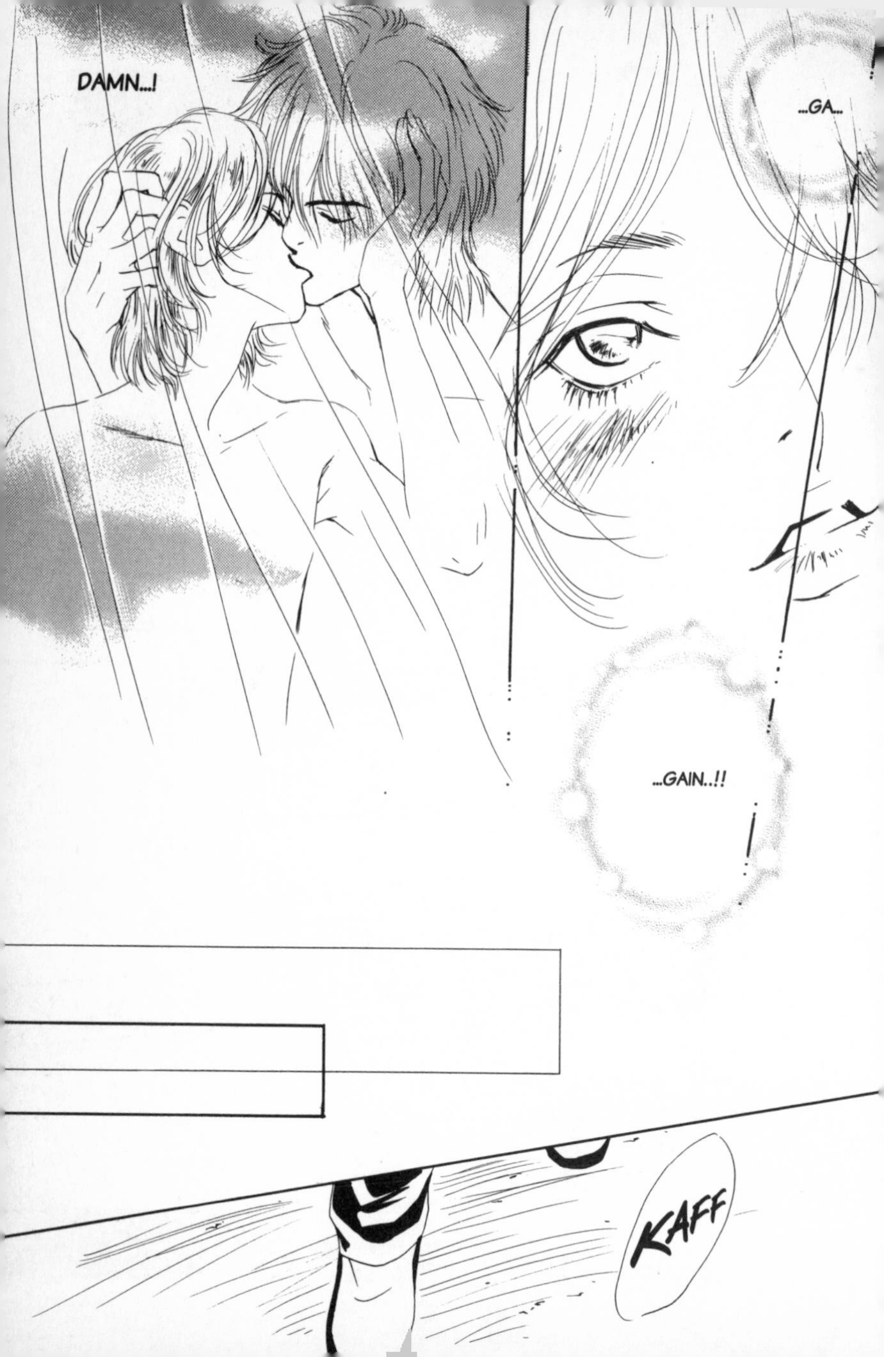
...GA...
...GAIN..!!
DAMN...!
KAFF

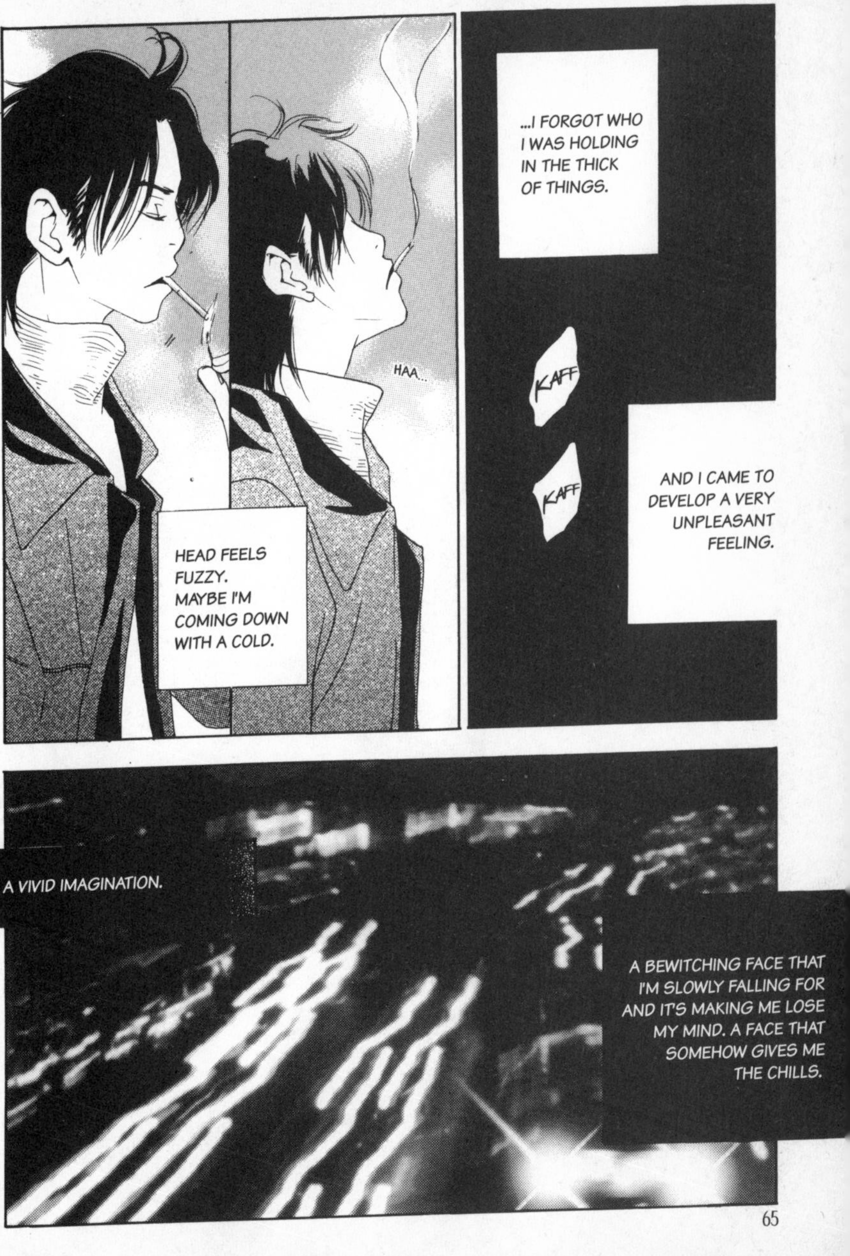
...I FORGOT WHO I WAS HOLDING IN THE THICK OF THINGS.
KAFF
KAFF
AND I CAME TO DEVELOP A VERY UNPLEASANT FEELING.
HAA...
HEAD FEELS FUZZY. MAYBE I'M COMING DOWN WITH A COLD.
A BEWITCHING FACE THAT I'M SLOWLY FALLING FOR AND IT'S MAKING ME LOSE MY MIND. A FACE THAT SOMEHOW GIVES ME THE CHILLS.
A VIVID IMAGINATION.

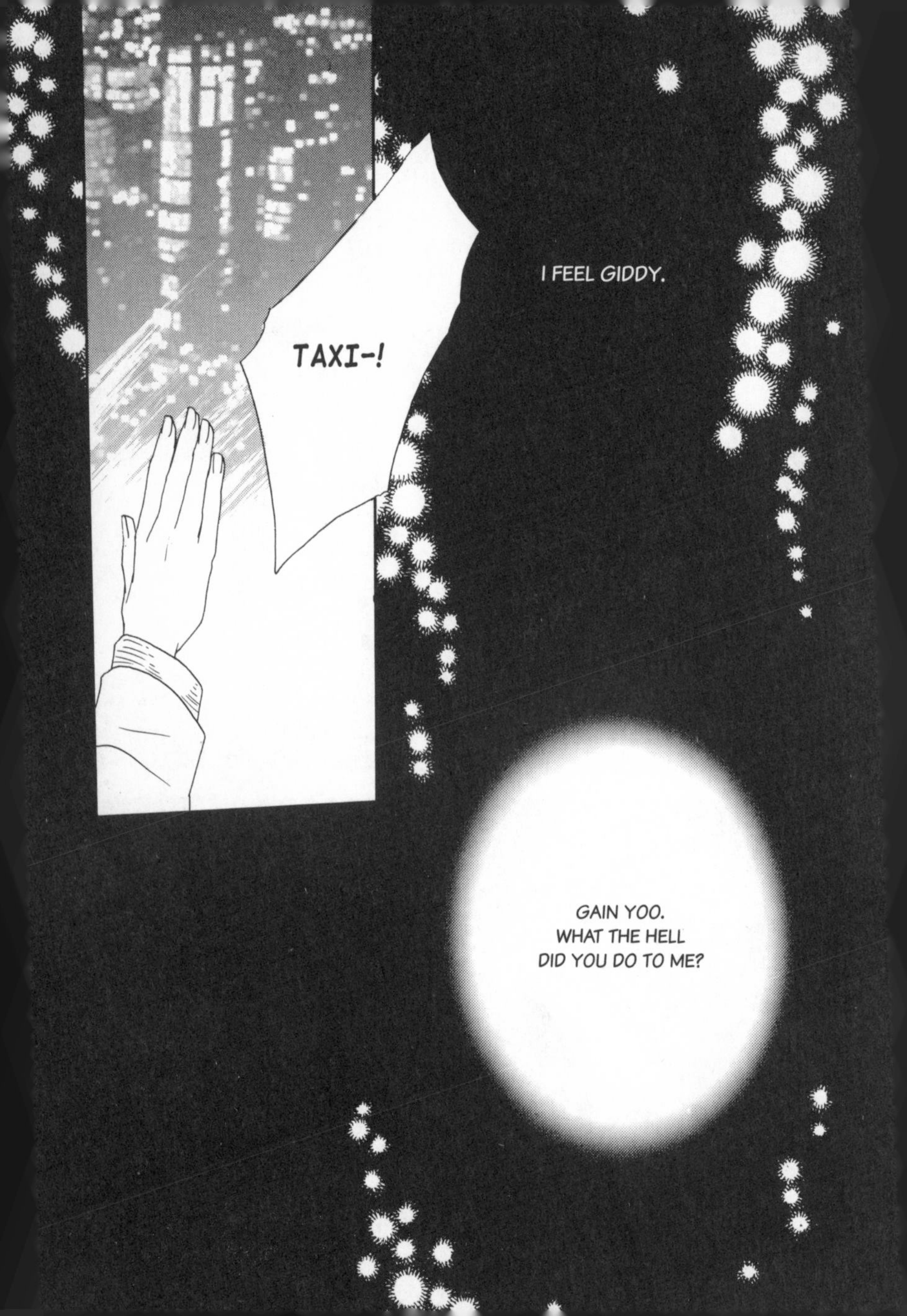
TAXI-!
I FEEL GIDDY.
GAIN YOO.
WHAT THE HELL
DID YOU DO TO ME?

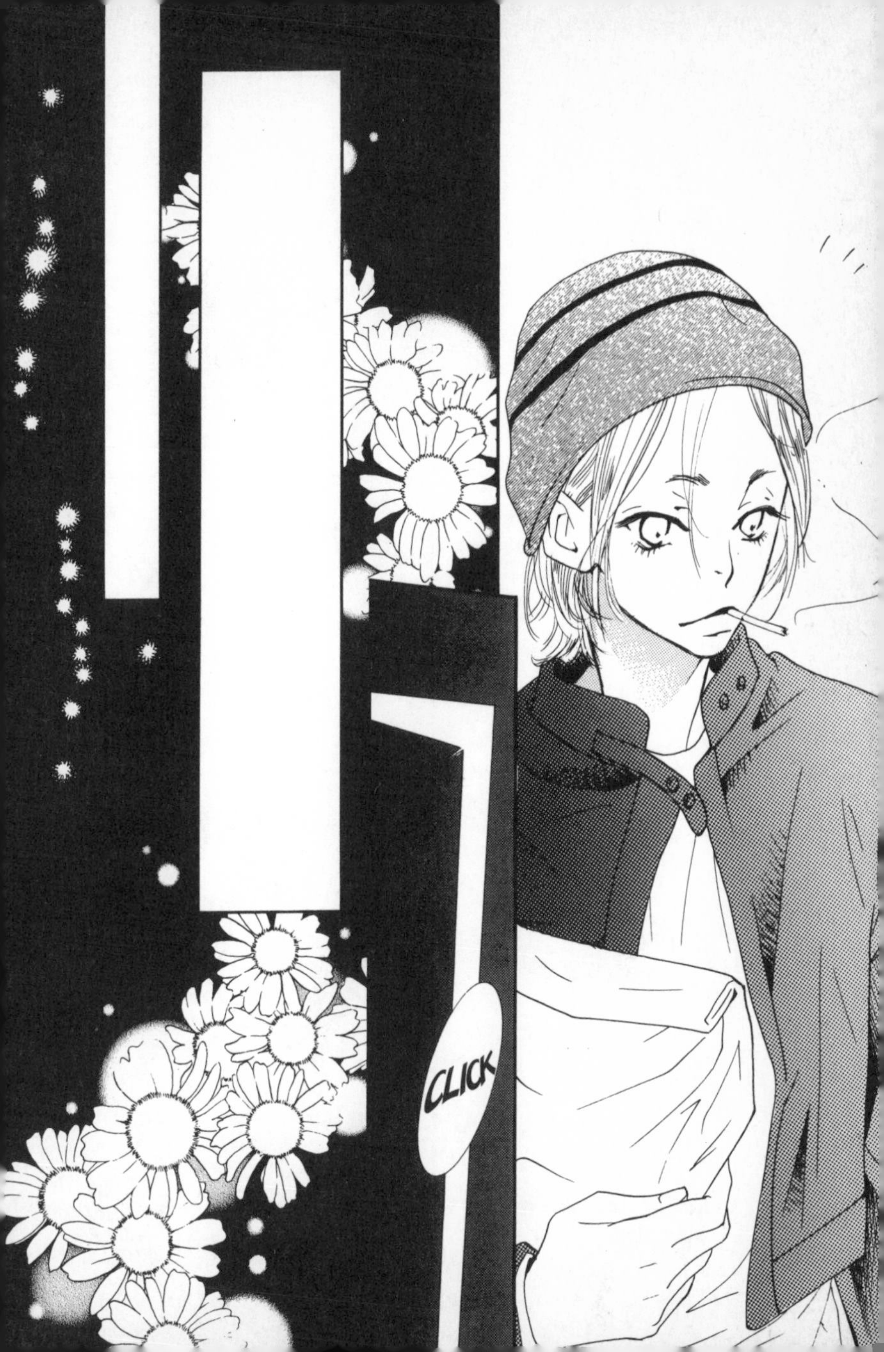
CLICK

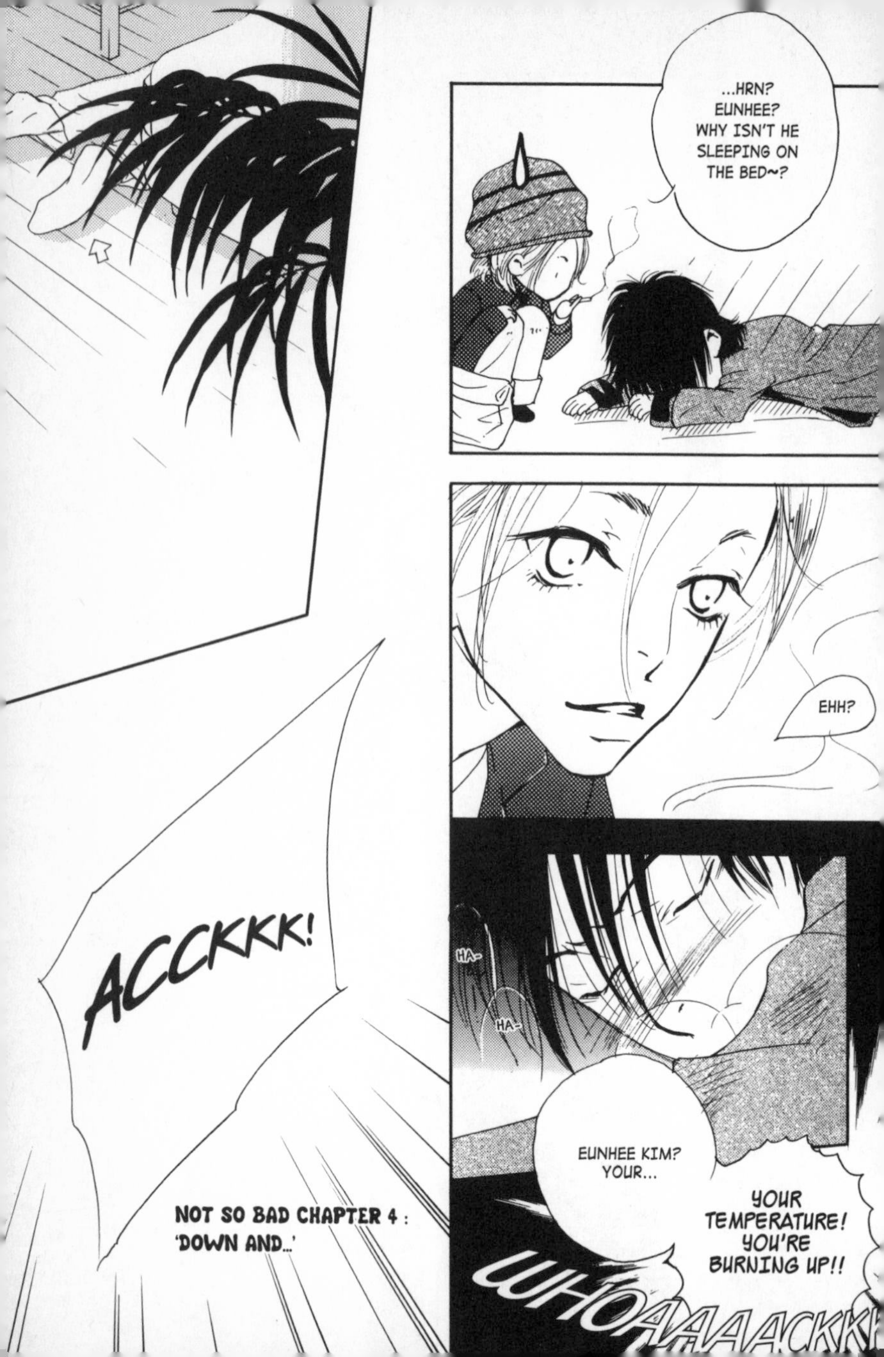
ACCKKK!
NOT SO BAD CHAPTER 4 :
'DOWN AND...'
...HRN? EUNHEE? WHY ISN'T HE SLEEPING ON THE BED~?
EHH?
HA-
HA-
EUNHEE KIM? YOUR...
YOUR TEMPERATURE! YOU'RE BURNING UP!!
WHOAAAAACKK

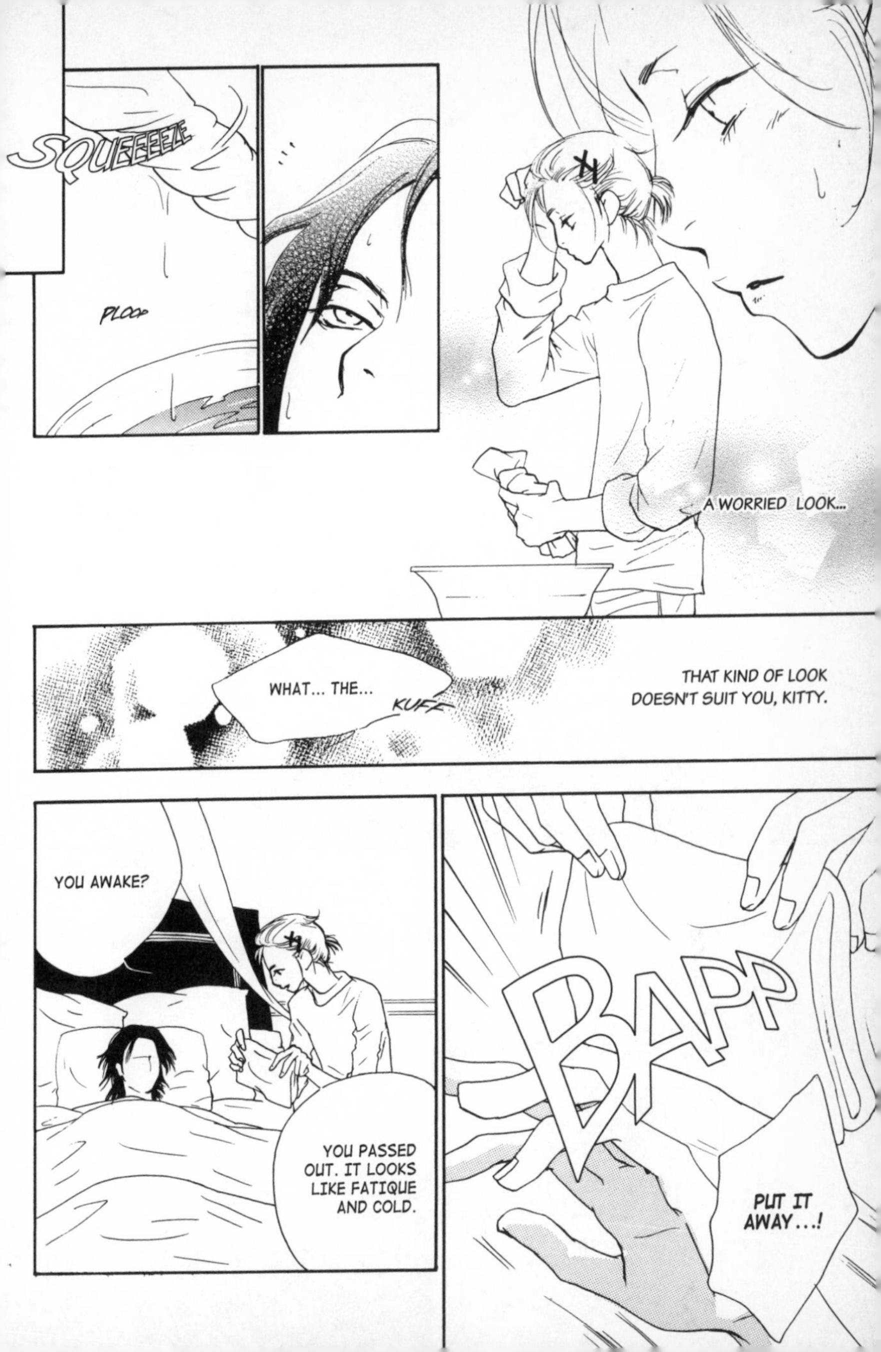
SQUEEEEEZE
PLOOP
...
A WORRIED LOOK...
THAT KIND OF LOOK DOESN'T SUIT YOU, KITTY.
WHAT... THE...
KUFF
YOU AWAKE?
YOU PASSED OUT. IT LOOKS LIKE FATIQUE AND COLD.
BAPP
PUT IT AWAY...!

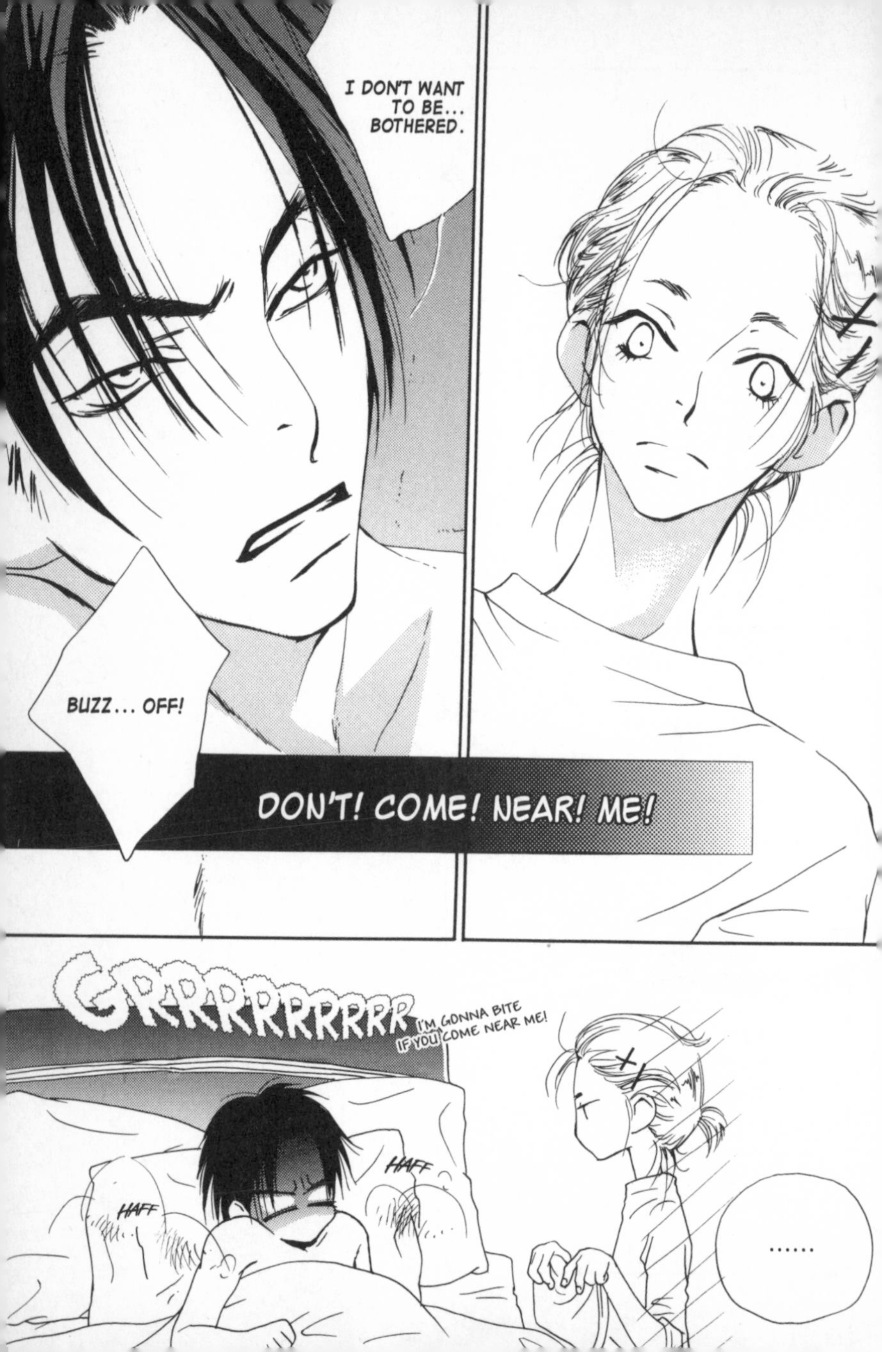
I DON'T WANT TO BE... BOTHERED.
BUZZ... OFF!
DON'T! COME! NEAR! ME!
GRRRRRRRRRR
I'M GONNA BITE IF YOU COME NEAR ME!
HAFF
HAFF
......

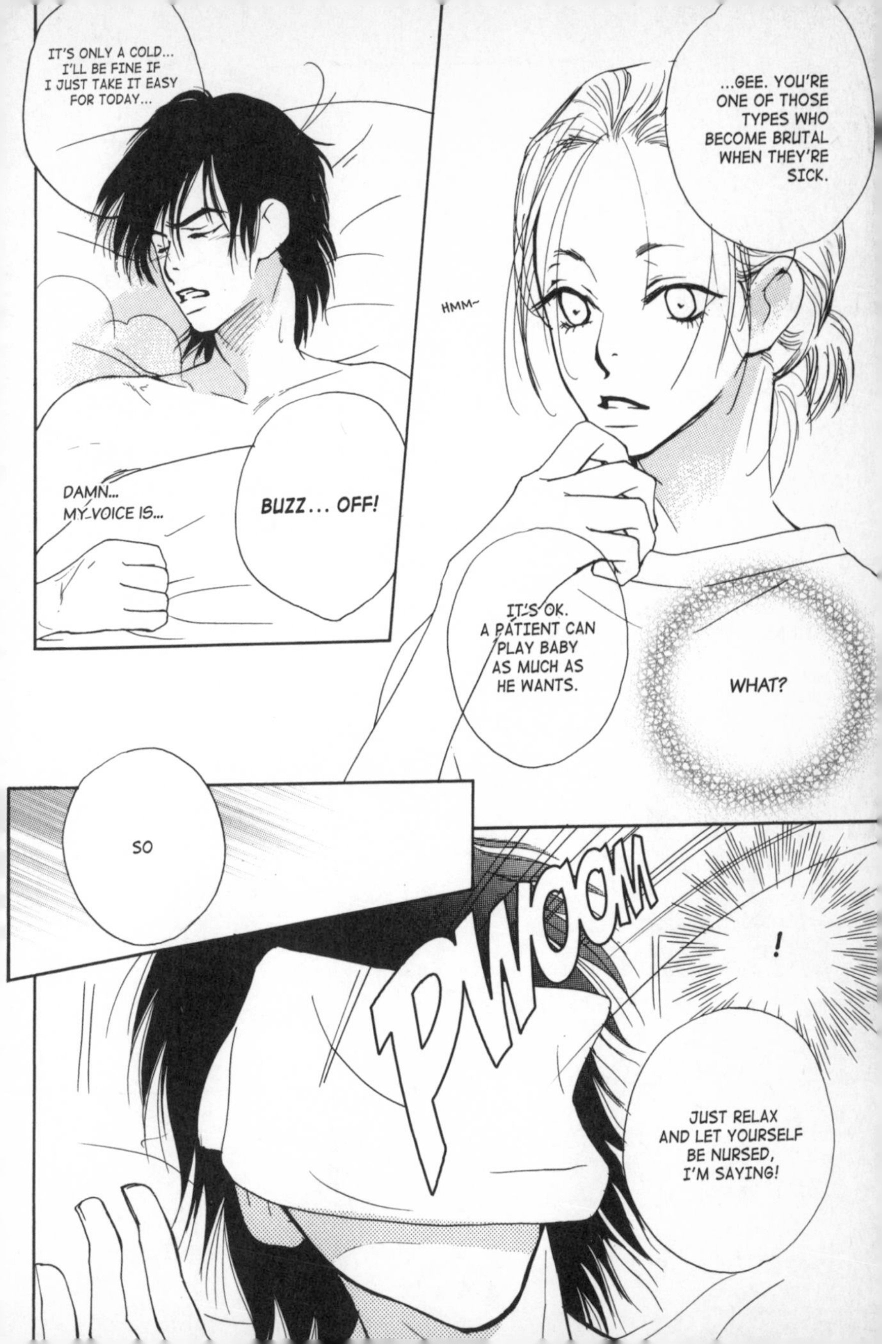
IT'S ONLY A COLD... I'LL BE FINE IF I JUST TAKE IT EASY FOR TODAY...
BUZZ... OFF!
DAMN... MY VOICE IS...
...GEE. YOU'RE ONE OF THOSE TYPES WHO BECOME BRUTAL WHEN THEY'RE SICK.
HMM~
IT'S OK. A PATIENT CAN PLAY BABY AS MUCH AS HE WANTS.
WHAT?
SO
PWOOM
!
JUST RELAX AND LET YOURSELF BE NURSED, I'M SAYING!

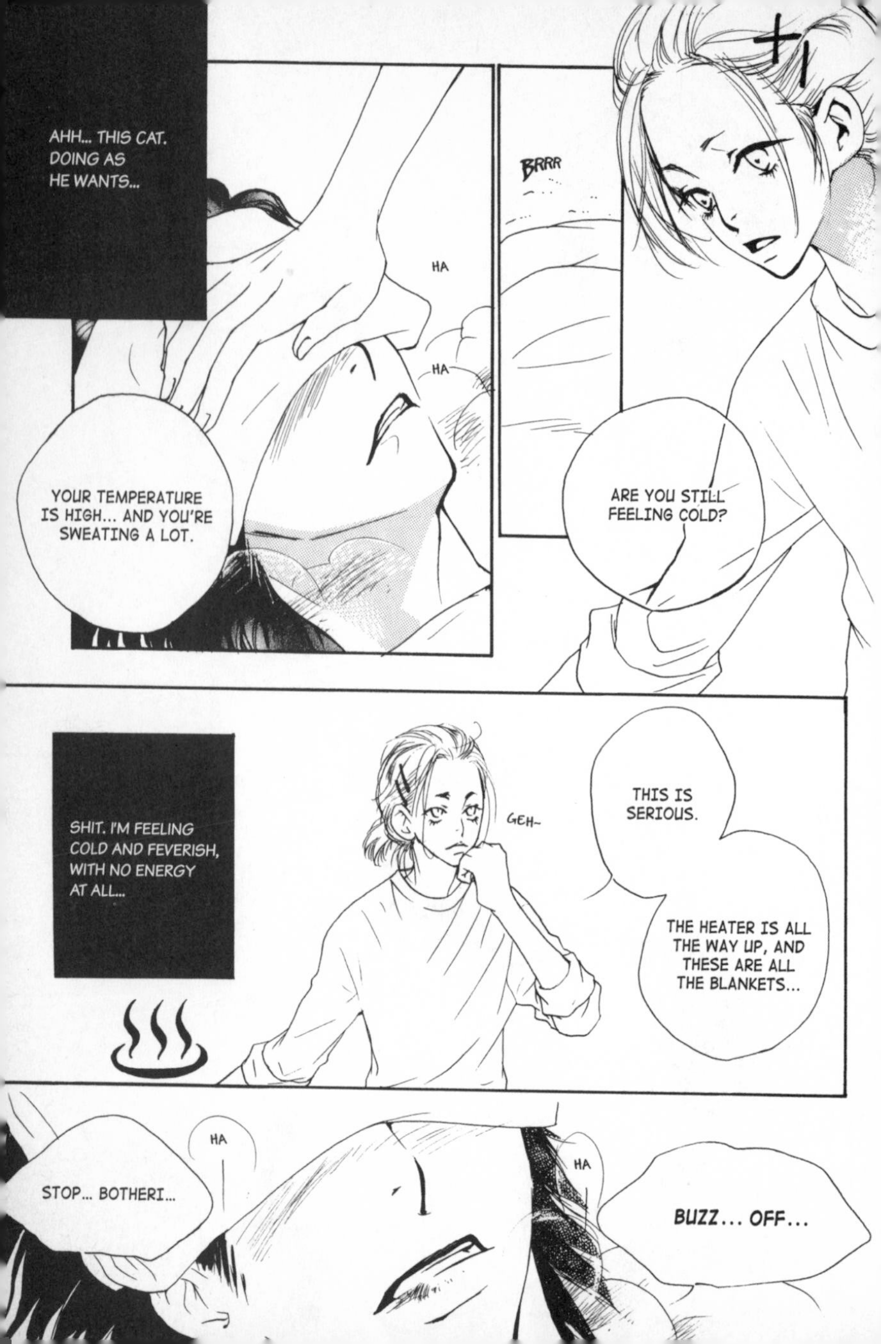
AHH... THIS CAT. DOING AS HE WANTS...
HA
HA
YOUR TEMPERATURE IS HIGH... AND YOU'RE SWEATING A LOT.
BRRR
ARE YOU STILL FEELING COLD?
SHIT. I'M FEELING COLD AND FEVERISH, WITH NO ENERGY AT ALL...
GEH~
THIS IS SERIOUS.
THE HEATER IS ALL THE WAY UP, AND THESE ARE ALL THE BLANKETS...
STOP... BOTHERI...
HA
HA
BUZZ... OFF...

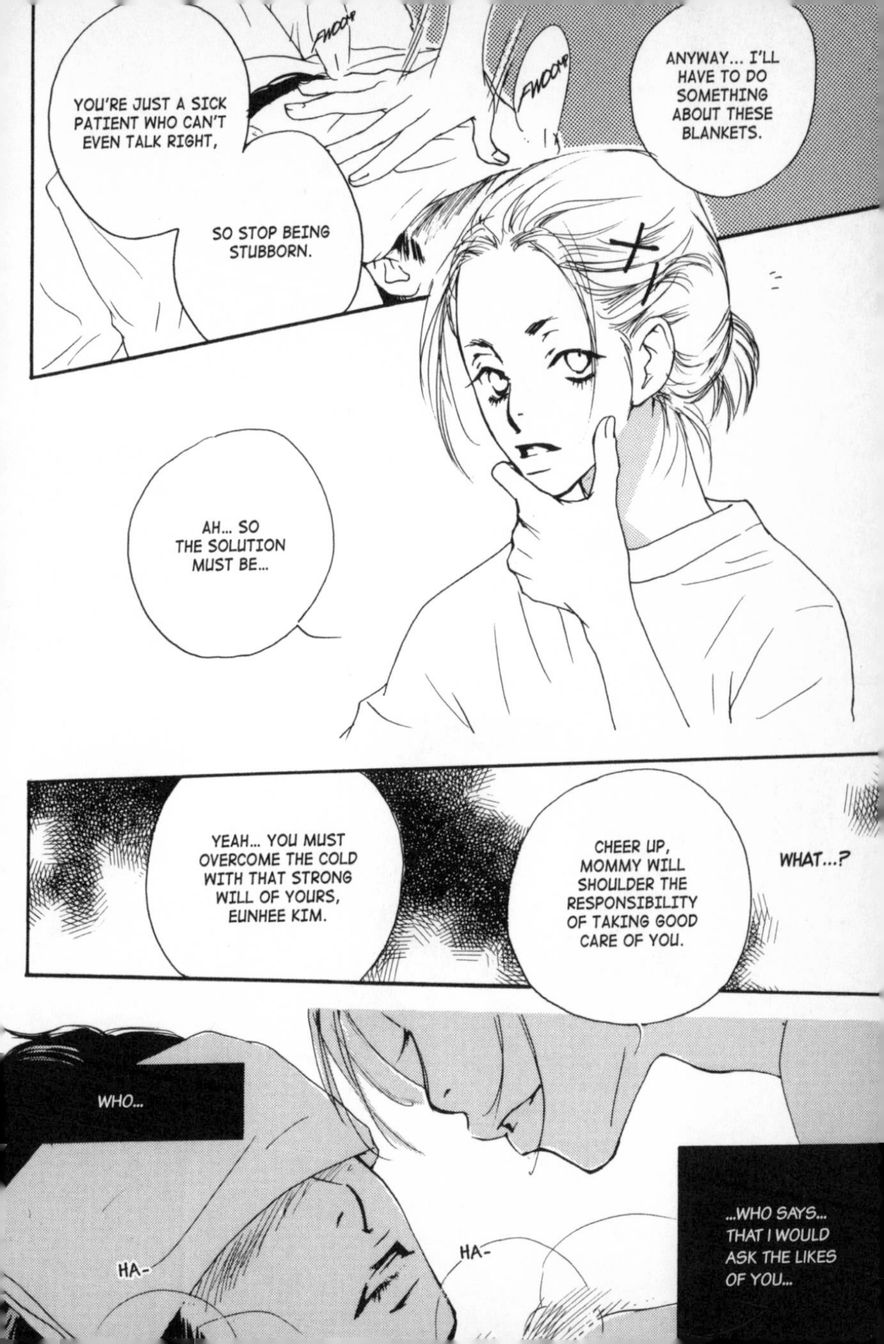
YOU'RE JUST A SICK PATIENT WHO CAN'T EVEN TALK RIGHT,
SO STOP BEING STUBBORN.
FWOOMP
FWOOMP
ANYWAY... I'LL HAVE TO DO SOMETHING ABOUT THESE BLANKETS.
AH... SO THE SOLUTION MUST BE...
YEAH... YOU MUST OVERCOME THE COLD WITH THAT STRONG WILL OF YOURS, EUNHEE KIM.
CHEER UP, MOMMY WILL SHOULDER THE RESPONSIBILITY OF TAKING GOOD CARE OF YOU.
WHAT...?
WHO...
HA-
HA-
...WHO SAYS... THAT I WOULD ASK THE LIKES OF YOU...

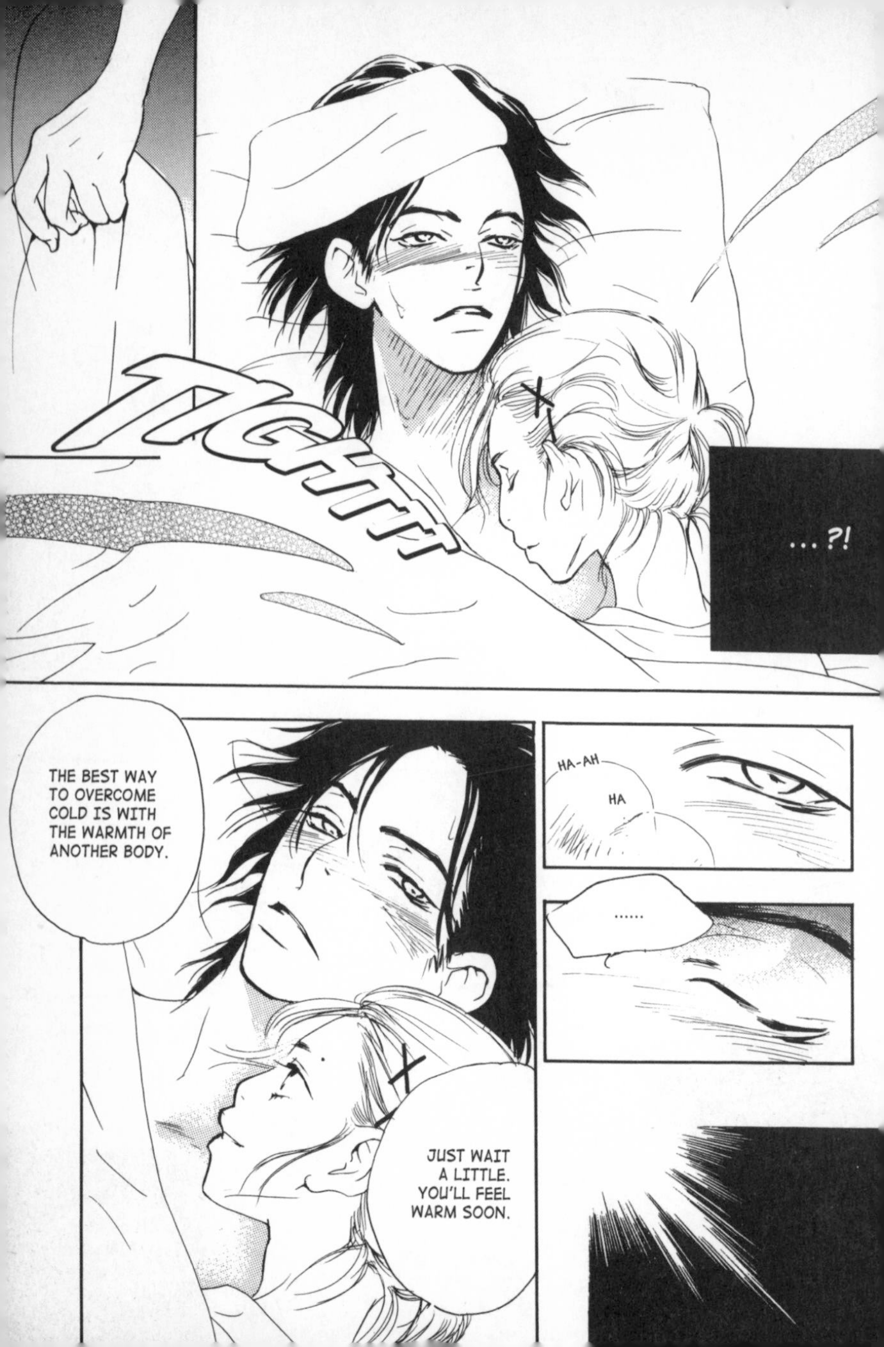
TIGHT
...?!
THE BEST WAY TO OVERCOME COLD IS WITH THE WARMTH OF ANOTHER BODY.
HA-AH
HA
......
JUST WAIT A LITTLE. YOU'LL FEEL WARM SOON.

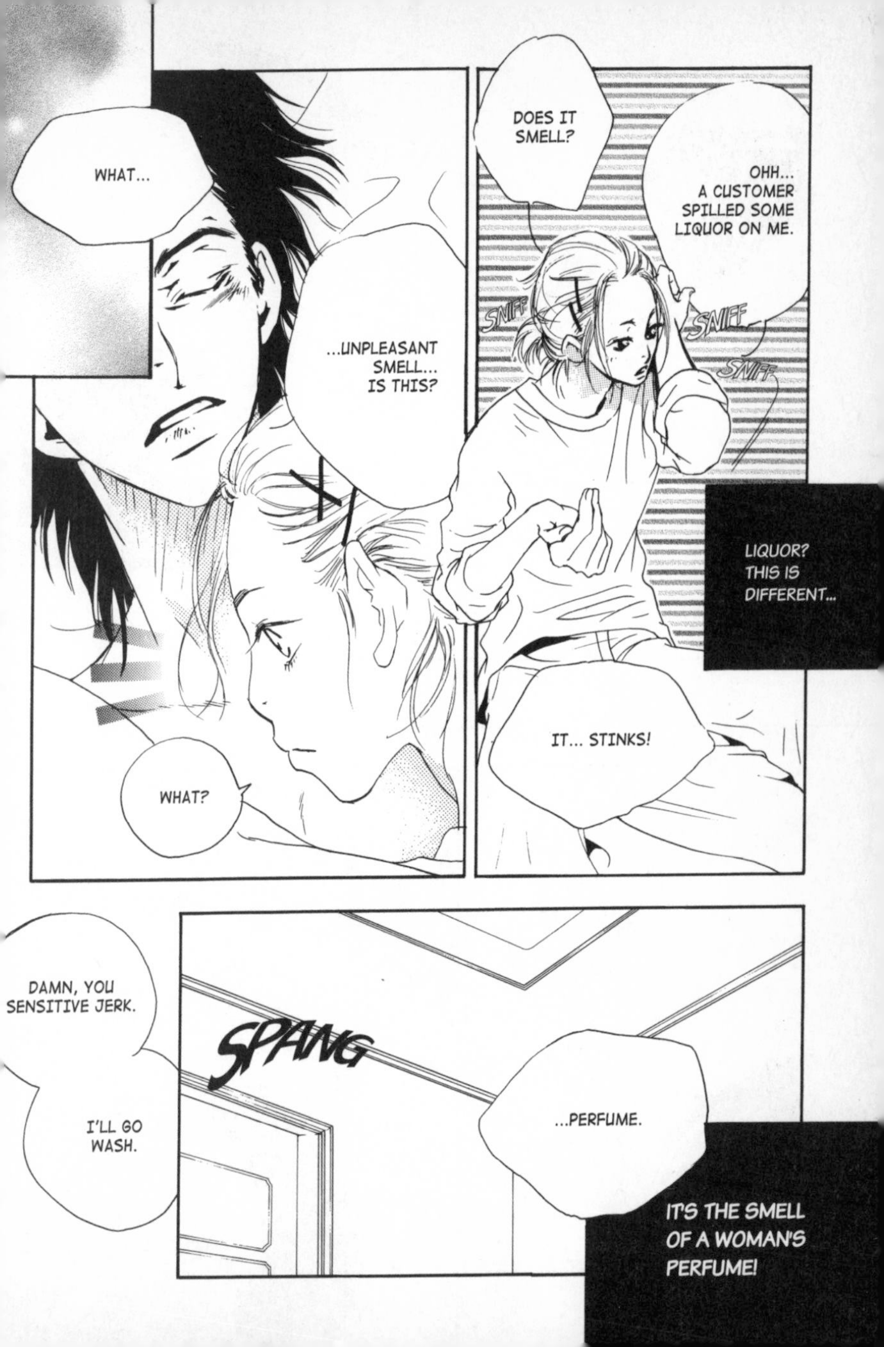

WHAT...
...UNPLEASANT SMELL... IS THIS?
WHAT?
DOES IT SMELL?
OHH... A CUSTOMER SPILLED SOME LIQUOR ON ME.
SNIFF
SNIFF
SNIFF
LIQUOR? THIS IS DIFFERENT...
IT... STINKS!
...PERFUME.
IT'S THE SMELL OF A WOMAN'S PERFUME!
DAMN, YOU SENSITIVE JERK.
I'LL GO WASH.
SPANG

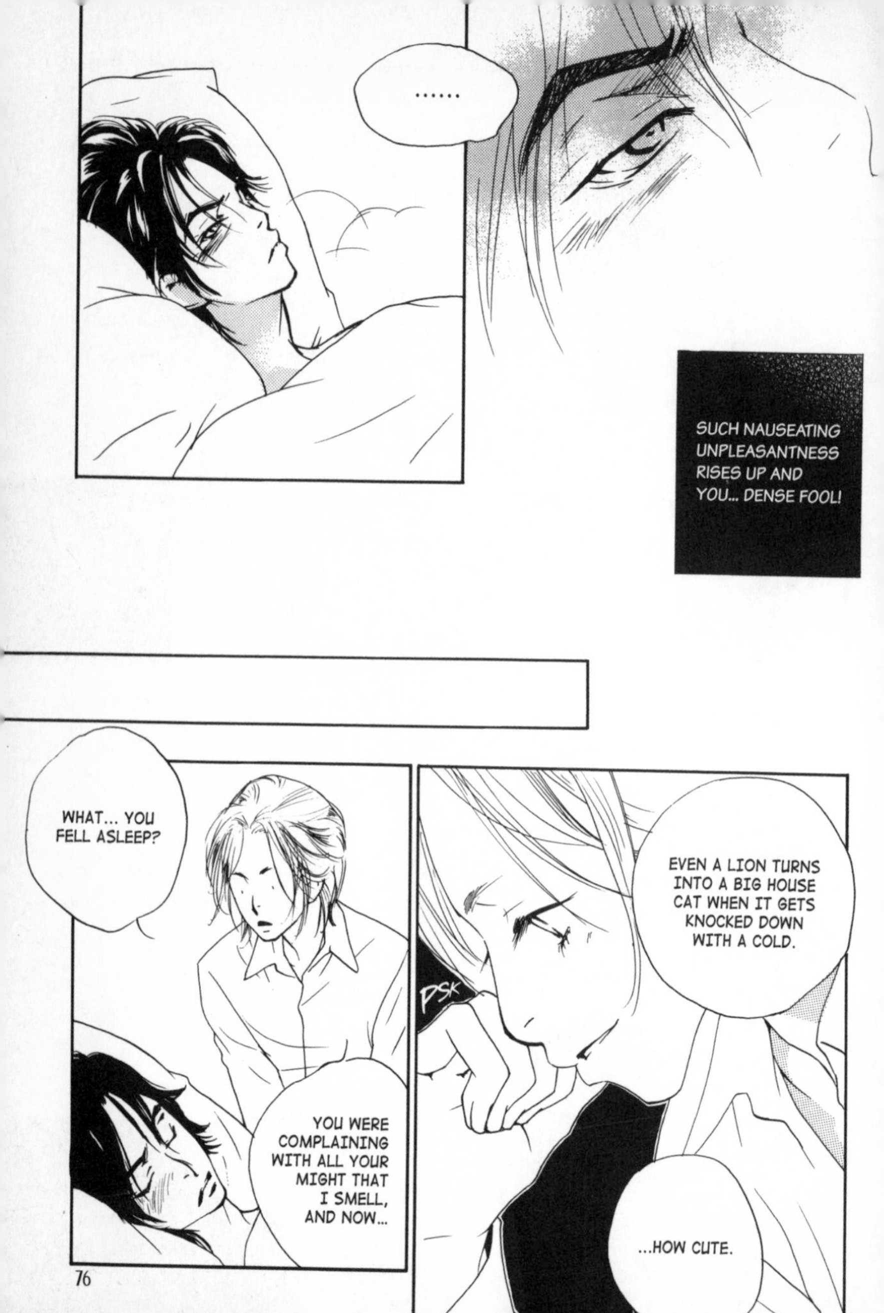
......
SUCH NAUSEATING UNPLEASANTNESS RISES UP AND YOU... DENSE FOOL!
WHAT... YOU FELL ASLEEP?
YOU WERE COMPLAINING WITH ALL YOUR MIGHT THAT I SMELL, AND NOW...
EVEN A LION TURNS INTO A BIG HOUSE CAT WHEN IT GETS KNOCKED DOWN WITH A COLD.
...HOW CUTE.
PSK

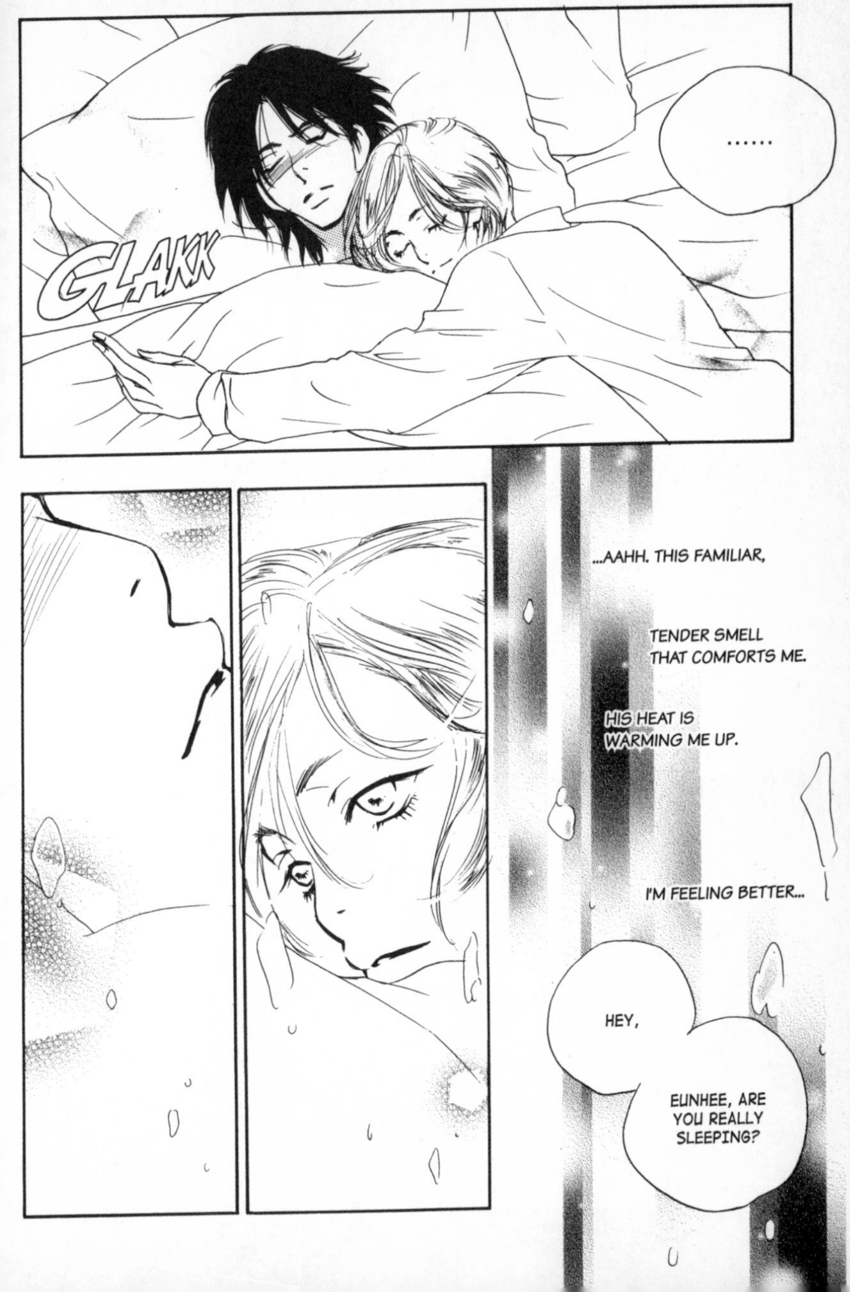

GLAKK
......
...AAHH. THIS FAMILIAR,
TENDER SMELL THAT COMFORTS ME.
HIS HEAT IS WARMING ME UP.
I'M FEELING BETTER...
HEY,
EUNHEE, ARE YOU REALLY SLEEPING?

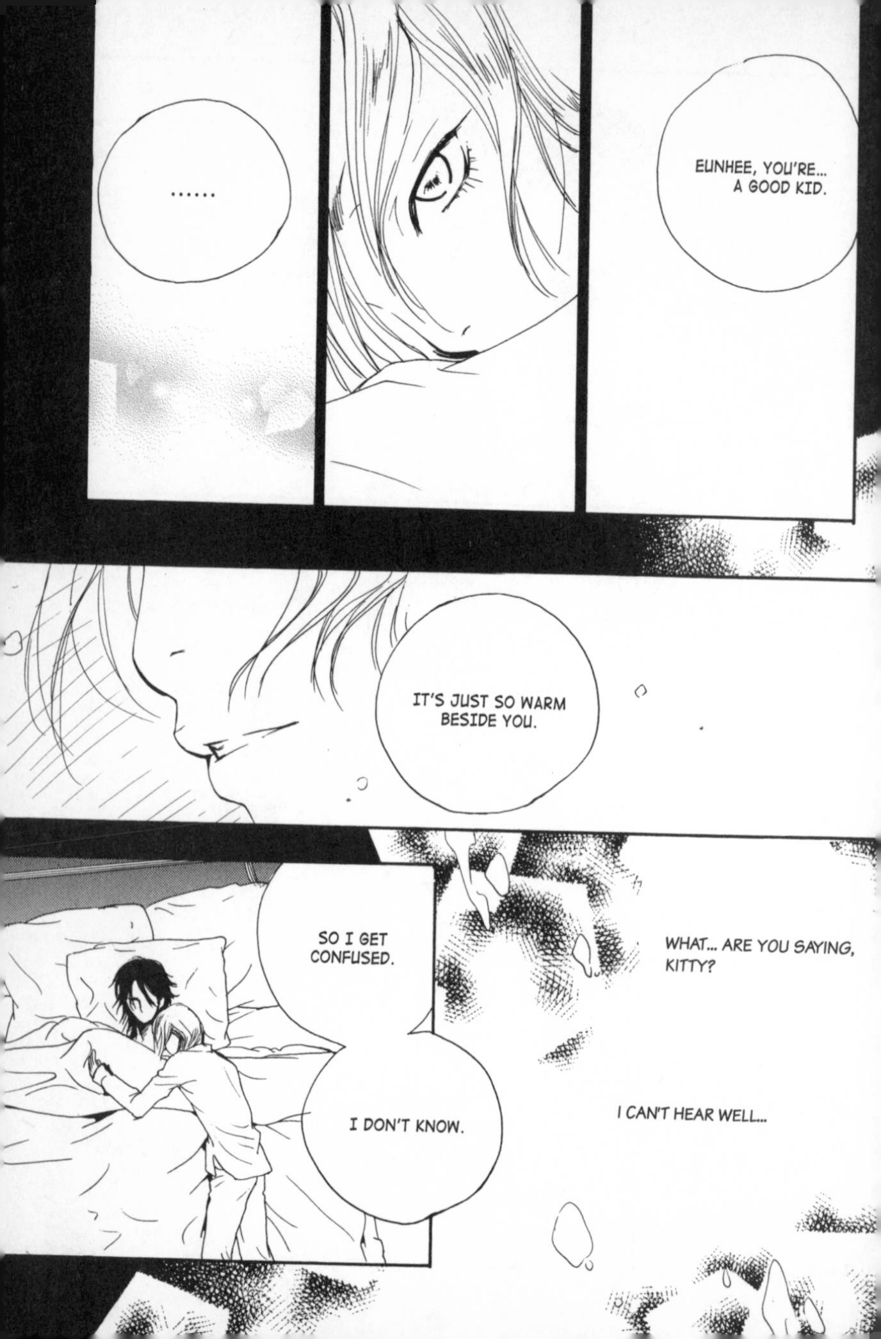
EUNHEE, YOU'RE... A GOOD KID.
......
IT'S JUST SO WARM BESIDE YOU.
WHAT... ARE YOU SAYING, KITTY?
I CAN'T HEAR WELL...
SO I GET CONFUSED.
I DON'T KNOW.

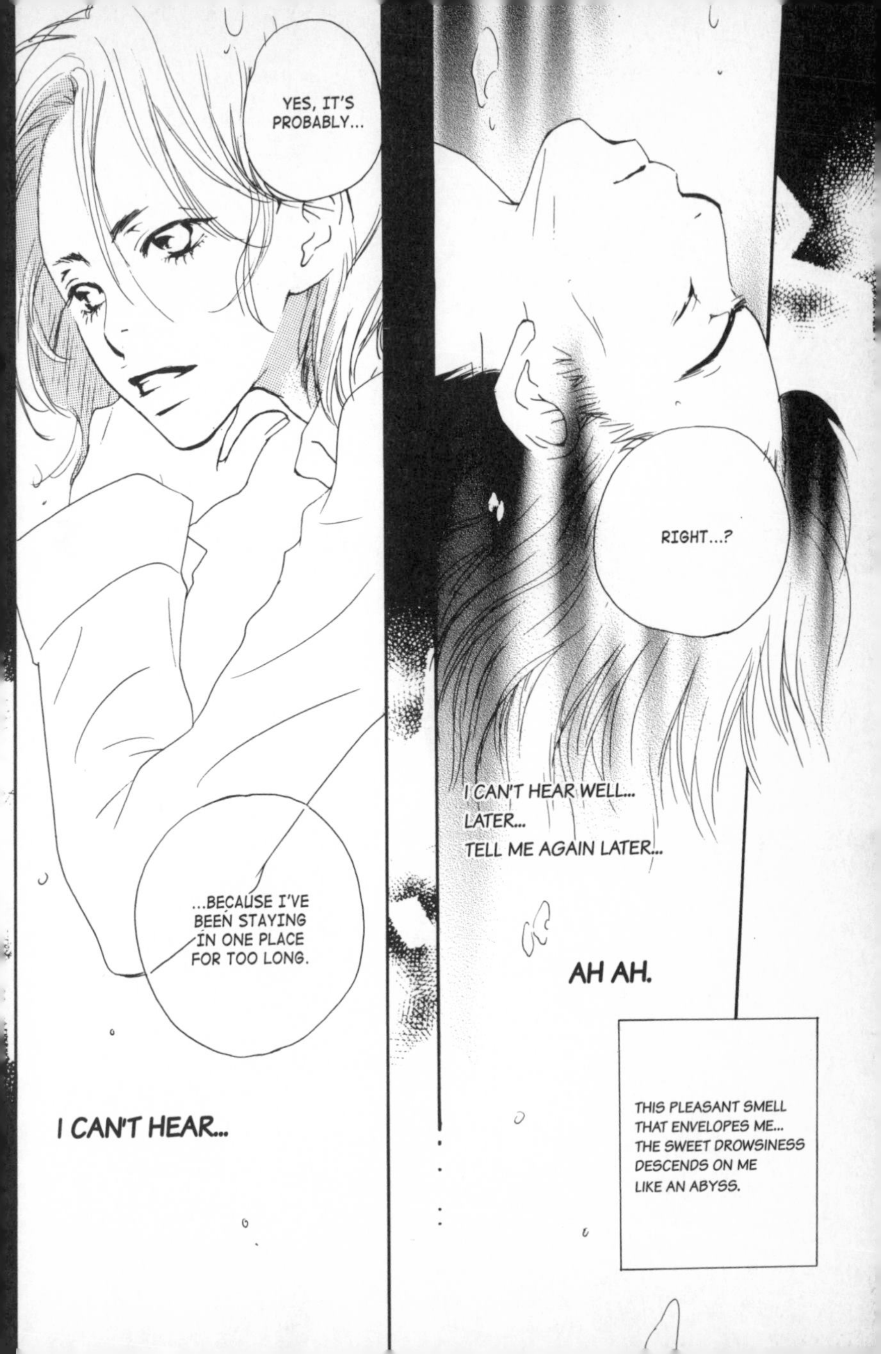
RIGHT...?
I CAN'T HEAR WELL... LATER... TELL ME AGAIN LATER...
AH AH.
THIS PLEASANT SMELL THAT ENVELOPES ME... THE SWEET DROWSINESS DESCENDS ON ME LIKE AN ABYSS.
YES, IT'S PROBABLY...
...BECAUSE I'VE BEEN STAYING IN ONE PLACE FOR TOO LONG.
I CAN'T HEAR...

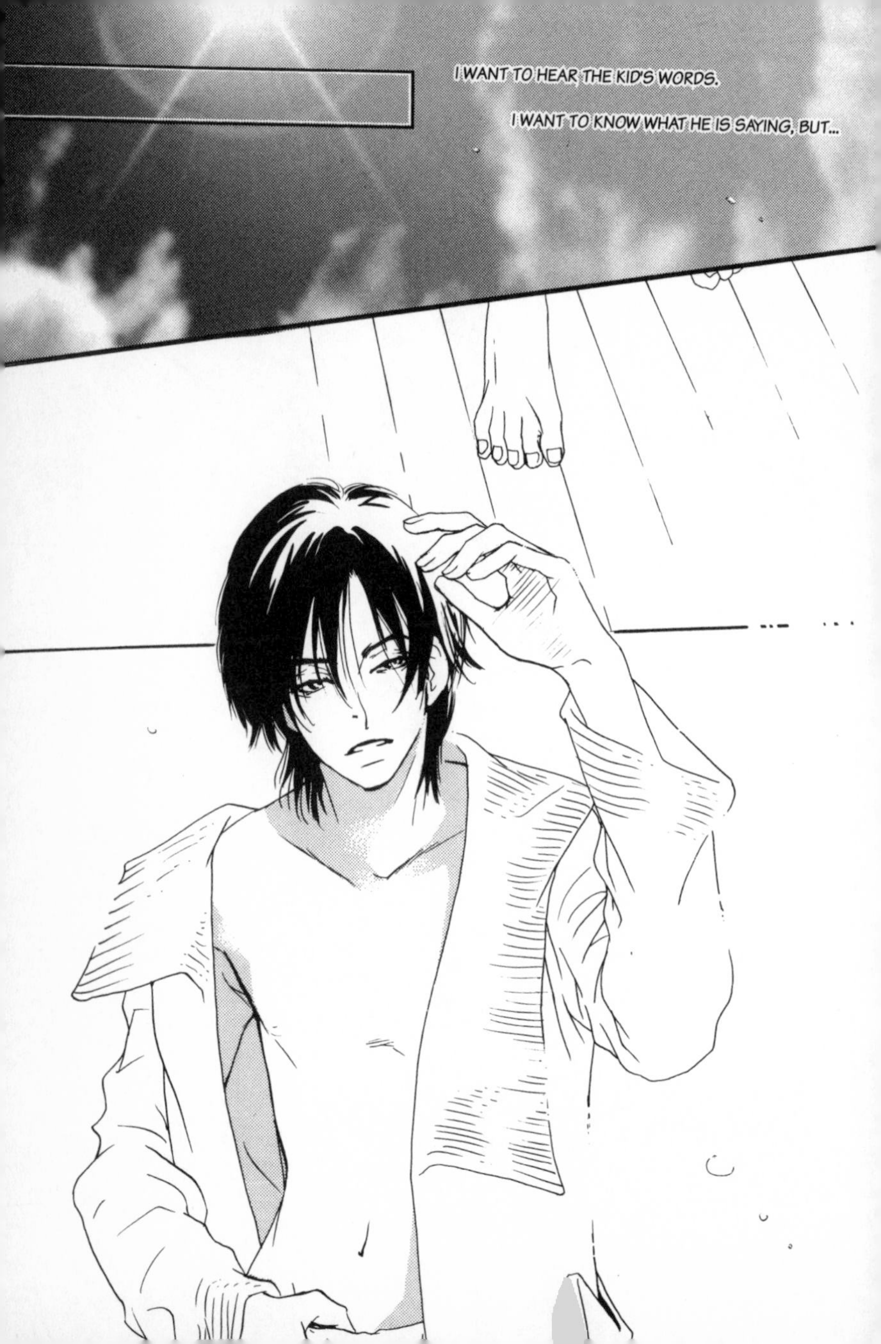
I WANT TO HEAR THE KID'S WORDS.
I WANT TO KNOW WHAT HE IS SAYING, BUT...

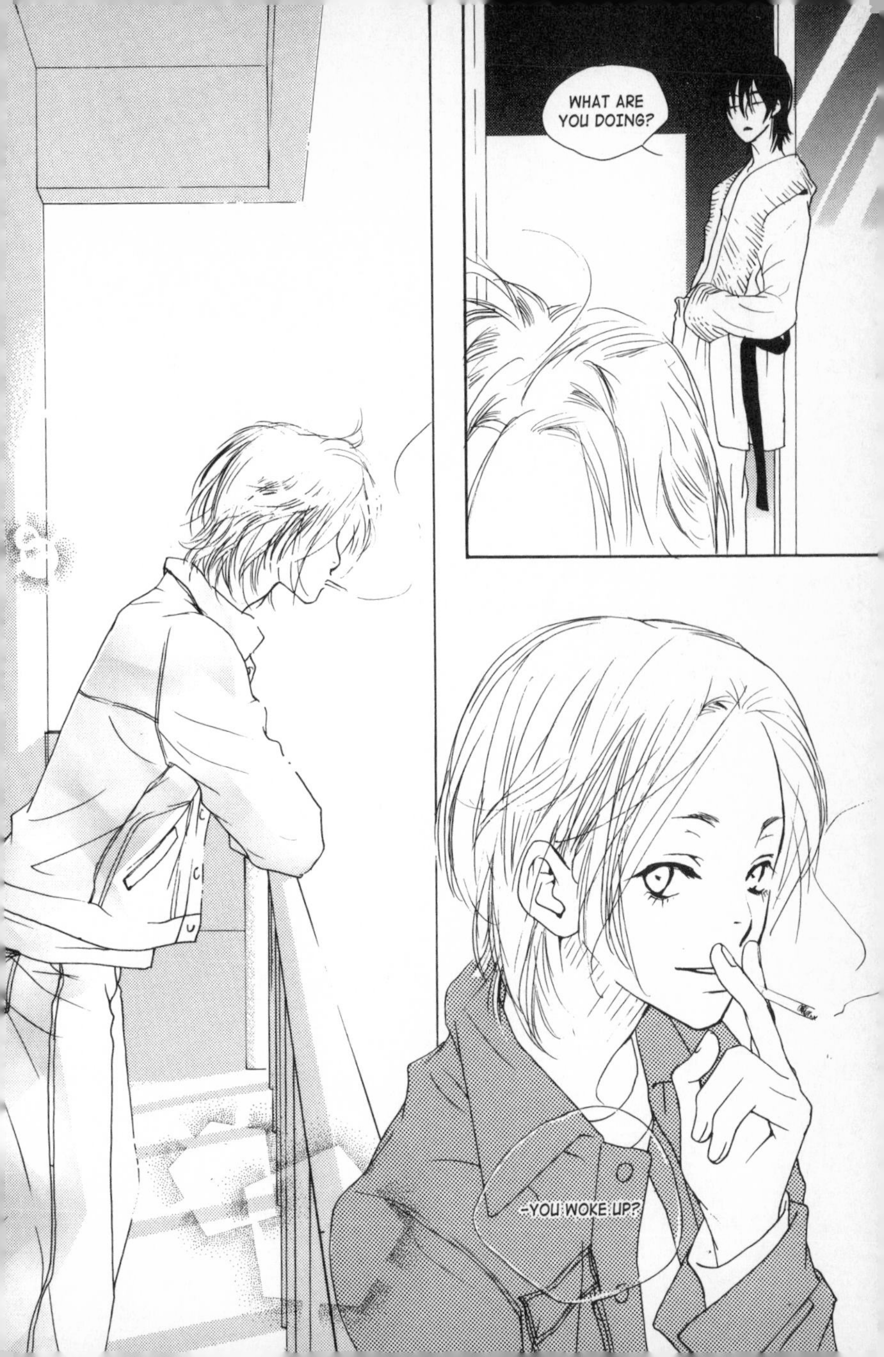
WHAT ARE YOU DOING?
-YOU WOKE UP?

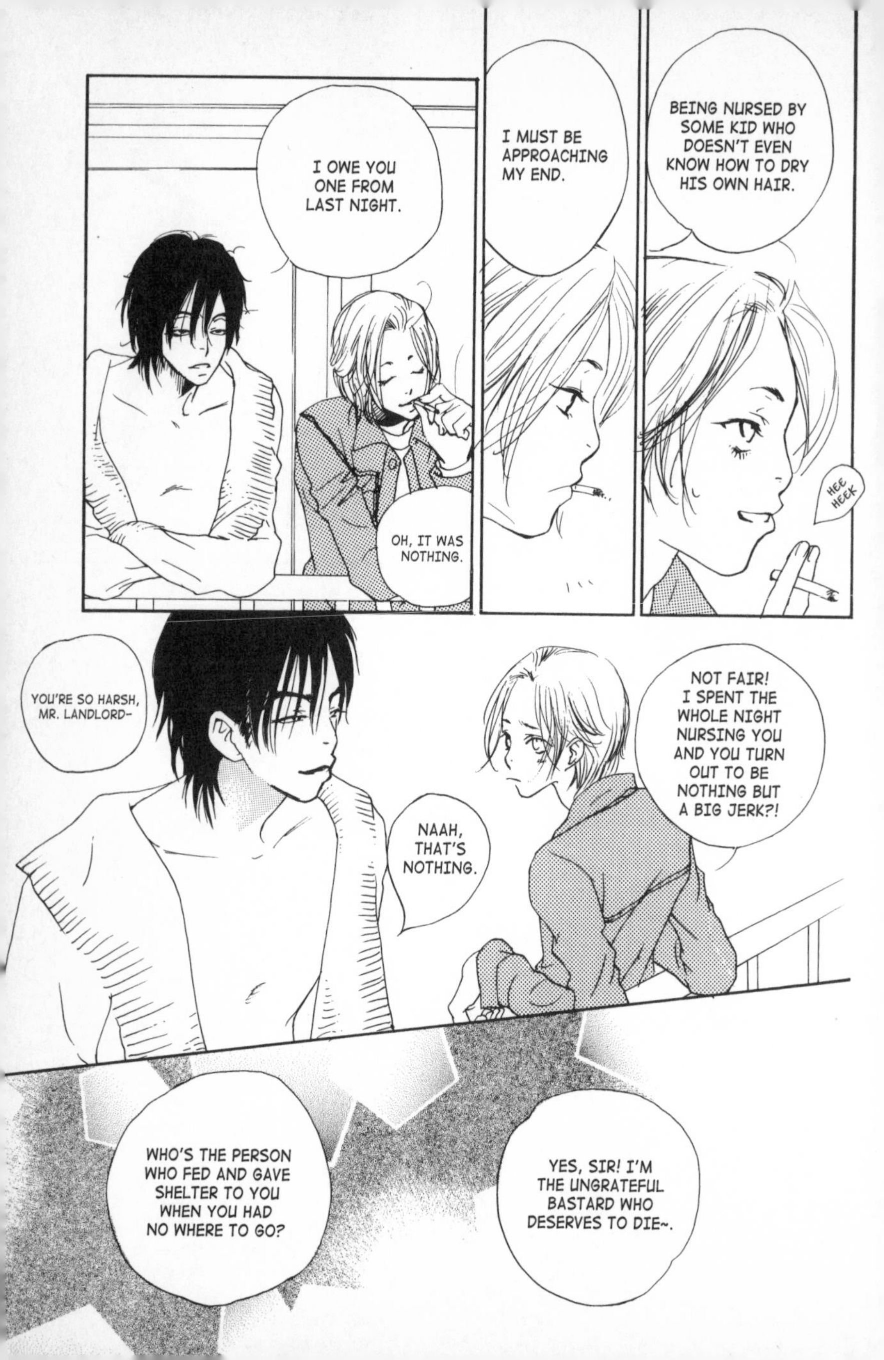
I OWE YOU ONE FROM LAST NIGHT.
OH, IT WAS NOTHING.
I MUST BE APPROACHING MY END.
BEING NURSED BY SOME KID WHO DOESN'T EVEN KNOW HOW TO DRY HIS OWN HAIR.
HEE HEEK
YOU'RE SO HARSH, MR. LANDLORD~
NAAH, THAT'S NOTHING.
NOT FAIR! I SPENT THE WHOLE NIGHT NURSING YOU AND YOU TURN OUT TO BE NOTHING BUT A BIG JERK?!
WHO'S THE PERSON WHO FED AND GAVE SHELTER TO YOU WHEN YOU HAD NO WHERE TO GO?
YES, SIR! I'M THE UNGRATEFUL BASTARD WHO DESERVES TO DIE~.

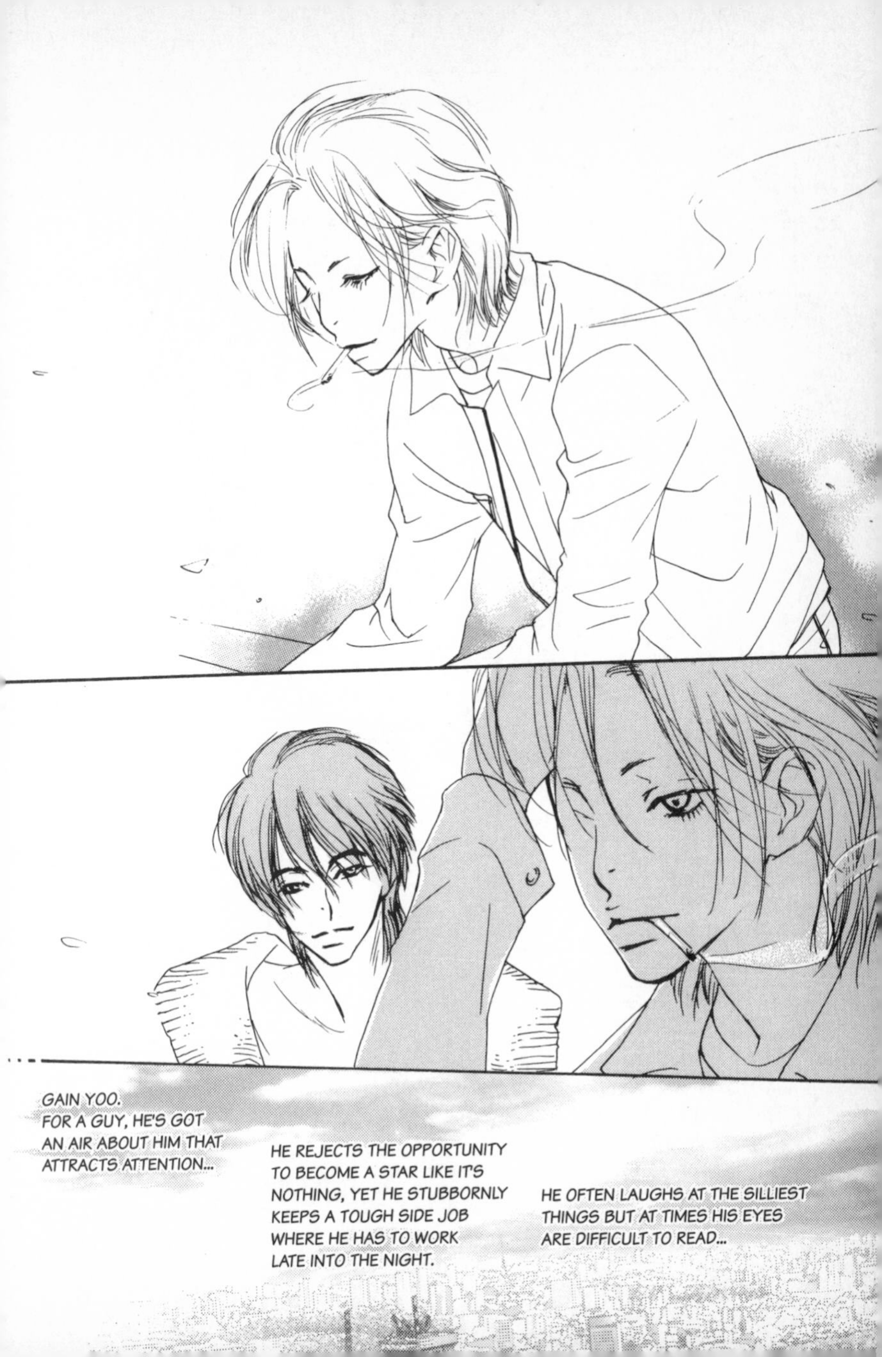
GAIN YOO.
FOR A GUY, HE'S GOT
AN AIR ABOUT HIM THAT
ATTRACTS ATTENTION...
HE REJECTS THE OPPORTUNITY
TO BECOME A STAR LIKE IT'S
NOTHING, YET HE STUBBORNLY
KEEPS A TOUGH SIDE JOB
WHERE HE HAS TO WORK
LATE INTO THE NIGHT.
HE OFTEN LAUGHS AT THE SILLIEST
THINGS BUT AT TIMES HIS EYES
ARE DIFFICULT TO READ...

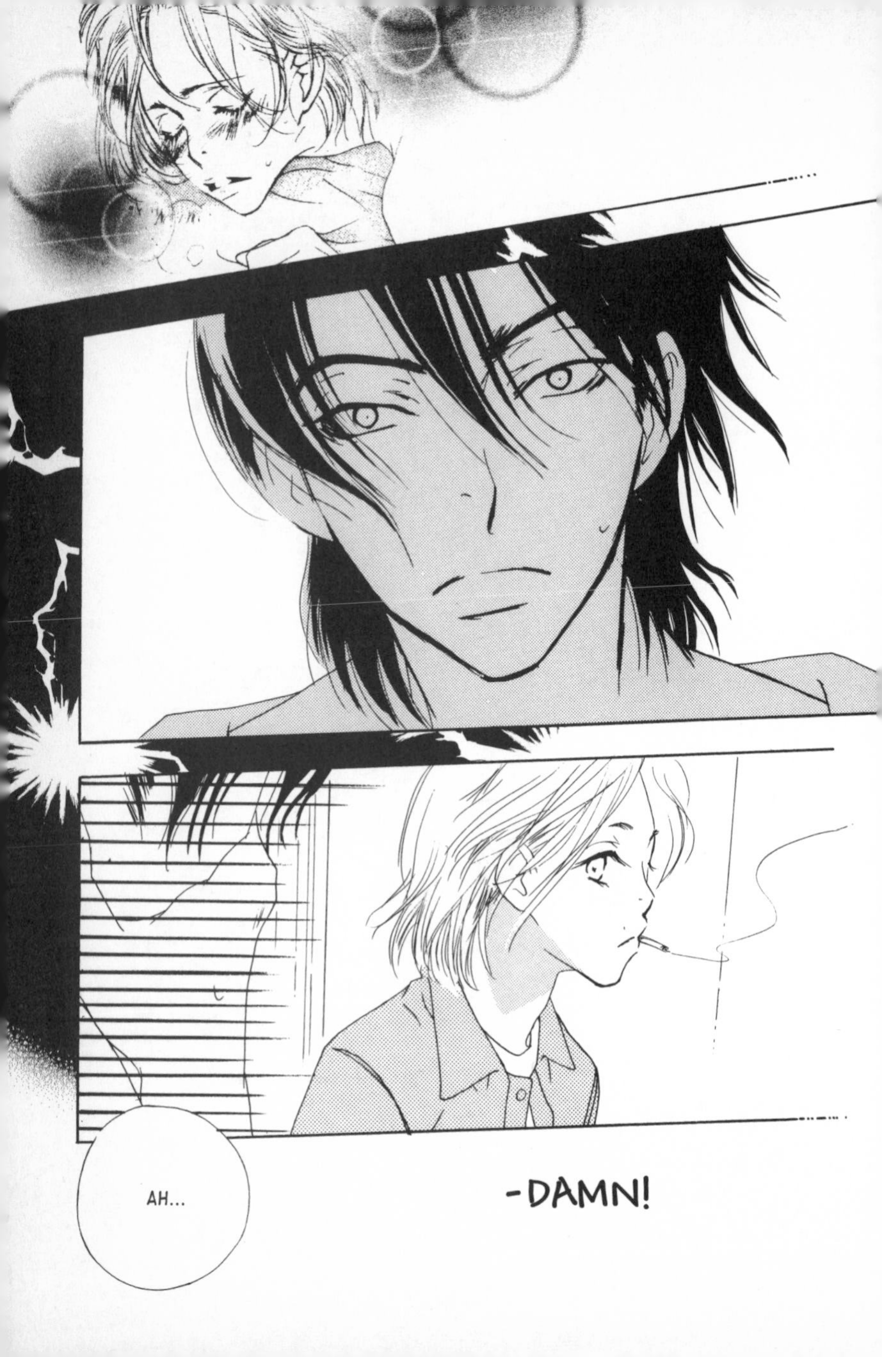
-DAMN!
AH...

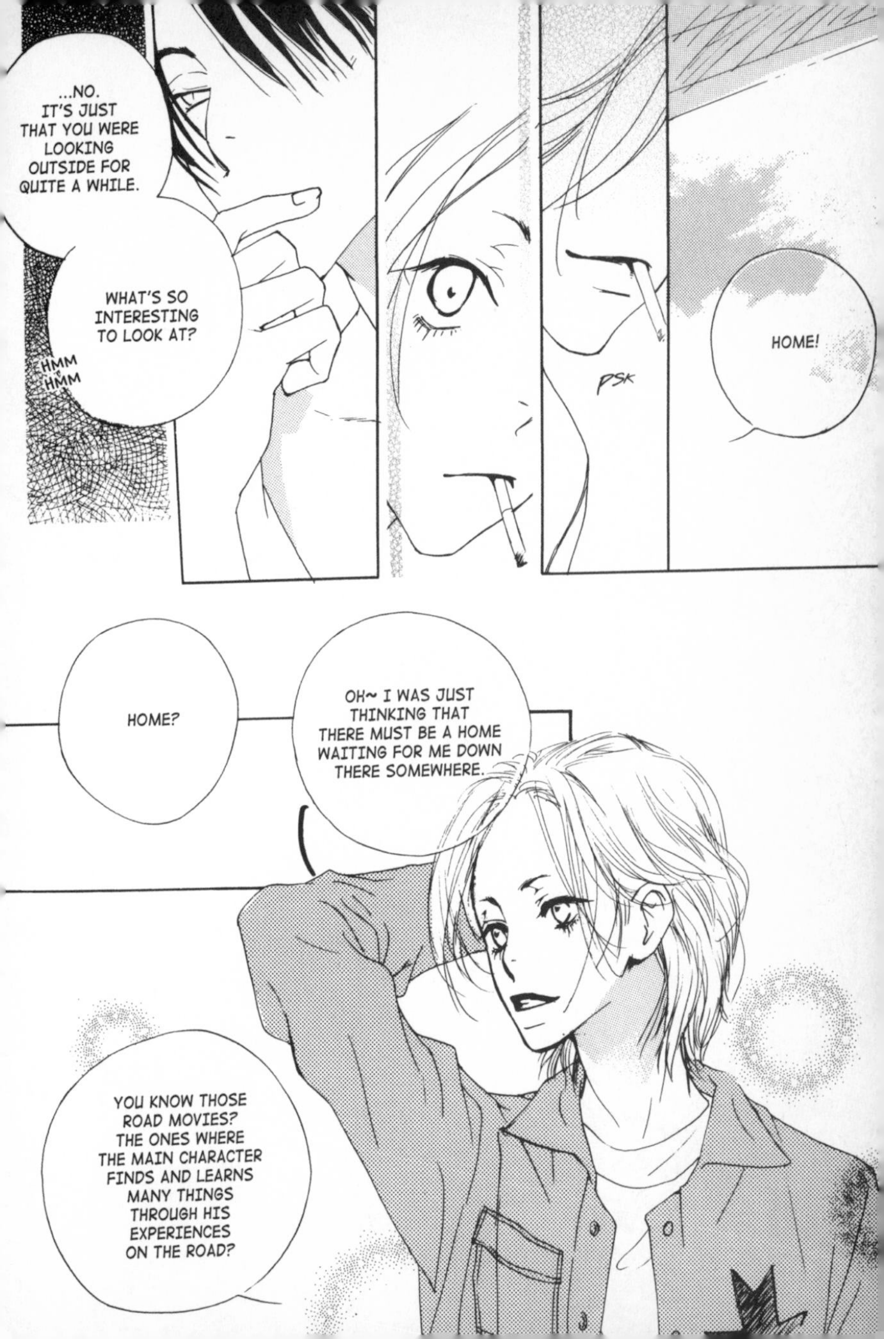

...NO. IT'S JUST THAT YOU WERE LOOKING OUTSIDE FOR QUITE A WHILE.
WHAT'S SO INTERESTING TO LOOK AT?
HMM HMM
PSK
HOME!
HOME?
OH~ I WAS JUST THINKING THAT THERE MUST BE A HOME WAITING FOR ME DOWN THERE SOMEWHERE.
YOU KNOW THOSE ROAD MOVIES? THE ONES WHERE THE MAIN CHARACTER FINDS AND LEARNS MANY THINGS THROUGH HIS EXPERIENCES ON THE ROAD?

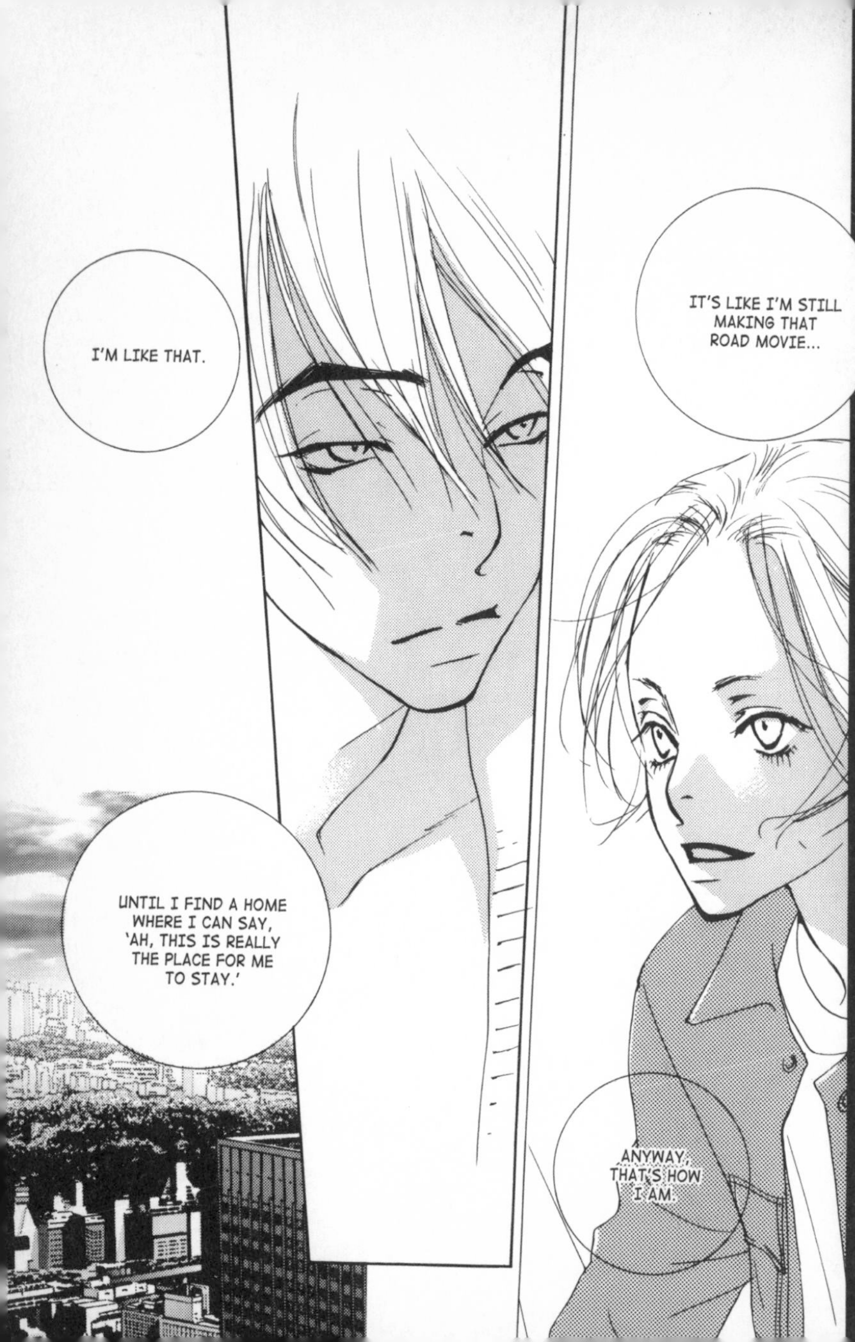
IT'S LIKE I'M STILL MAKING THAT ROAD MOVIE...
I'M LIKE THAT.
UNTIL I FIND A HOME WHERE I CAN SAY, 'AH, THIS IS REALLY THE PLACE FOR ME TO STAY.'
ANYWAY, THAT'S HOW I AM.

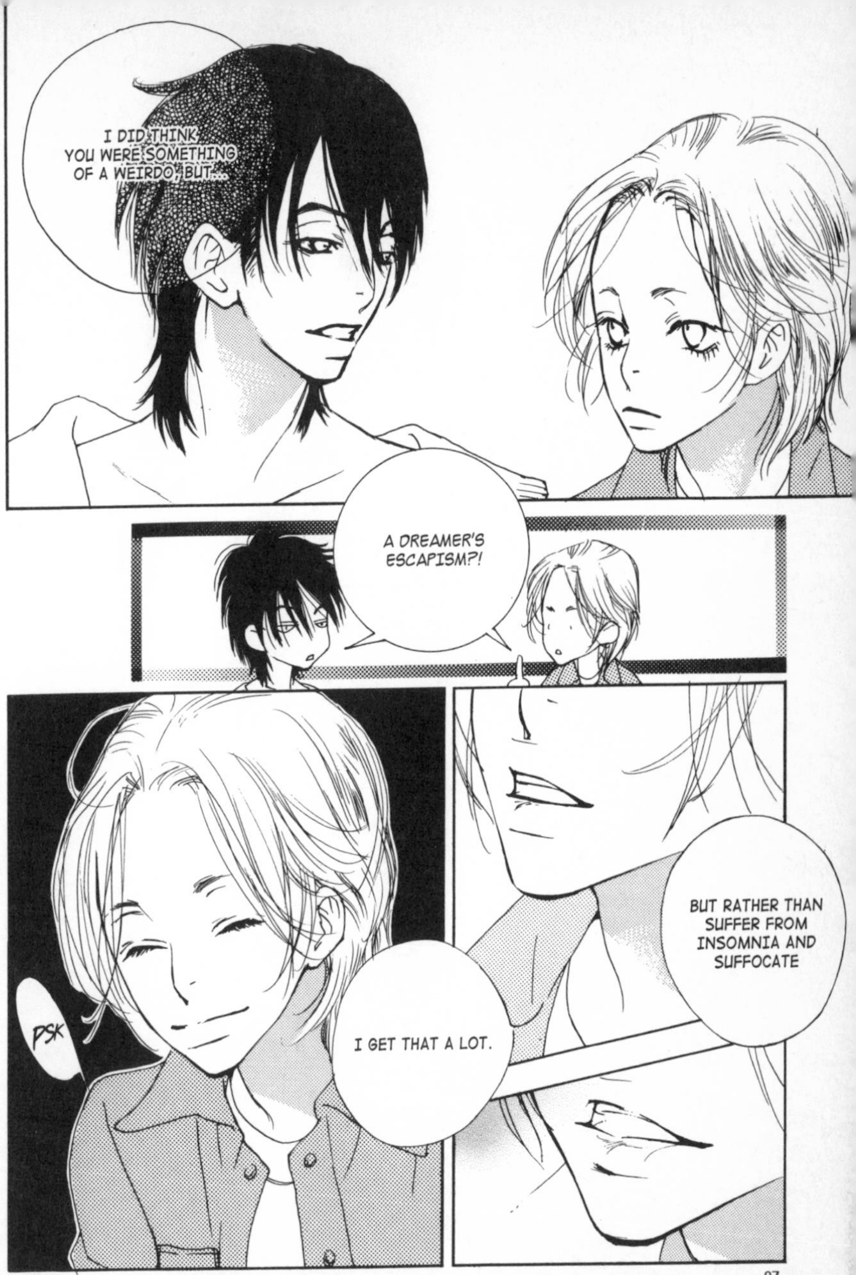
I DID THINK YOU WERE SOMETHING OF A WEIRDO, BUT...
A DREAMER'S ESCAPISM?!
BUT RATHER THAN SUFFER FROM INSOMNIA AND SUFFOCATE
I GET THAT A LOT.
PSK

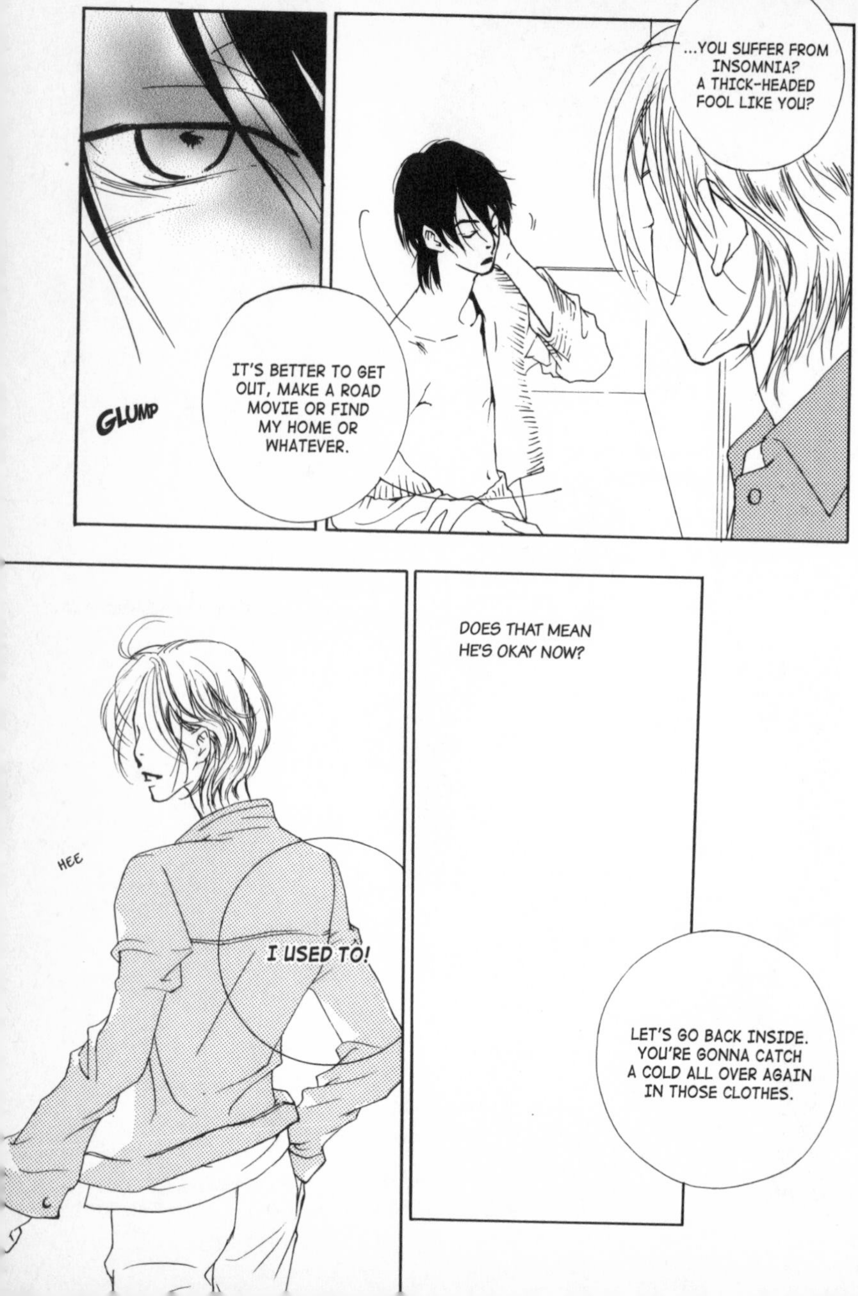
...YOU SUFFER FROM INSOMNIA? A THICK-HEADED FOOL LIKE YOU?
IT'S BETTER TO GET OUT, MAKE A ROAD MOVIE OR FIND MY HOME OR WHATEVER.
GLUMP
DOES THAT MEAN HE'S OKAY NOW?
I USED TO!
HEE
LET'S GO BACK INSIDE. YOU'RE GONNA CATCH A COLD ALL OVER AGAIN IN THOSE CLOTHES.

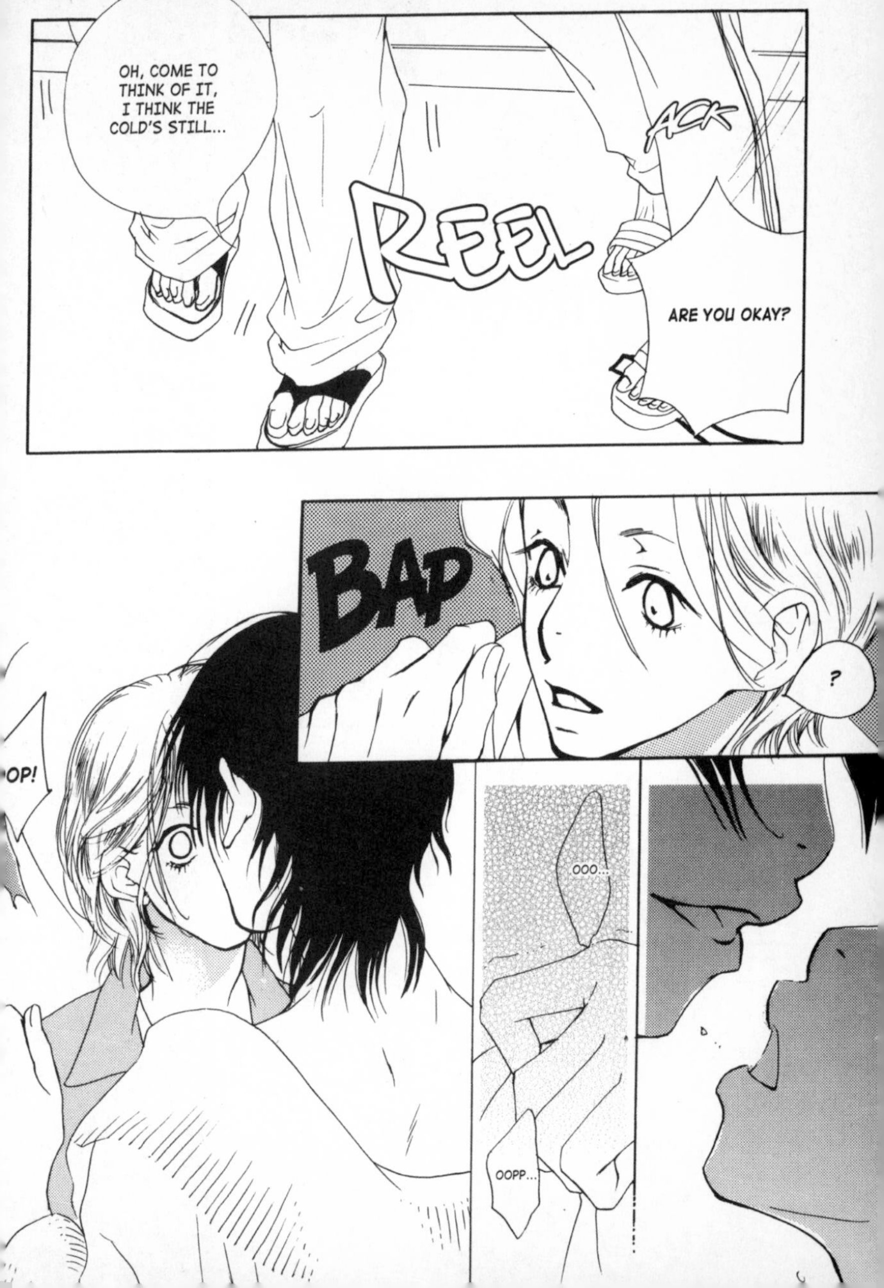
OH, COME TO THINK OF IT, I THINK THE COLD'S STILL...
REEL
ACK
ARE YOU OKAY?
BAP
?
D...
OOO...
OOPP...
OP!

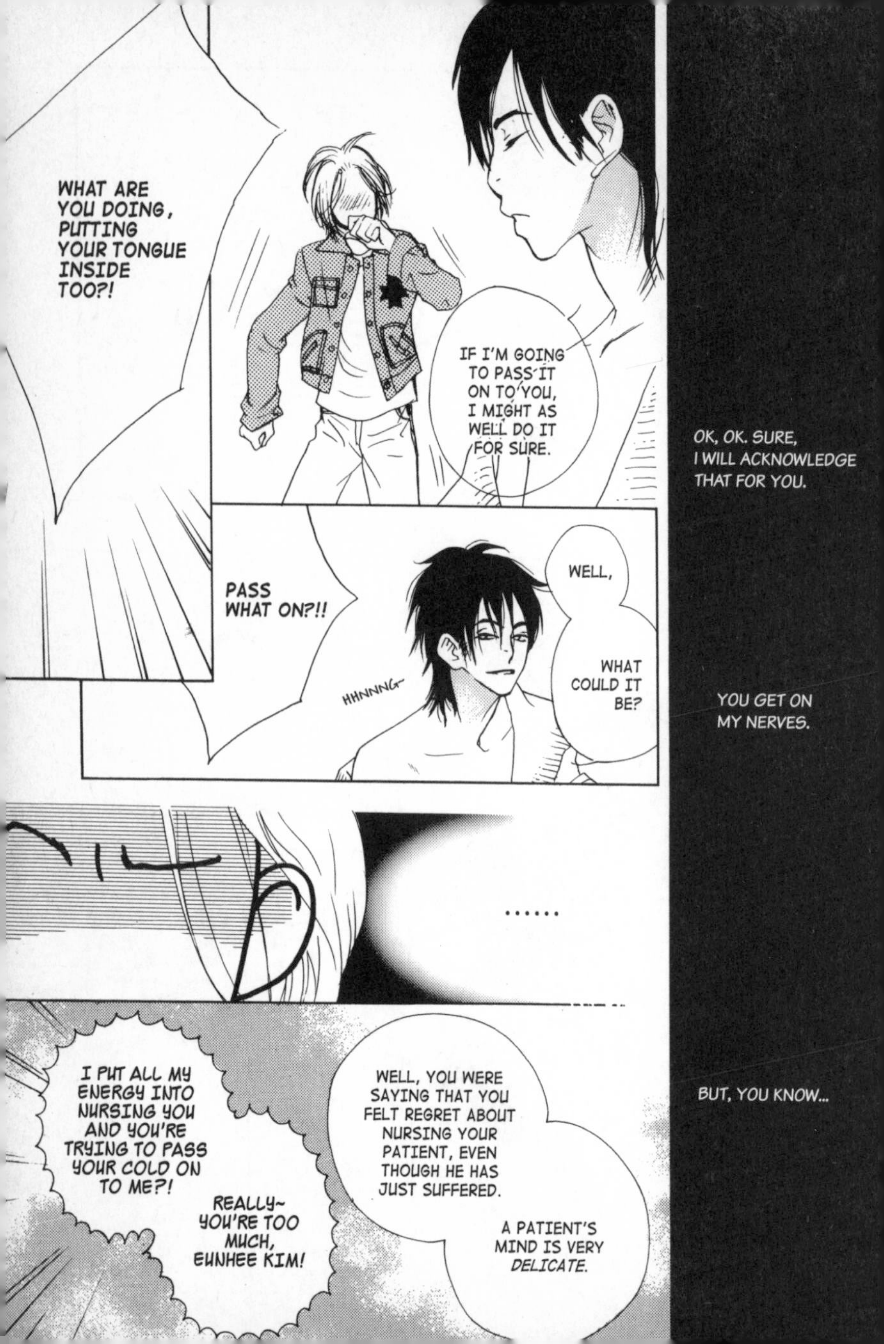
WHAT ARE YOU DOING, PUTTING YOUR TONGUE INSIDE TOO?!
IF I'M GOING TO PASS IT ON TO YOU, I MIGHT AS WELL DO IT FOR SURE.
OK, OK. SURE, I WILL ACKNOWLEDGE THAT FOR YOU.
PASS WHAT ON?!!
WELL,
WHAT COULD IT BE?
HHNNNG~
YOU GET ON MY NERVES.
......
I PUT ALL MY ENERGY INTO NURSING YOU AND YOU'RE TRYING TO PASS YOUR COLD ON TO ME?!
REALLY~ YOU'RE TOO MUCH, EUNHEE KIM!
WELL, YOU WERE SAYING THAT YOU FELT REGRET ABOUT NURSING YOUR PATIENT, EVEN THOUGH HE HAS JUST SUFFERED.
A PATIENT'S MIND IS VERY *DELICATE*.
BUT, YOU KNOW...

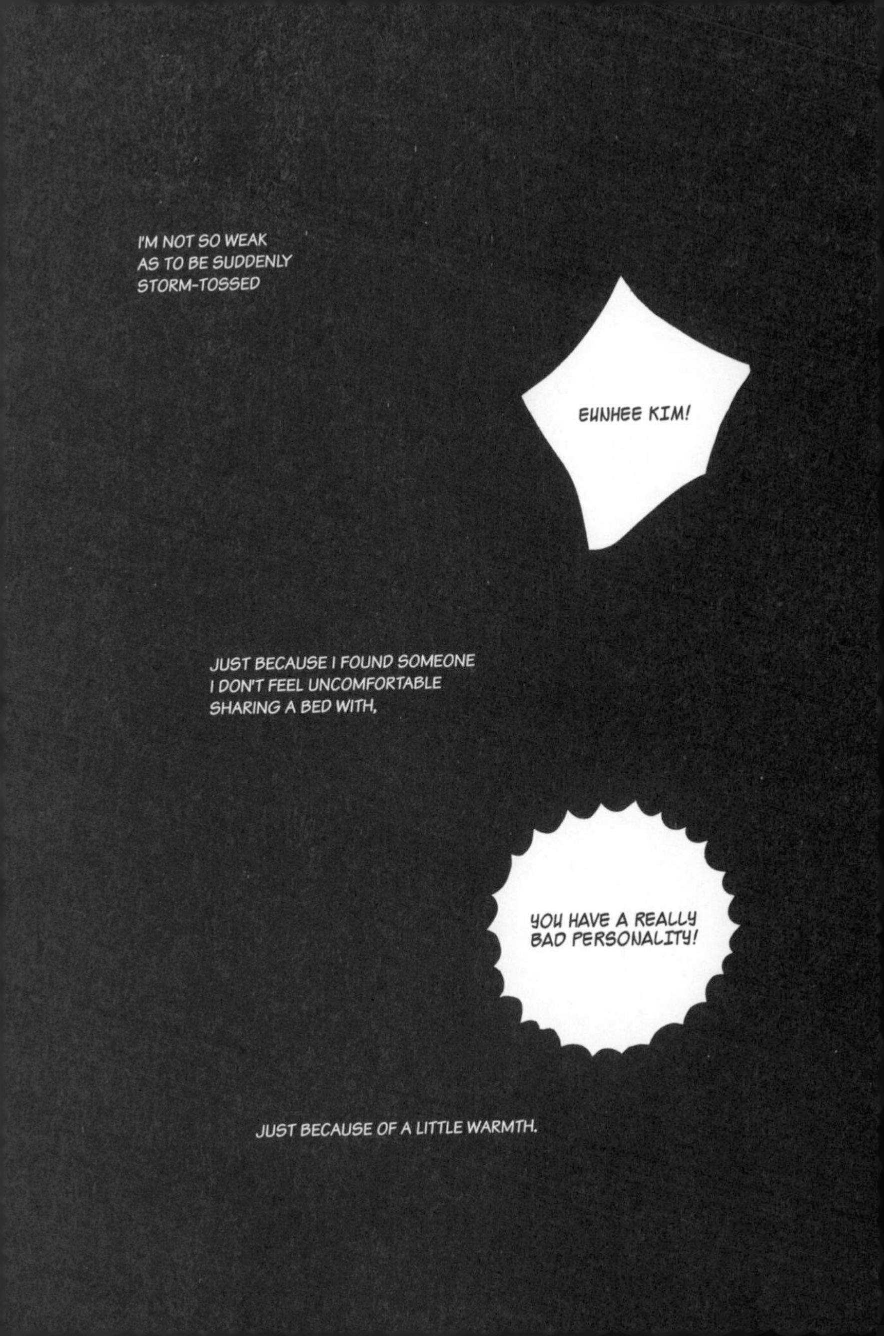
I'M NOT SO WEAK
AS TO BE SUDDENLY
STORM-TOSSED
EUNHEE KIM!
JUST BECAUSE I FOUND SOMEONE
I DON'T FEEL UNCOMFORTABLE
SHARING A BED WITH,
YOU HAVE A REALLY
BAD PERSONALITY!
JUST BECAUSE OF A LITTLE WARMTH.

NOT SO BAD

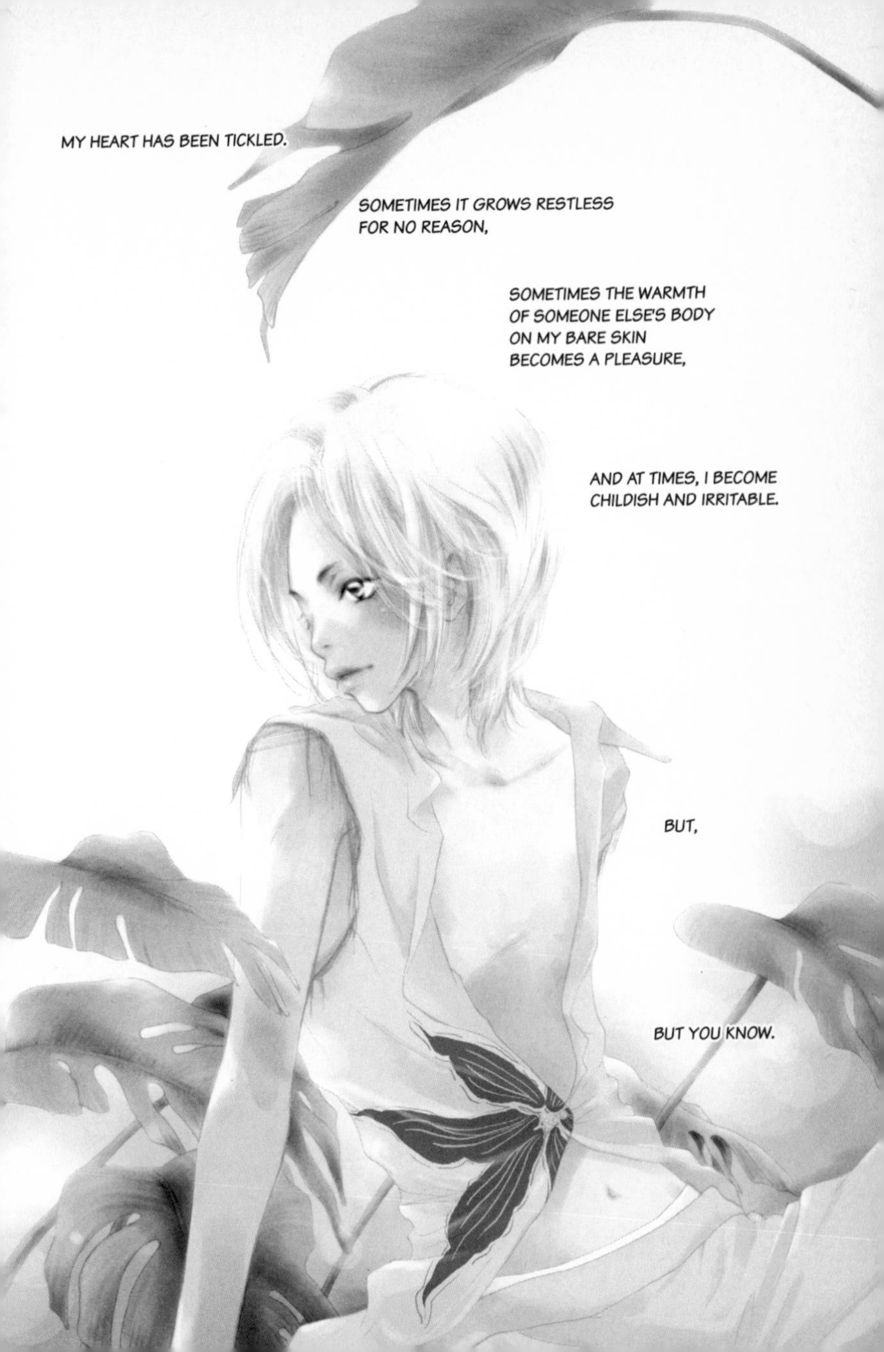
MY HEART HAS BEEN TICKLED.
SOMETIMES IT GROWS RESTLESS FOR NO REASON,
SOMETIMES THE WARMTH OF SOMEONE ELSE'S BODY ON MY BARE SKIN BECOMES A PLEASURE,
AND AT TIMES, I BECOME CHILDISH AND IRRITABLE.
BUT,
BUT YOU KNOW.

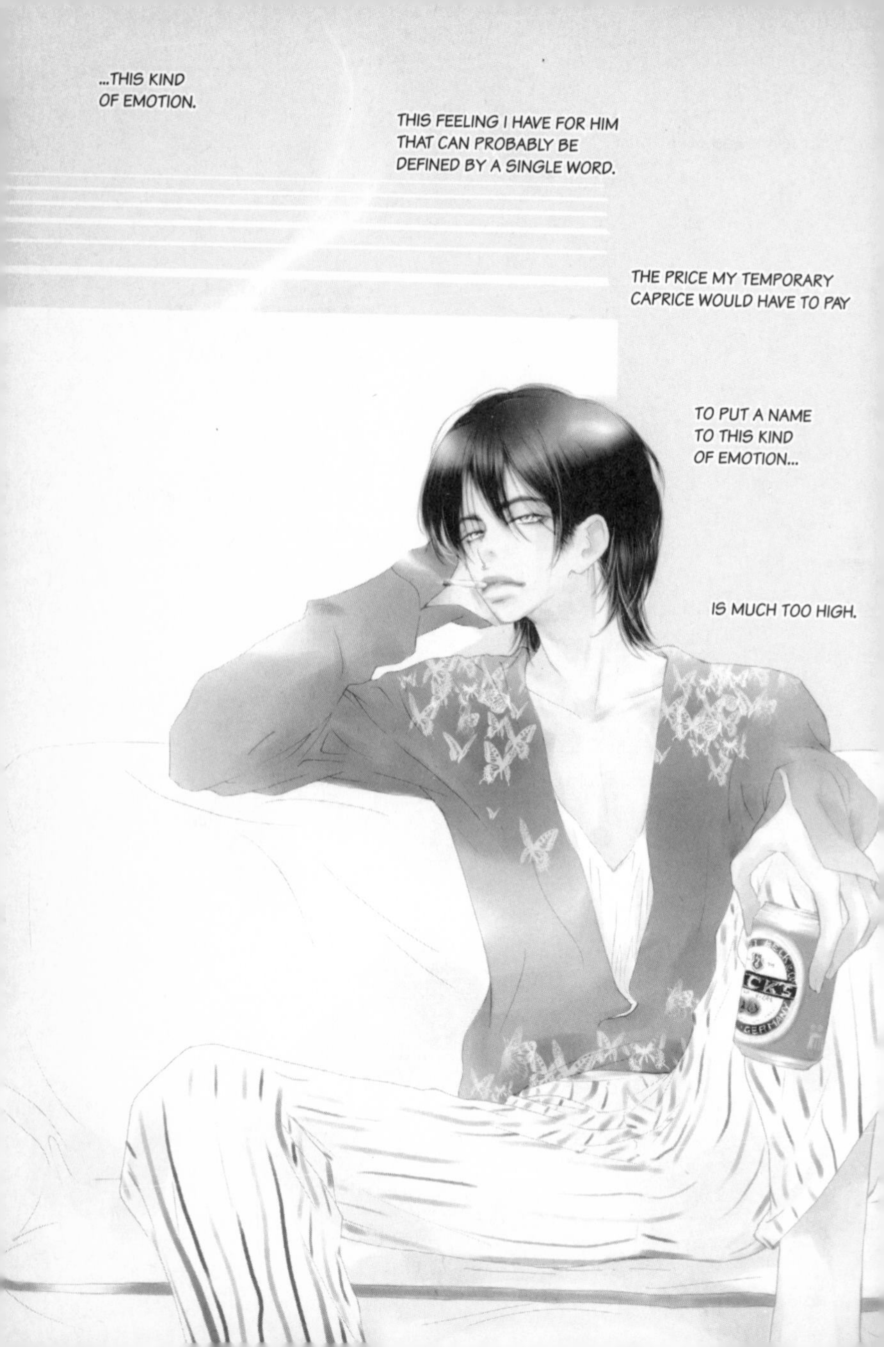
...THIS KIND OF EMOTION.
THIS FEELING I HAVE FOR HIM THAT CAN PROBABLY BE DEFINED BY A SINGLE WORD.
THE PRICE MY TEMPORARY CAPRICE WOULD HAVE TO PAY
TO PUT A NAME TO THIS KIND OF EMOTION...
IS MUCH TOO HIGH.

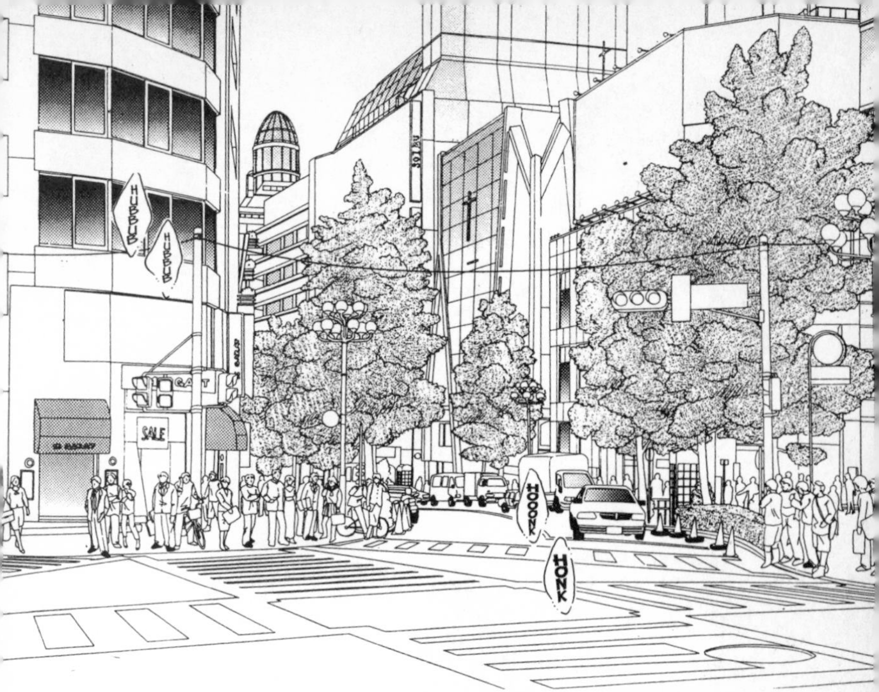
HUBBUB
HUBBUB
SALE
HOOONK
HONK

NOT SO BAD CHAPTER 5 : 'THE GLASS RINGS'

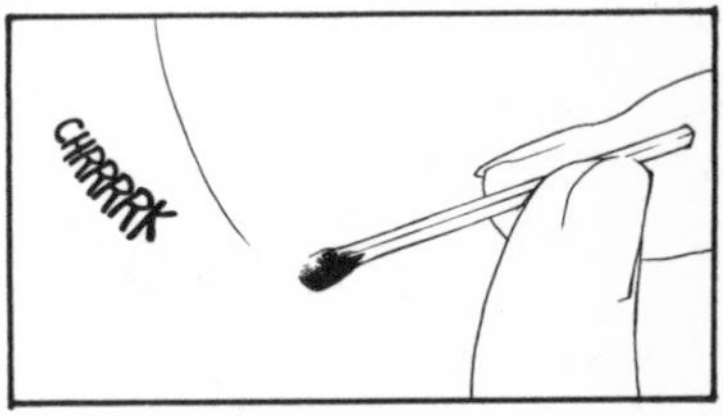
CHRRRRK

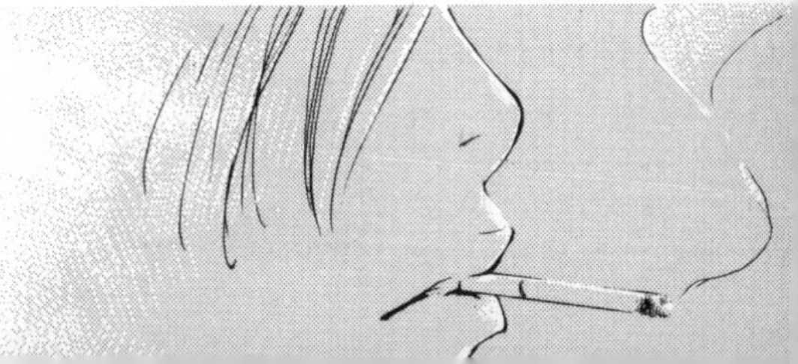

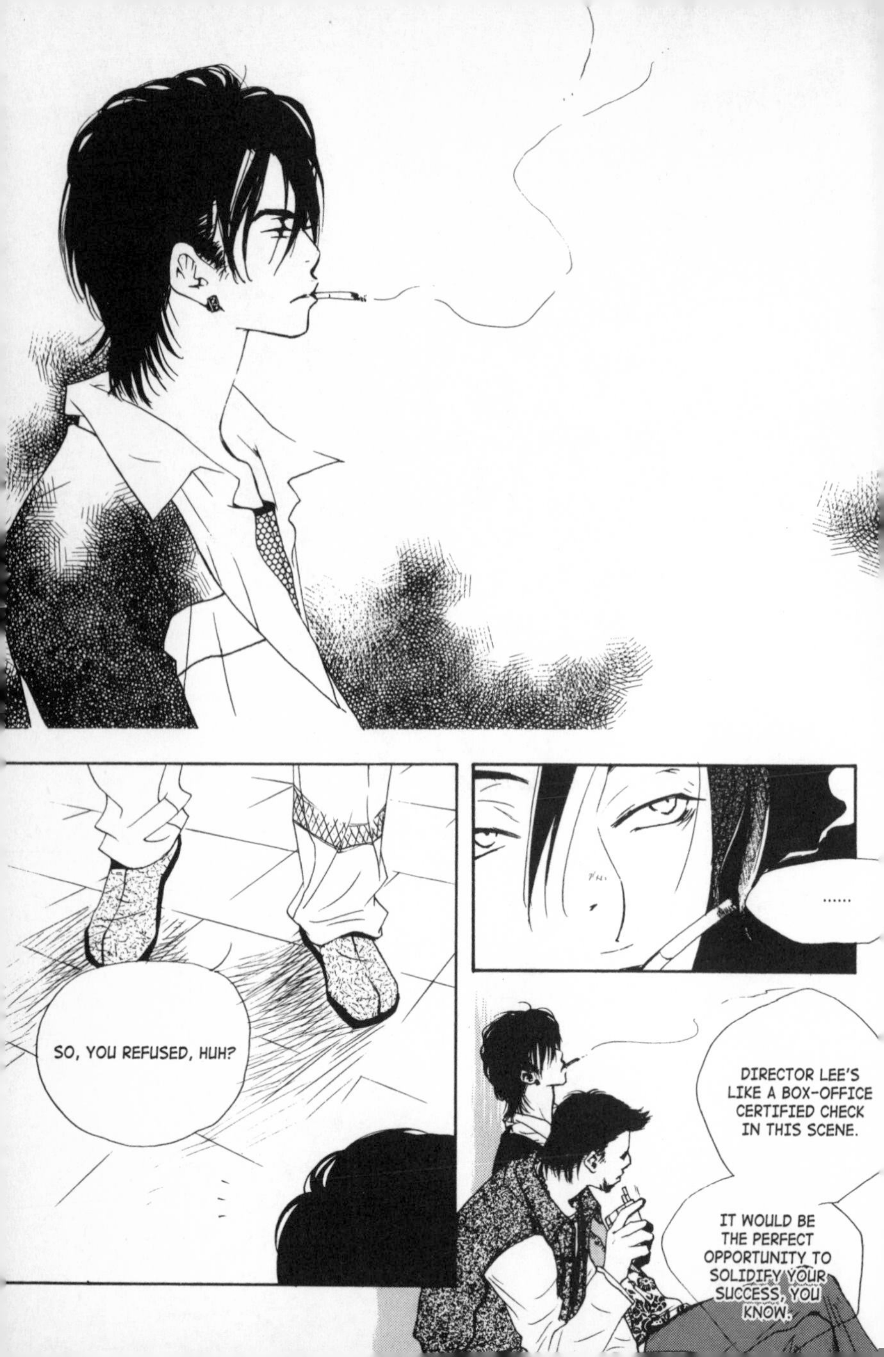
......
SO, YOU REFUSED, HUH?
DIRECTOR LEE'S LIKE A BOX-OFFICE CERTIFIED CHECK IN THIS SCENE.
IT WOULD BE THE PERFECT OPPORTUNITY TO SOLIDIFY YOUR SUCCESS, YOU KNOW.

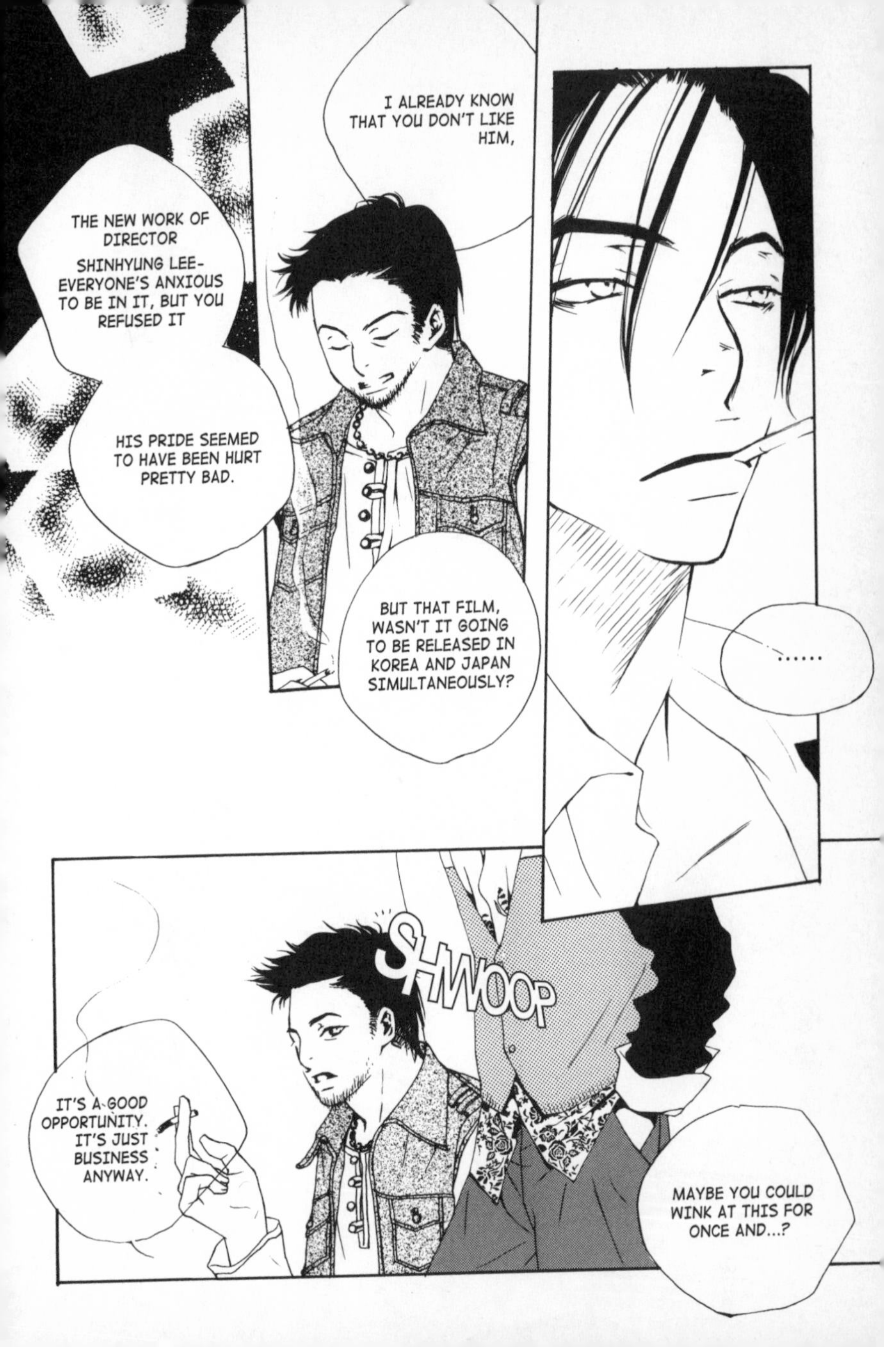

THE NEW WORK OF DIRECTOR
SHINHYUNG LEE- EVERYONE'S ANXIOUS TO BE IN IT, BUT YOU REFUSED IT
HIS PRIDE SEEMED TO HAVE BEEN HURT PRETTY BAD.
I ALREADY KNOW THAT YOU DON'T LIKE HIM,
BUT THAT FILM, WASN'T IT GOING TO BE RELEASED IN KOREA AND JAPAN SIMULTANEOUSLY?
......
SHWOOP
IT'S A GOOD OPPORTUNITY. IT'S JUST BUSINESS ANYWAY.
MAYBE YOU COULD WINK AT THIS FOR ONCE AND...?

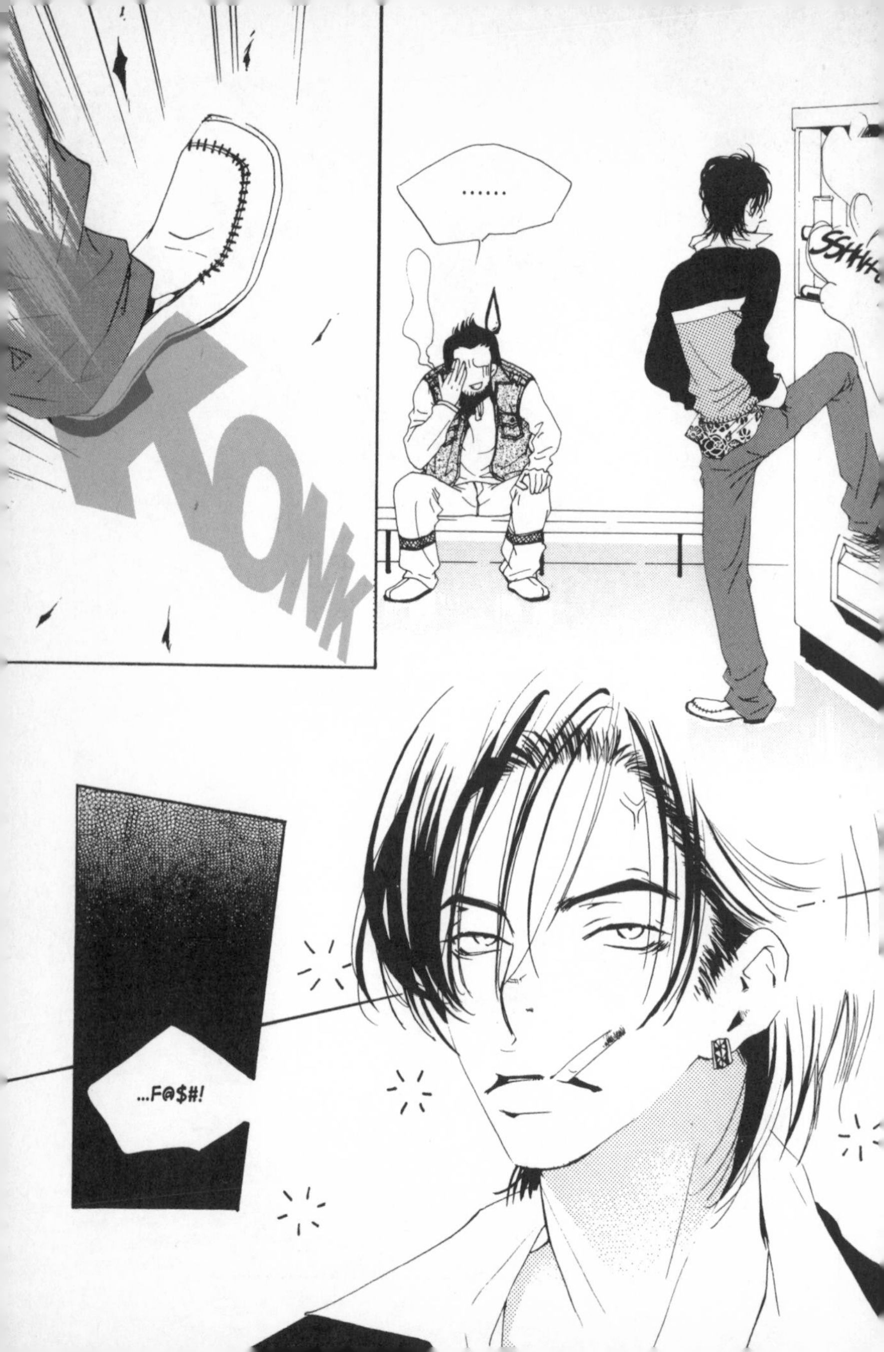
TONK
SSHWF
......
...F@$#!

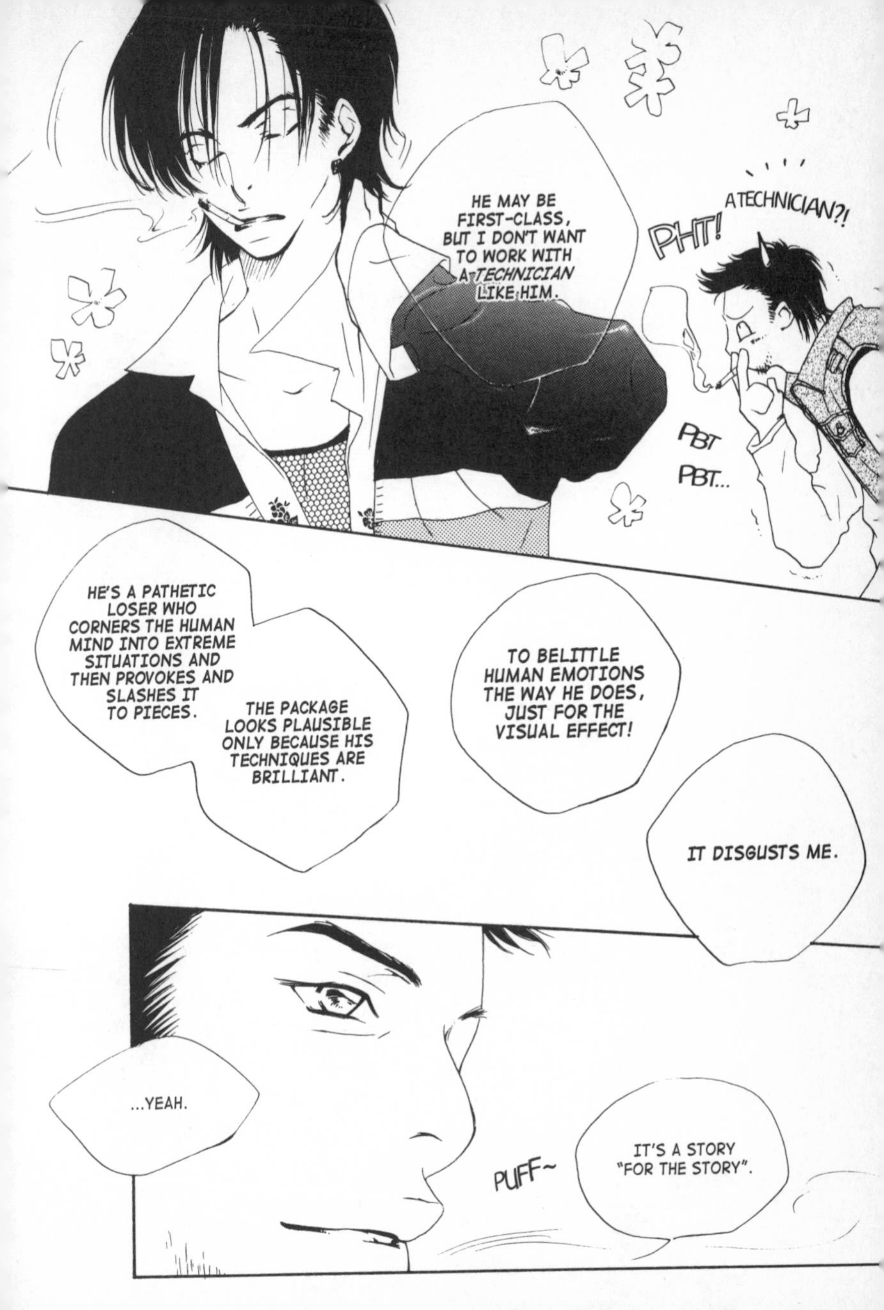
HE MAY BE FIRST-CLASS, BUT I DON'T WANT TO WORK WITH A TECHNICIAN LIKE HIM.
A TECHNICIAN?!
PHT!
PBT PBT...
HE'S A PATHETIC LOSER WHO CORNERS THE HUMAN MIND INTO EXTREME SITUATIONS AND THEN PROVOKES AND SLASHES IT TO PIECES.
THE PACKAGE LOOKS PLAUSIBLE ONLY BECAUSE HIS TECHNIQUES ARE BRILLIANT.
TO BELITTLE HUMAN EMOTIONS THE WAY HE DOES, JUST FOR THE VISUAL EFFECT!
IT DISGUSTS ME.
IT'S A STORY "FOR THE STORY".
PUFF~
...YEAH.

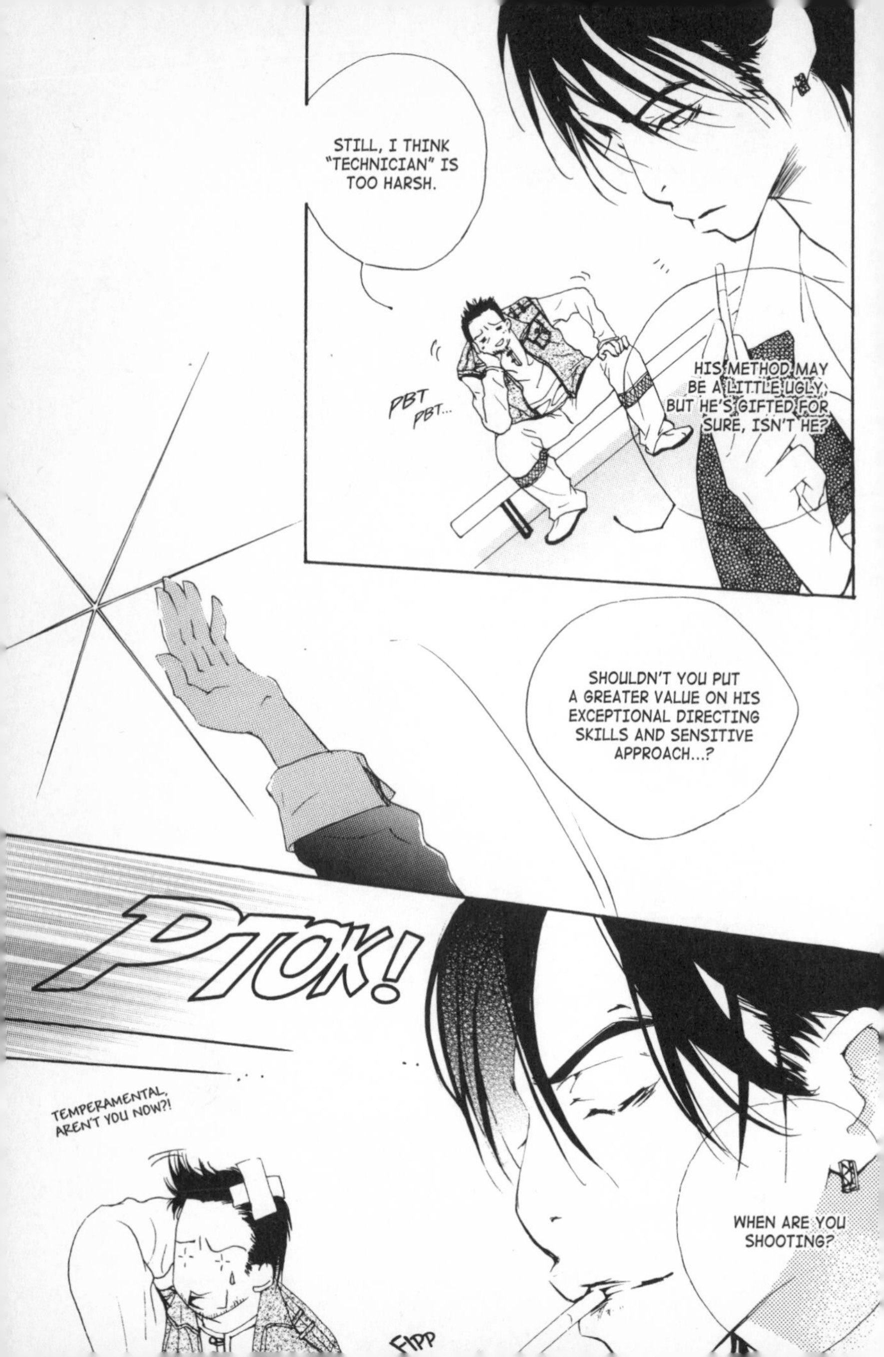
STILL, I THINK "TECHNICIAN" IS TOO HARSH.
HIS METHOD MAY BE A LITTLE UGLY, BUT HE'S GIFTED FOR SURE, ISN'T HE?
PBT PBT...
SHOULDN'T YOU PUT A GREATER VALUE ON HIS EXCEPTIONAL DIRECTING SKILLS AND SENSITIVE APPROACH...?
PTOK!
...
...
TEMPERAMENTAL, AREN'T YOU NOW?!
WHEN ARE YOU SHOOTING?
FIPP

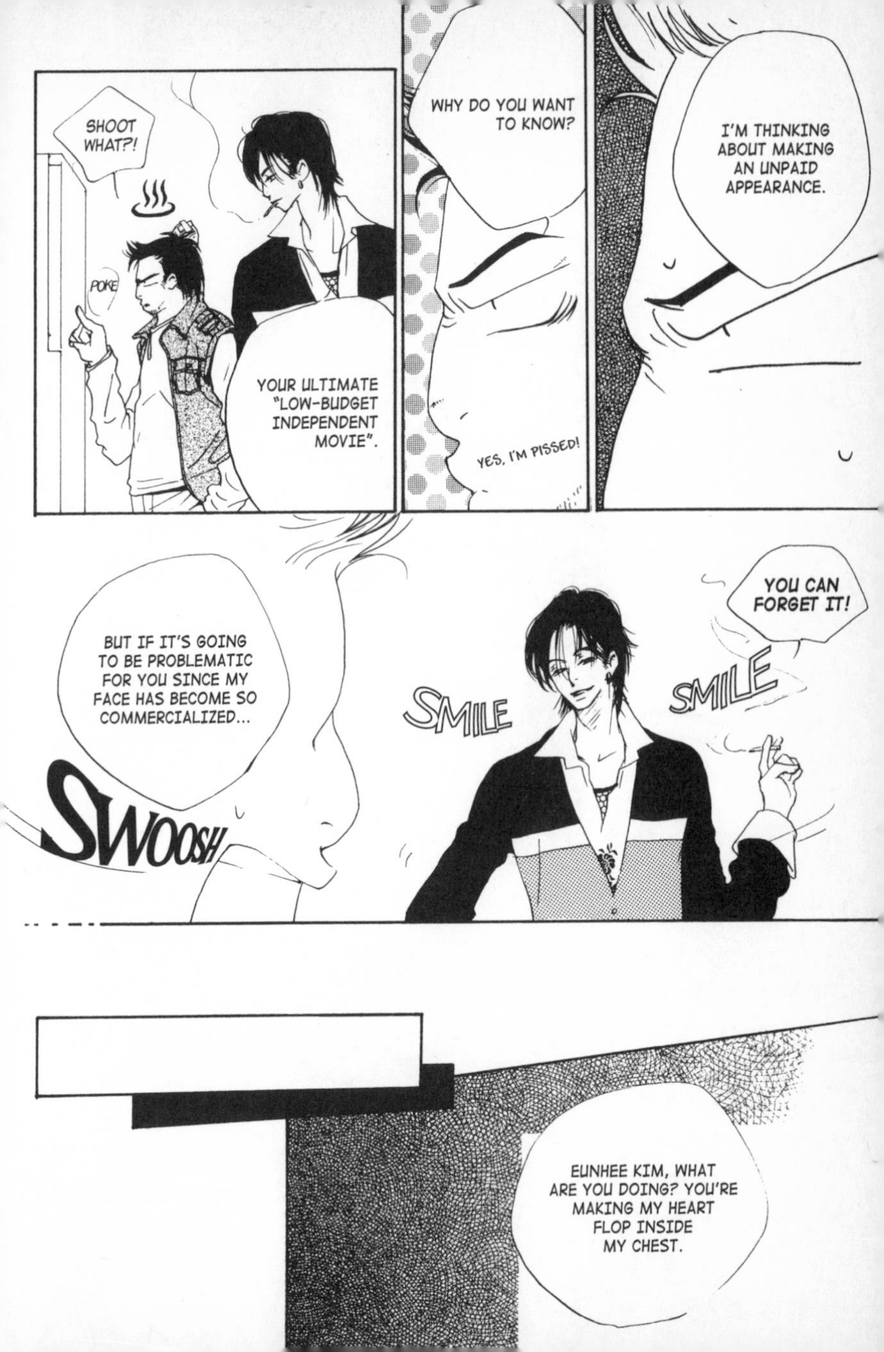
SHOOT WHAT?!
POKE
YOUR ULTIMATE "LOW-BUDGET INDEPENDENT MOVIE".
WHY DO YOU WANT TO KNOW?
YES, I'M PISSED!
I'M THINKING ABOUT MAKING AN UNPAID APPEARANCE.
BUT IF IT'S GOING TO BE PROBLEMATIC FOR YOU SINCE MY FACE HAS BECOME SO COMMERCIALIZED...
SWOOSH
SMILE
SMILE
YOU CAN FORGET IT!
EUNHEE KIM, WHAT ARE YOU DOING? YOU'RE MAKING MY HEART FLOP INSIDE MY CHEST.

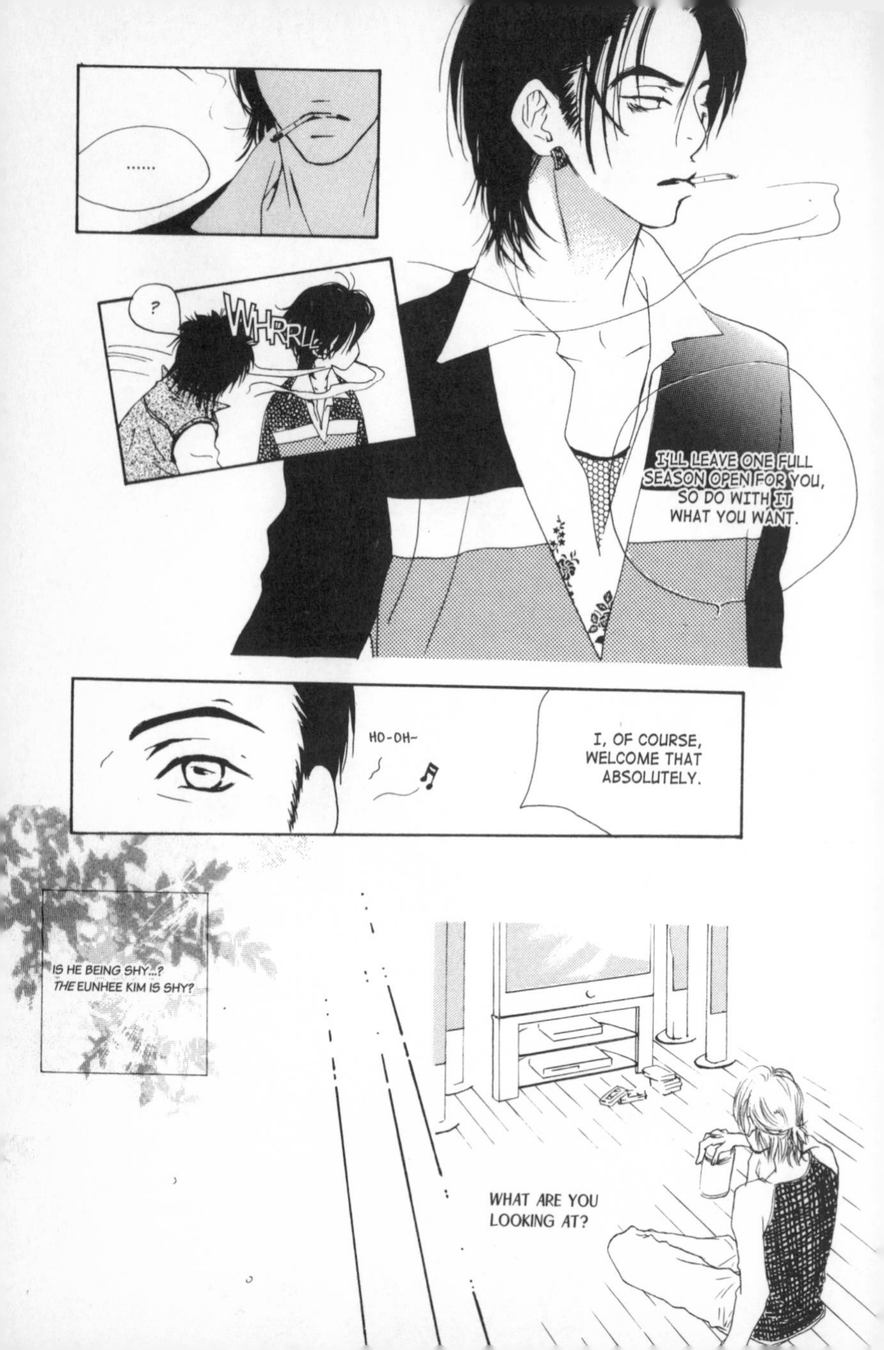
......
?
WHRRLL
I'LL LEAVE ONE FULL SEASON OPEN FOR YOU, SO DO WITH IT WHAT YOU WANT.
HO-OH~
I, OF COURSE, WELCOME THAT ABSOLUTELY.
IS HE BEING SHY...? THE EUNHEE KIM IS SHY?
WHAT ARE YOU LOOKING AT?

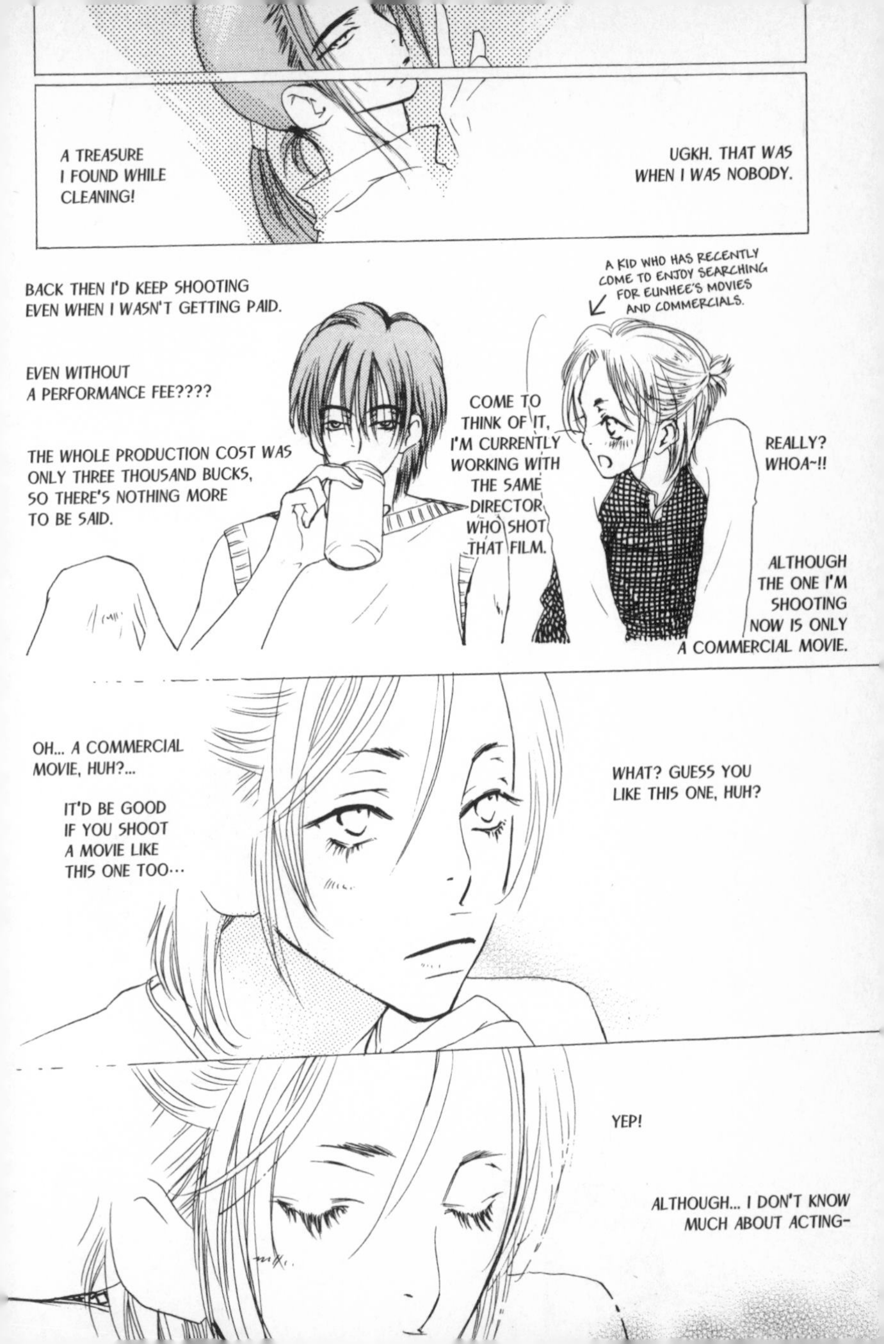
A TREASURE I FOUND WHILE CLEANING!
UGKH. THAT WAS WHEN I WAS NOBODY.
BACK THEN I'D KEEP SHOOTING EVEN WHEN I WASN'T GETTING PAID.
EVEN WITHOUT A PERFORMANCE FEE????
THE WHOLE PRODUCTION COST WAS ONLY THREE THOUSAND BUCKS, SO THERE'S NOTHING MORE TO BE SAID.
A KID WHO HAS RECENTLY COME TO ENJOY SEARCHING FOR EUNHEE'S MOVIES AND COMMERCIALS.
COME TO THINK OF IT, I'M CURRENTLY WORKING WITH THE SAME DIRECTOR WHO SHOT THAT FILM.
REALLY? WHOA~!!
ALTHOUGH THE ONE I'M SHOOTING NOW IS ONLY A COMMERCIAL MOVIE.
OH... A COMMERCIAL MOVIE, HUH?...
IT'D BE GOOD IF YOU SHOOT A MOVIE LIKE THIS ONE TOO...
WHAT? GUESS YOU LIKE THIS ONE, HUH?
YEP!
ALTHOUGH... I DON'T KNOW MUCH ABOUT ACTING-

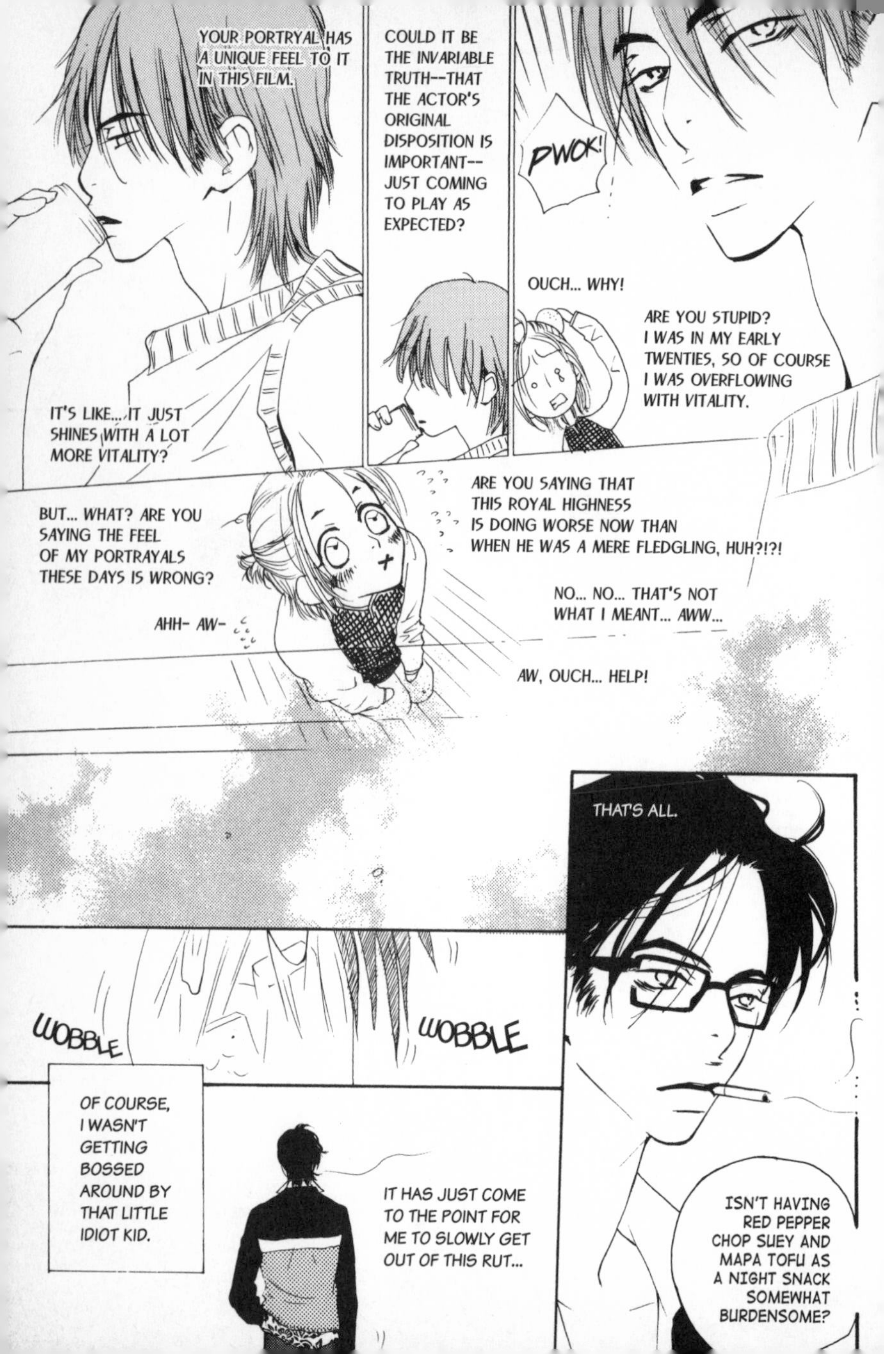
YOUR PORTRYAL HAS A UNIQUE FEEL TO IT IN THIS FILM.
IT'S LIKE... IT JUST SHINES WITH A LOT MORE VITALITY?
COULD IT BE THE INVARIABLE TRUTH--THAT THE ACTOR'S ORIGINAL DISPOSITION IS IMPORTANT-- JUST COMING TO PLAY AS EXPECTED?
PWOK!
OUCH... WHY!
ARE YOU STUPID? I WAS IN MY EARLY TWENTIES, SO OF COURSE I WAS OVERFLOWING WITH VITALITY.
BUT... WHAT? ARE YOU SAYING THE FEEL OF MY PORTRAYALS THESE DAYS IS WRONG?
ARE YOU SAYING THAT THIS ROYAL HIGHNESS IS DOING WORSE NOW THAN WHEN HE WAS A MERE FLEDGLING, HUH?!?!
AHH- AW-
NO... NO... THAT'S NOT WHAT I MEANT... AWW...
AW, OUCH... HELP!
THAT'S ALL.
WOBBLE
WOBBLE
OF COURSE, I WASN'T GETTING BOSSED AROUND BY THAT LITTLE IDIOT KID.
IT HAS JUST COME TO THE POINT FOR ME TO SLOWLY GET OUT OF THIS RUT...
ISN'T HAVING RED PEPPER CHOP SUEY AND MAPA TOFU AS A NIGHT SNACK SOMEWHAT BURDENSOME?

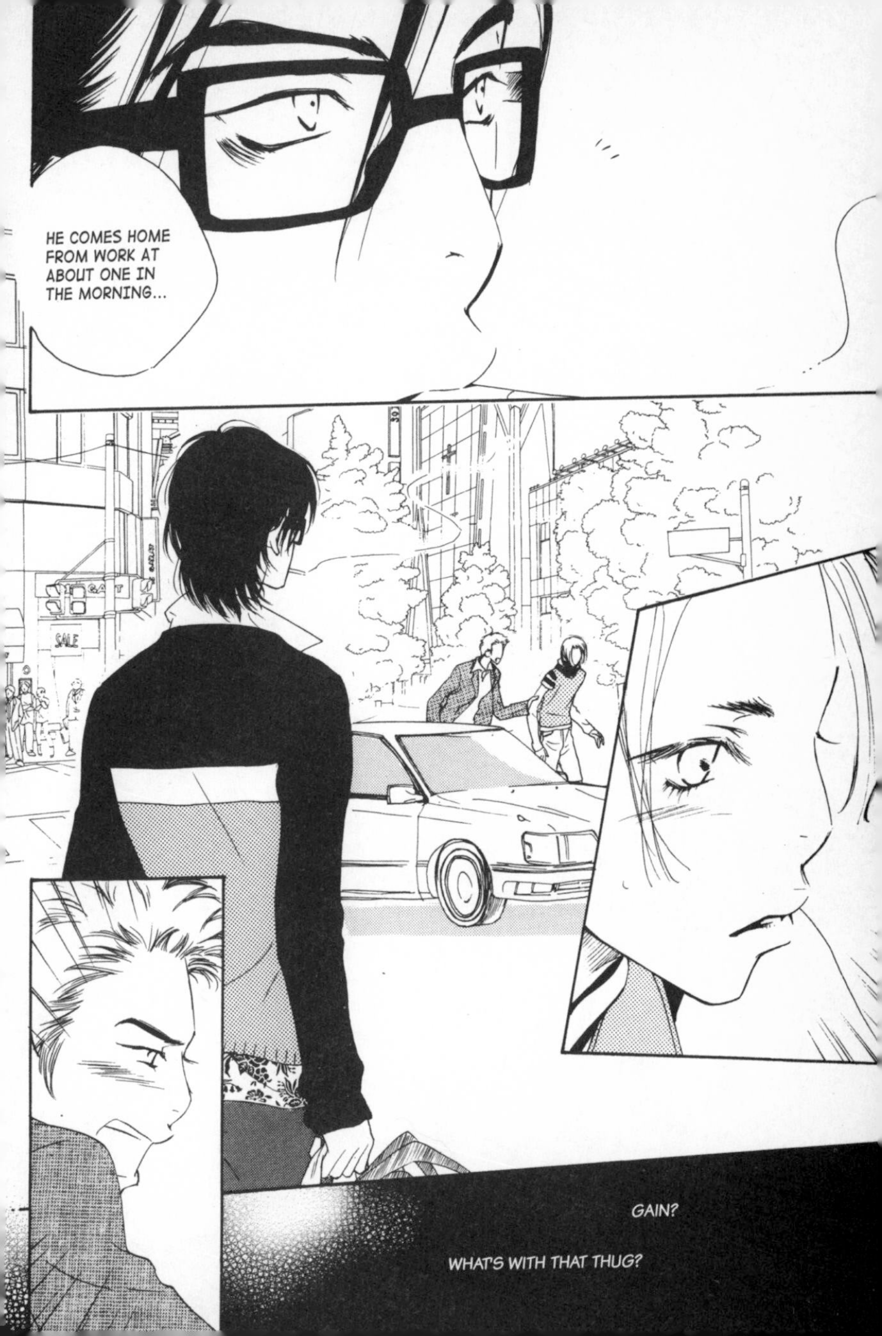
HE COMES HOME FROM WORK AT ABOUT ONE IN THE MORNING...
SALE
GAIN?
WHAT'S WITH THAT THUG?

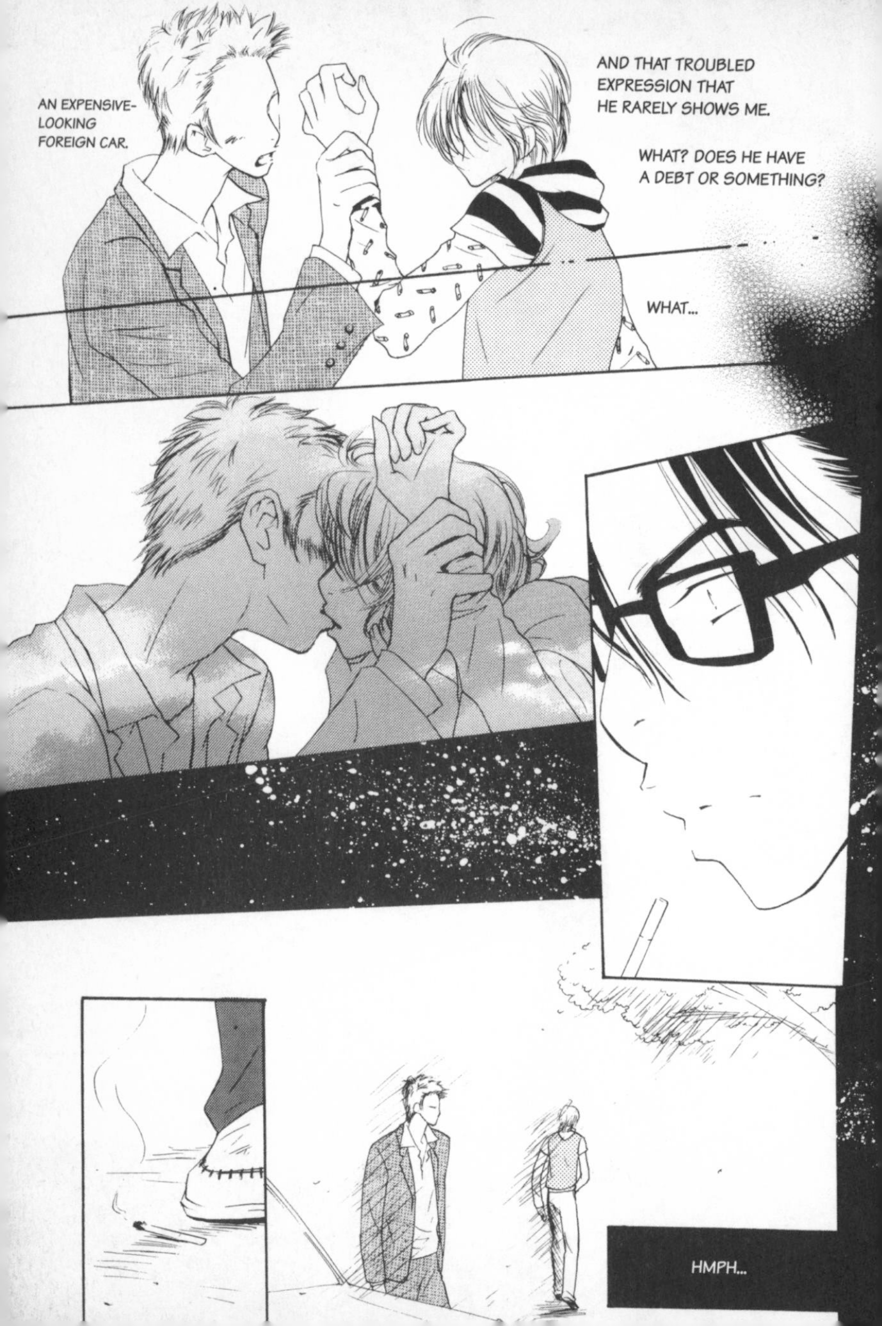
AN EXPENSIVE-LOOKING FOREIGN CAR.
AND THAT TROUBLED EXPRESSION THAT HE RARELY SHOWS ME.
WHAT? DOES HE HAVE A DEBT OR SOMETHING?
WHAT...
HMPH...

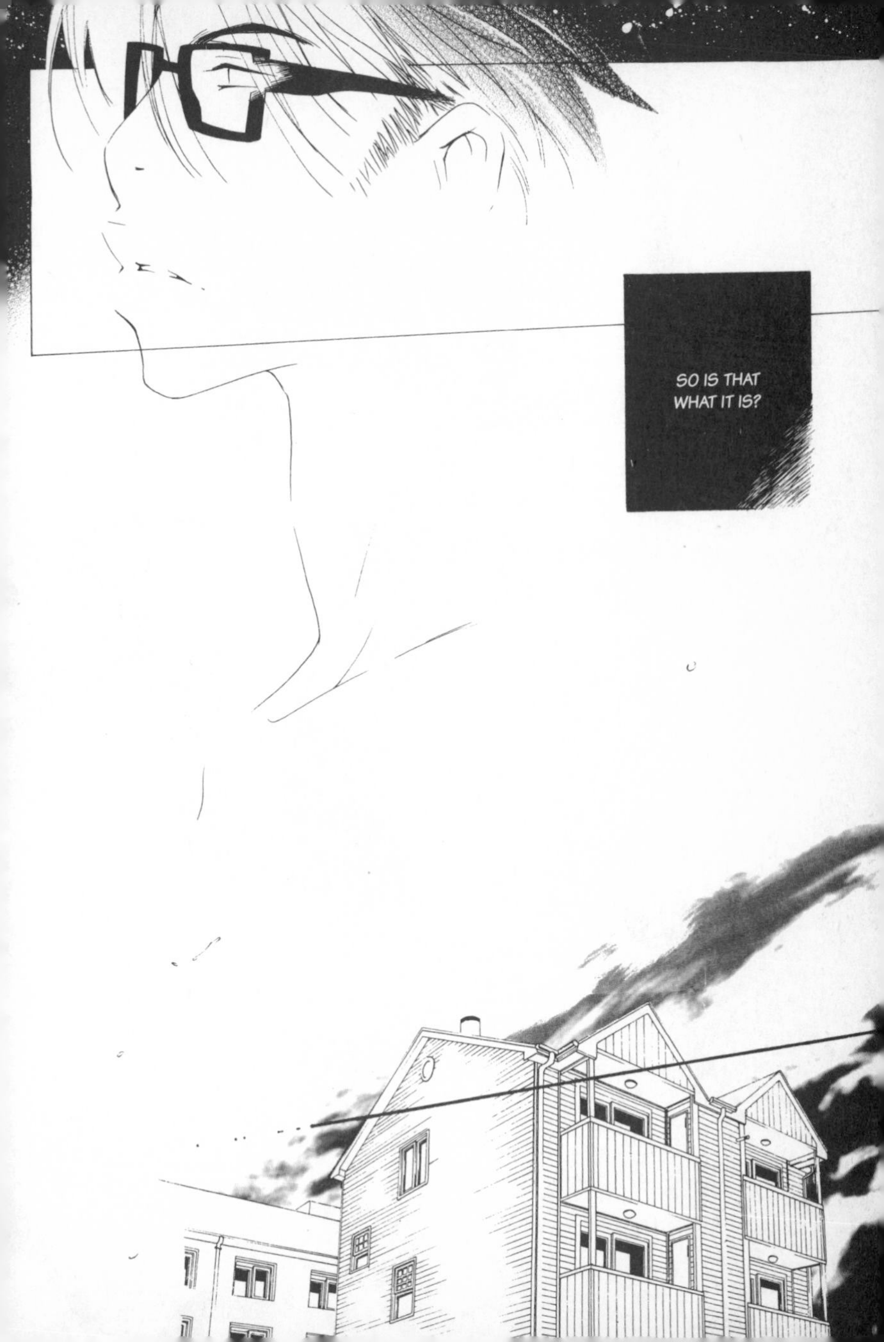
SO IS THAT WHAT IT IS?

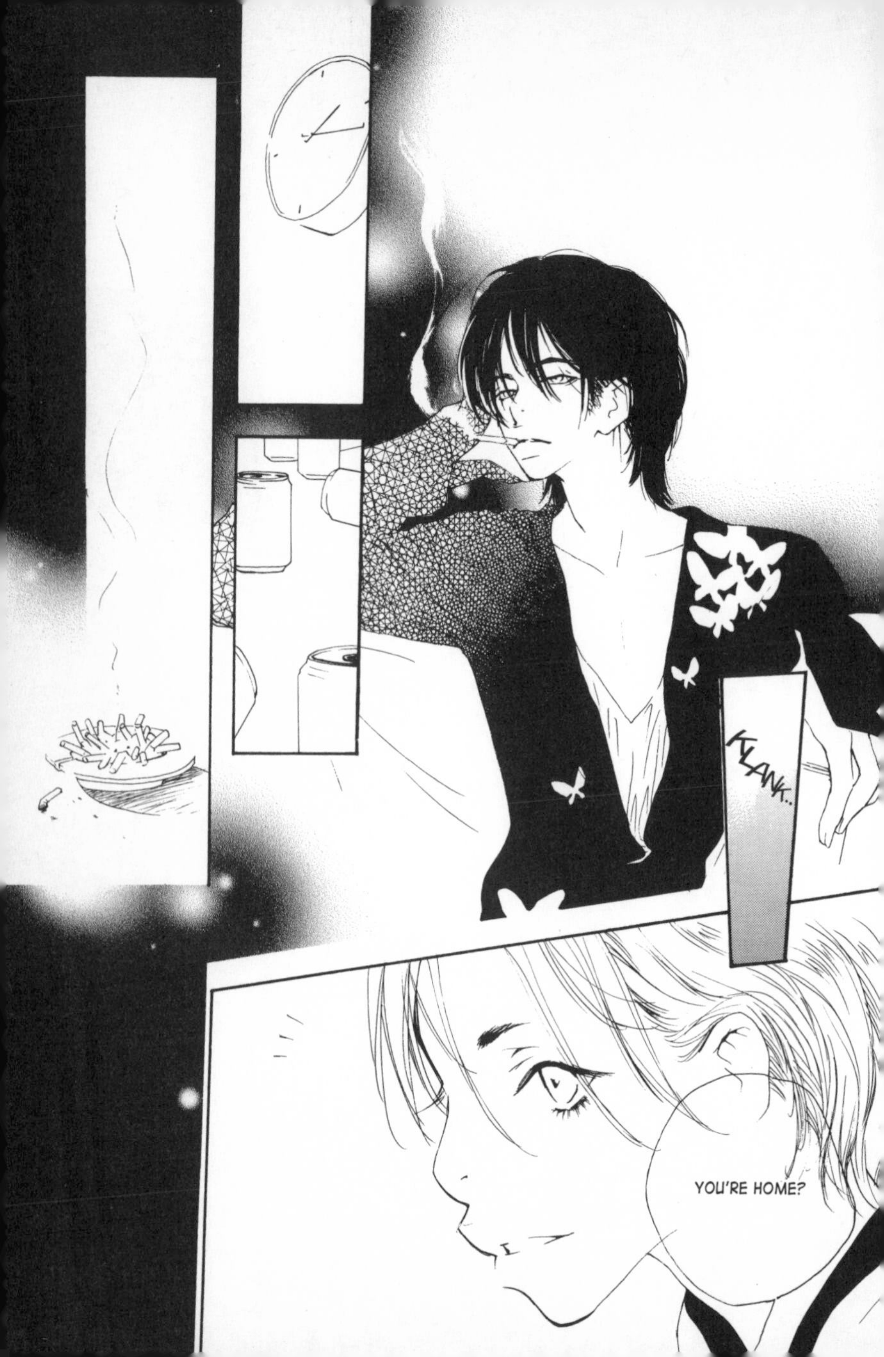
KLANK..
YOU'RE HOME?

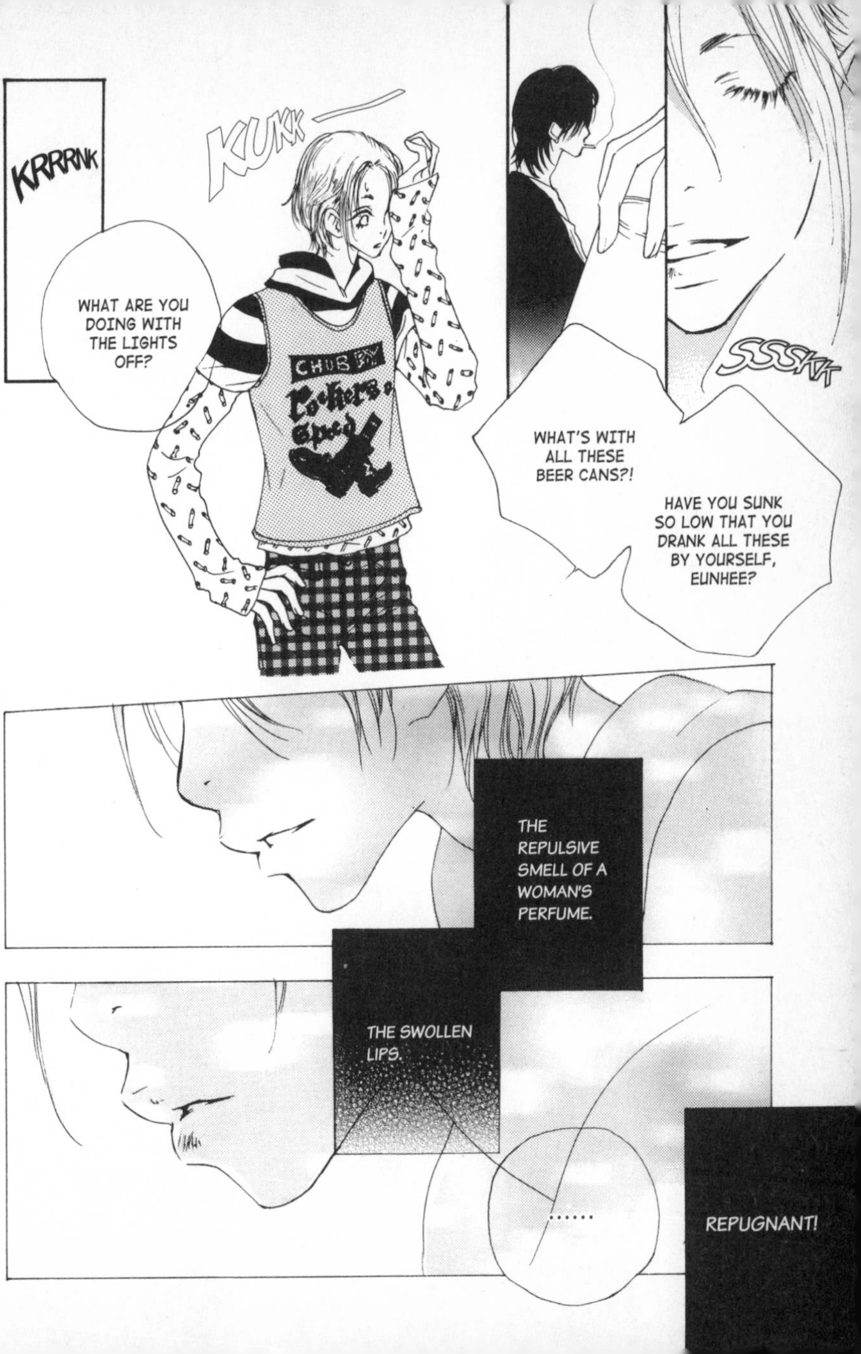
KRRRNK
KUKK
WHAT ARE YOU DOING WITH THE LIGHTS OFF?
SSSKK
WHAT'S WITH ALL THESE BEER CANS?!
HAVE YOU SUNK SO LOW THAT YOU DRANK ALL THESE BY YOURSELF, EUNHEE?
THE REPULSIVE SMELL OF A WOMAN'S PERFUME.
THE SWOLLEN LIPS.
......
REPUGNANT!

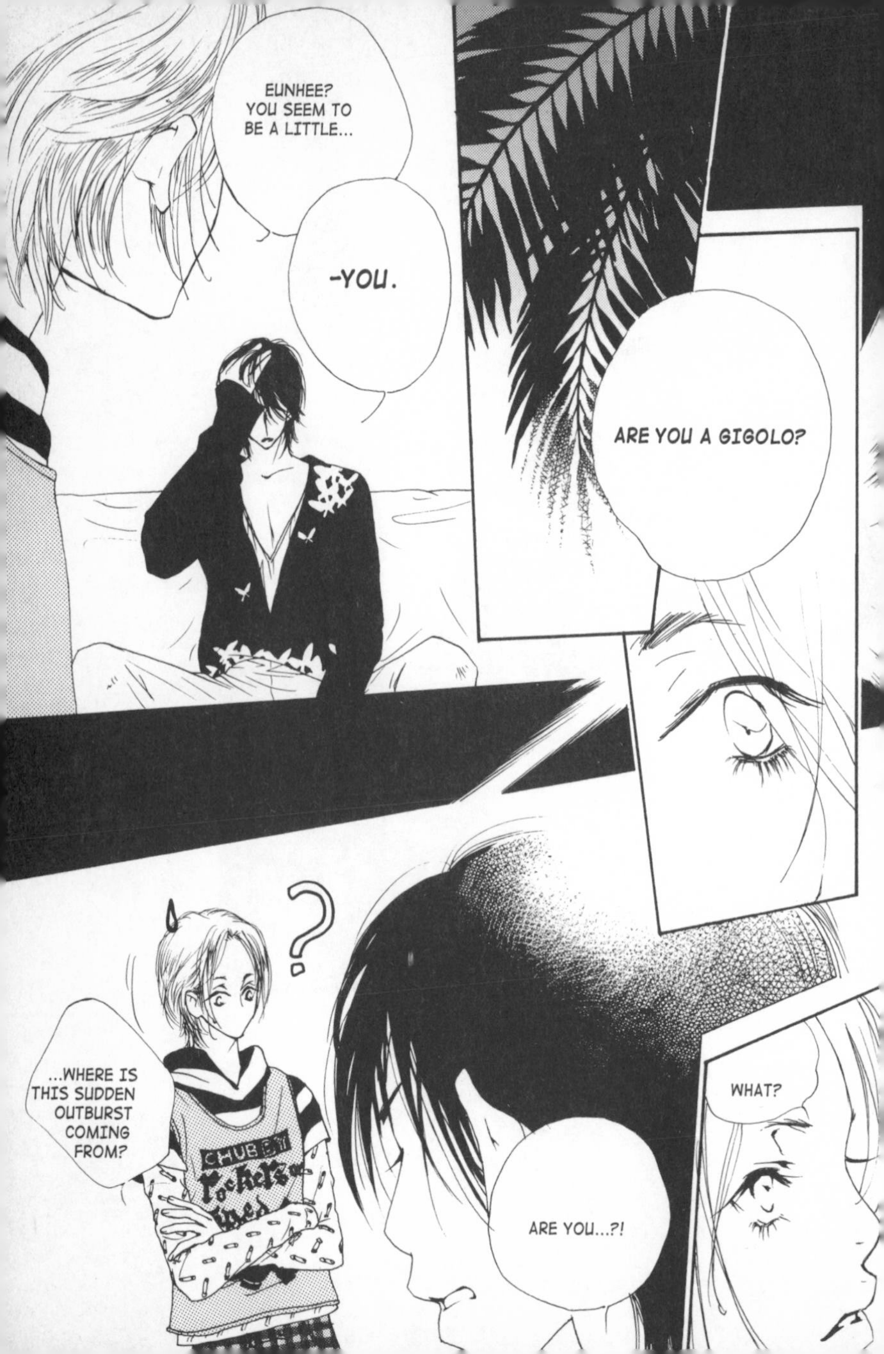
EUNHEE? YOU SEEM TO BE A LITTLE...
-YOU.
ARE YOU A GIGOLO?
ARE YOU...?!
WHAT?
...WHERE IS THIS SUDDEN OUTBURST COMING FROM?

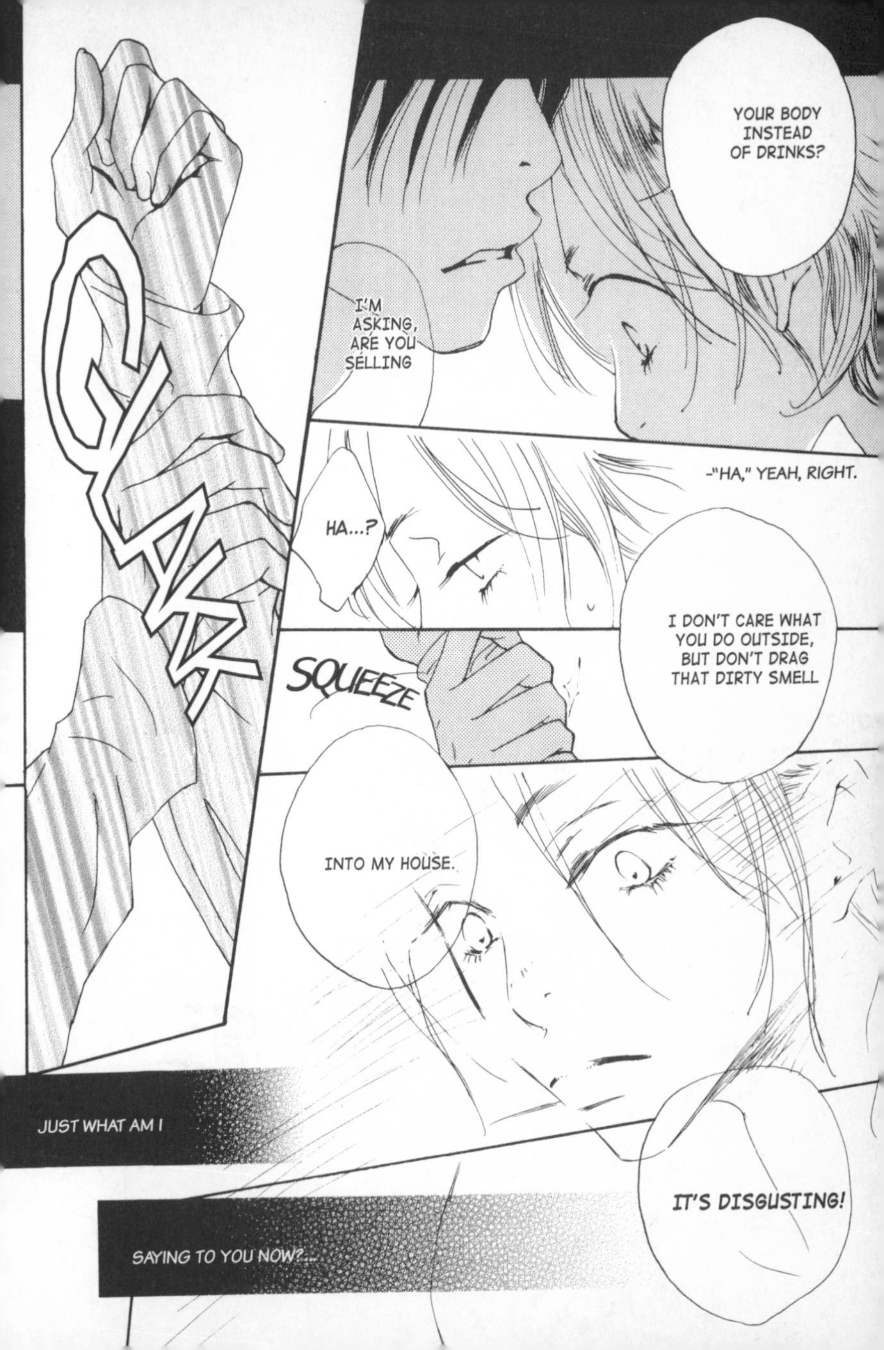
I'M ASKING, ARE YOU SELLING
YOUR BODY INSTEAD OF DRINKS?
-"HA," YEAH, RIGHT.
HA...?
I DON'T CARE WHAT YOU DO OUTSIDE, BUT DON'T DRAG THAT DIRTY SMELL
SQUEEZE
INTO MY HOUSE.
IT'S DISGUSTING!
JUST WHAT AM I
SAYING TO YOU NOW?...

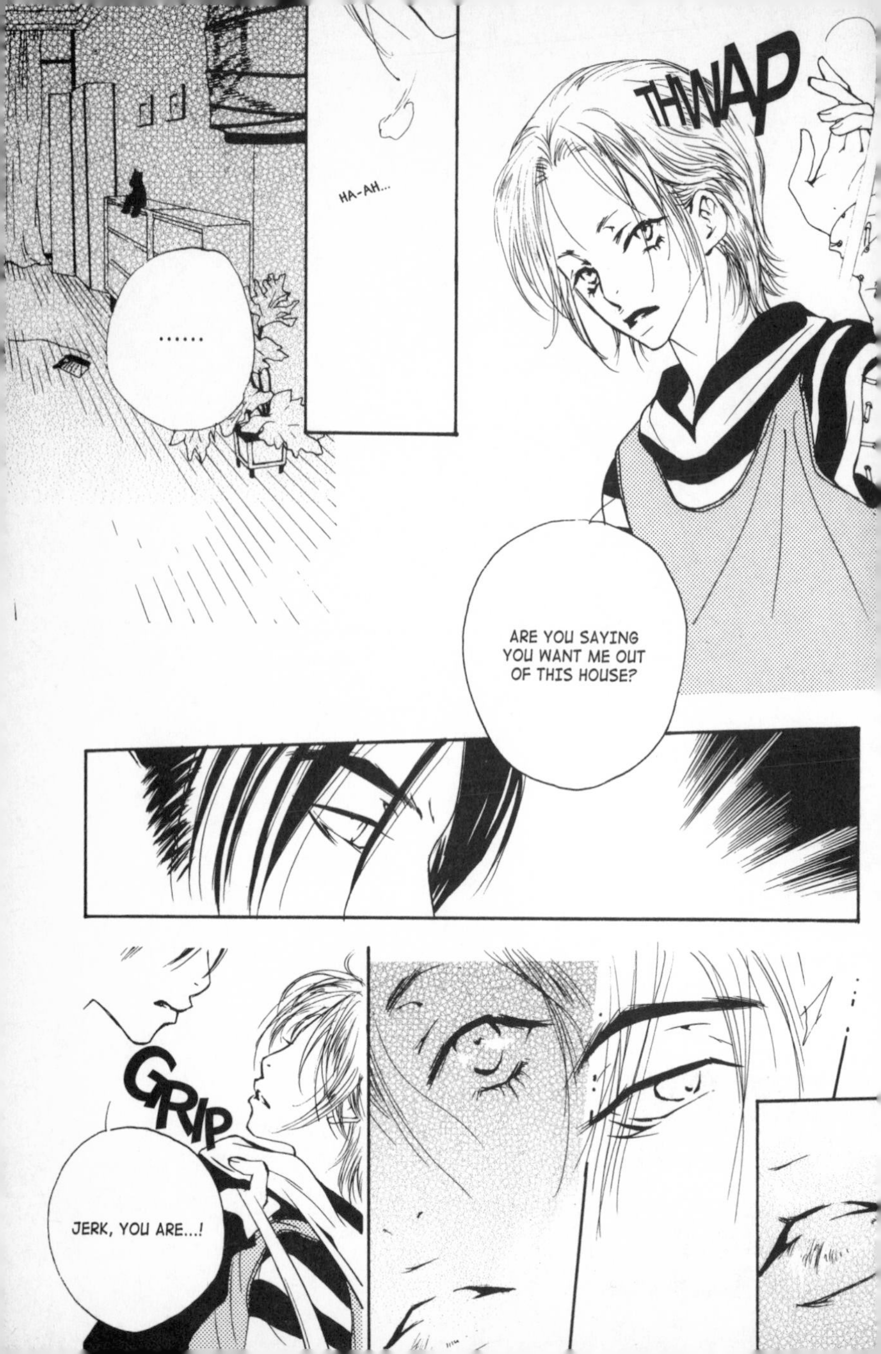
THWAP
HA-AH...
......
ARE YOU SAYING YOU WANT ME OUT OF THIS HOUSE?
GRIP
JERK, YOU ARE...!

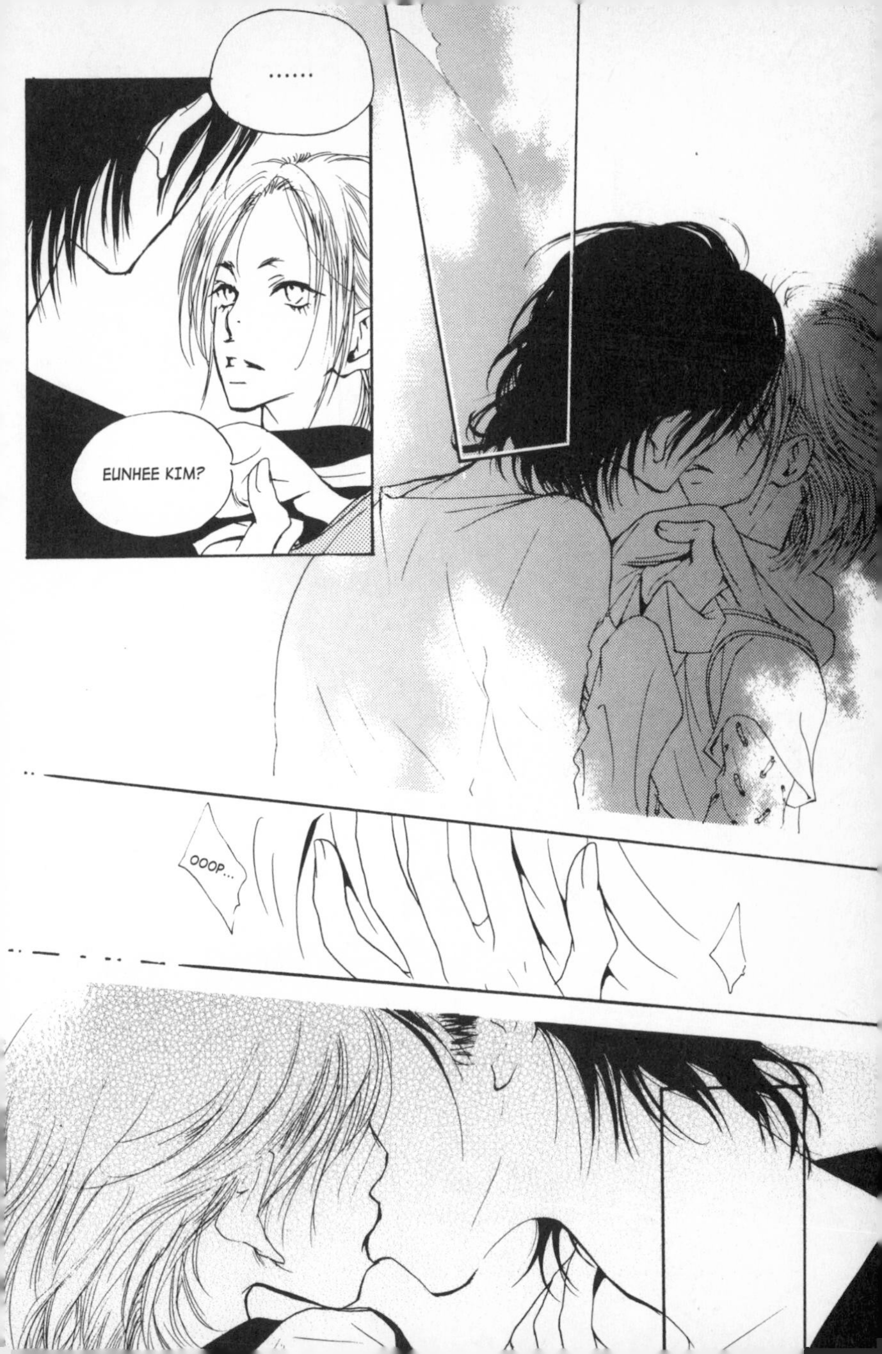
......
EUNHEE KIM?
OOOP...

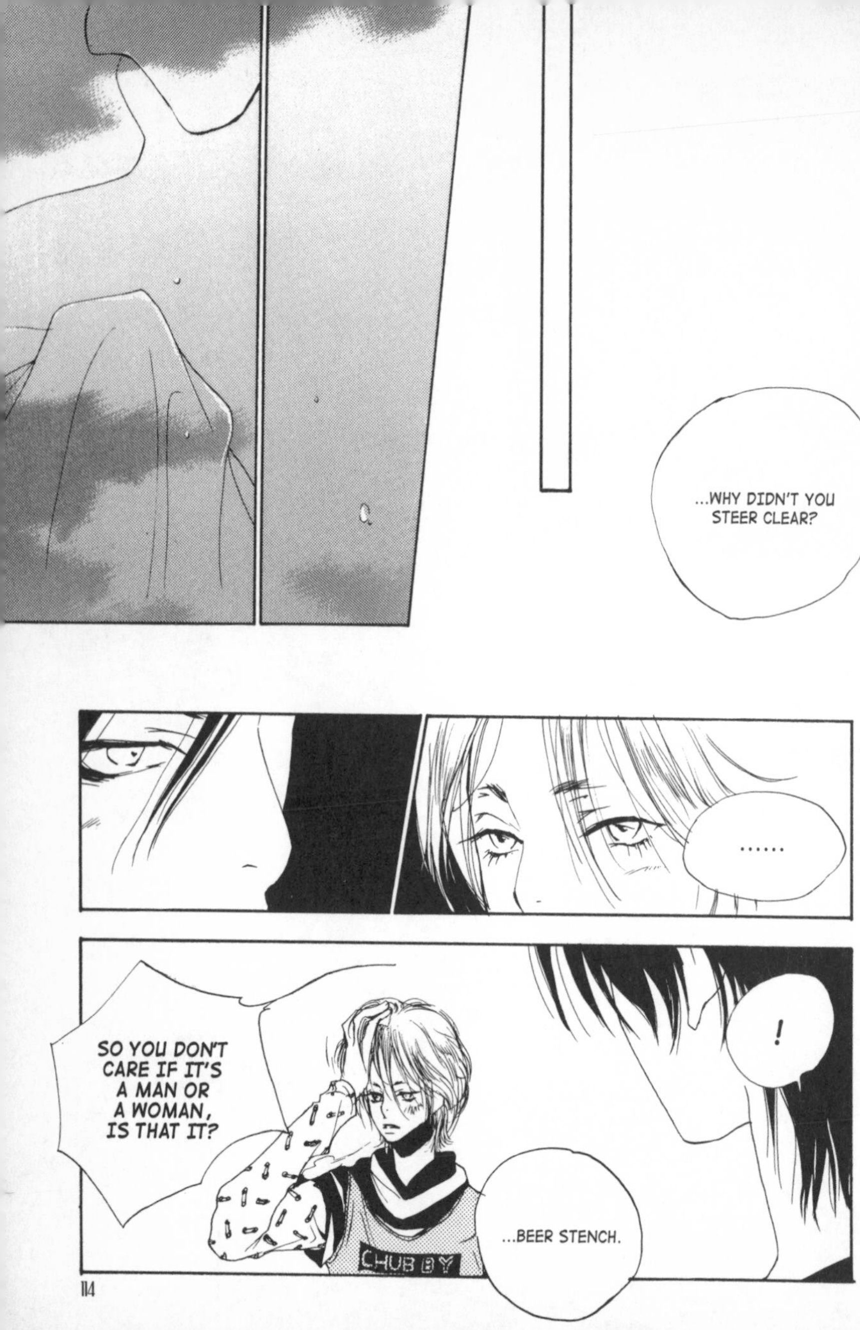
...WHY DIDN'T YOU STEER CLEAR?
......
!
SO YOU DON'T CARE IF IT'S A MAN OR A WOMAN, IS THAT IT?
...BEER STENCH.
CHUBBY

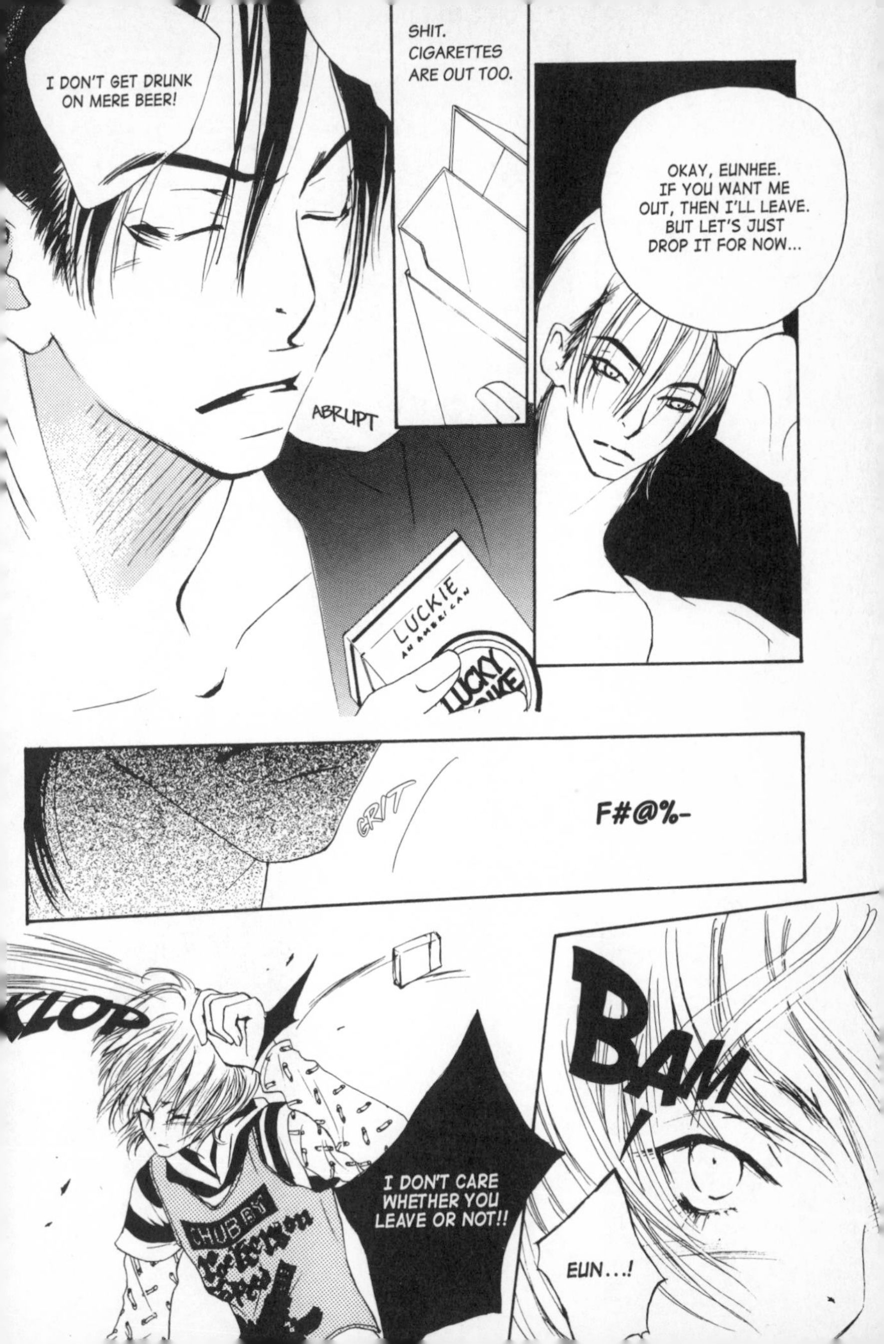
I DON'T GET DRUNK ON MERE BEER!
SHIT. CIGARETTES ARE OUT TOO.
ABRUPT
LUCKIE
OKAY, EUNHEE. IF YOU WANT ME OUT, THEN I'LL LEAVE. BUT LET'S JUST DROP IT FOR NOW...
GRIT
F#@%-
KLOP
BAM
I DON'T CARE WHETHER YOU LEAVE OR NOT!!
EUN...!

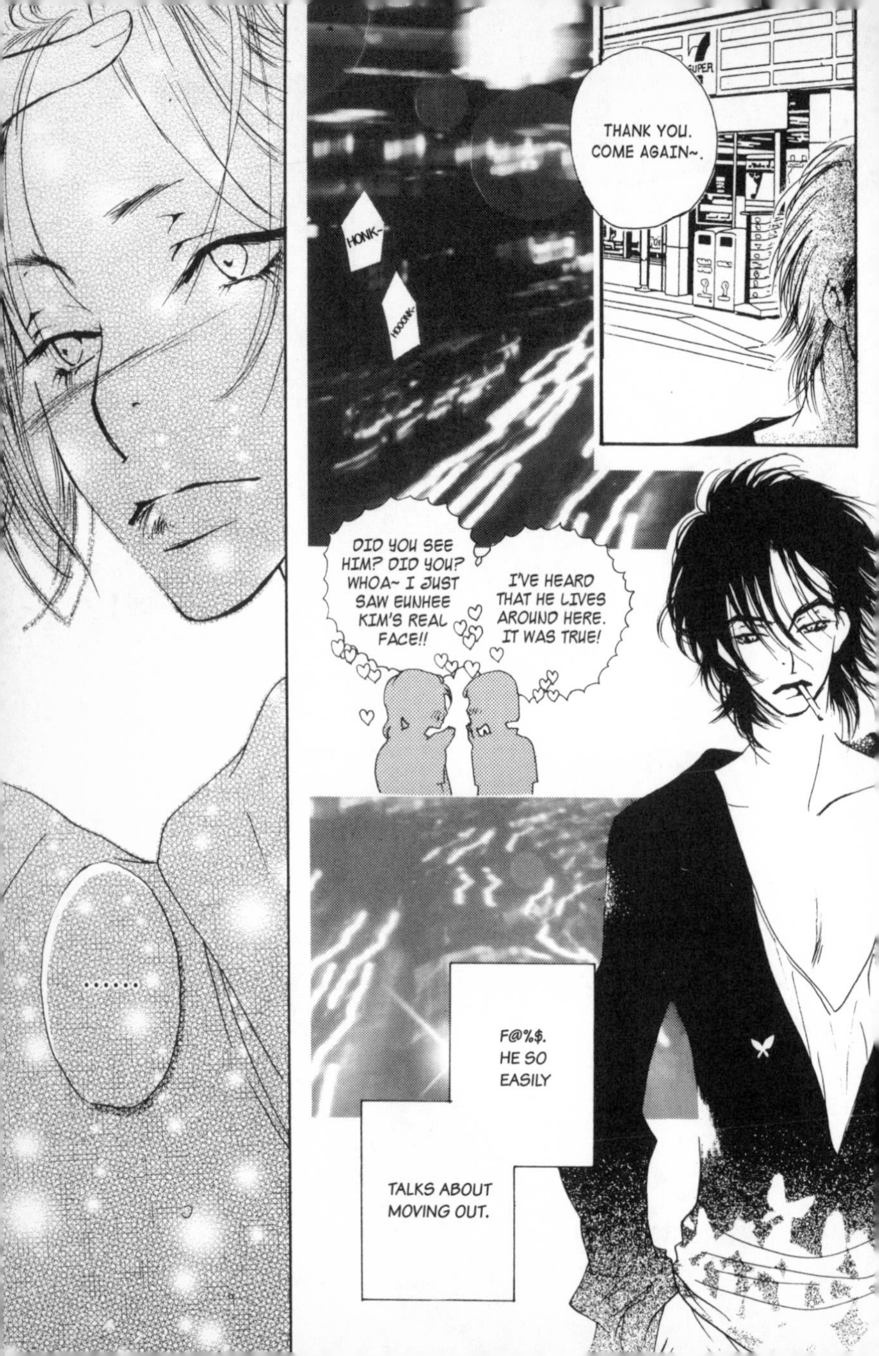
......
HONK~
HOOONK~
THANK YOU. COME AGAIN~.
DID YOU SEE HIM? DID YOU? WHOA~ I JUST SAW EUNHEE KIM'S REAL FACE!!
I'VE HEARD THAT HE LIVES AROUND HERE. IT WAS TRUE!
F@%$. HE SO EASILY
TALKS ABOUT MOVING OUT.

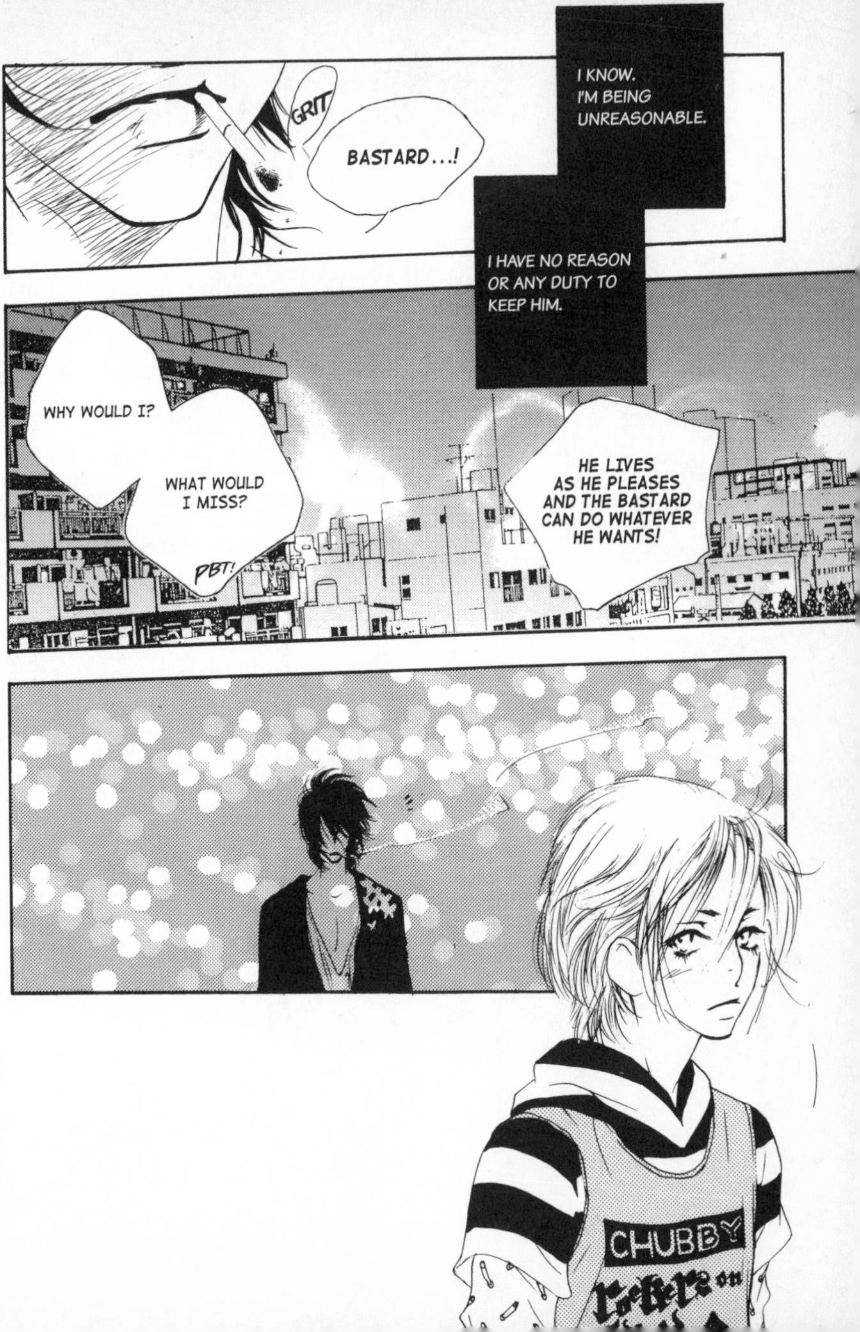
I KNOW.
I'M BEING
UNREASONABLE.
GRIT
BASTARD...!
I HAVE NO REASON
OR ANY DUTY TO
KEEP HIM.
HE LIVES
AS HE PLEASES
AND THE BASTARD
CAN DO WHATEVER
HE WANTS!
WHY WOULD I?
WHAT WOULD
I MISS?
PBT!
CHUBBY

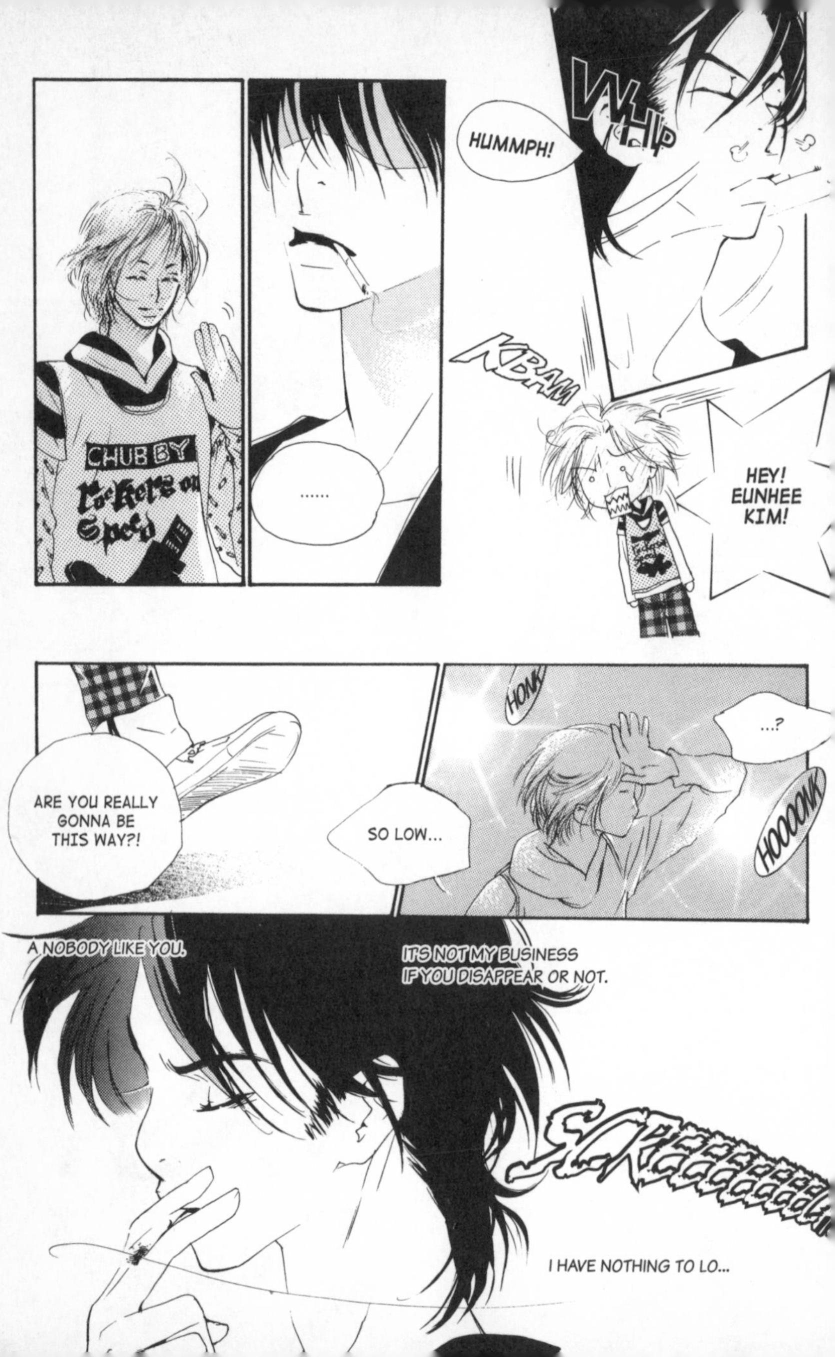
CHUBBY
Rockers on Speed
......
HUMMPH!
WHIP
KBAM
HEY! EUNHEE KIM!
ARE YOU REALLY GONNA BE THIS WAY?!
SO LOW...
HONK
...?
HOOOONK
A NOBODY LIKE YOU.
IT'S NOT MY BUSINESS IF YOU DISAPPEAR OR NOT.
I HAVE NOTHING TO LO...

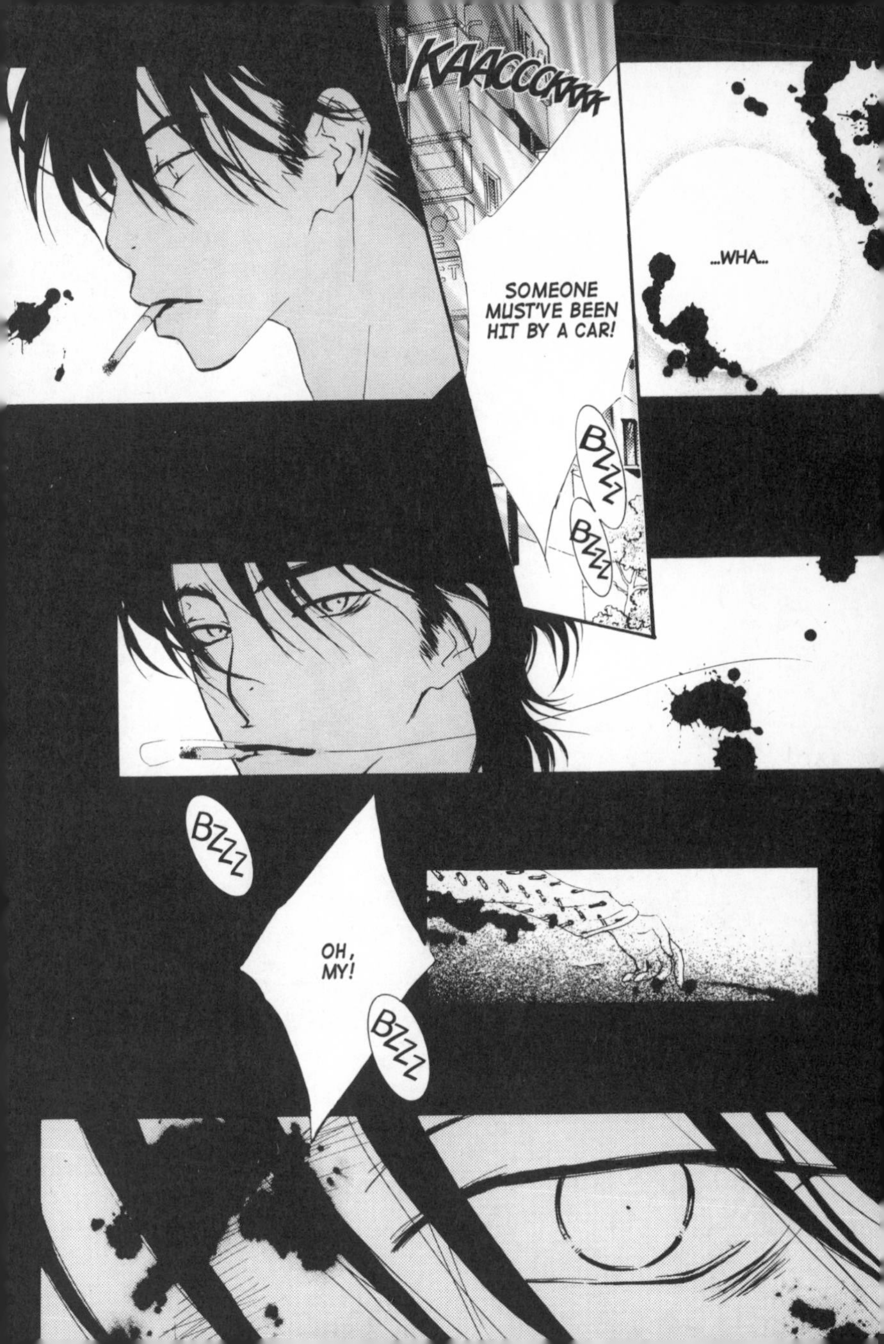
KAACCCKKKK
...WHA...
SOMEONE MUST'VE BEEN HIT BY A CAR!
BZZZ
BZZZ
BZZZ
OH, MY!
BZZZ

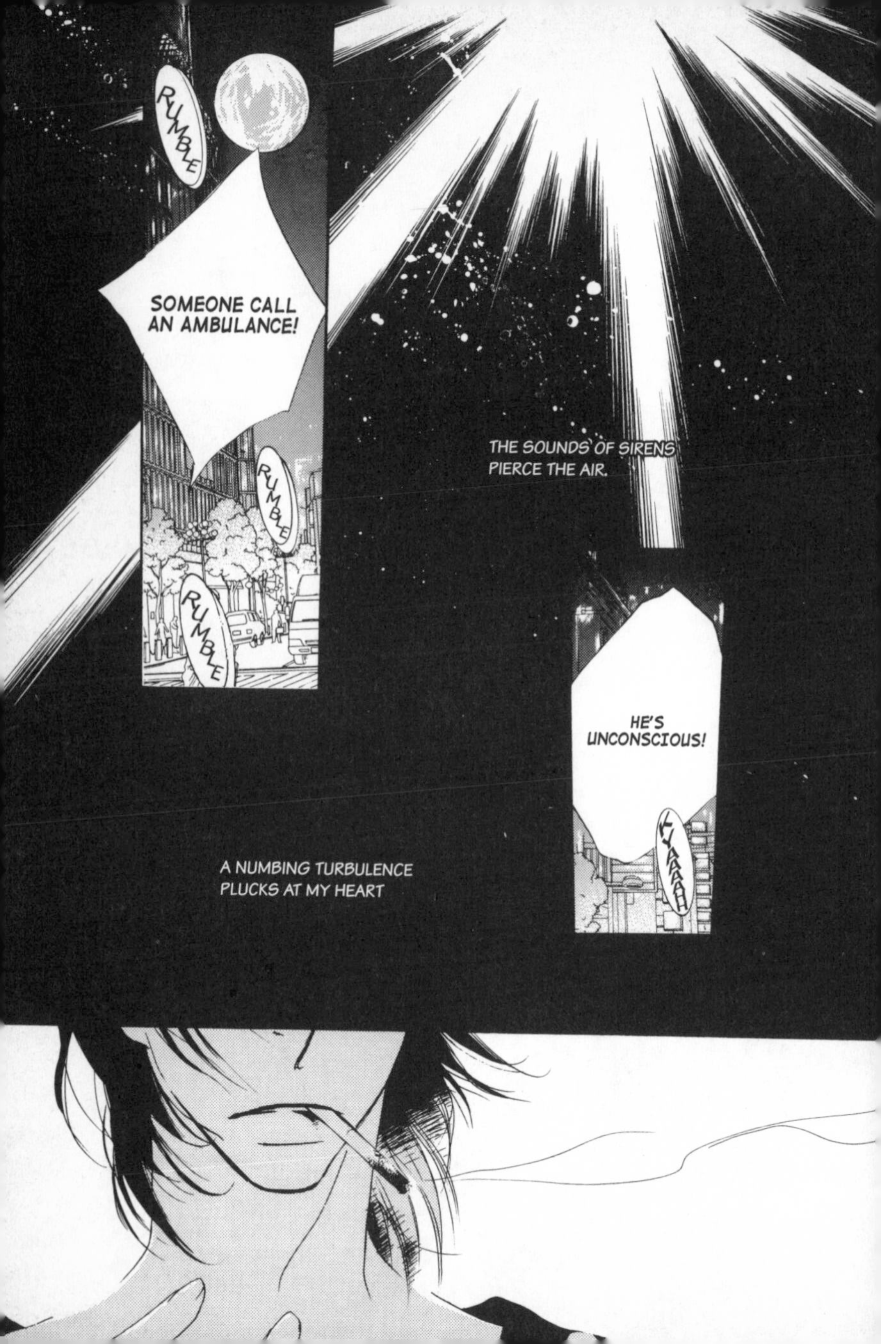
THE SOUNDS OF SIRENS PIERCE THE AIR.
RUMBLE
SOMEONE CALL AN AMBULANCE!
RUMBLE
RUMBLE
HE'S UNCONSCIOUS!
KYAAAAH
A NUMBING TURBULENCE PLUCKS AT MY HEART

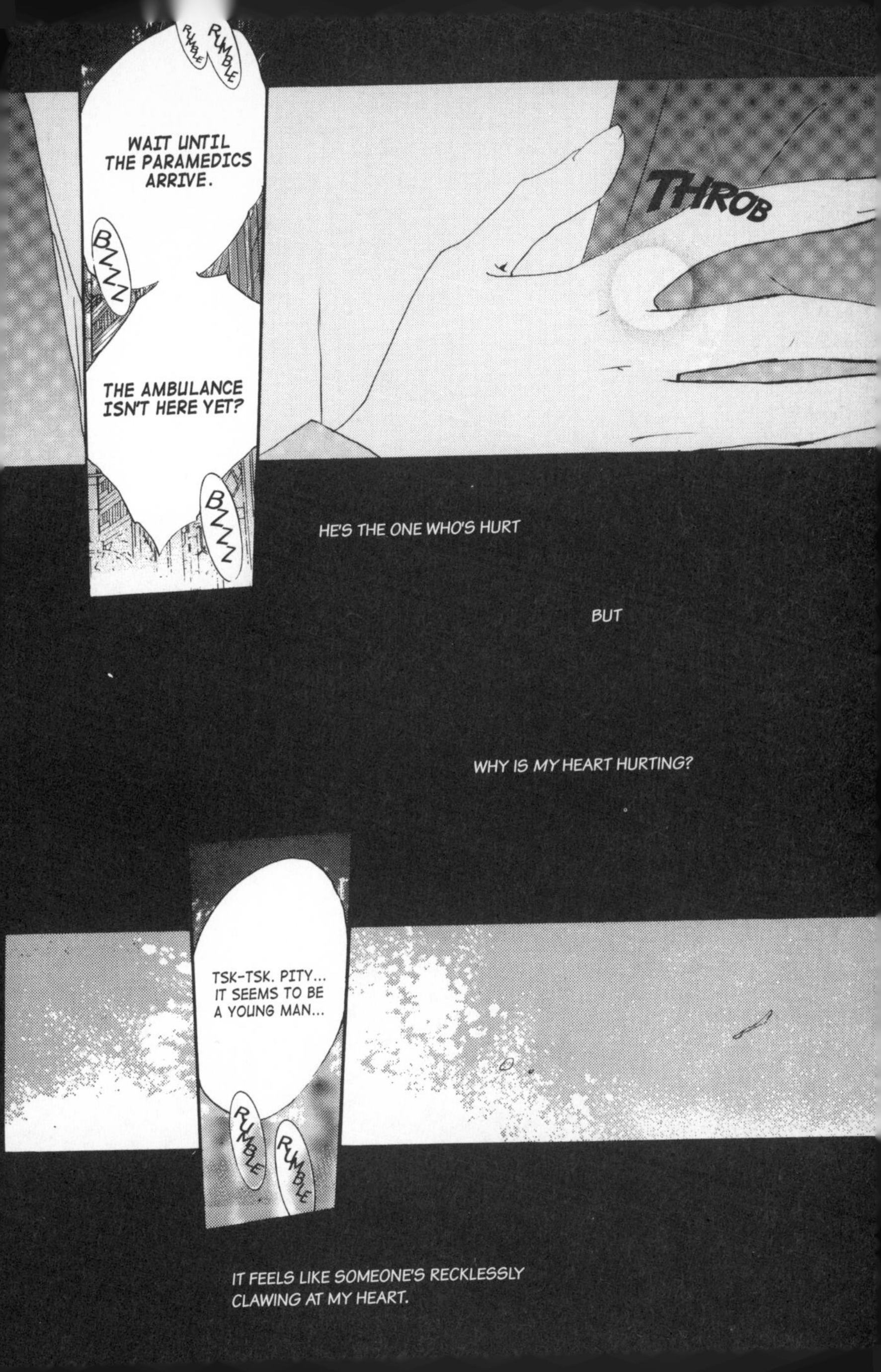

THROB
RUMBLE
RUMBLE
WAIT UNTIL THE PARAMEDICS ARRIVE.
BZZZ
THE AMBULANCE ISN'T HERE YET?
BZZZ
HE'S THE ONE WHO'S HURT
BUT
WHY IS MY HEART HURTING?
TSK-TSK. PITY... IT SEEMS TO BE A YOUNG MAN...
RUMBLE
RUMBLE
IT FEELS LIKE SOMEONE'S RECKLESSLY CLAWING AT MY HEART.

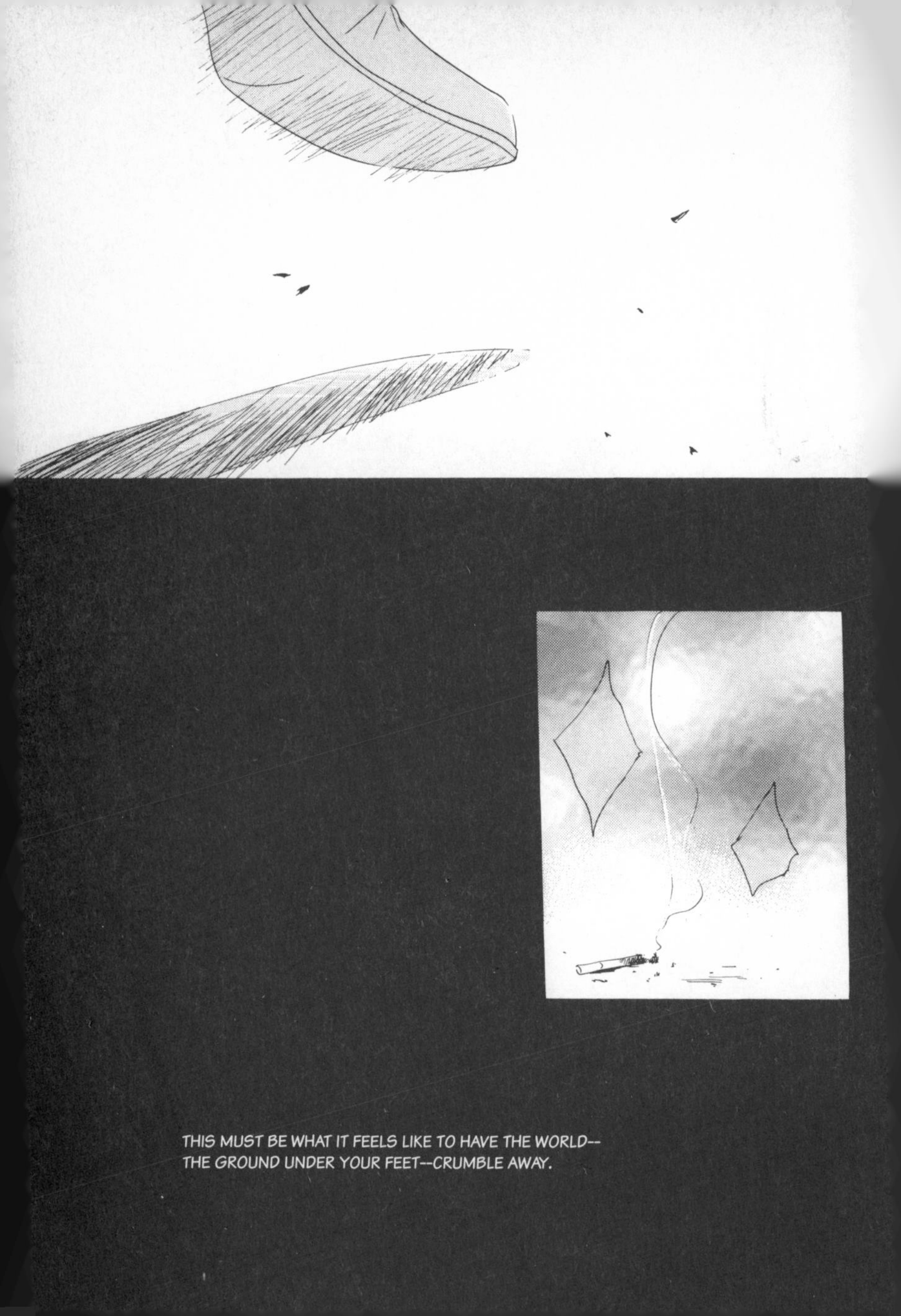
THIS MUST BE WHAT IT FEELS LIKE TO HAVE THE WORLD--
THE GROUND UNDER YOUR FEET--CRUMBLE AWAY.

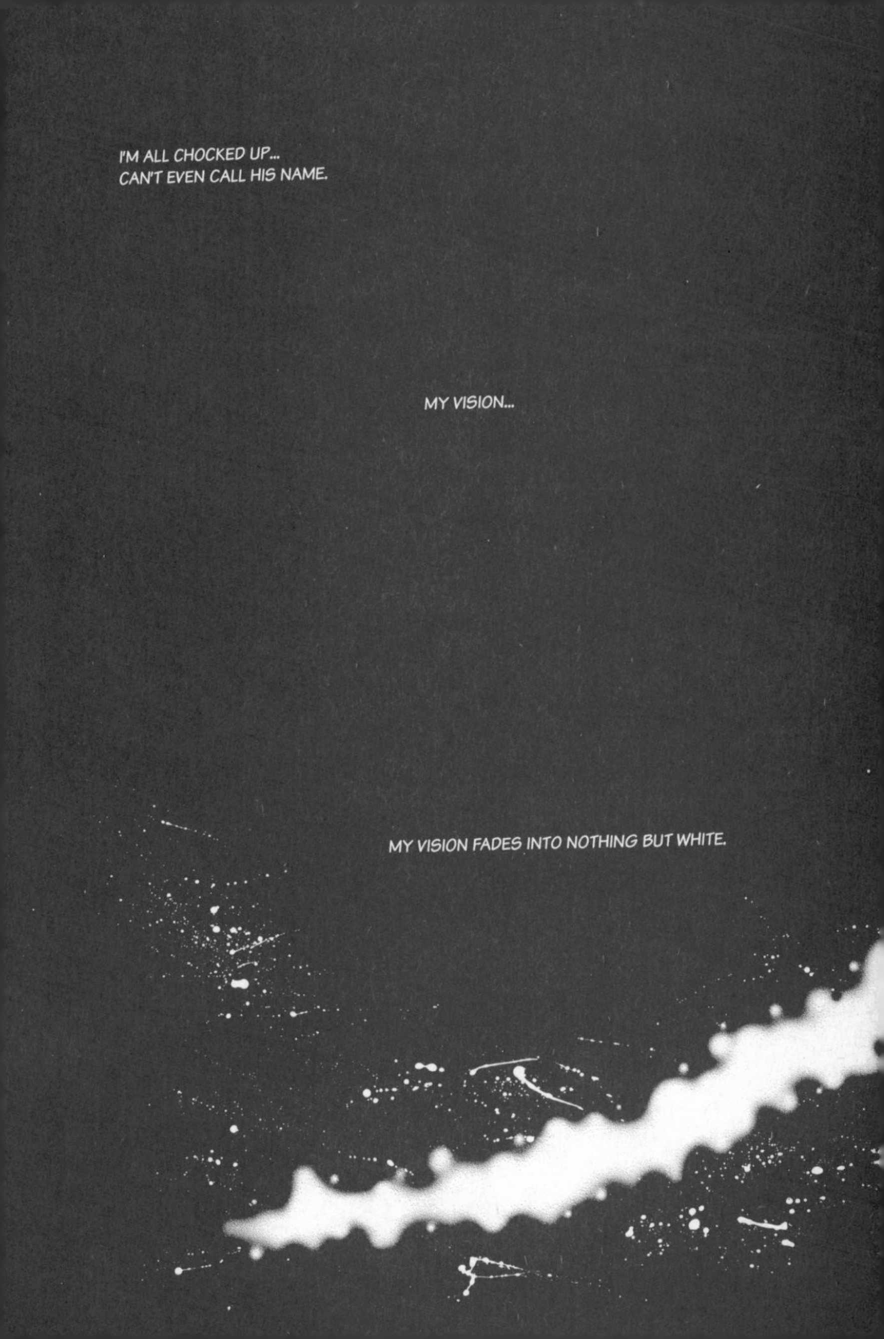
I'M ALL CHOCKED UP...
CAN'T EVEN CALL HIS NAME.
MY VISION...
MY VISION FADES INTO NOTHING BUT WHITE.

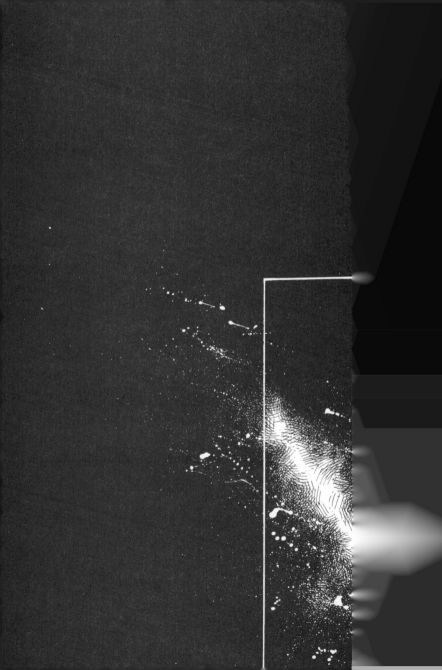

6

"THE LONG AND WINDING ROAD"

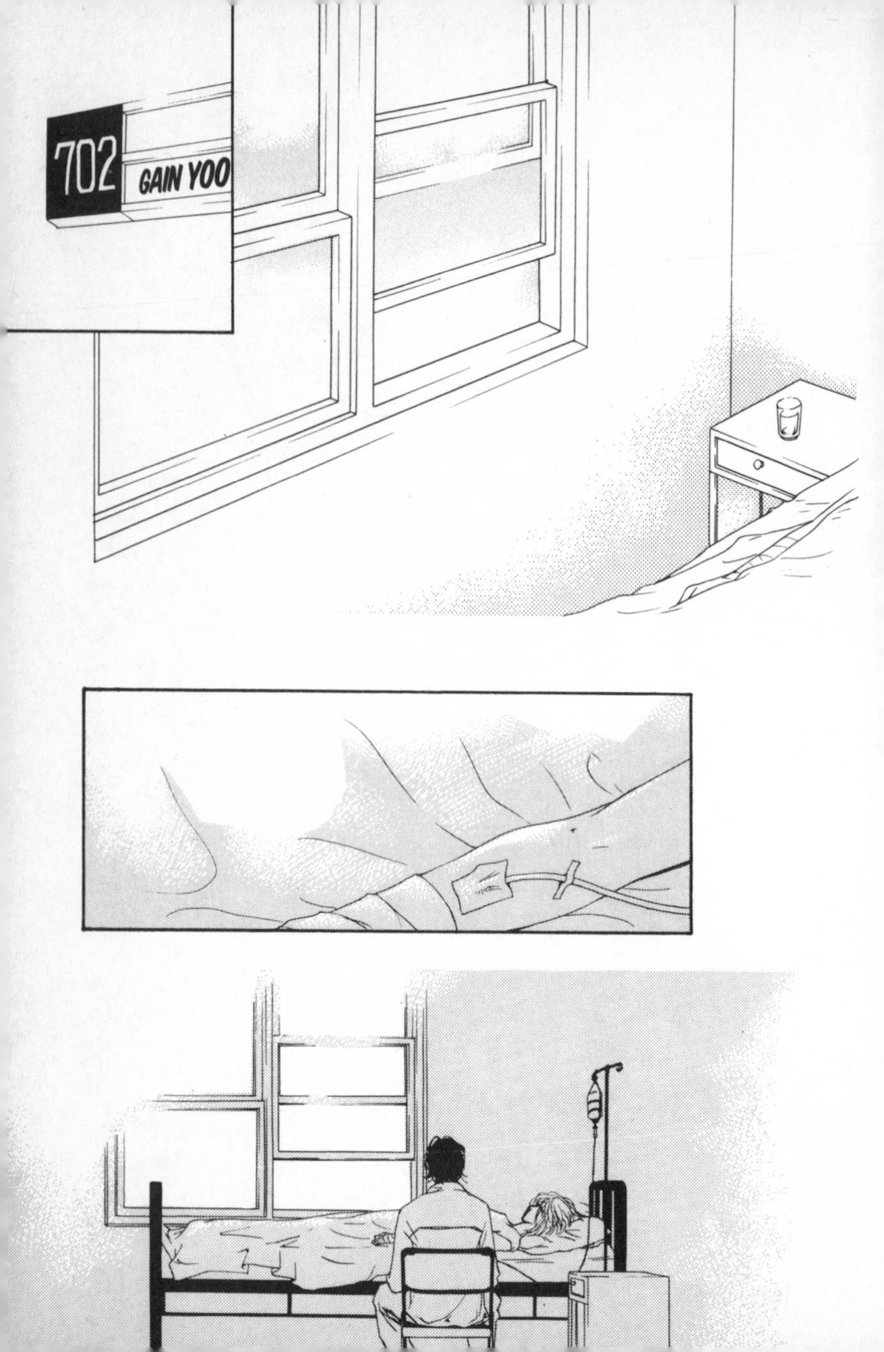
702
GAIN YOO

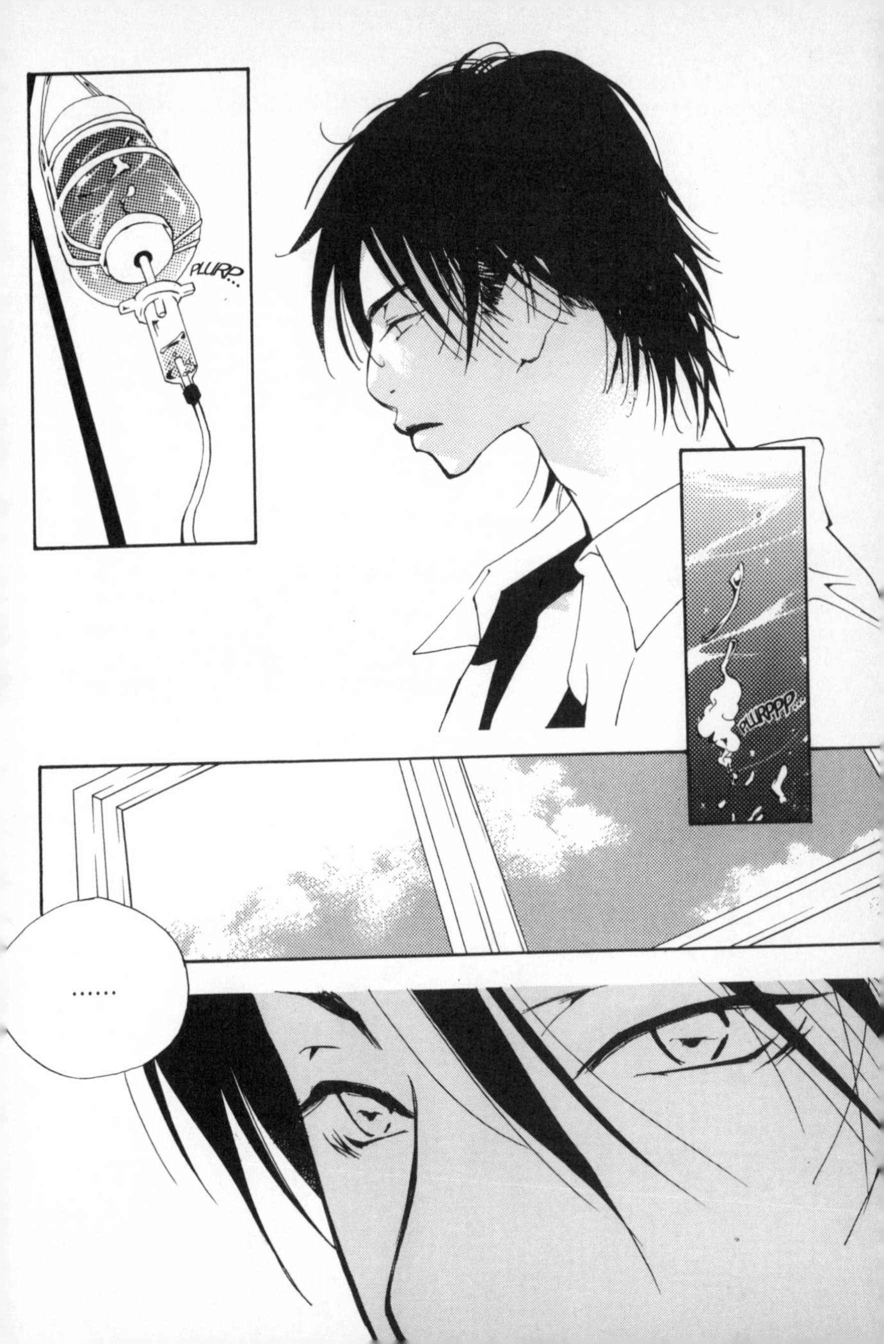
PLURP...
PLURPPP...
......

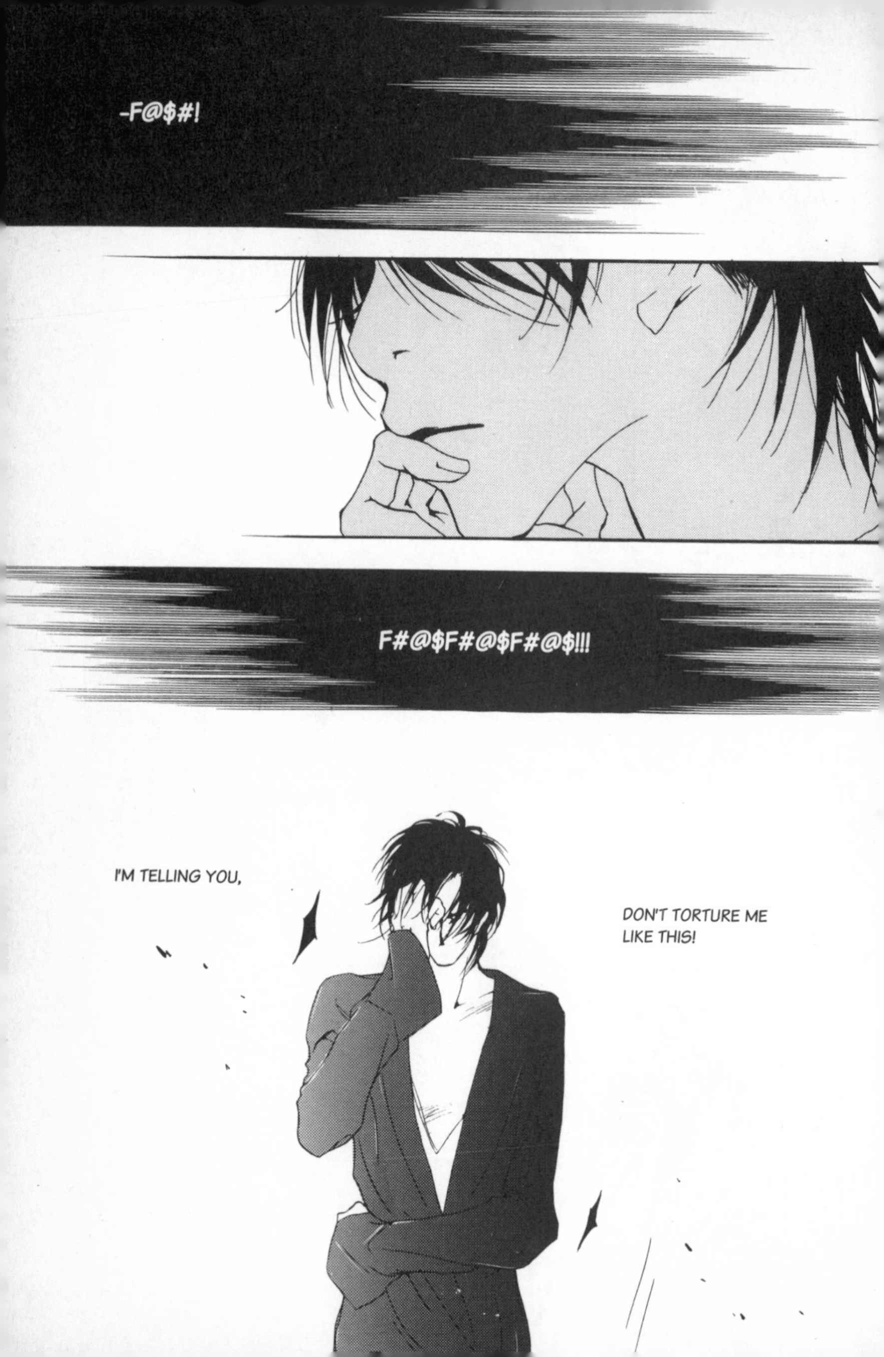
-F@$#!
F#@$F#@$F#@$!!!
I'M TELLING YOU,
DON'T TORTURE ME
LIKE THIS!

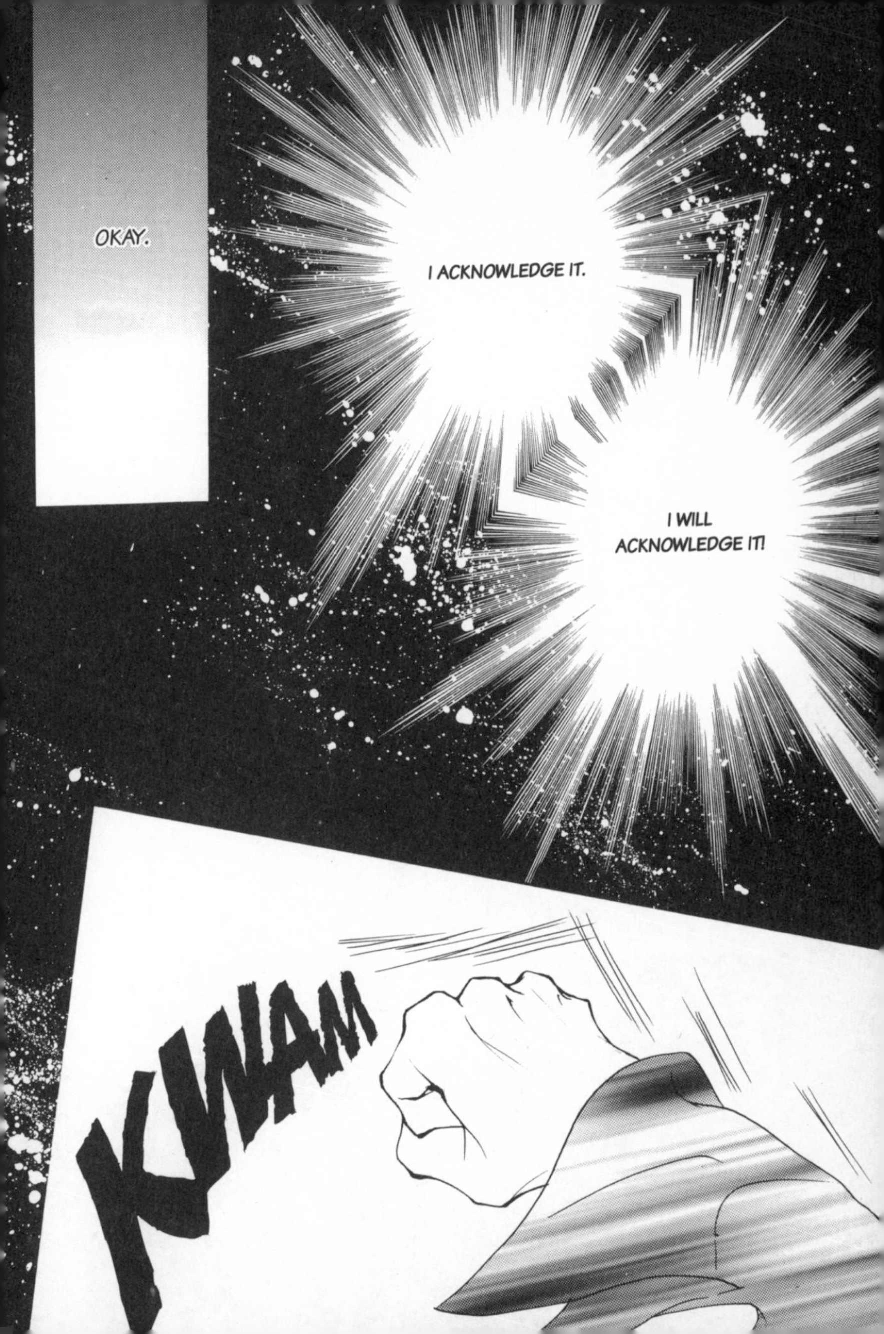
OKAY.
I ACKNOWLEDGE IT.
I WILL ACKNOWLEDGE IT!
KWAM

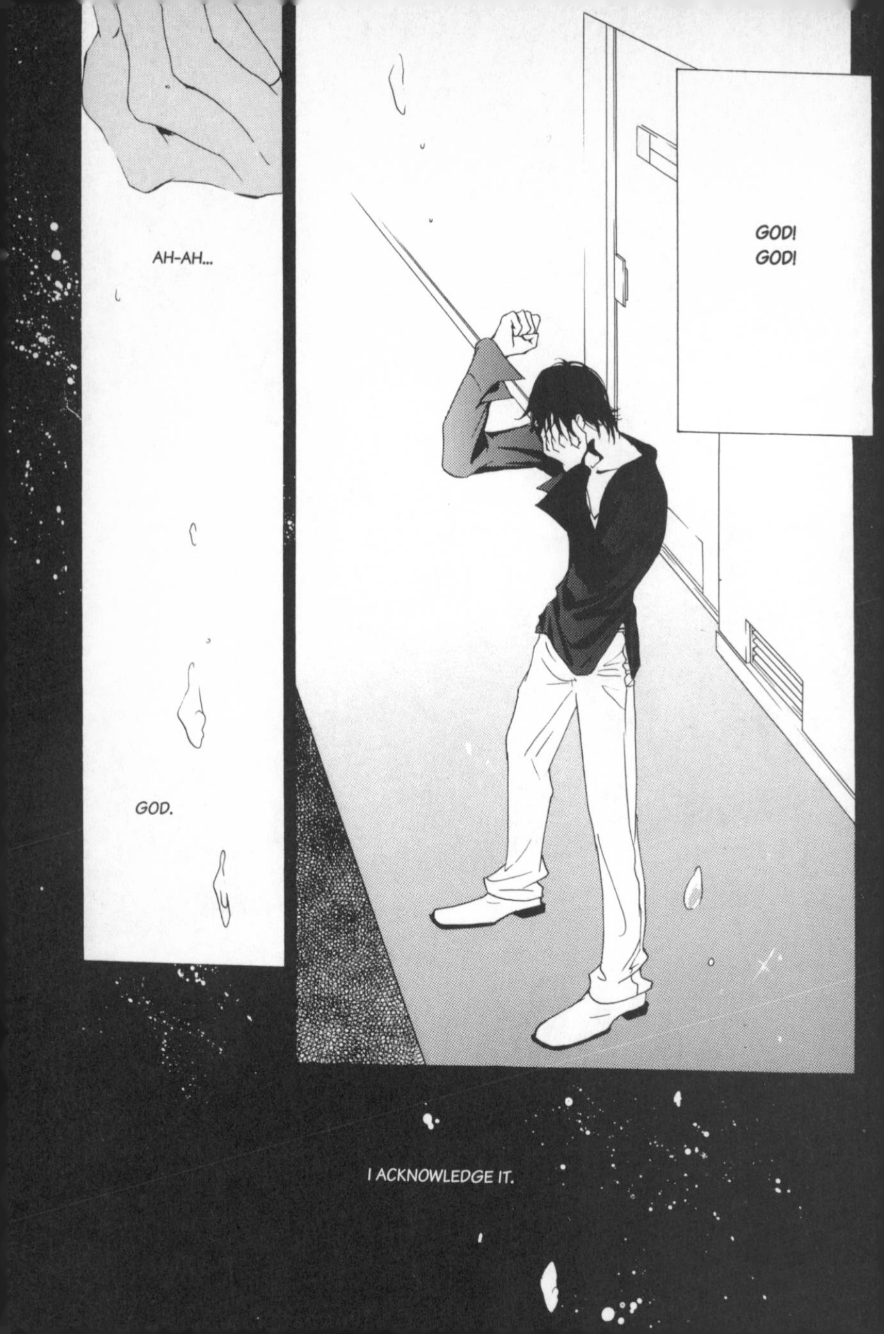
GOD!
GOD!
AH-AH...
GOD.
I ACKNOWLEDGE IT.

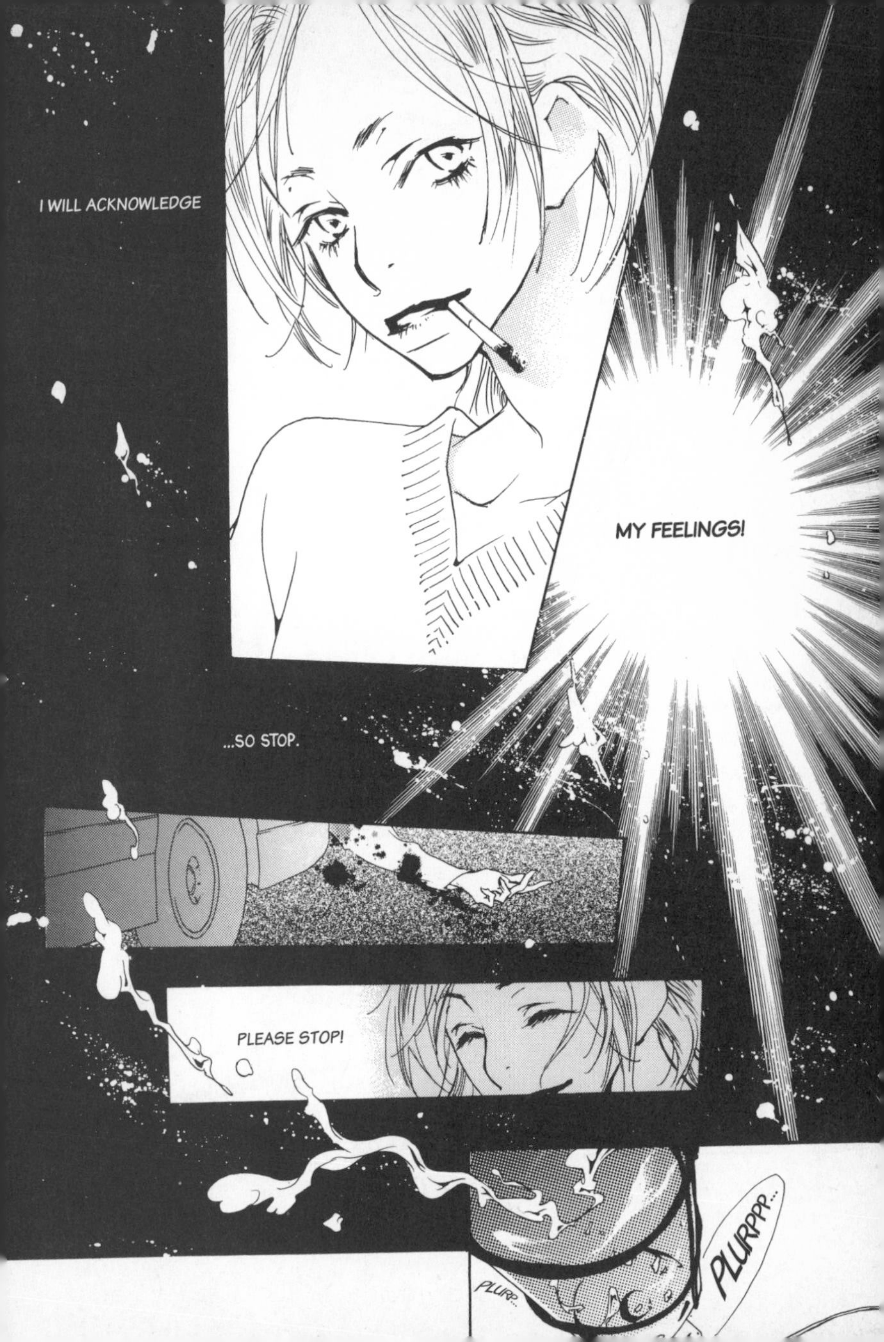
I WILL ACKNOWLEDGE
MY FEELINGS!
...SO STOP.
PLEASE STOP!
PLURPPP...
PLURP...

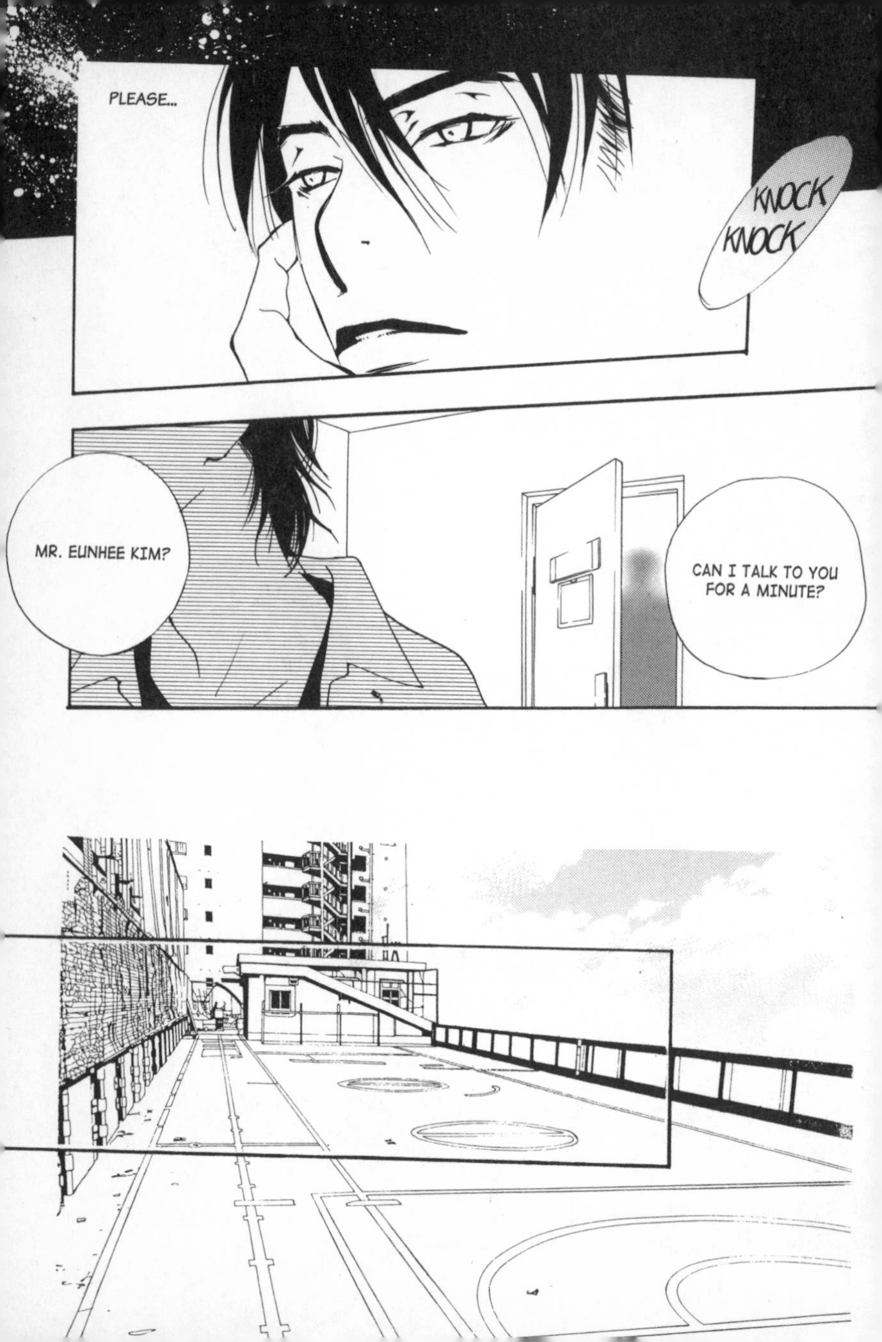
KNOCK KNOCK
PLEASE...
CAN I TALK TO YOU FOR A MINUTE?
MR. EUNHEE KIM?

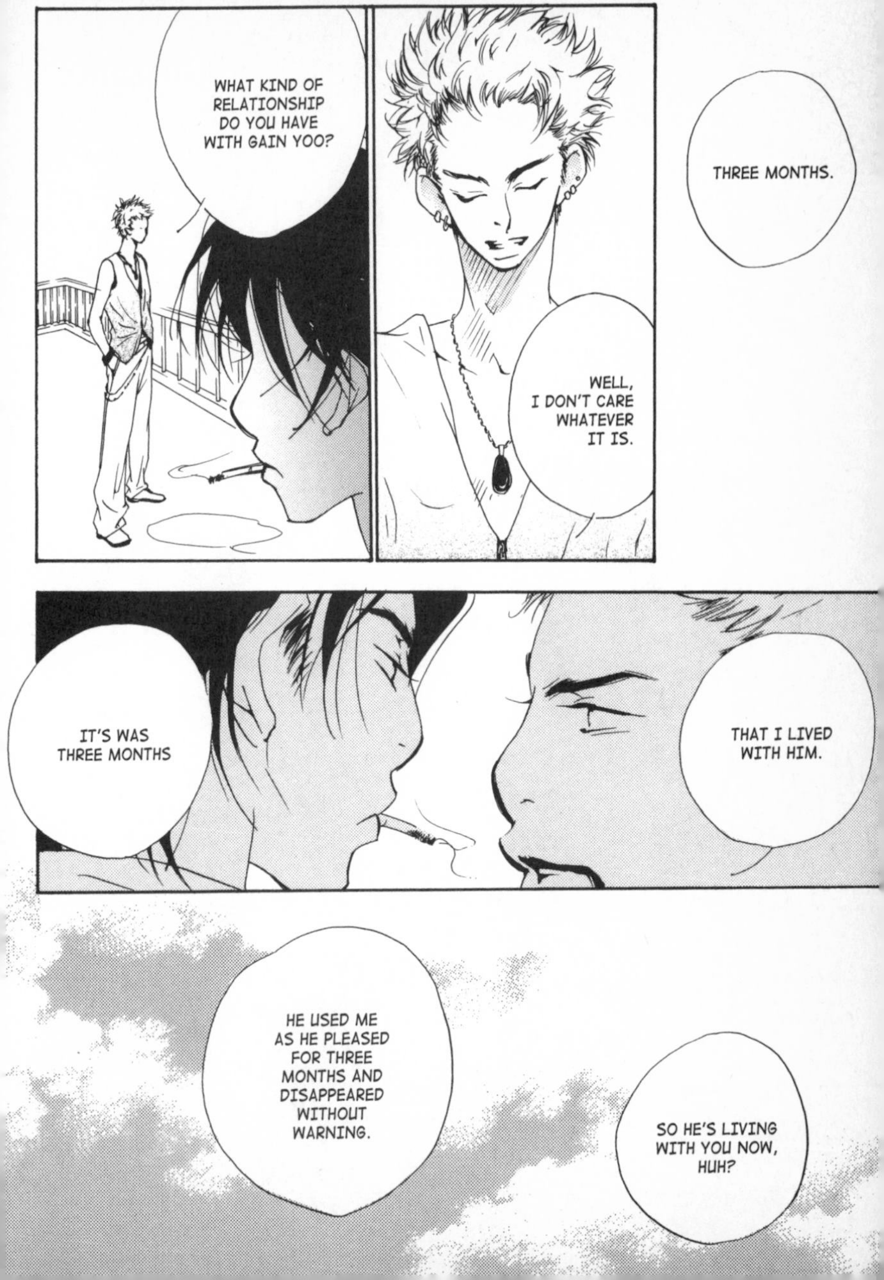
WHAT KIND OF RELATIONSHIP DO YOU HAVE WITH GAIN YOO?
WELL, I DON'T CARE WHATEVER IT IS.
THREE MONTHS.
IT'S WAS THREE MONTHS
THAT I LIVED WITH HIM.
HE USED ME AS HE PLEASED FOR THREE MONTHS AND DISAPPEARED WITHOUT WARNING.
SO HE'S LIVING WITH YOU NOW, HUH?

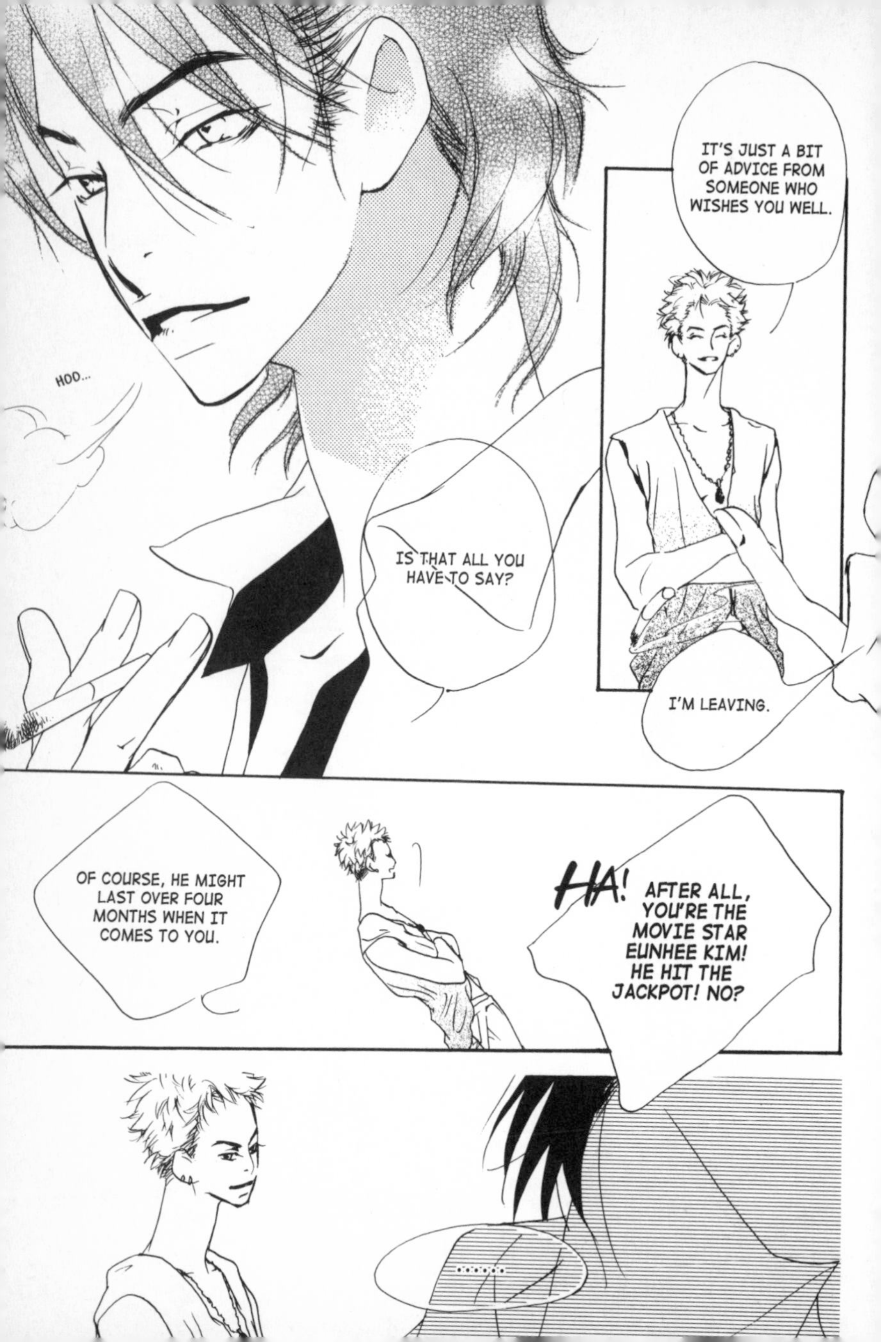
IT'S JUST A BIT OF ADVICE FROM SOMEONE WHO WISHES YOU WELL.
HOO...
IS THAT ALL YOU HAVE TO SAY?
I'M LEAVING.
HA!
AFTER ALL, YOU'RE THE MOVIE STAR EUNHEE KIM! HE HIT THE JACKPOT! NO?
OF COURSE, HE MIGHT LAST OVER FOUR MONTHS WHEN IT COMES TO YOU.
......

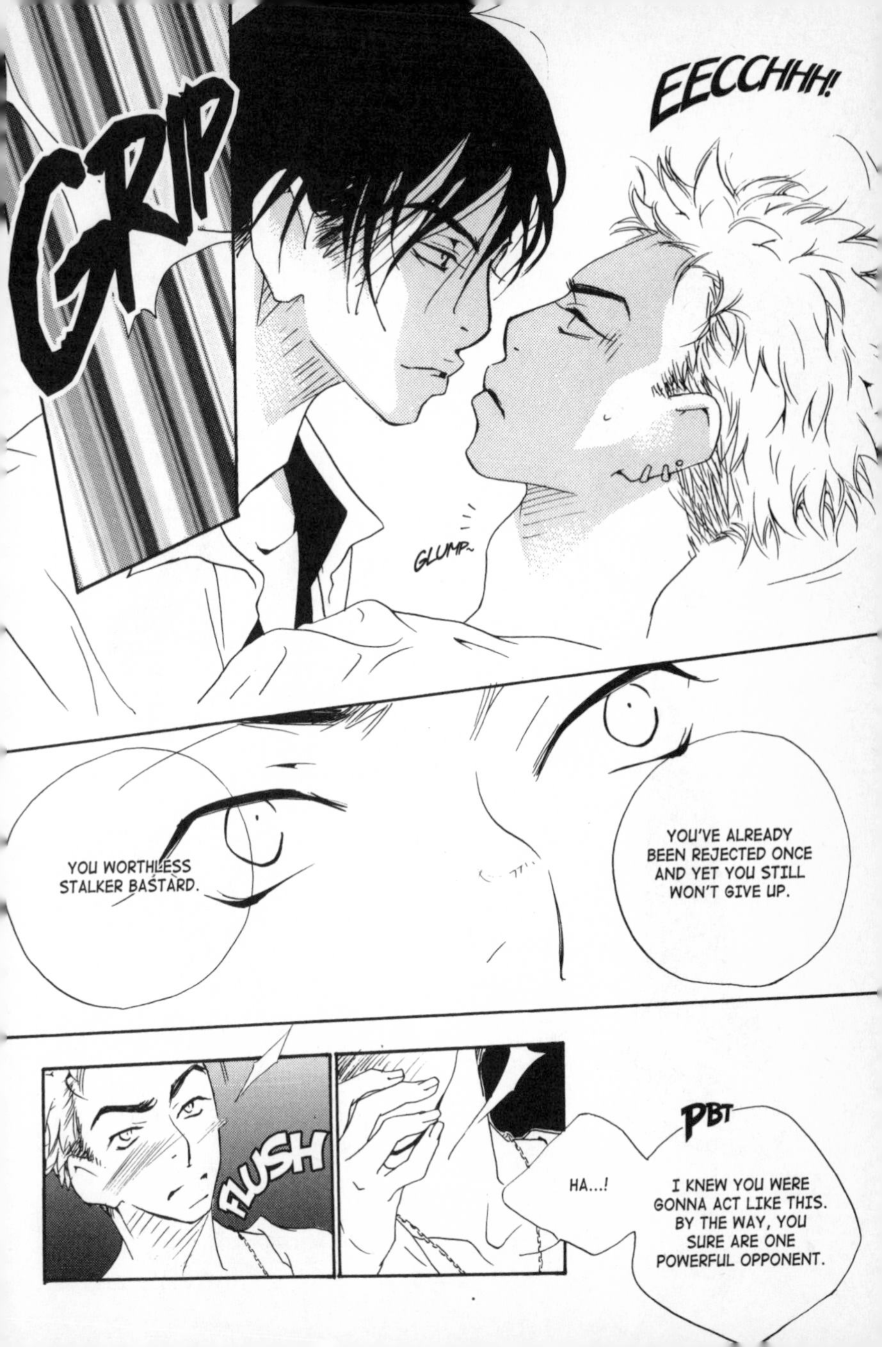
EECCHHH!
GRIP
GLUMP~
YOU'VE ALREADY BEEN REJECTED ONCE AND YET YOU STILL WON'T GIVE UP.
YOU WORTHLESS STALKER BASTARD.
PBT
I KNEW YOU WERE GONNA ACT LIKE THIS. BY THE WAY, YOU SURE ARE ONE POWERFUL OPPONENT.
HA...!
FLUSH

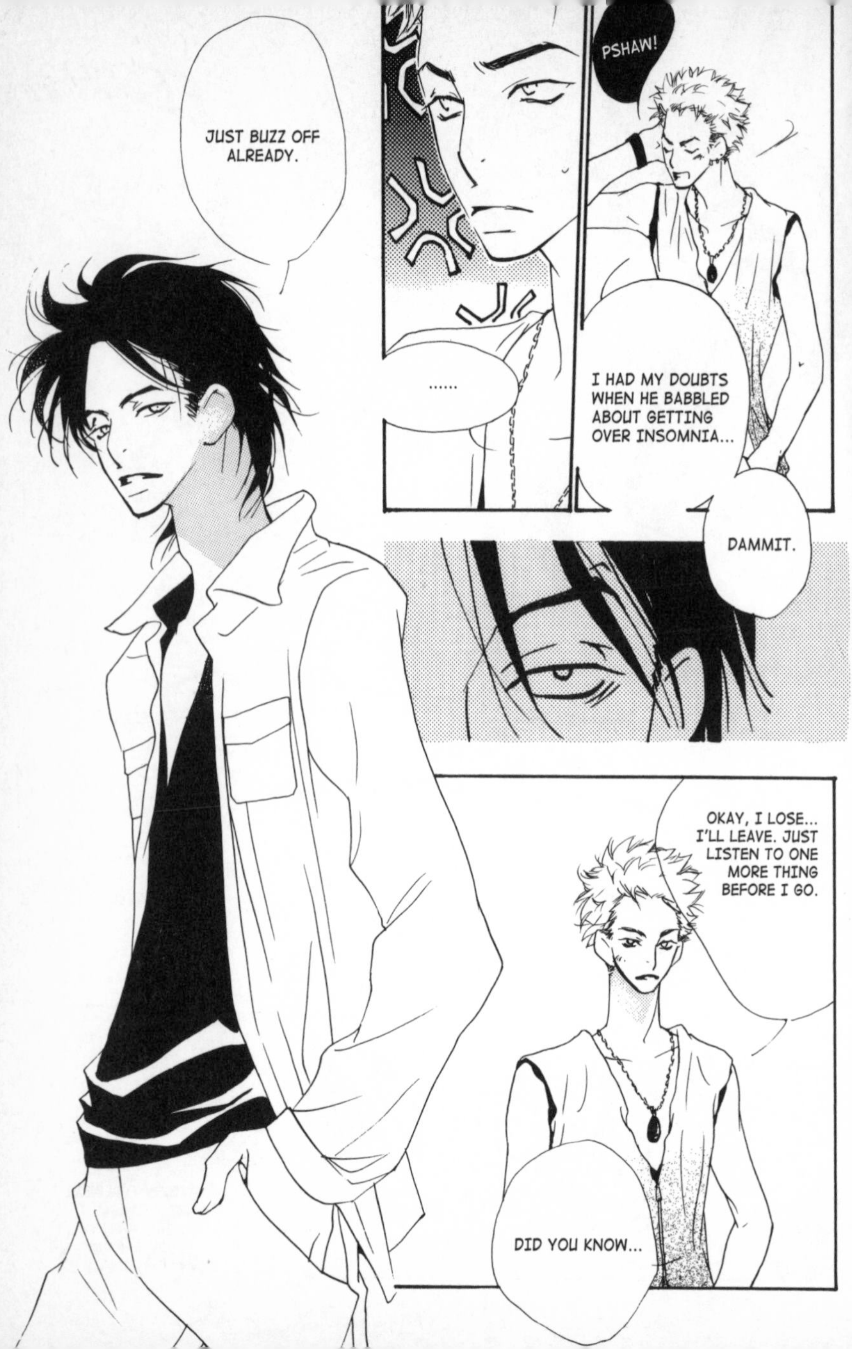
PSHAW!
I HAD MY DOUBTS WHEN HE BABBLED ABOUT GETTING OVER INSOMNIA...
DAMMIT.
......
JUST BUZZ OFF ALREADY.
OKAY, I LOSE... I'LL LEAVE. JUST LISTEN TO ONE MORE THING BEFORE I GO.
DID YOU KNOW...

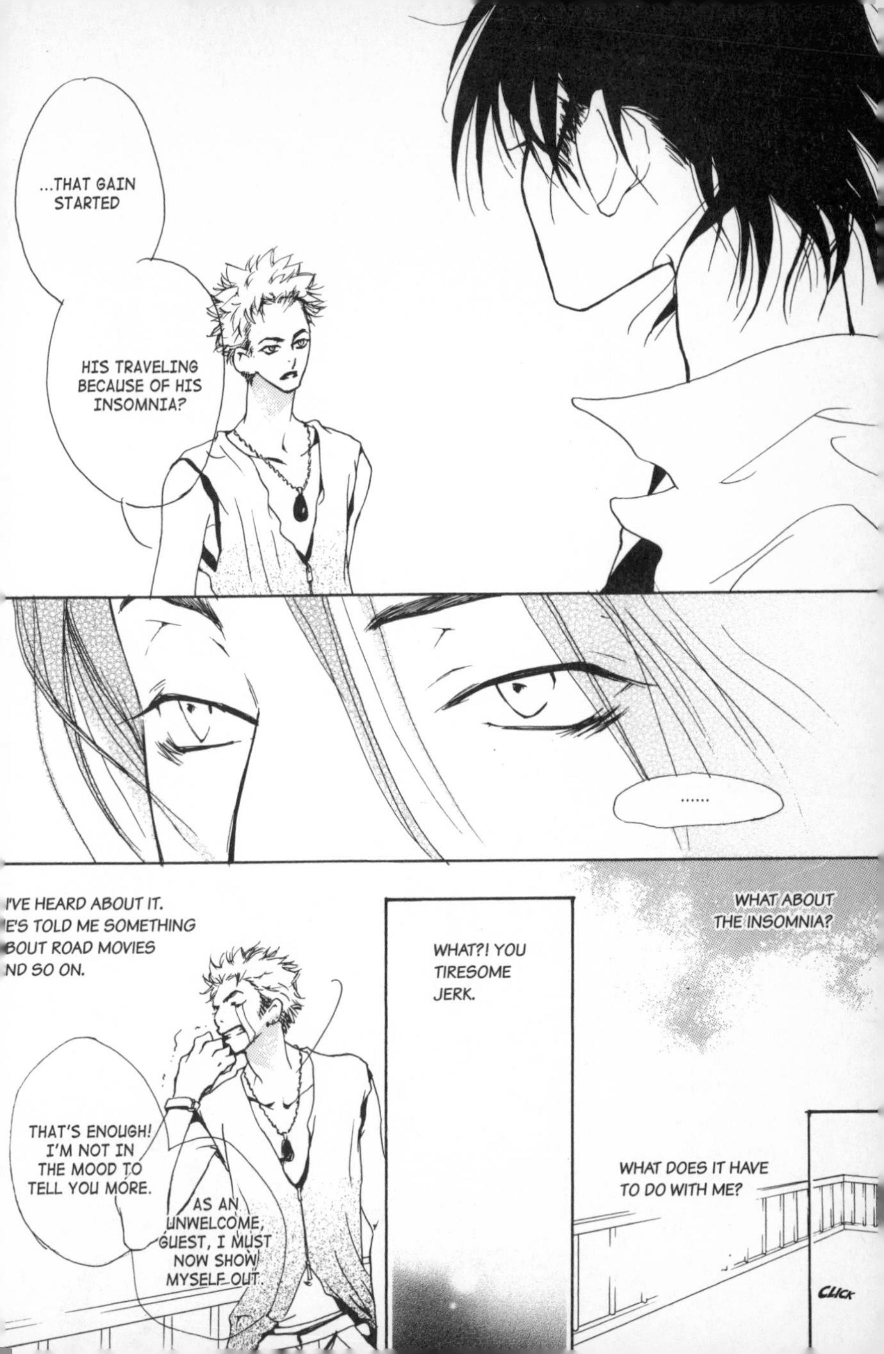
...THAT GAIN STARTED
HIS TRAVELING BECAUSE OF HIS INSOMNIA?
......
WHAT ABOUT THE INSOMNIA?
WHAT?! YOU TIRESOME JERK.
I'VE HEARD ABOUT IT. E'S TOLD ME SOMETHING BOUT ROAD MOVIES ND SO ON.
THAT'S ENOUGH! I'M NOT IN THE MOOD TO TELL YOU MORE.
AS AN UNWELCOME GUEST, I MUST NOW SHOW MYSELF OUT.
WHAT DOES IT HAVE TO DO WITH ME?
CLICK

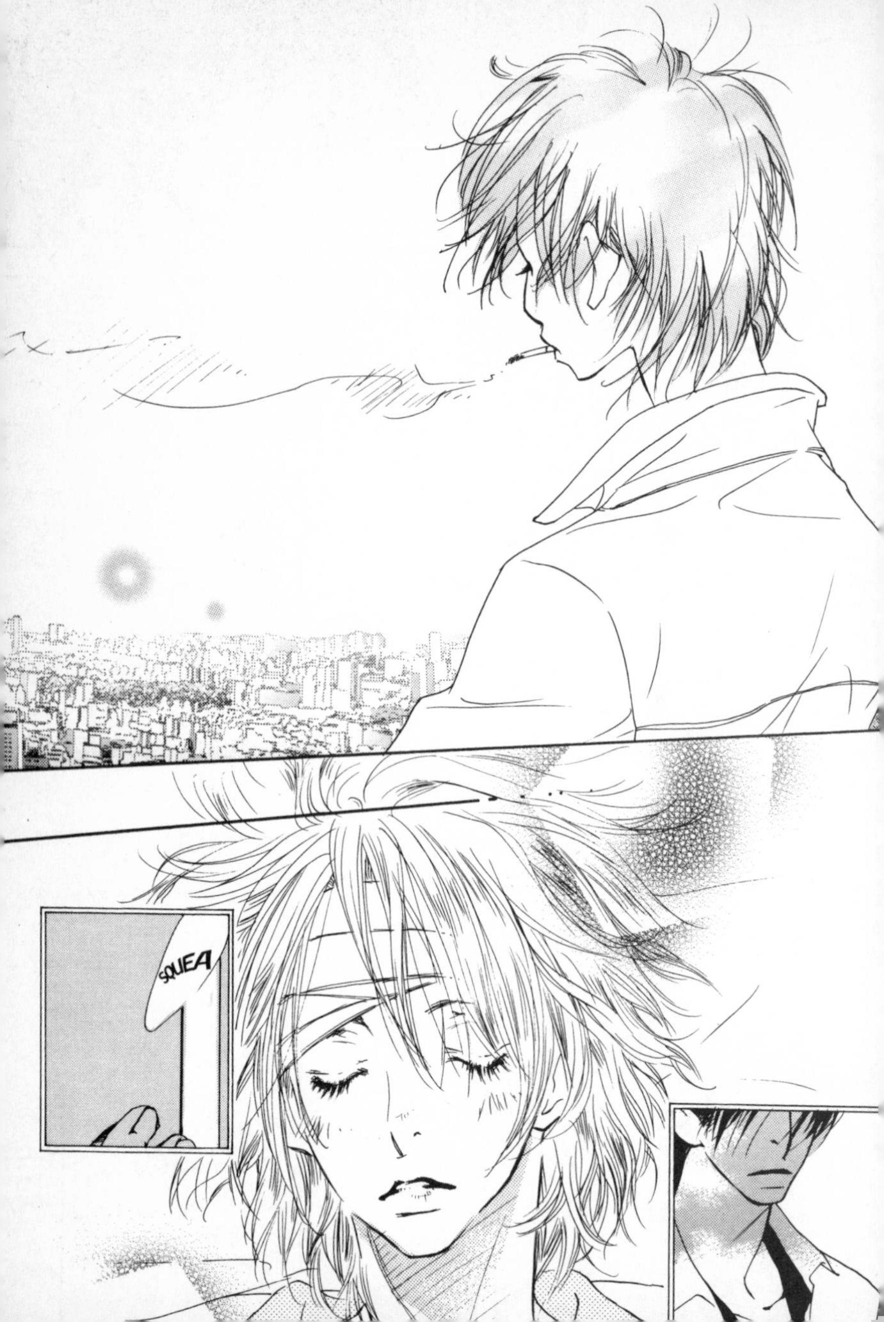
SQUEA

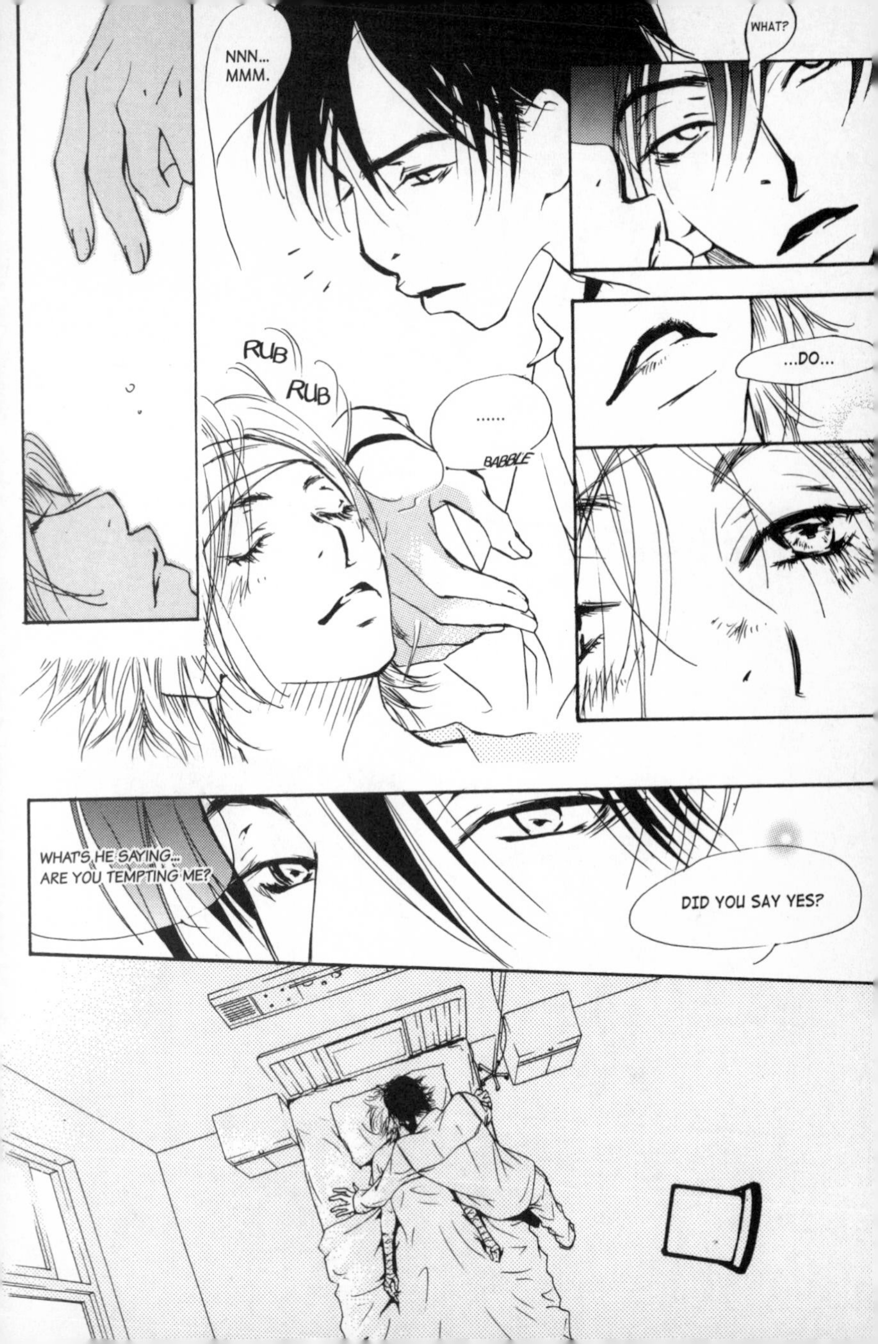
NNN... MMM.
RUB
RUB
......
BABBLE
WHAT?
...DO...
DID YOU SAY YES?
WHAT'S HE SAYING... ARE YOU TEMPTING ME?

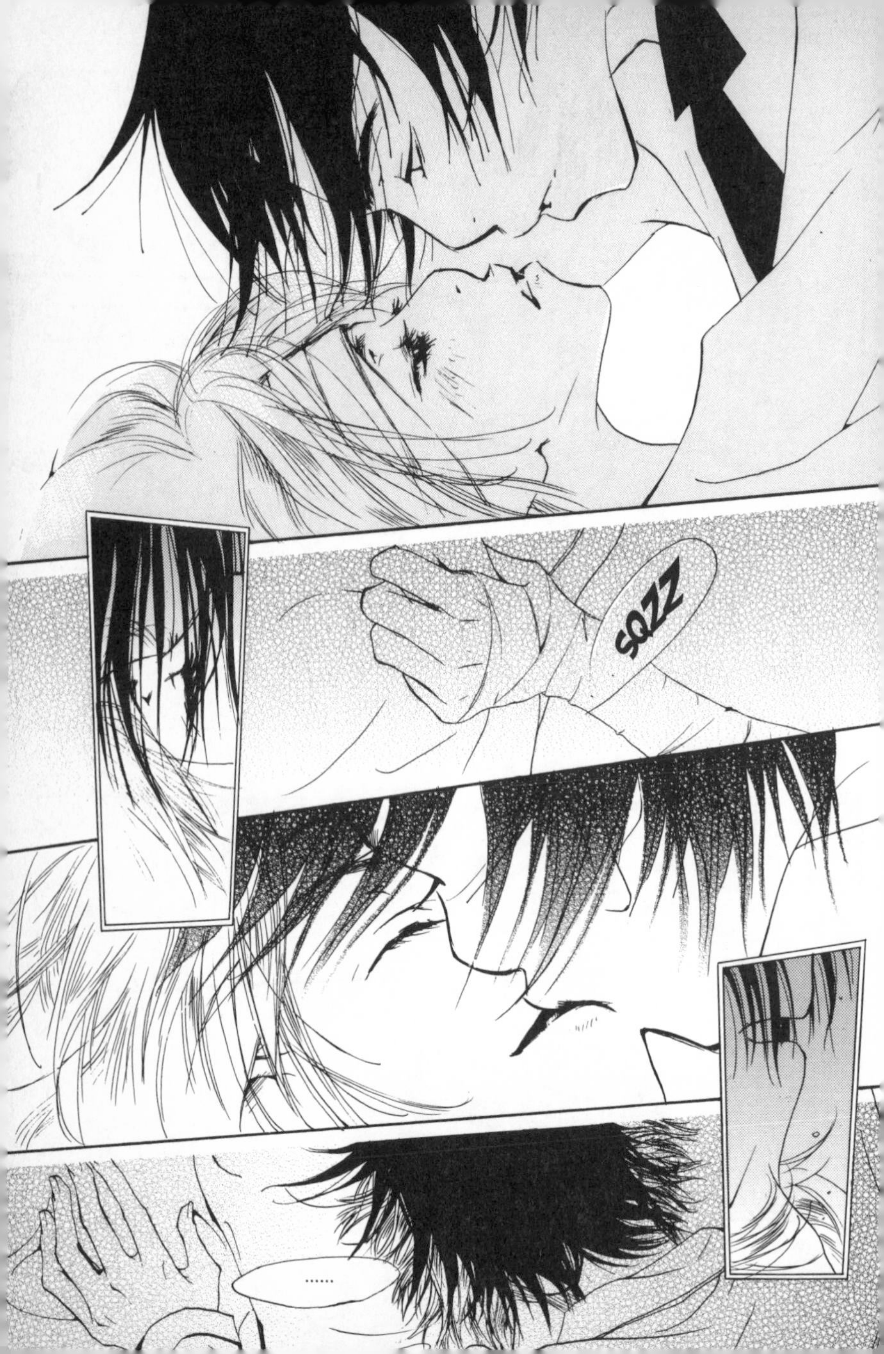
SQZZ
......

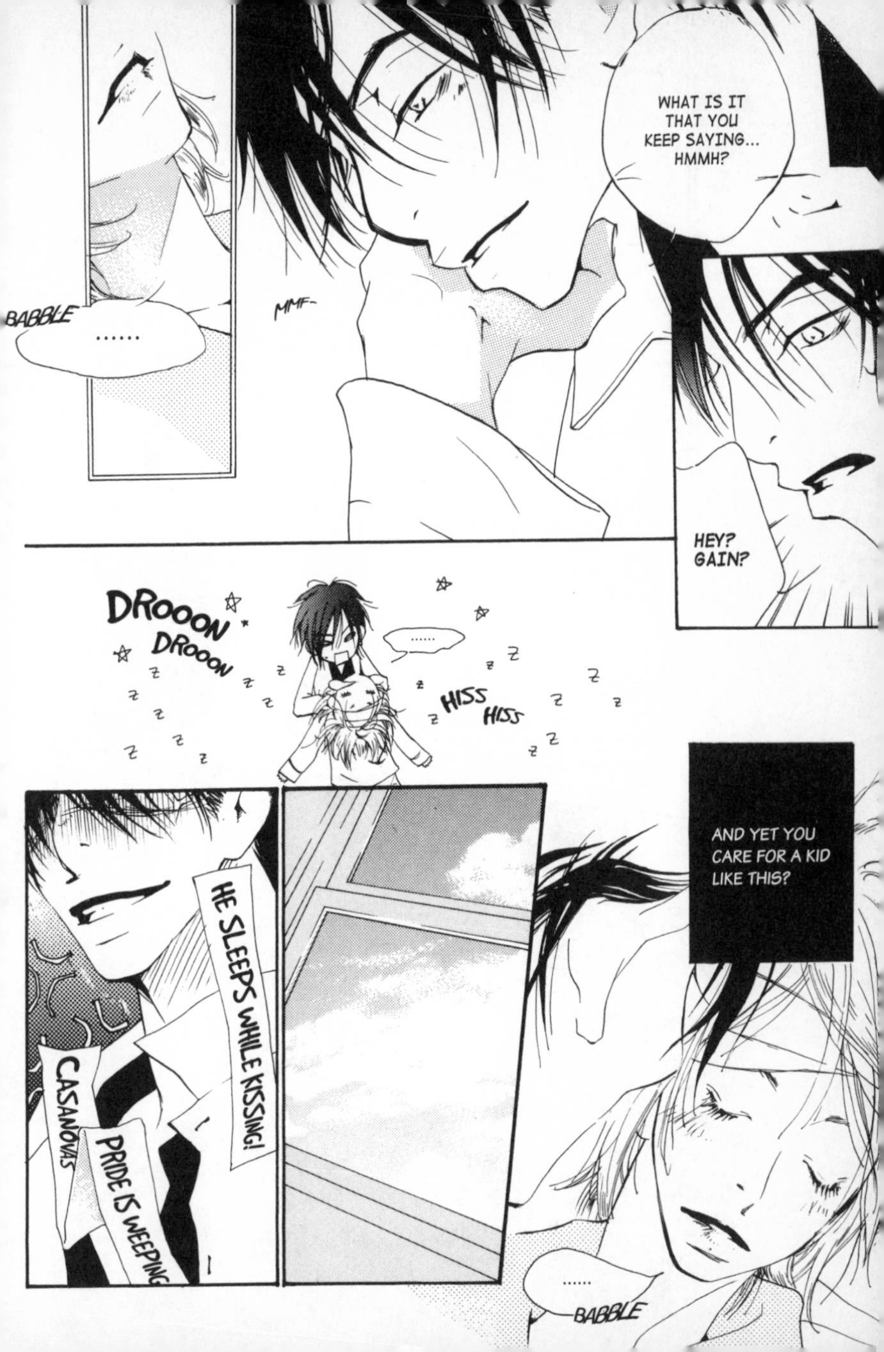
WHAT IS IT THAT YOU KEEP SAYING... HMMH?
MMF-
BABBLE
....
HEY? GAIN?
DROOON DROOON
......
HISS HISS
AND YET YOU CARE FOR A KID LIKE THIS?
......
BABBLE
HE SLEEPS WHILE KISSING!
CASANOVA'S PRIDE IS WEEPING

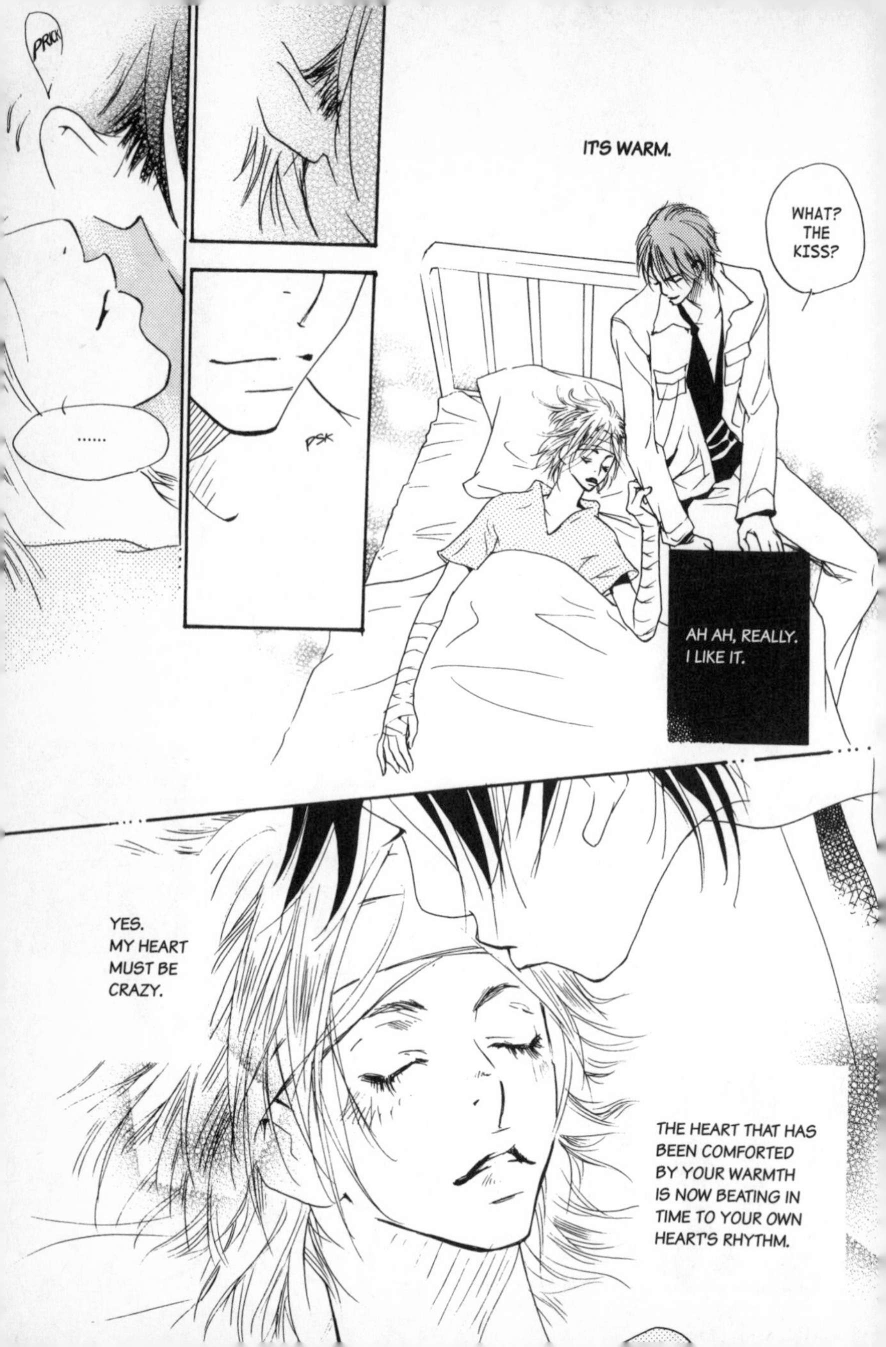
IT'S WARM.
WHAT? THE KISS?
AH AH, REALLY. I LIKE IT.
PSK
PRICK
......
THE HEART THAT HAS BEEN COMFORTED BY YOUR WARMTH IS NOW BEATING IN TIME TO YOUR OWN HEART'S RHYTHM.
YES. MY HEART MUST BE CRAZY.

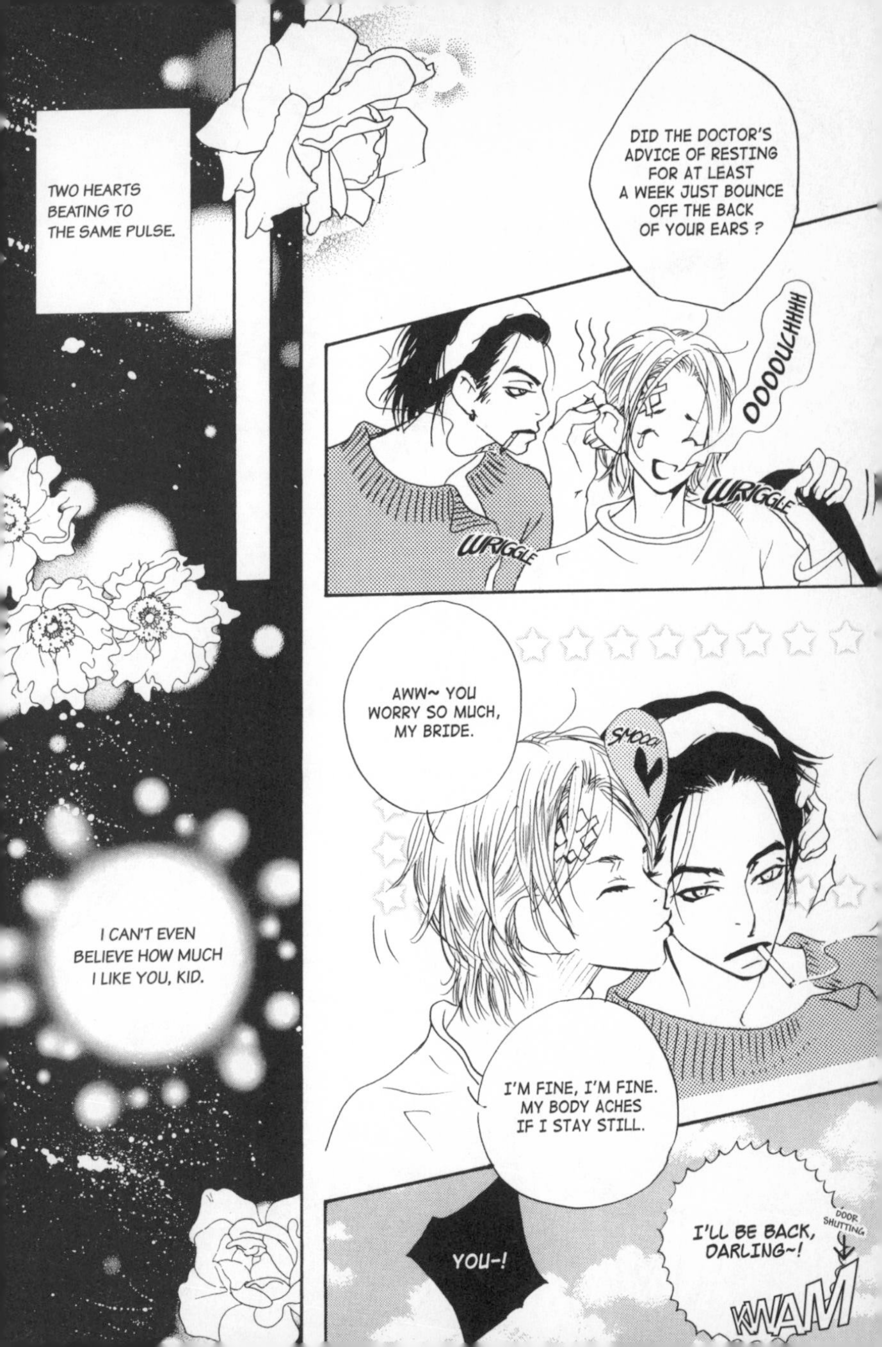
DID THE DOCTOR'S ADVICE OF RESTING FOR AT LEAST A WEEK JUST BOUNCE OFF THE BACK OF YOUR EARS ?
OOOOOUCHHHH
WRIGGLE
WRIGGLE
AWW~ YOU WORRY SO MUCH, MY BRIDE.
I'M FINE, I'M FINE. MY BODY ACHES IF I STAY STILL.
I'LL BE BACK, DARLING~!
DOOR SHUTTING
KWAM
YOU-!
TWO HEARTS BEATING TO THE SAME PULSE.
I CAN'T EVEN BELIEVE HOW MUCH I LIKE YOU, KID.

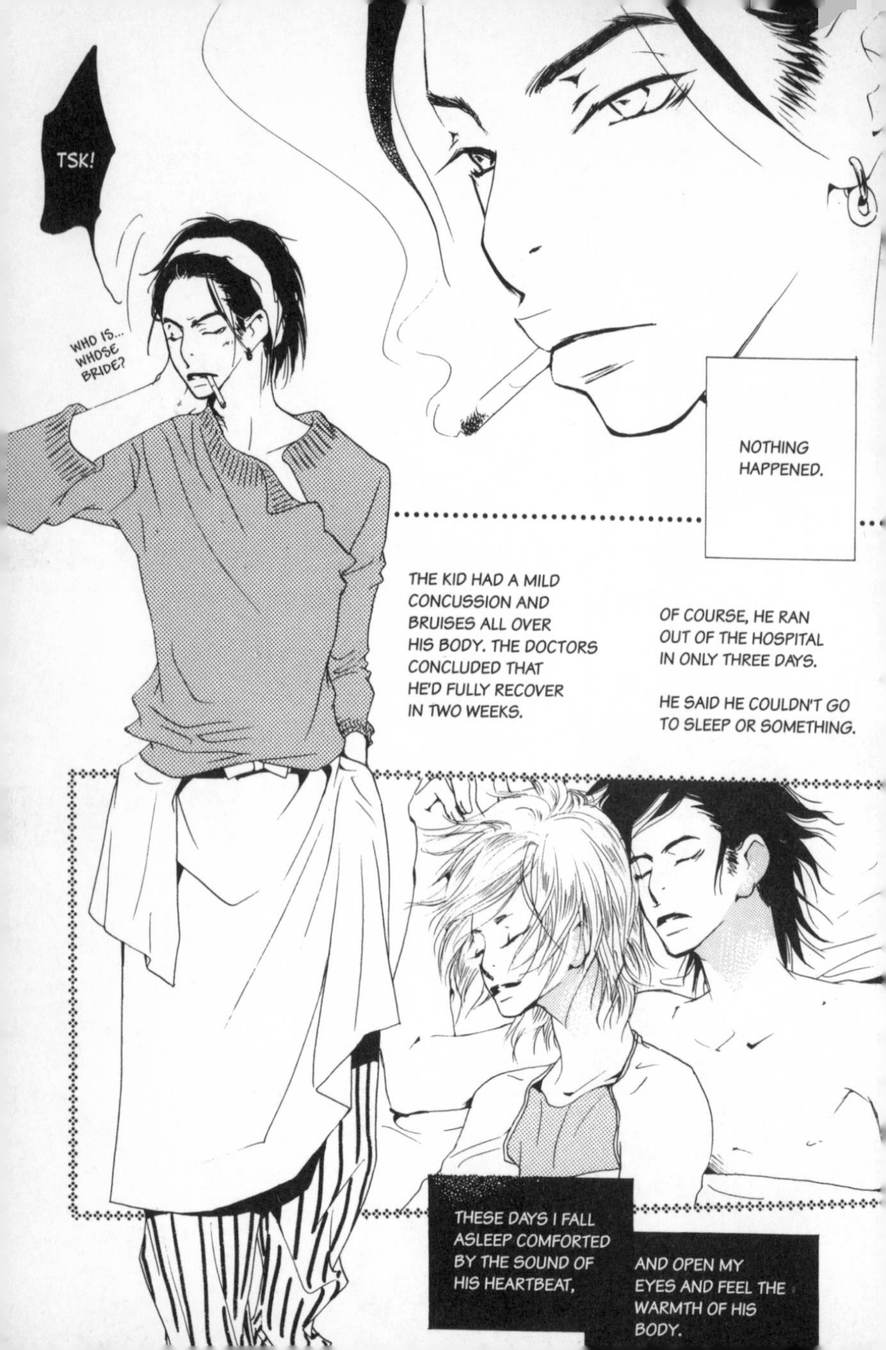
TSK!
WHO IS... WHOSE BRIDE?
NOTHING HAPPENED.
THE KID HAD A MILD CONCUSSION AND BRUISES ALL OVER HIS BODY. THE DOCTORS CONCLUDED THAT HE'D FULLY RECOVER IN TWO WEEKS.
OF COURSE, HE RAN OUT OF THE HOSPITAL IN ONLY THREE DAYS.
HE SAID HE COULDN'T GO TO SLEEP OR SOMETHING.
THESE DAYS I FALL ASLEEP COMFORTED BY THE SOUND OF HIS HEARTBEAT,
AND OPEN MY EYES AND FEEL THE WARMTH OF HIS BODY.

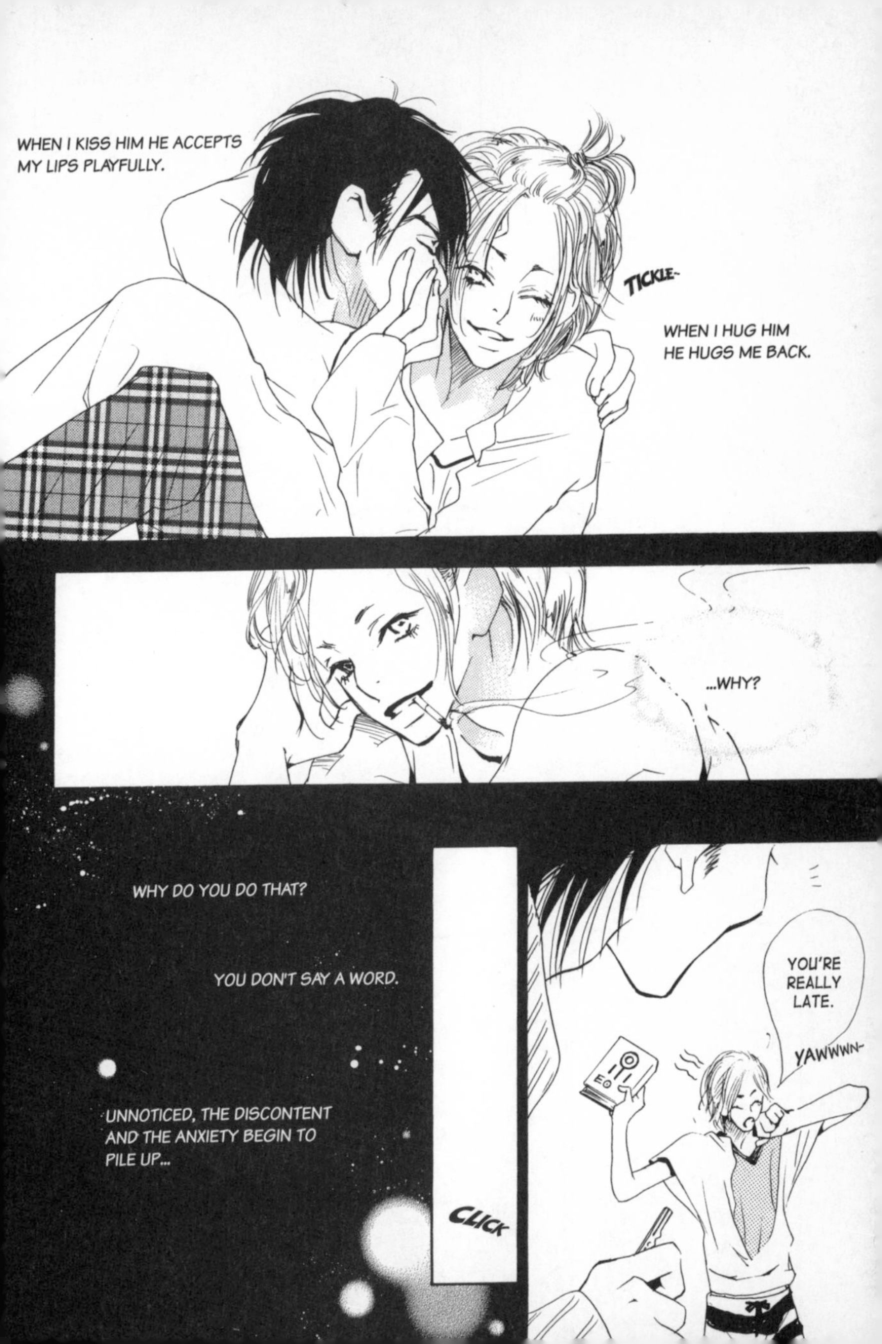
WHEN I KISS HIM HE ACCEPTS MY LIPS PLAYFULLY.
TICKLE-
WHEN I HUG HIM HE HUGS ME BACK.
...WHY?
WHY DO YOU DO THAT?
YOU DON'T SAY A WORD.
UNNOTICED, THE DISCONTENT AND THE ANXIETY BEGIN TO PILE UP...
CLICK
YOU'RE REALLY LATE.
YAWWWN-

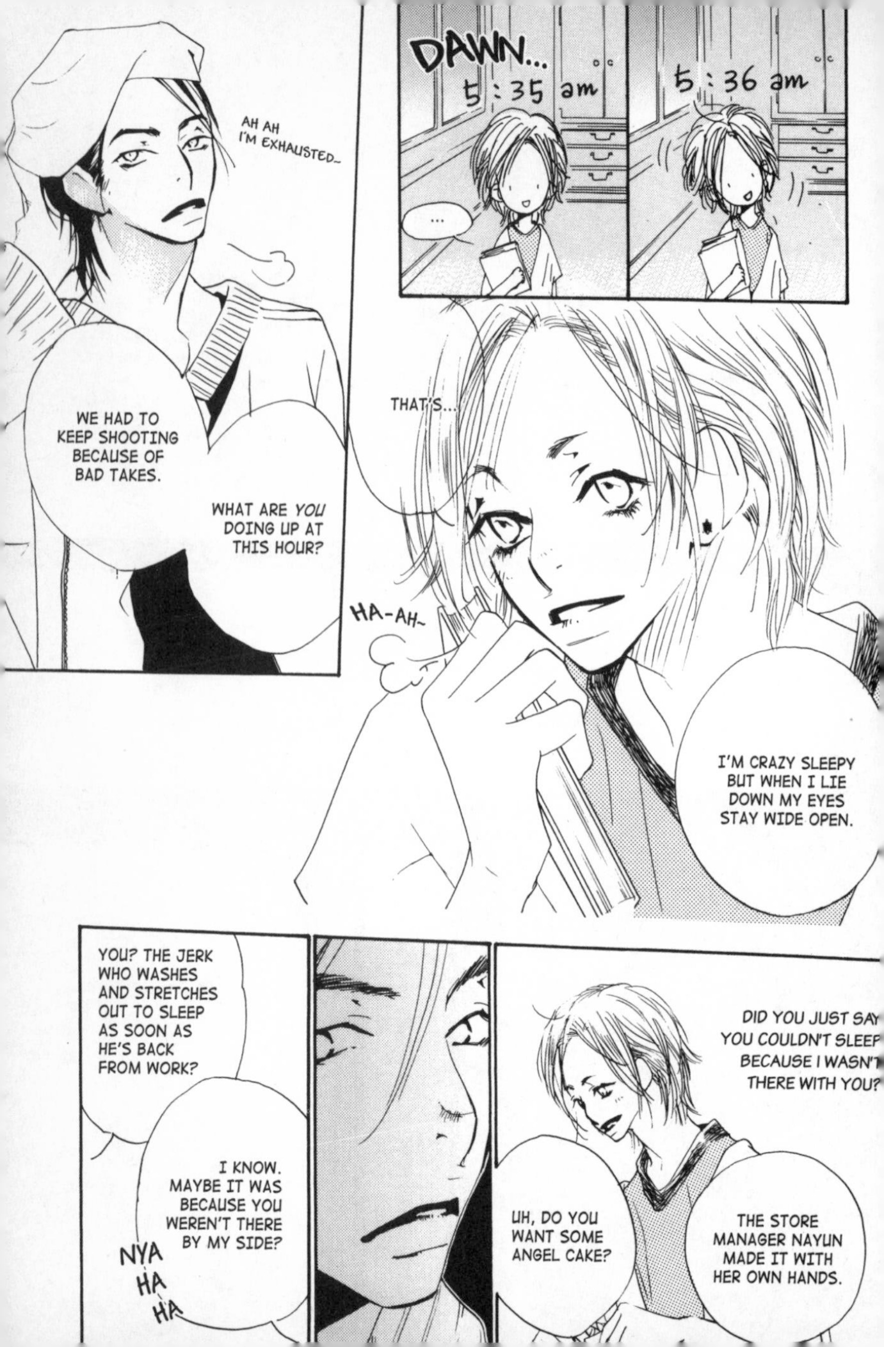
DAWN...
5:35 am
...
5:36 am
AH AH
I'M EXHAUSTED~
WE HAD TO KEEP SHOOTING BECAUSE OF BAD TAKES.
WHAT ARE *YOU* DOING UP AT THIS HOUR?
THAT'S...
HA-AH~
I'M CRAZY SLEEPY BUT WHEN I LIE DOWN MY EYES STAY WIDE OPEN.
YOU? THE JERK WHO WASHES AND STRETCHES OUT TO SLEEP AS SOON AS HE'S BACK FROM WORK?
I KNOW. MAYBE IT WAS BECAUSE YOU WEREN'T THERE BY MY SIDE?
NYA HA HA
DID YOU JUST SAY YOU COULDN'T SLEEP BECAUSE I WASN'T THERE WITH YOU?
UH, DO YOU WANT SOME ANGEL CAKE?
THE STORE MANAGER NAYUN MADE IT WITH HER OWN HANDS.

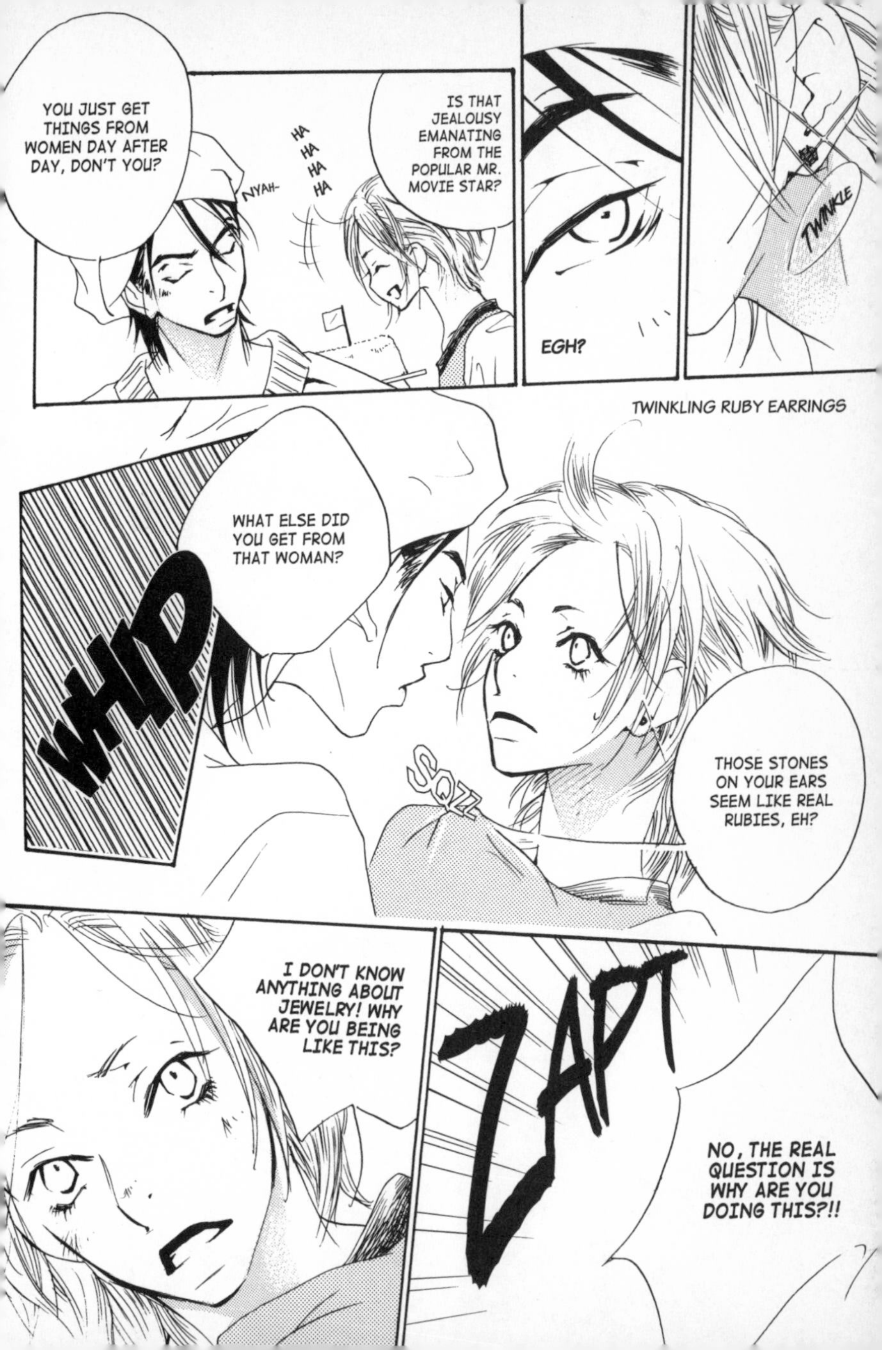
YOU JUST GET THINGS FROM WOMEN DAY AFTER DAY, DON'T YOU?
NYAH-
HA HA HA HA
IS THAT JEALOUSY EMANATING FROM THE POPULAR MR. MOVIE STAR?
EGH?
TWINKLE
TWINKLING RUBY EARRINGS
WHIP
WHAT ELSE DID YOU GET FROM THAT WOMAN?
SQZZ
THOSE STONES ON YOUR EARS SEEM LIKE REAL RUBIES, EH?
I DON'T KNOW ANYTHING ABOUT JEWELRY! WHY ARE YOU BEING LIKE THIS?
ZAP
NO, THE REAL QUESTION IS WHY ARE YOU DOING THIS?!!

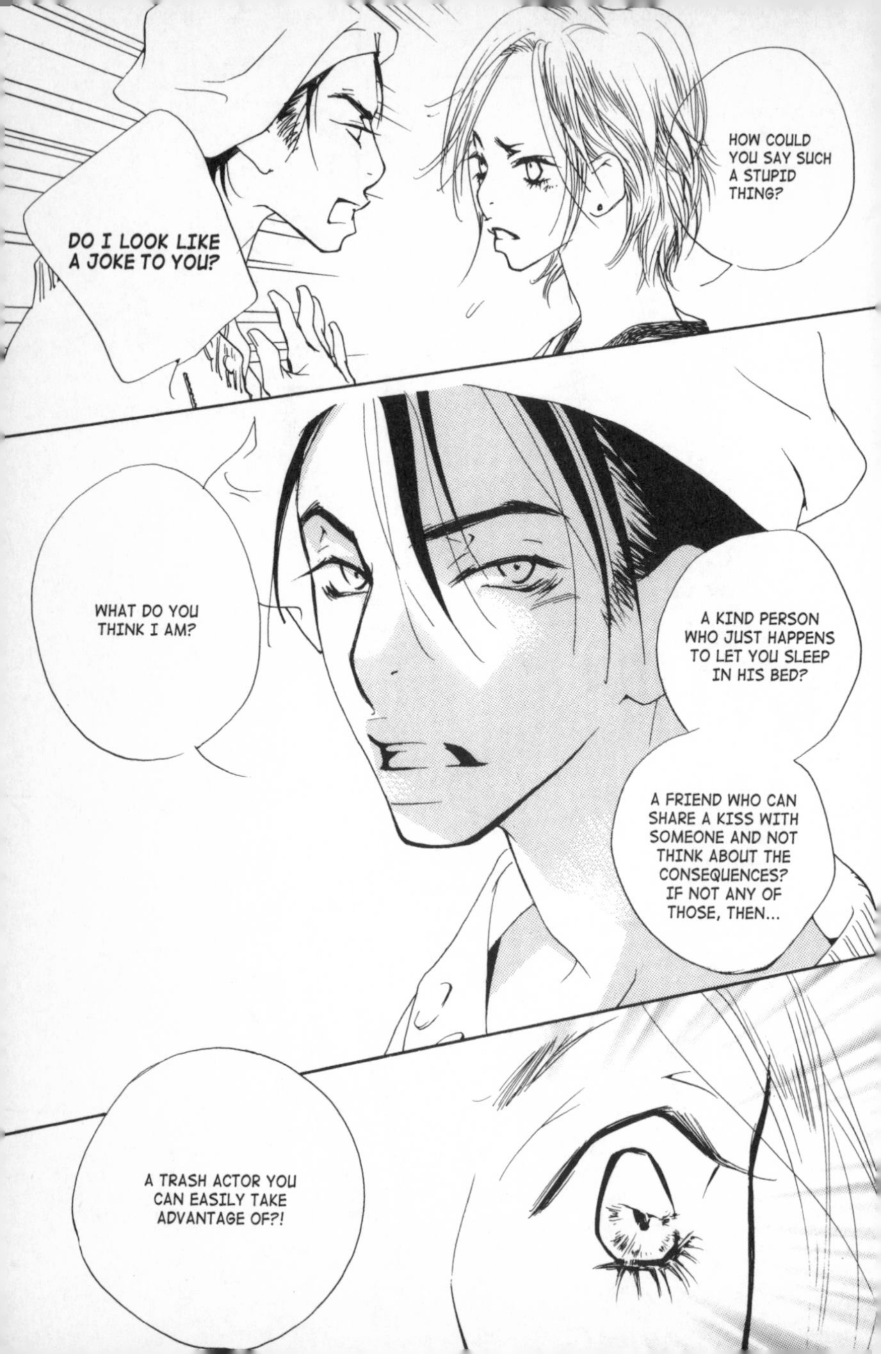

HOW COULD YOU SAY SUCH A STUPID THING?
DO I LOOK LIKE A JOKE TO YOU?
A KIND PERSON WHO JUST HAPPENS TO LET YOU SLEEP IN HIS BED?
A FRIEND WHO CAN SHARE A KISS WITH SOMEONE AND NOT THINK ABOUT THE CONSEQUENCES? IF NOT ANY OF THOSE, THEN...
WHAT DO YOU THINK I AM?
A TRASH ACTOR YOU CAN EASILY TAKE ADVANTAGE OF?!

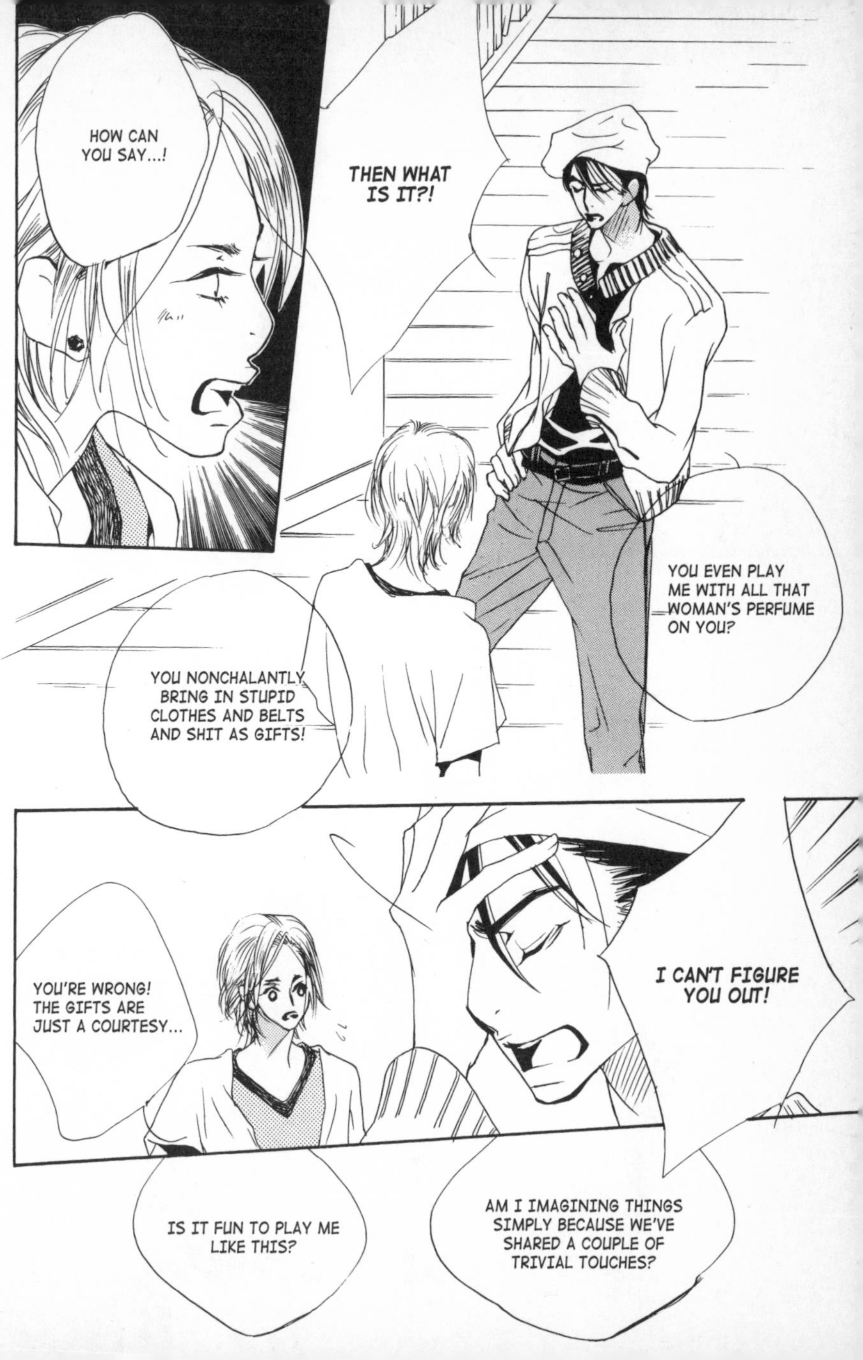

HOW CAN YOU SAY...!
THEN WHAT IS IT?!
YOU NONCHALANTLY BRING IN STUPID CLOTHES AND BELTS AND SHIT AS GIFTS!
YOU EVEN PLAY ME WITH ALL THAT WOMAN'S PERFUME ON YOU?
YOU'RE WRONG! THE GIFTS ARE JUST A COURTESY...
I CAN'T FIGURE YOU OUT!
IS IT FUN TO PLAY ME LIKE THIS?
AM I IMAGINING THINGS SIMPLY BECAUSE WE'VE SHARED A COUPLE OF TRIVIAL TOUCHES?

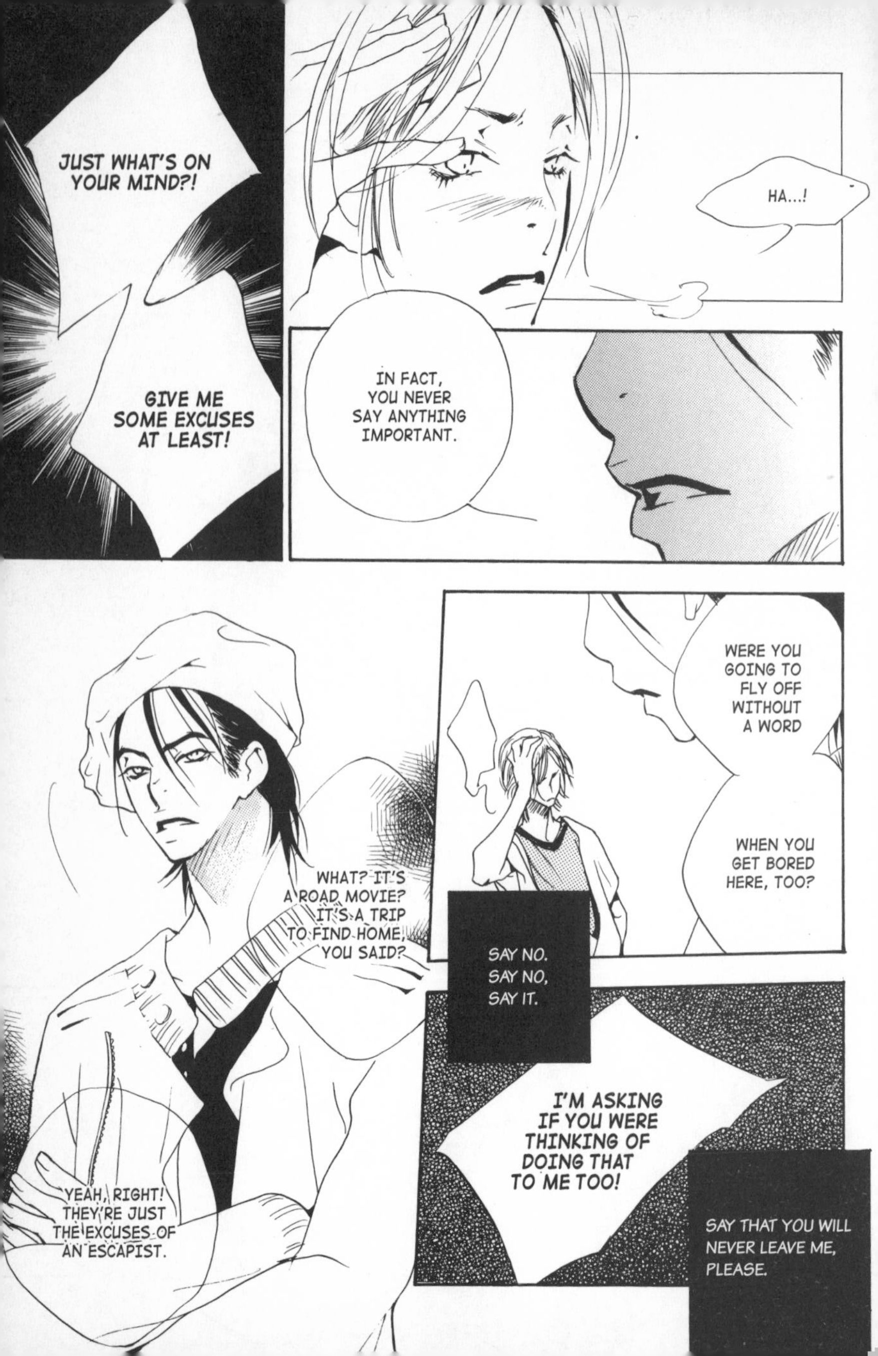
JUST WHAT'S ON YOUR MIND?!
GIVE ME SOME EXCUSES AT LEAST!
HA...!
IN FACT, YOU NEVER SAY ANYTHING IMPORTANT.
WHAT? IT'S A ROAD MOVIE? IT'S A TRIP TO FIND HOME, YOU SAID?
YEAH, RIGHT! THEY'RE JUST THE EXCUSES OF AN ESCAPIST.
WERE YOU GOING TO FLY OFF WITHOUT A WORD
WHEN YOU GET BORED HERE, TOO?
SAY NO. SAY NO, SAY IT.
I'M ASKING IF YOU WERE THINKING OF DOING THAT TO ME TOO!
SAY THAT YOU WILL NEVER LEAVE ME, PLEASE.

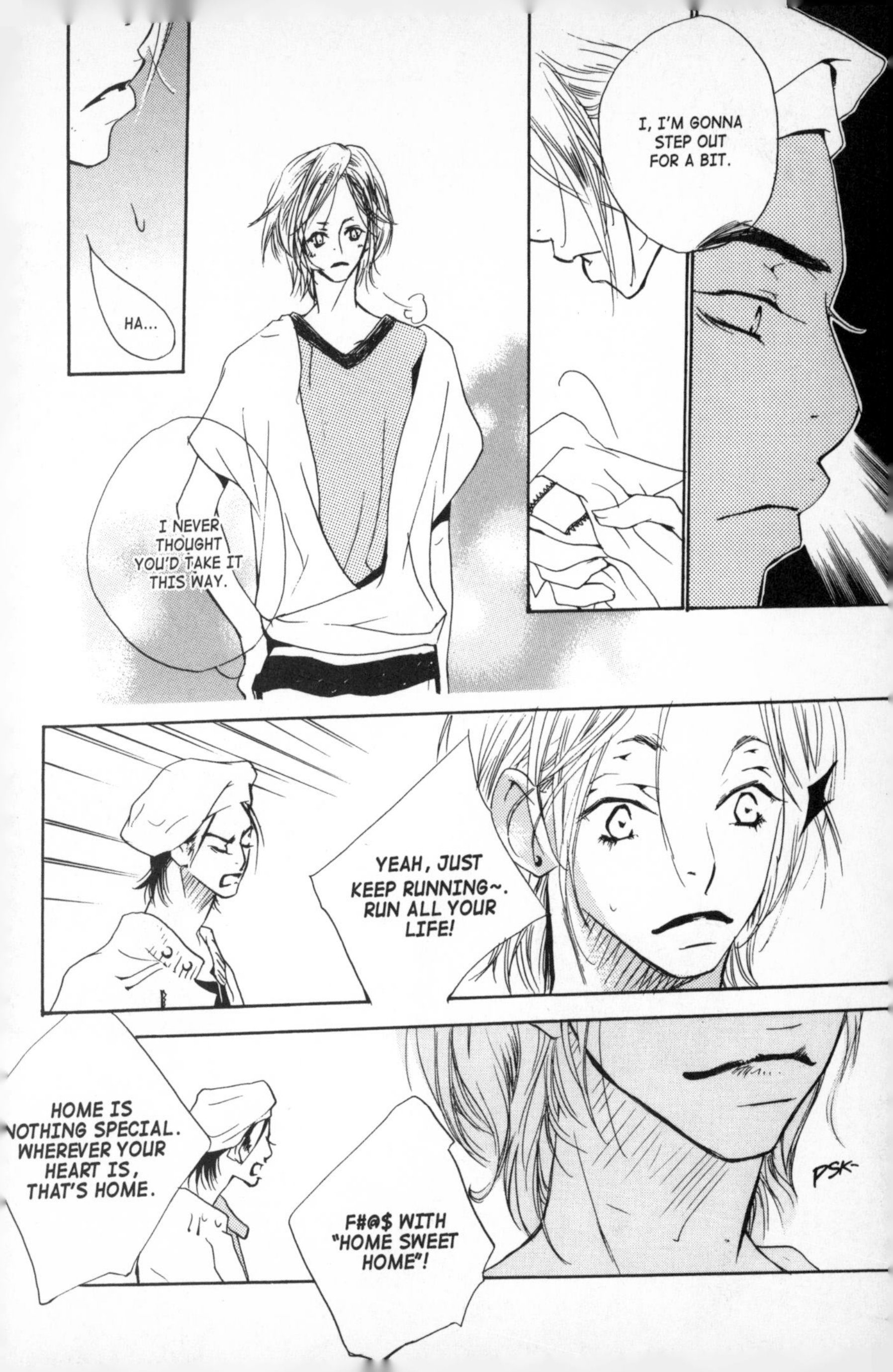
I, I'M GONNA STEP OUT FOR A BIT.
HA...
I NEVER THOUGHT YOU'D TAKE IT THIS WAY.
YEAH, JUST KEEP RUNNING~. RUN ALL YOUR LIFE!
PSK-
F#@$ WITH "HOME SWEET HOME"!
HOME IS NOTHING SPECIAL. WHEREVER YOUR HEART IS, THAT'S HOME.

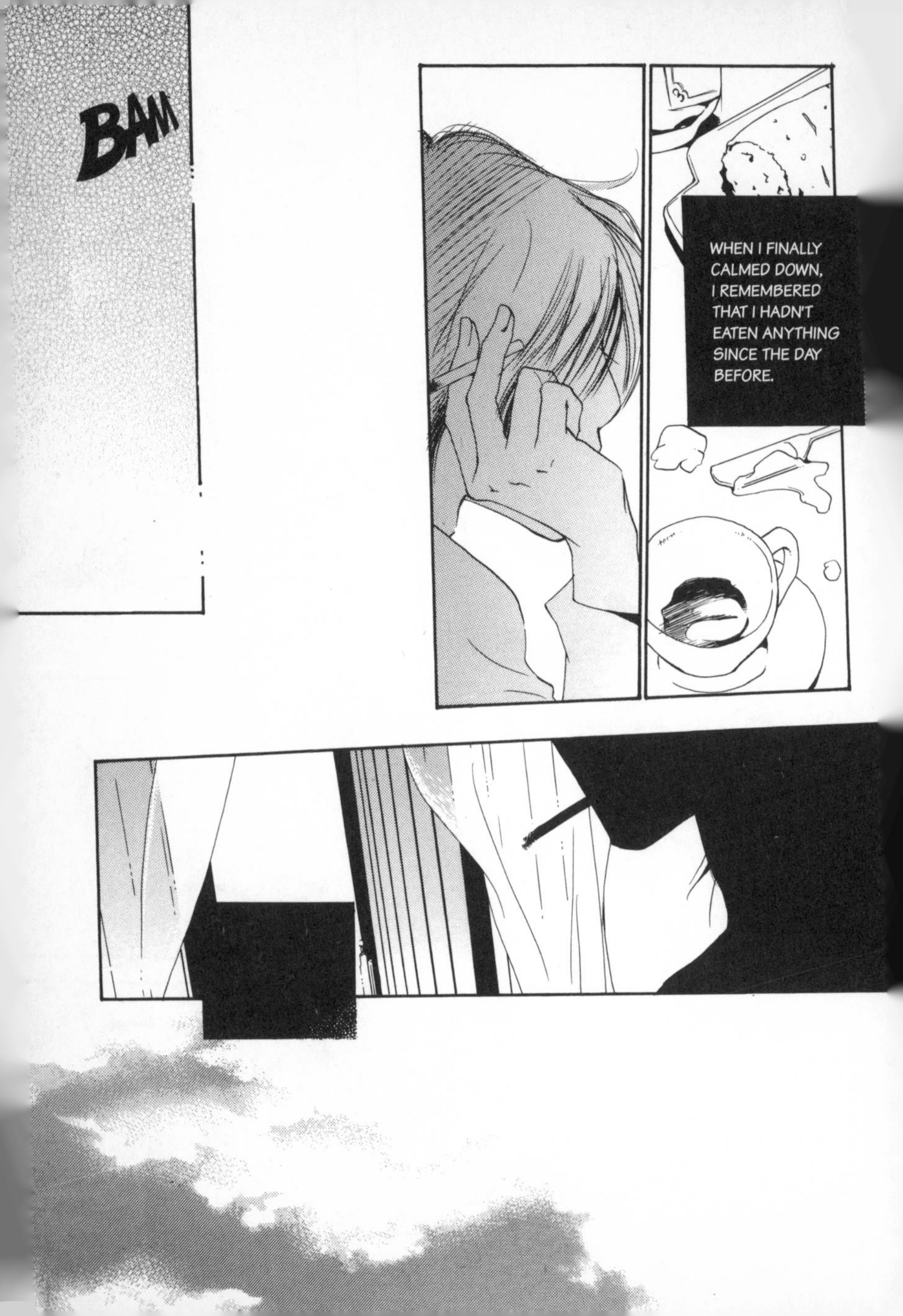
BAM
WHEN I FINALLY CALMED DOWN, I REMEMBERED THAT I HADN'T EATEN ANYTHING SINCE THE DAY BEFORE.

BUT

THAT DAY, THE NEXT DAY,
AND THE DAY AFTER THAT...

THE KID STILL HADN'T
COME BACK.

NOT SO BAD

NOT SO BAD CHAPTER 7 :
"WHAT IS THE IDEAL BED TEMPERATURE?" I

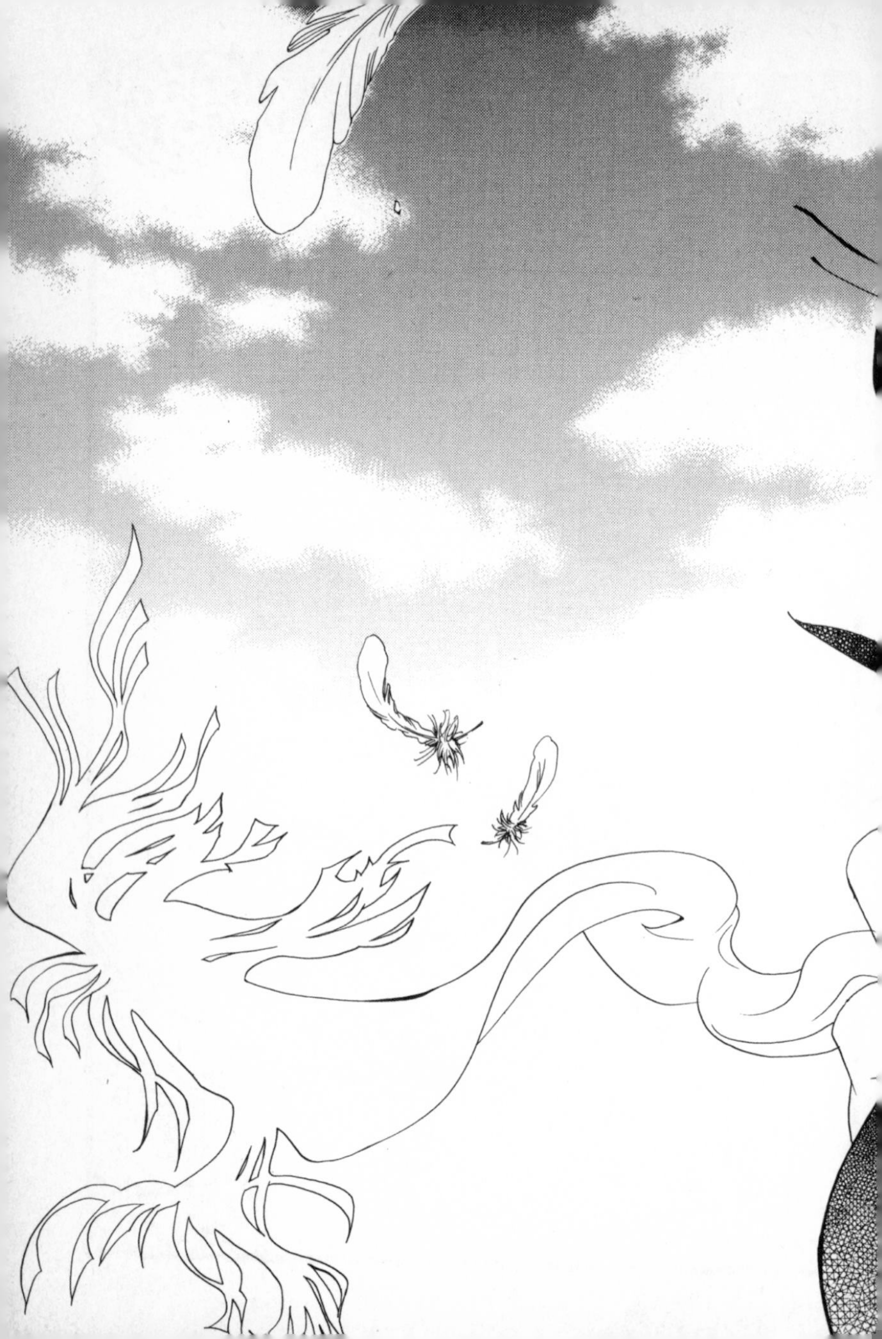

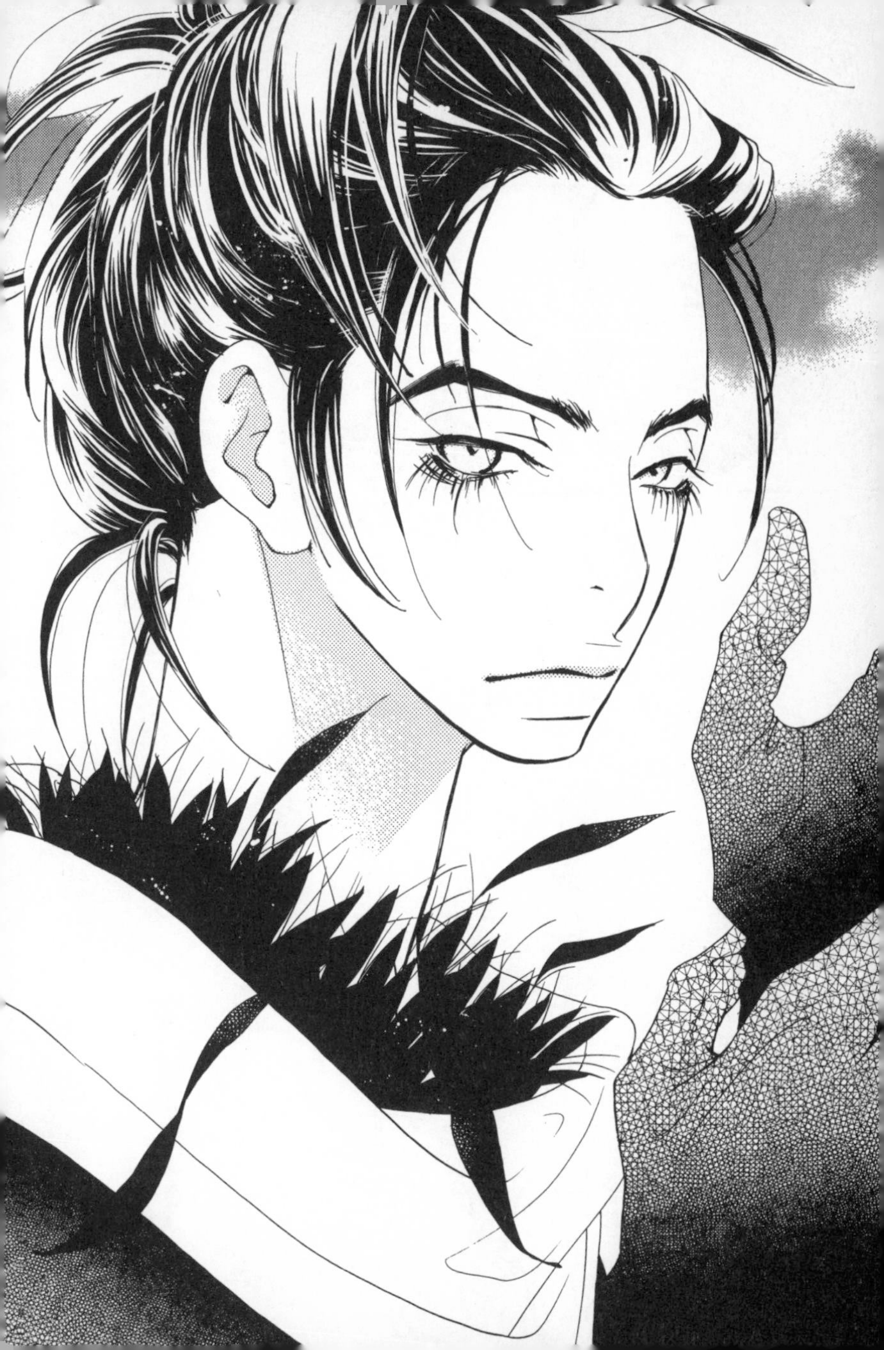

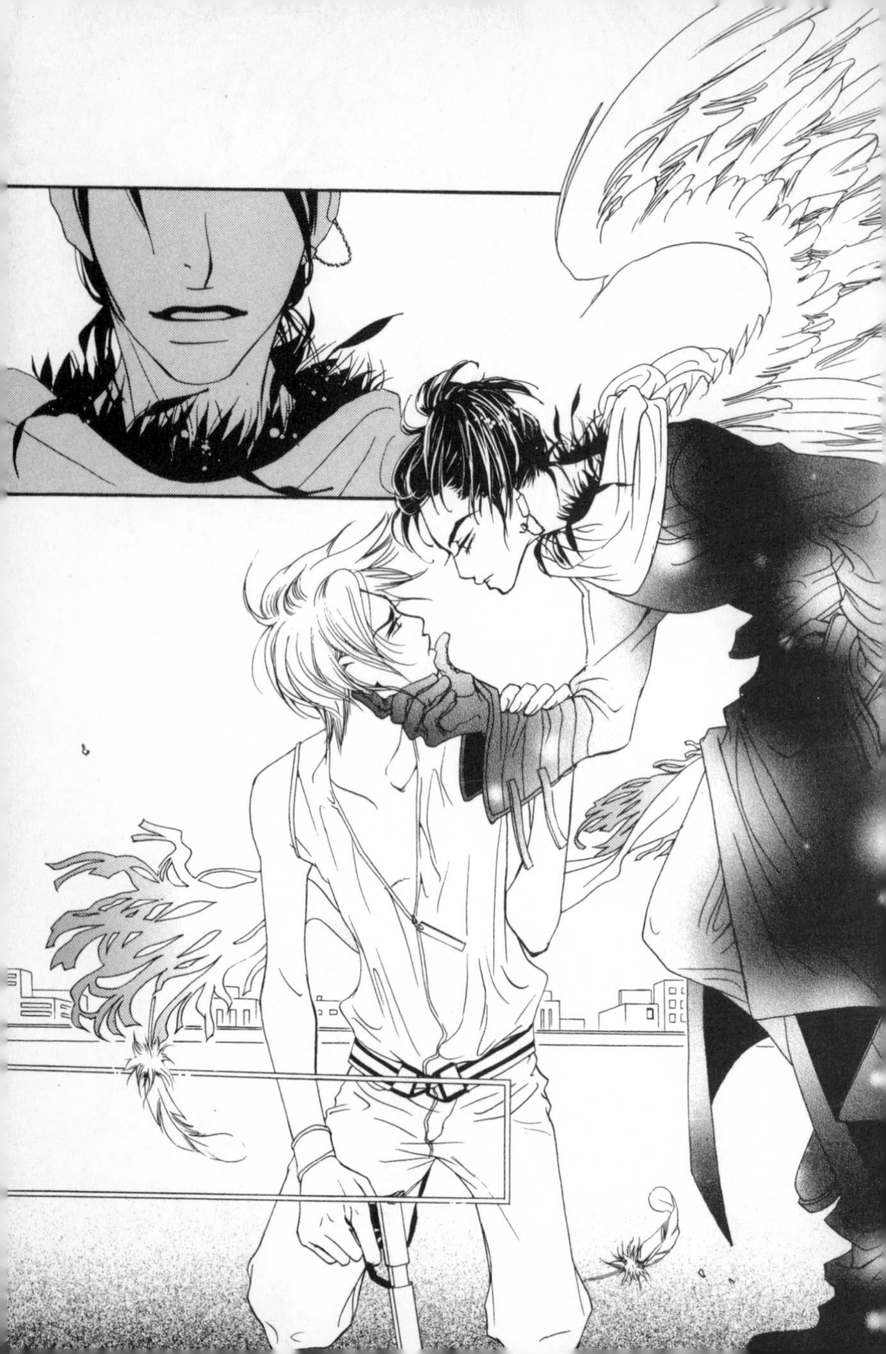

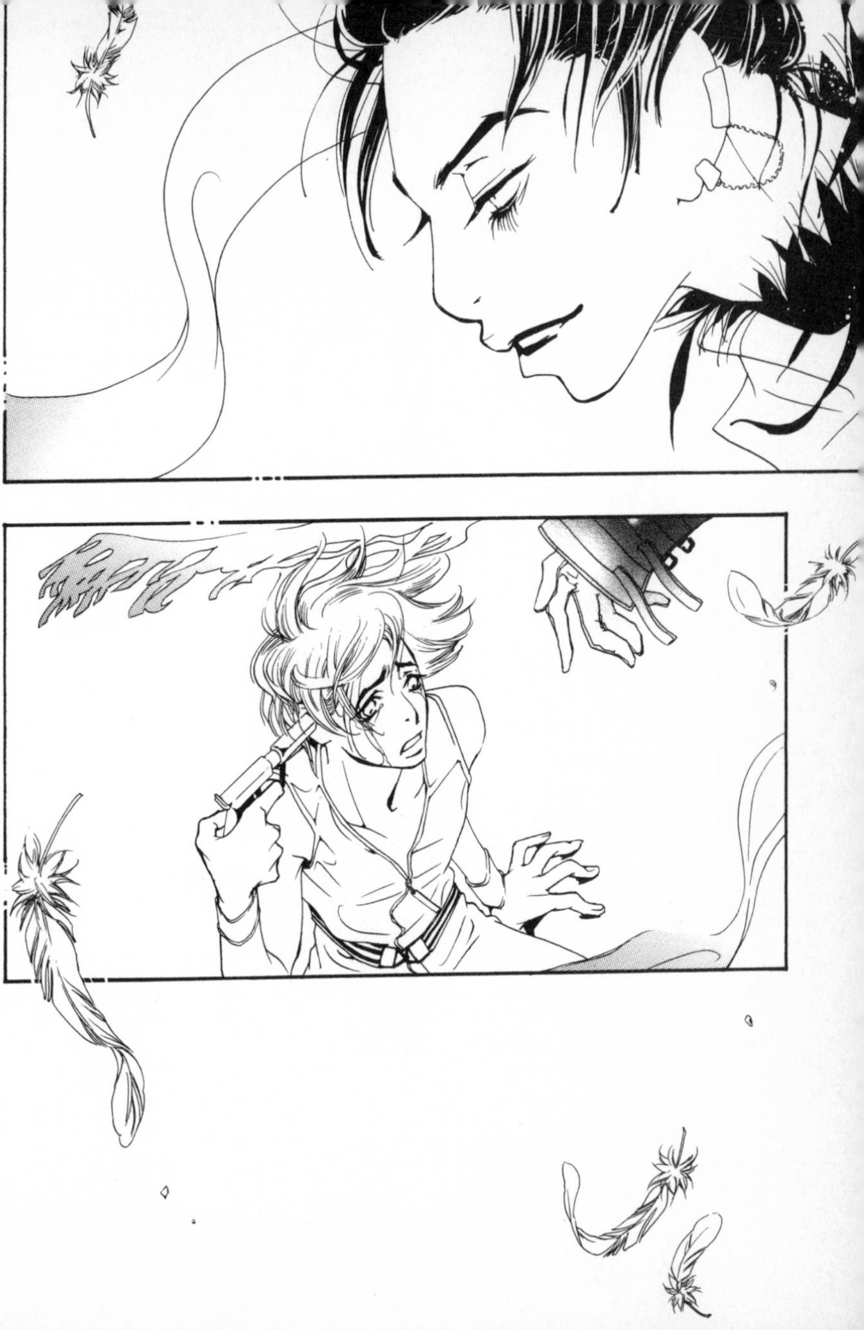

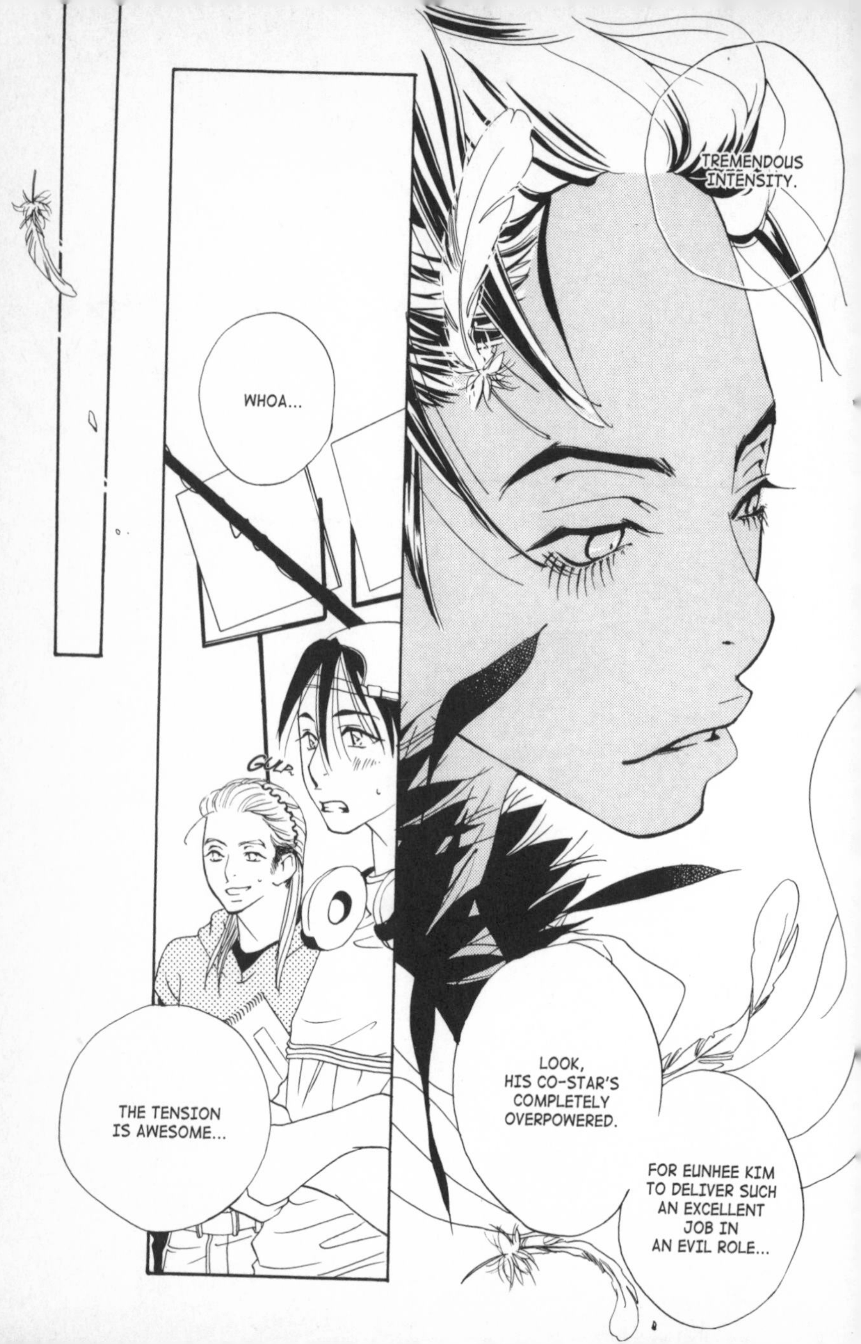
TREMENDOUS INTENSITY.
WHOA...
GULP
THE TENSION IS AWESOME...
LOOK, HIS CO-STAR'S COMPLETELY OVERPOWERED.
FOR EUNHEE KIM TO DELIVER SUCH AN EXCELLENT JOB IN AN EVIL ROLE...

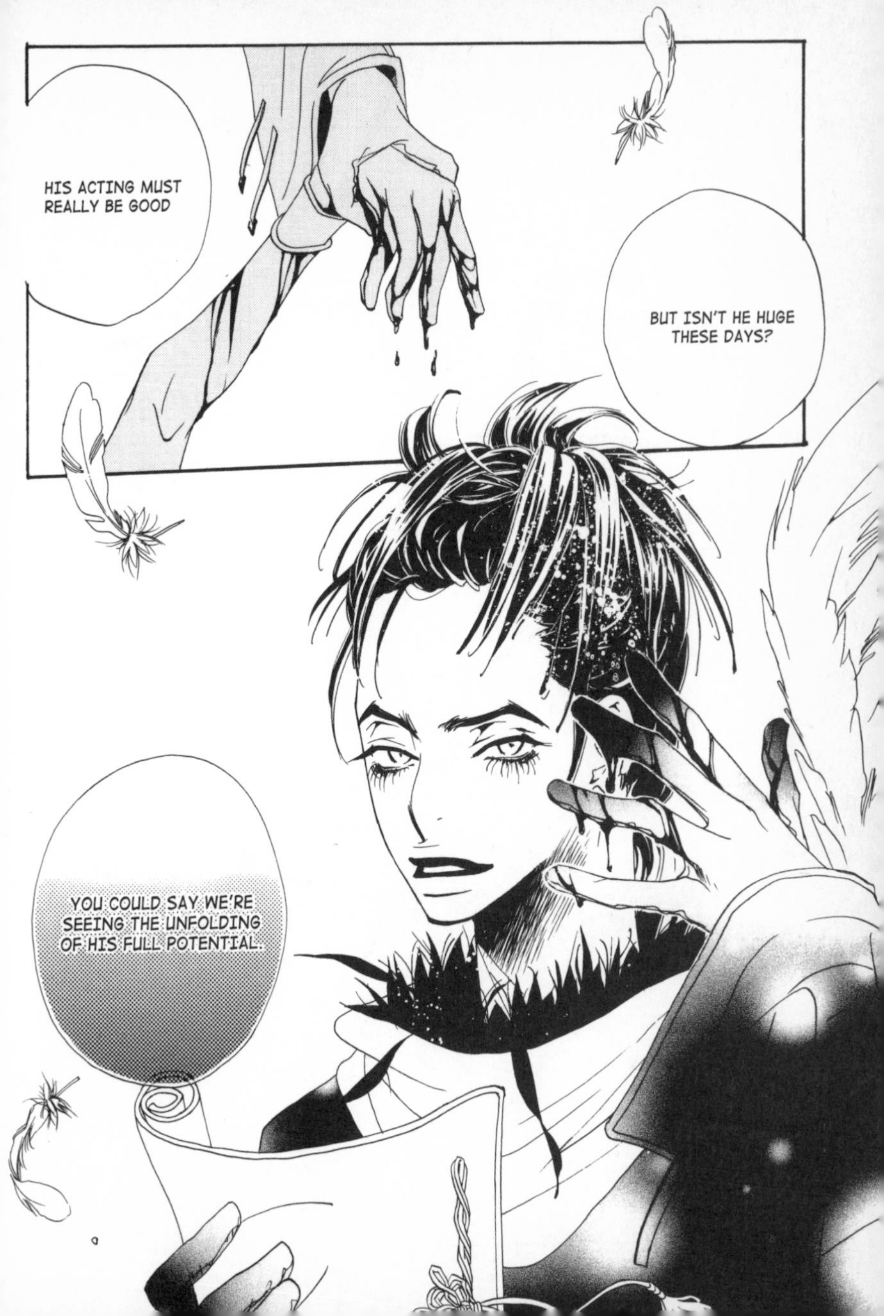
BUT ISN'T HE HUGE THESE DAYS?
HIS ACTING MUST REALLY BE GOOD
YOU COULD SAY WE'RE SEEING THE UNFOLDING OF HIS FULL POTENTIAL.

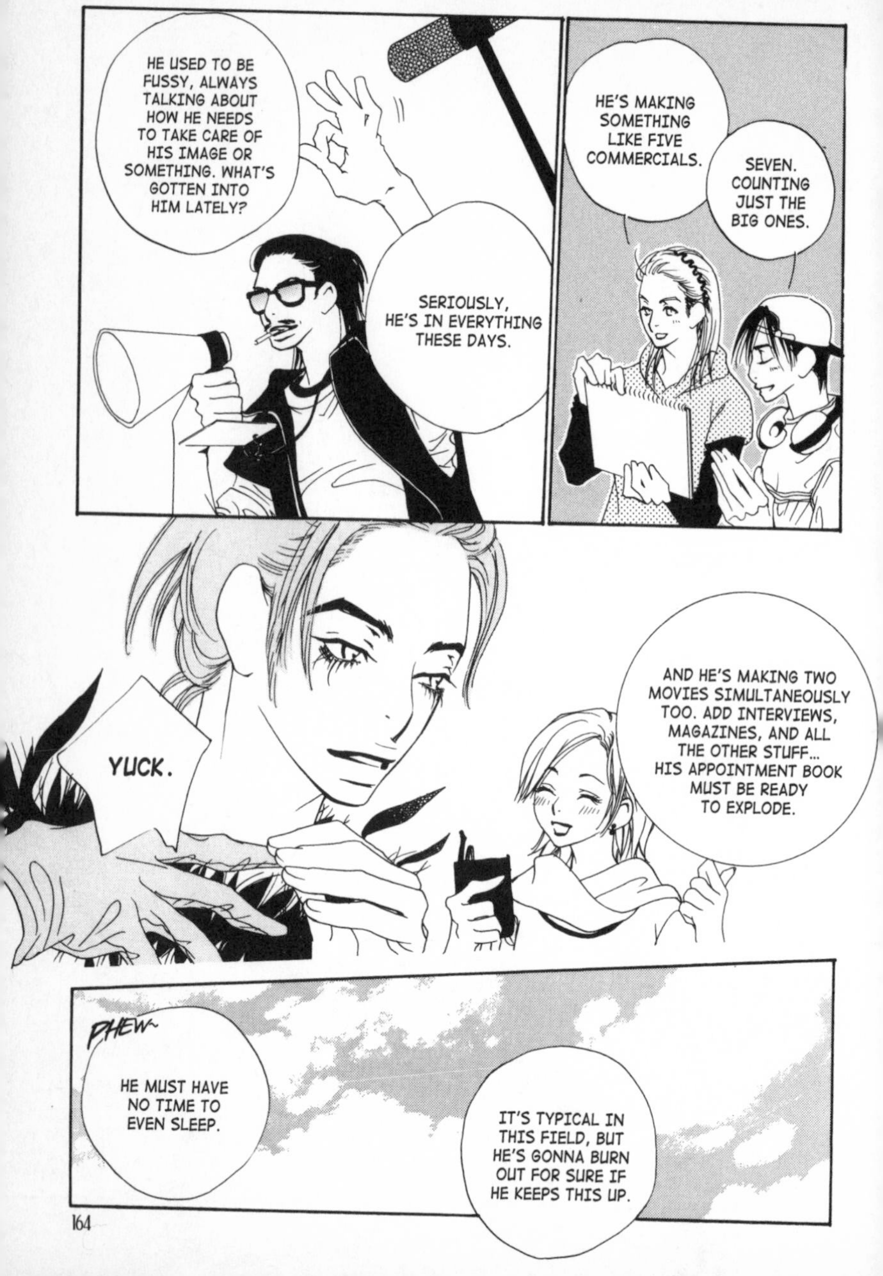
HE USED TO BE FUSSY, ALWAYS TALKING ABOUT HOW HE NEEDS TO TAKE CARE OF HIS IMAGE OR SOMETHING. WHAT'S GOTTEN INTO HIM LATELY?
SERIOUSLY, HE'S IN EVERYTHING THESE DAYS.
HE'S MAKING SOMETHING LIKE FIVE COMMERCIALS.
SEVEN. COUNTING JUST THE BIG ONES.
YUCK.
AND HE'S MAKING TWO MOVIES SIMULTANEOUSLY TOO. ADD INTERVIEWS, MAGAZINES, AND ALL THE OTHER STUFF... HIS APPOINTMENT BOOK MUST BE READY TO EXPLODE.
PHEW~
HE MUST HAVE NO TIME TO EVEN SLEEP.
IT'S TYPICAL IN THIS FIELD, BUT HE'S GONNA BURN OUT FOR SURE IF HE KEEPS THIS UP.

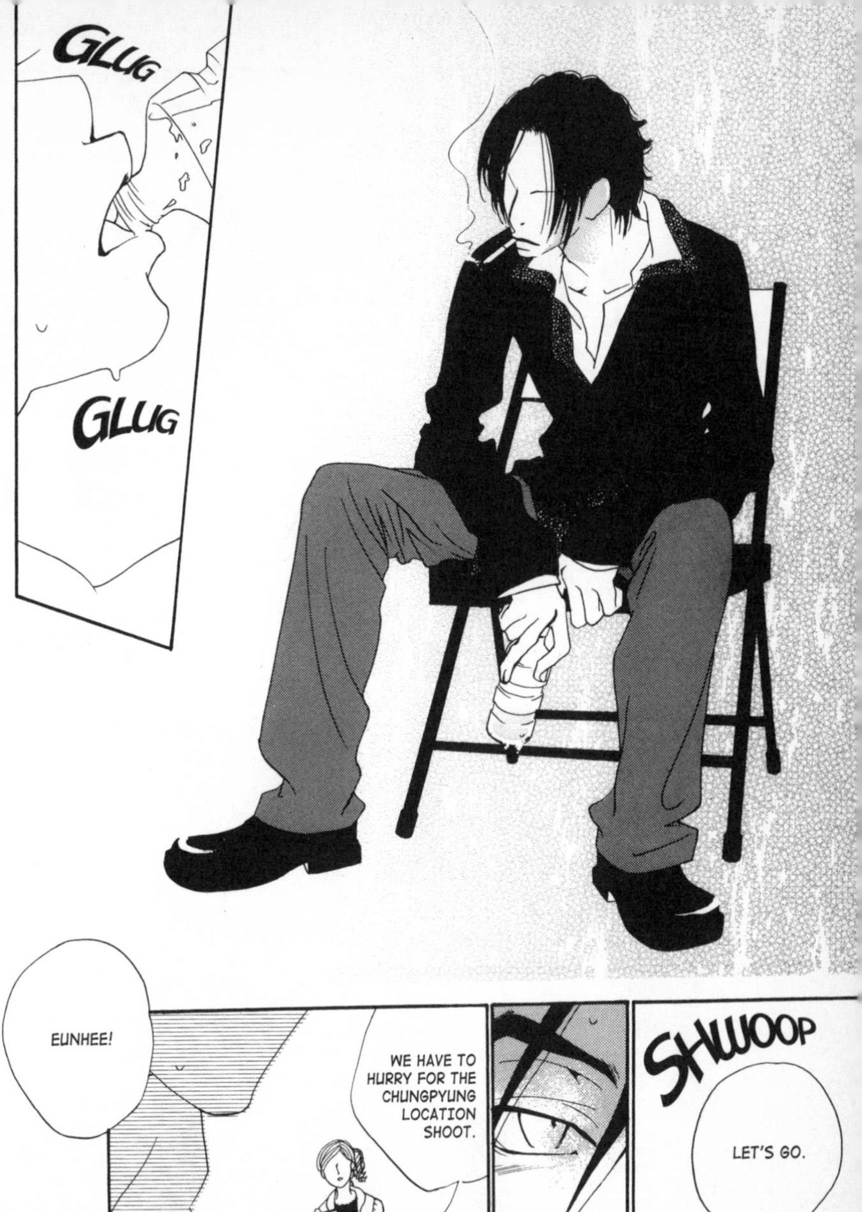
GLUG
GLUG
EUNHEE!
WE HAVE TO HURRY FOR THE CHUNGPYUNG LOCATION SHOOT.
SHWOOP
LET'S GO.

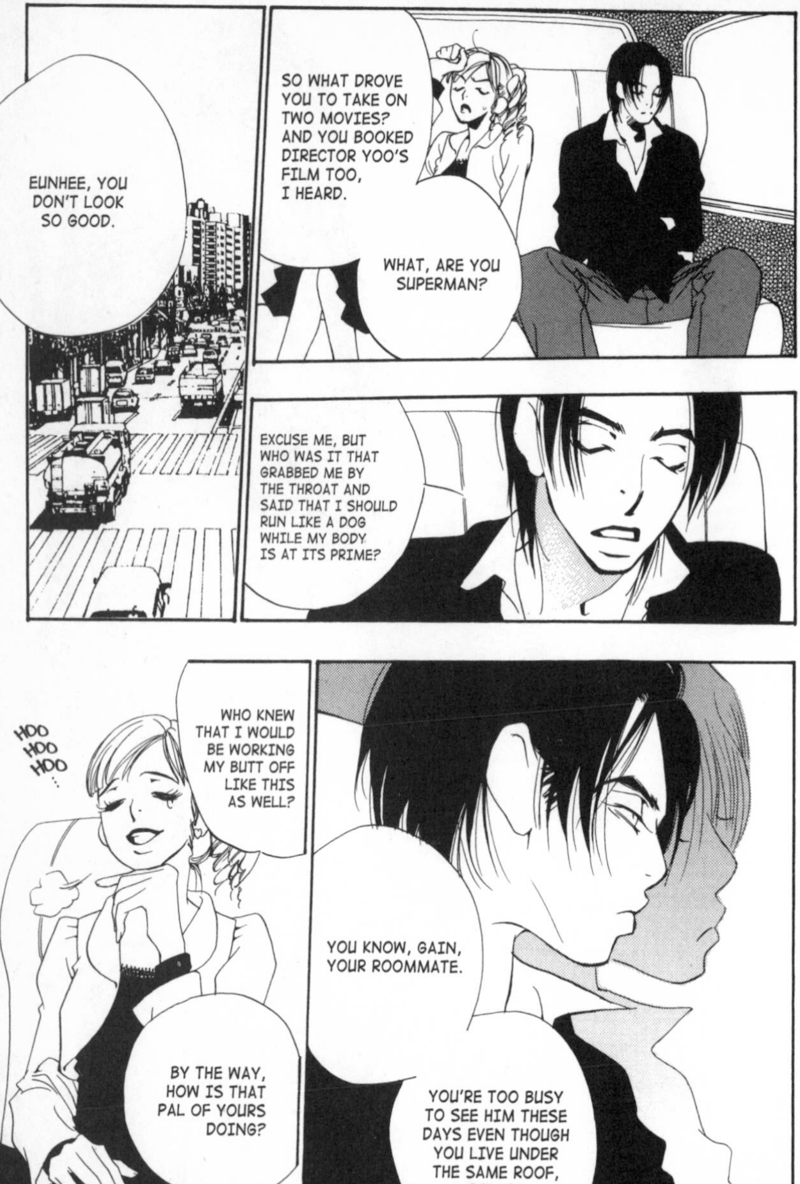
EUNHEE, YOU DON'T LOOK SO GOOD.
SO WHAT DROVE YOU TO TAKE ON TWO MOVIES? AND YOU BOOKED DIRECTOR YOO'S FILM TOO, I HEARD.
WHAT, ARE YOU SUPERMAN?
EXCUSE ME, BUT WHO WAS IT THAT GRABBED ME BY THE THROAT AND SAID THAT I SHOULD RUN LIKE A DOG WHILE MY BODY IS AT ITS PRIME?
WHO KNEW THAT I WOULD BE WORKING MY BUTT OFF LIKE THIS AS WELL?
HOO HOO HOO...
BY THE WAY, HOW IS THAT PAL OF YOURS DOING?
YOU KNOW, GAIN, YOUR ROOMMATE.
YOU'RE TOO BUSY TO SEE HIM THESE DAYS EVEN THOUGH YOU LIVE UNDER THE SAME ROOF, RIGHT?

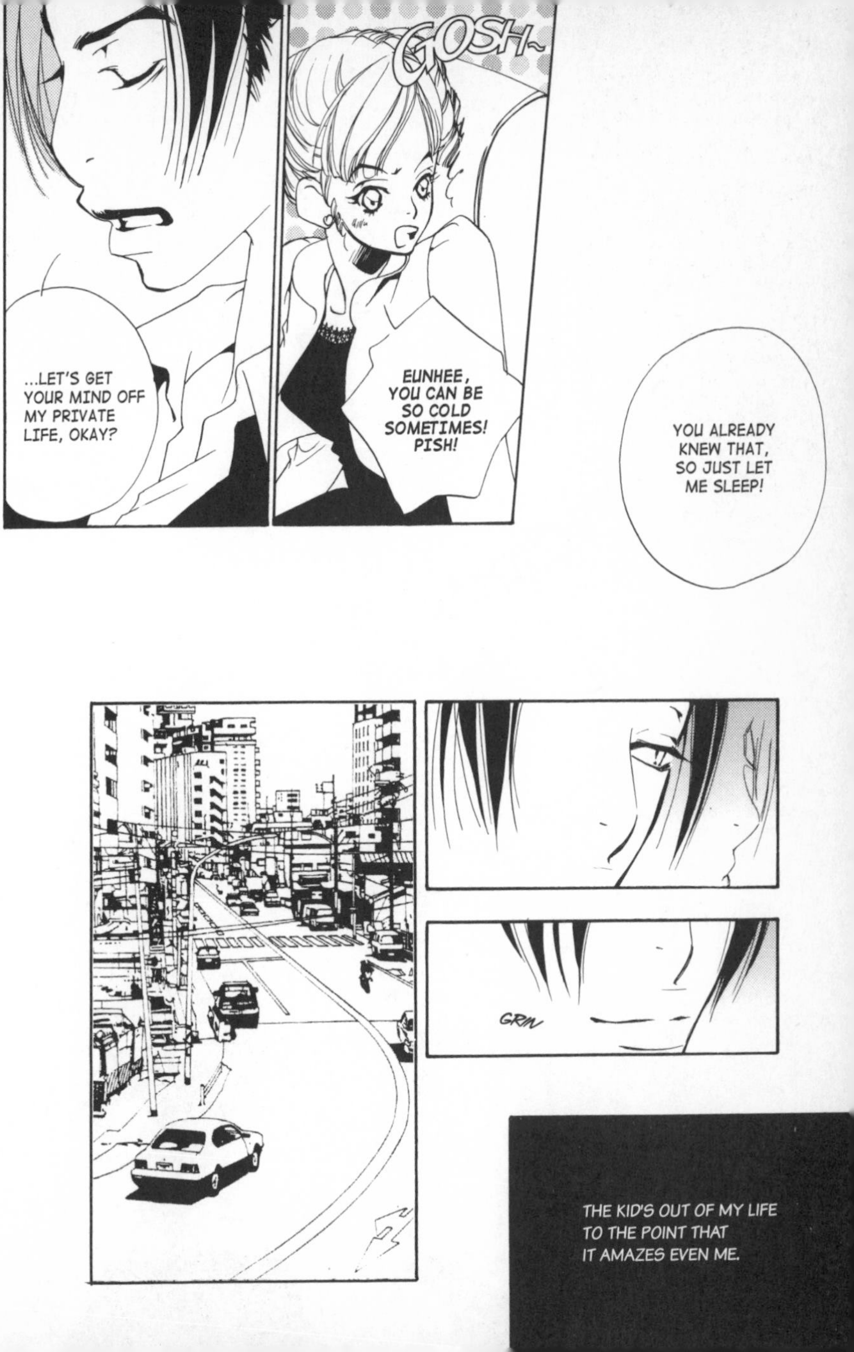
...LET'S GET YOUR MIND OFF MY PRIVATE LIFE, OKAY?
GOSH~
EUNHEE, YOU CAN BE SO COLD SOMETIMES! PISH!
YOU ALREADY KNEW THAT, SO JUST LET ME SLEEP!
GRIN
THE KID'S OUT OF MY LIFE TO THE POINT THAT IT AMAZES EVEN ME.

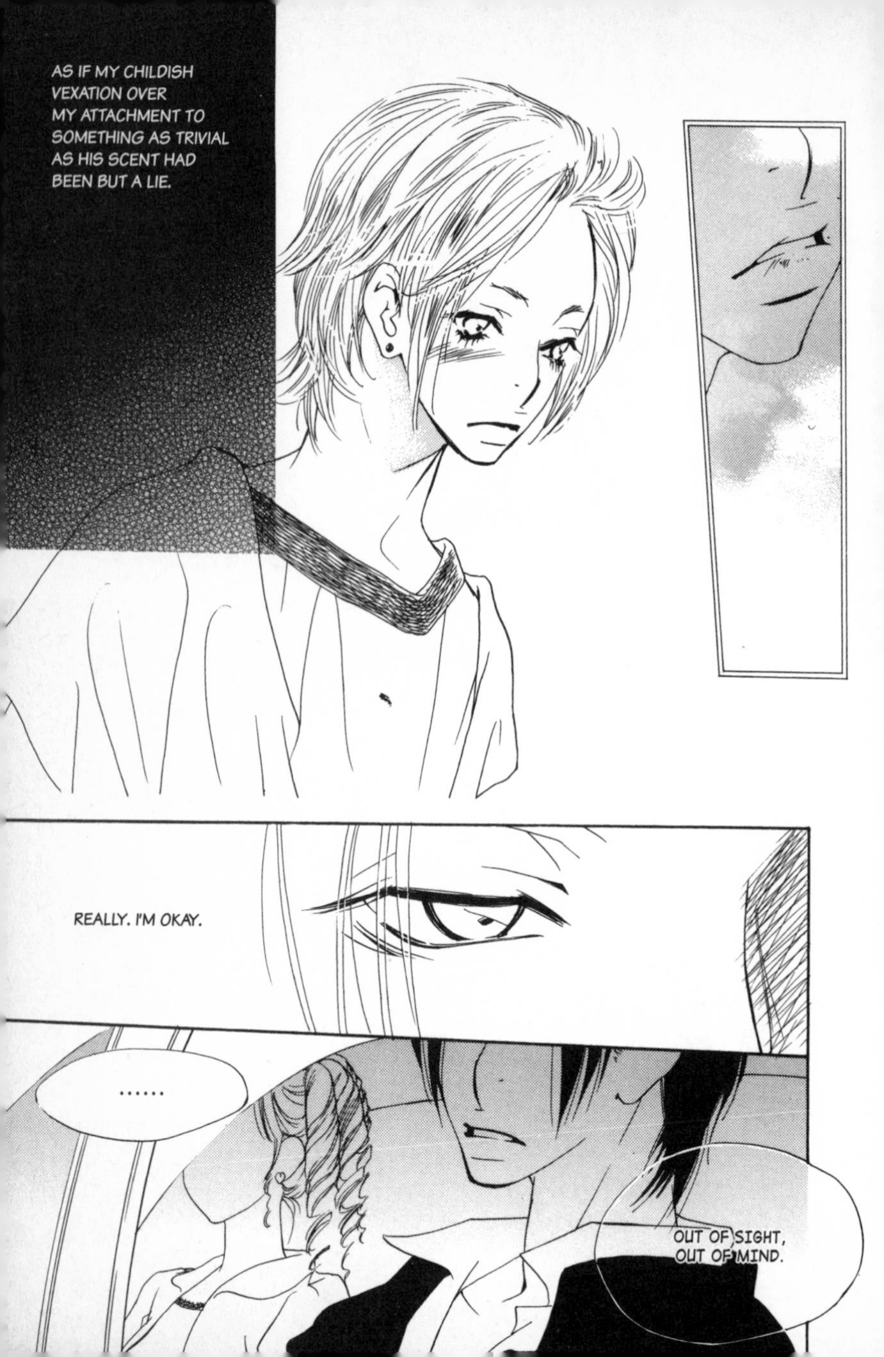
AS IF MY CHILDISH VEXATION OVER MY ATTACHMENT TO SOMETHING AS TRIVIAL AS HIS SCENT HAD BEEN BUT A LIE.
REALLY. I'M OKAY.
......
OUT OF SIGHT, OUT OF MIND.

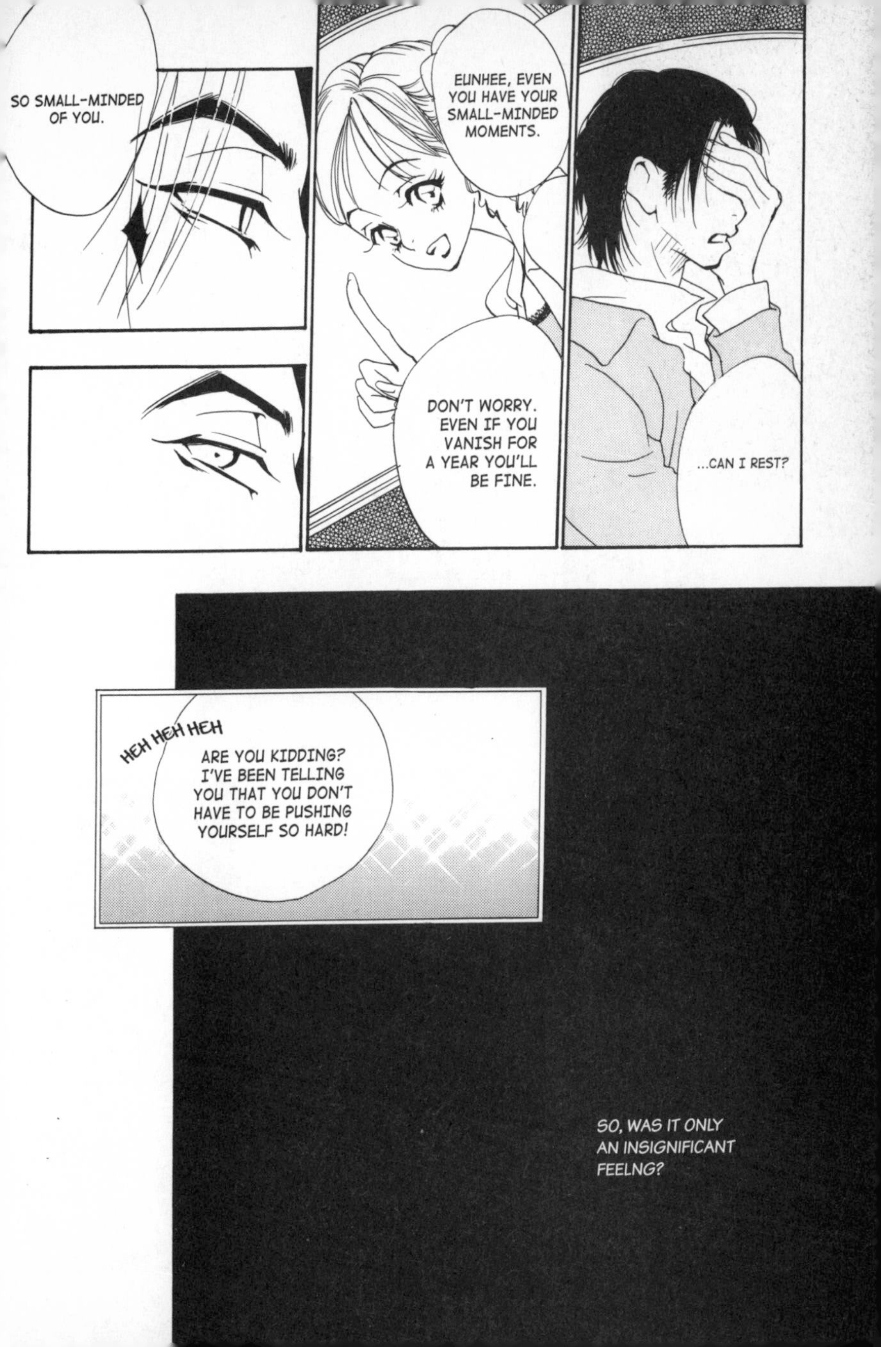
SO SMALL-MINDED OF YOU.
EUNHEE, EVEN YOU HAVE YOUR SMALL-MINDED MOMENTS.
DON'T WORRY. EVEN IF YOU VANISH FOR A YEAR YOU'LL BE FINE.
...CAN I REST?
HEH HEH HEH
ARE YOU KIDDING? I'VE BEEN TELLING YOU THAT YOU DON'T HAVE TO BE PUSHING YOURSELF SO HARD!
SO, WAS IT ONLY AN INSIGNIFICANT FEELNG?

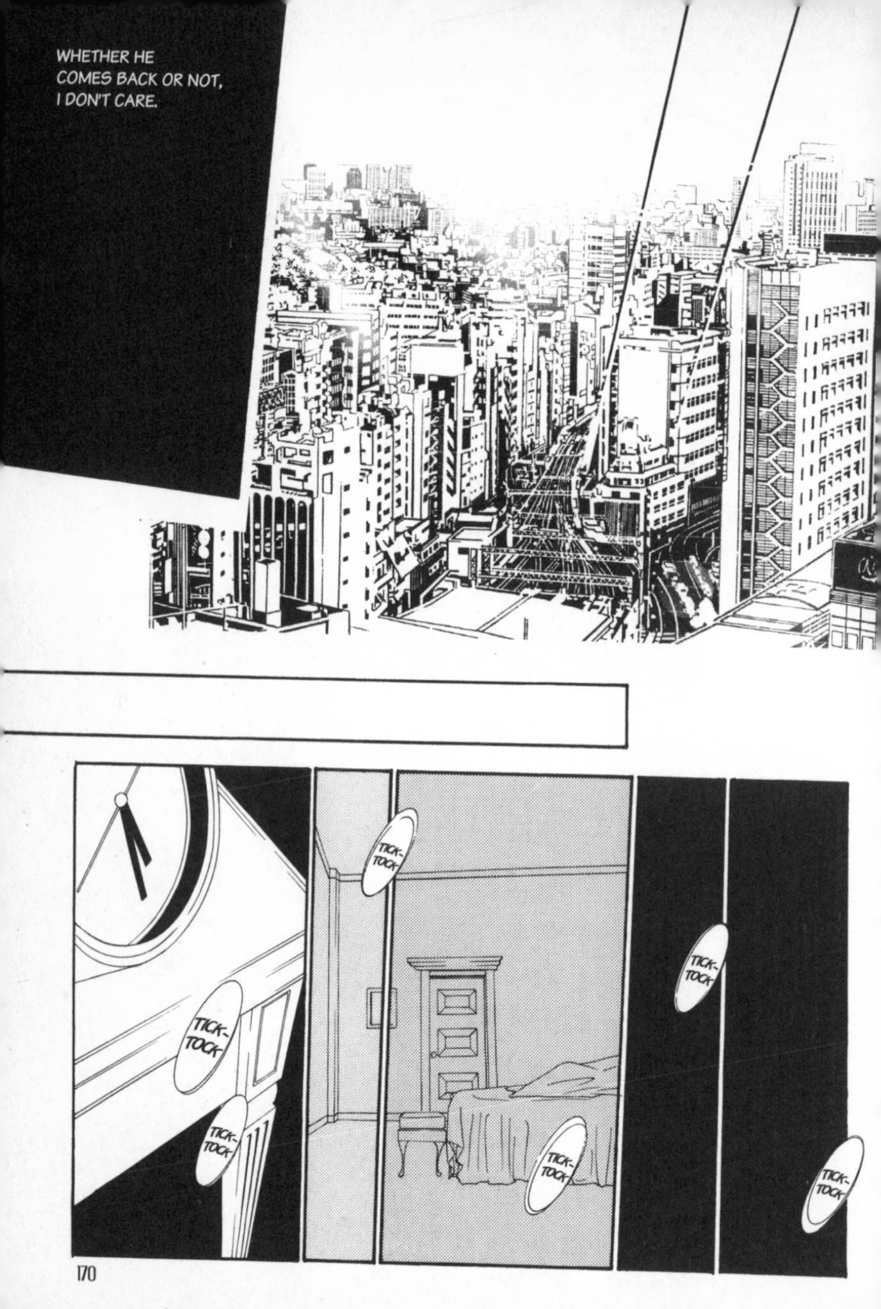
WHETHER HE COMES BACK OR NOT, I DON'T CARE.
TICK-TOCK
TICK-TOCK
TICK-TOCK
TICK-TOCK
TICK-TOCK
TICK-TOCK

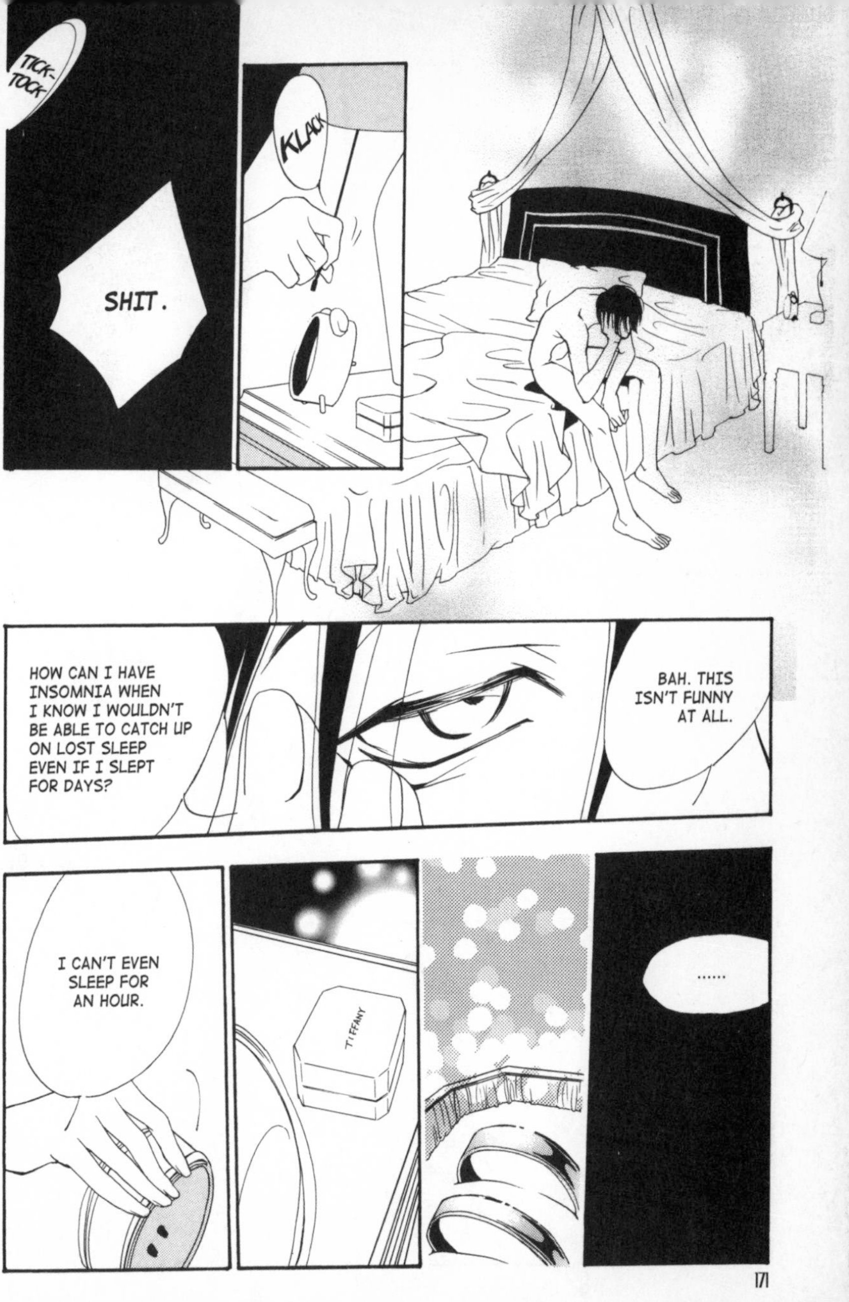
KLACK
TICK-TOCK
SHIT.
BAH. THIS ISN'T FUNNY AT ALL.
HOW CAN I HAVE INSOMNIA WHEN I KNOW I WOULDN'T BE ABLE TO CATCH UP ON LOST SLEEP EVEN IF I SLEPT FOR DAYS?
......
TIFFANY
I CAN'T EVEN SLEEP FOR AN HOUR.

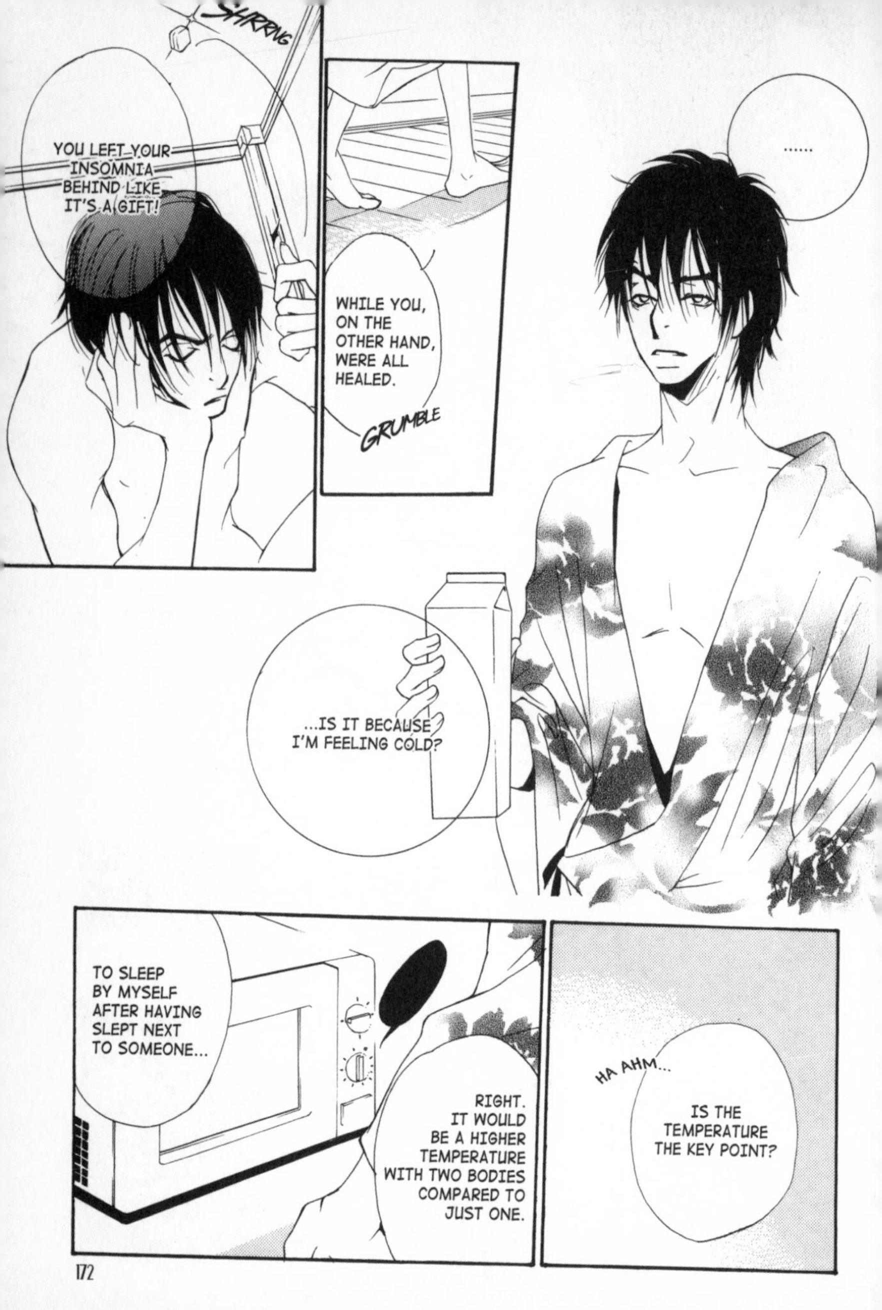
......
SHRRNG
YOU LEFT YOUR INSOMNIA BEHIND LIKE IT'S A GIFT!
WHILE YOU, ON THE OTHER HAND, WERE ALL HEALED.
GRUMBLE
...IS IT BECAUSE I'M FEELING COLD?
HA AHM...
IS THE TEMPERATURE THE KEY POINT?
RIGHT. IT WOULD BE A HIGHER TEMPERATURE WITH TWO BODIES COMPARED TO JUST ONE.
TO SLEEP BY MYSELF AFTER HAVING SLEPT NEXT TO SOMEONE...

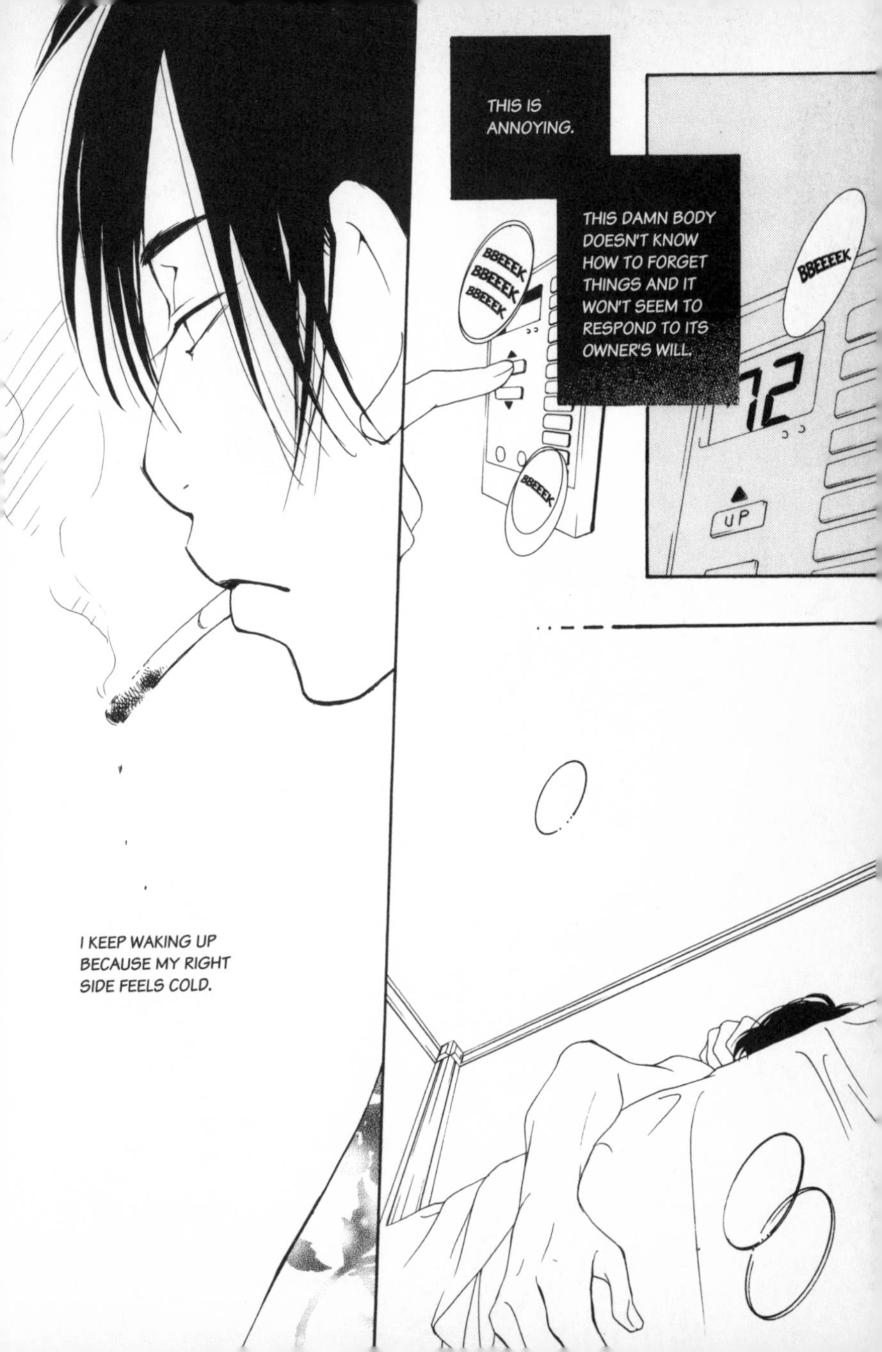
THIS IS ANNOYING.
THIS DAMN BODY DOESN'T KNOW HOW TO FORGET THINGS AND IT WON'T SEEM TO RESPOND TO ITS OWNER'S WILL.
BBEEEEK
BBEEEK BBEEEK BBEEEK
BBEEEK
72
UP
I KEEP WAKING UP BECAUSE MY RIGHT SIDE FEELS COLD.

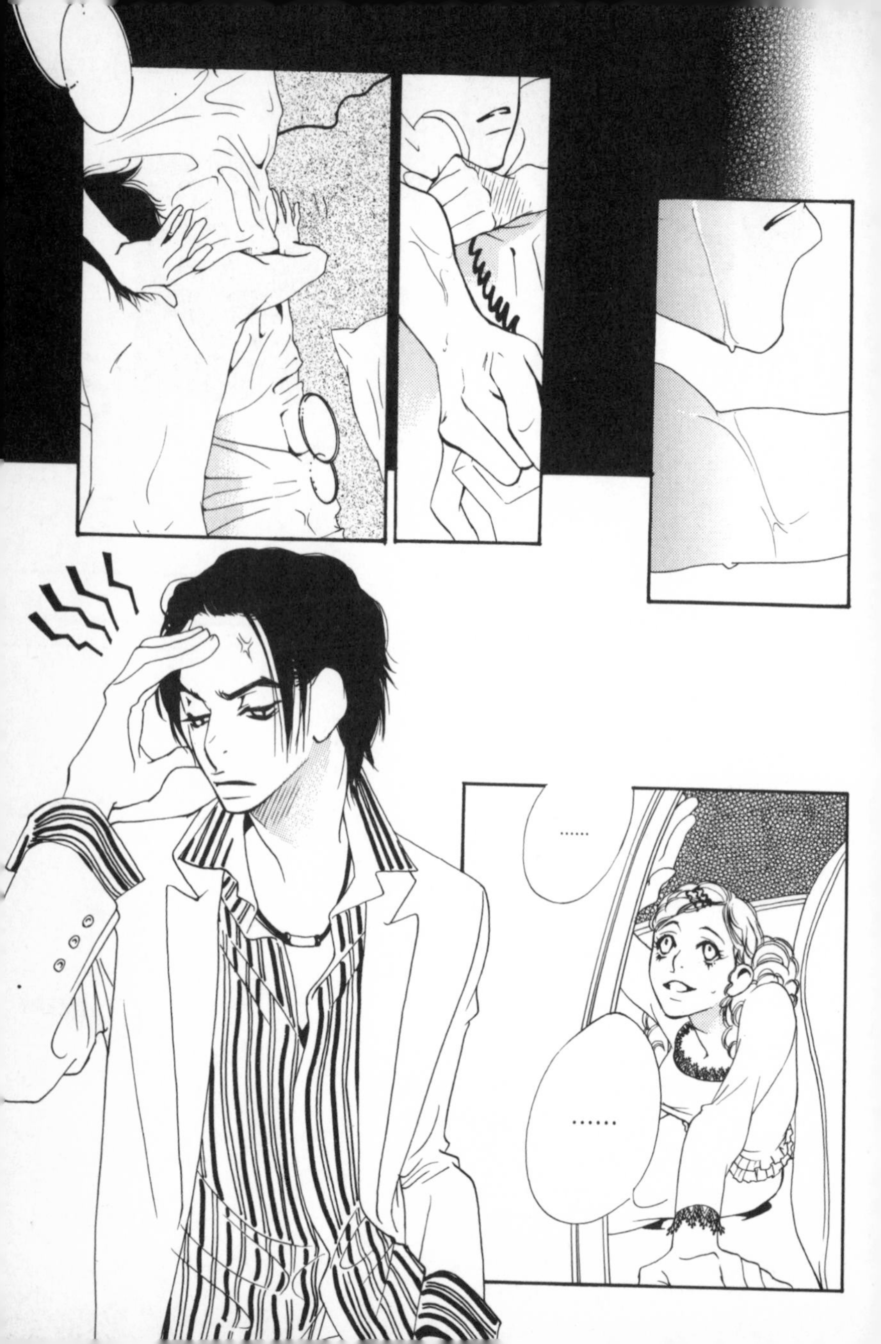
……
……

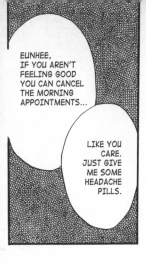

EUNHEE,
IF YOU AREN'T
FEELING GOOD
YOU CAN CANCEL
THE MORNING
APPOINTMENTS...

LIKE YOU
CARE.
JUST GIVE
ME SOME
HEADACHE
PILLS.

JEEZ!

JUST LISTEN
TO THE WAY
YOU TALK!

THANK YOU, FOLKS!
THE NEXT SHOOT
WON'T TAKE PLACE
UNTIL AFTER TWO
WEEKS SO WE CAN
ALL GET WASTED
TODAY!

OH
OH

YOU'RE DOING
THE SECOND
ROUND TOO,
RIGHT?

WHAT
BRINGS
YOU HERE?

I'LL BE
JOINING
YOU IN THE
NEXT SCENE.
DIDN'T YOU
KNOW?

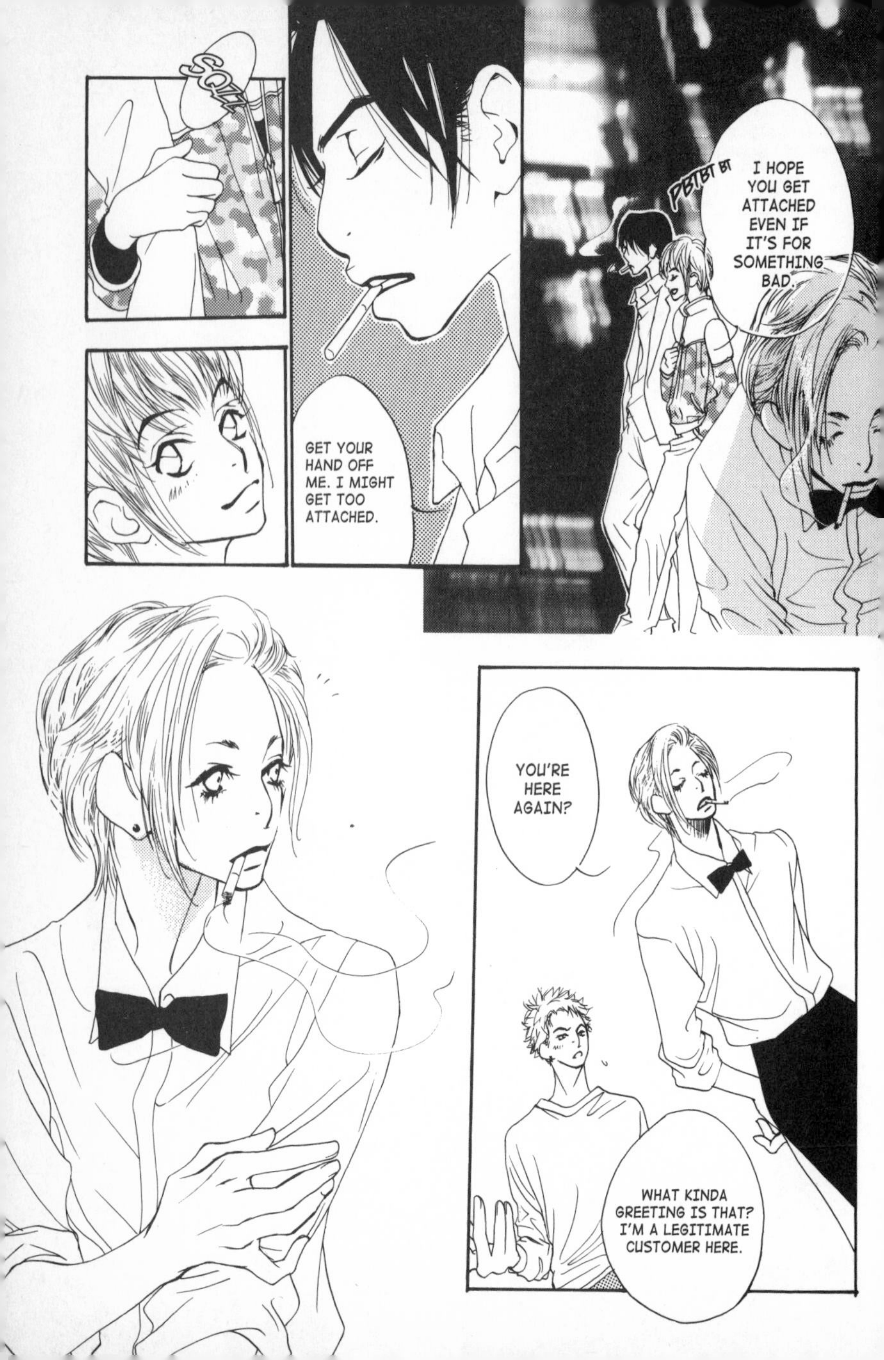
SQZZ
GET YOUR HAND OFF ME. I MIGHT GET TOO ATTACHED.
PBTBTBT BT
I HOPE YOU GET ATTACHED EVEN IF IT'S FOR SOMETHING BAD.
YOU'RE HERE AGAIN?
WHAT KINDA GREETING IS THAT? I'M A LEGITIMATE CUSTOMER HERE.

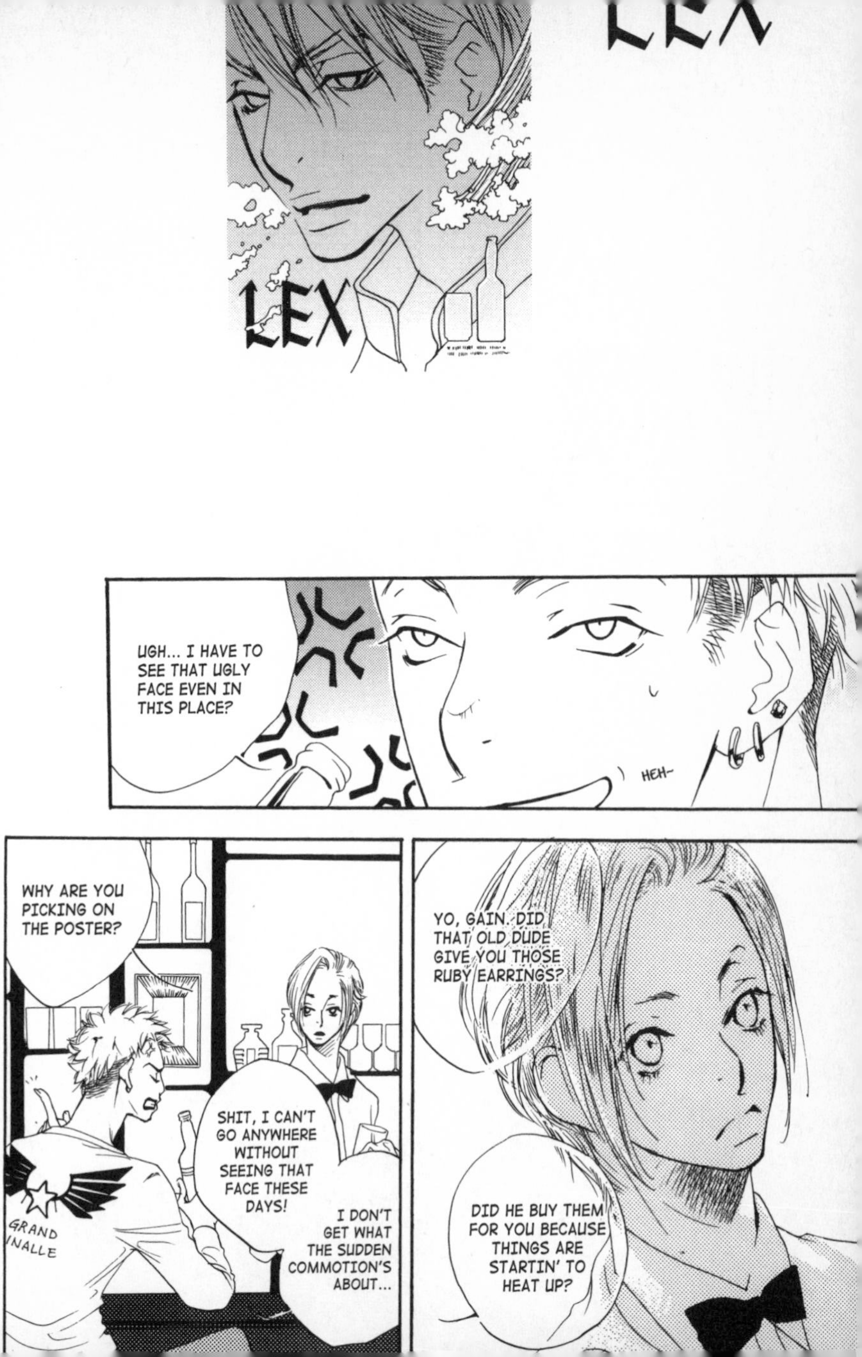
LEX
HEH~
UGH... I HAVE TO SEE THAT UGLY FACE EVEN IN THIS PLACE?
YO, GAIN. DID THAT OLD DUDE GIVE YOU THOSE RUBY EARRINGS?
DID HE BUY THEM FOR YOU BECAUSE THINGS ARE STARTIN' TO HEAT UP?
WHY ARE YOU PICKING ON THE POSTER?
SHIT, I CAN'T GO ANYWHERE WITHOUT SEEING THAT FACE THESE DAYS!
I DON'T GET WHAT THE SUDDEN COMMOTION'S ABOUT...
GRAND
INALLE

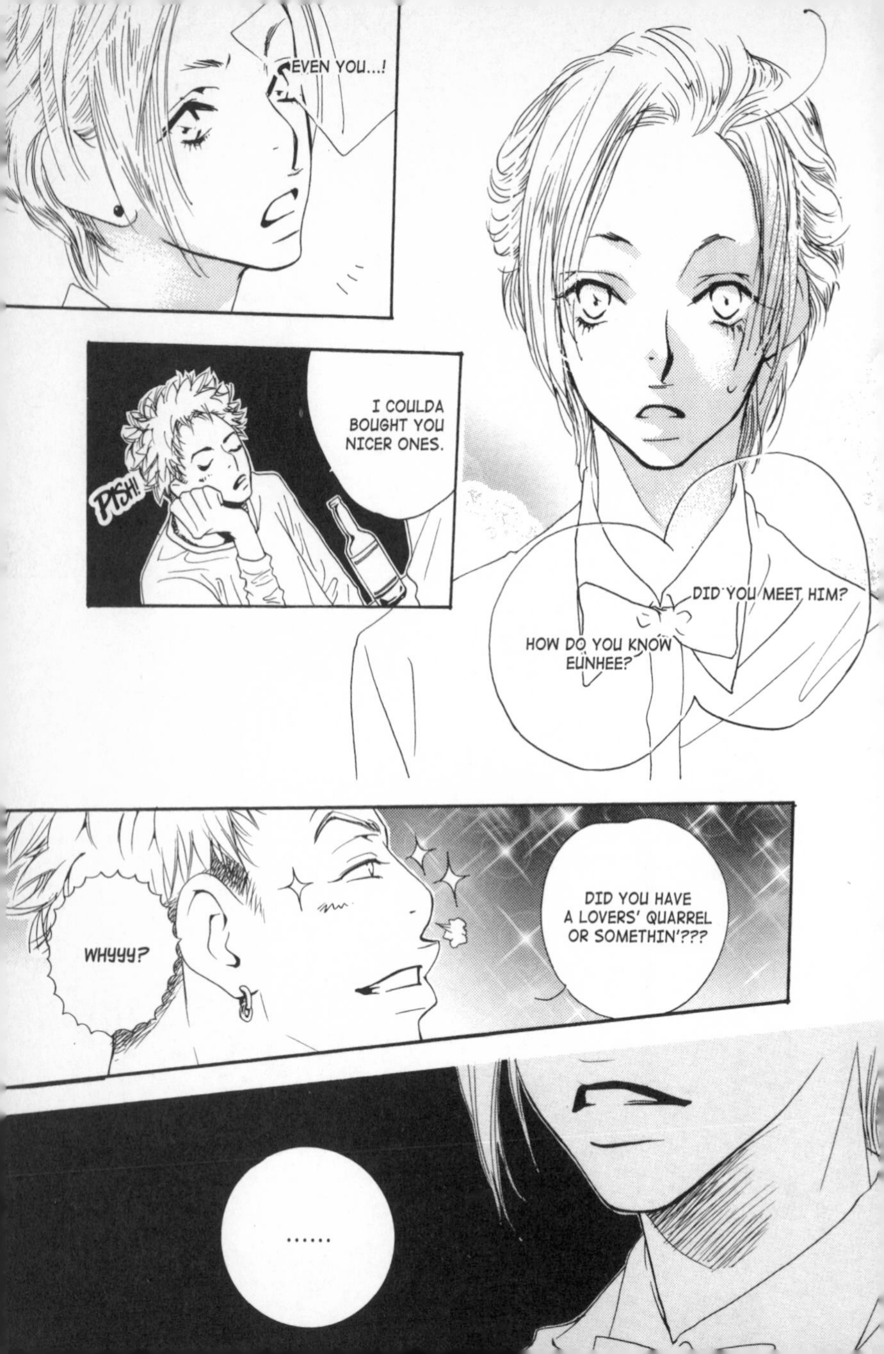
EVEN YOU...!
I COULDA BOUGHT YOU NICER ONES.
PISH!
DID YOU MEET HIM?
HOW DO YOU KNOW EUNHEE?
DID YOU HAVE A LOVERS' QUARREL OR SOMETHIN'???
WHYYY?
......

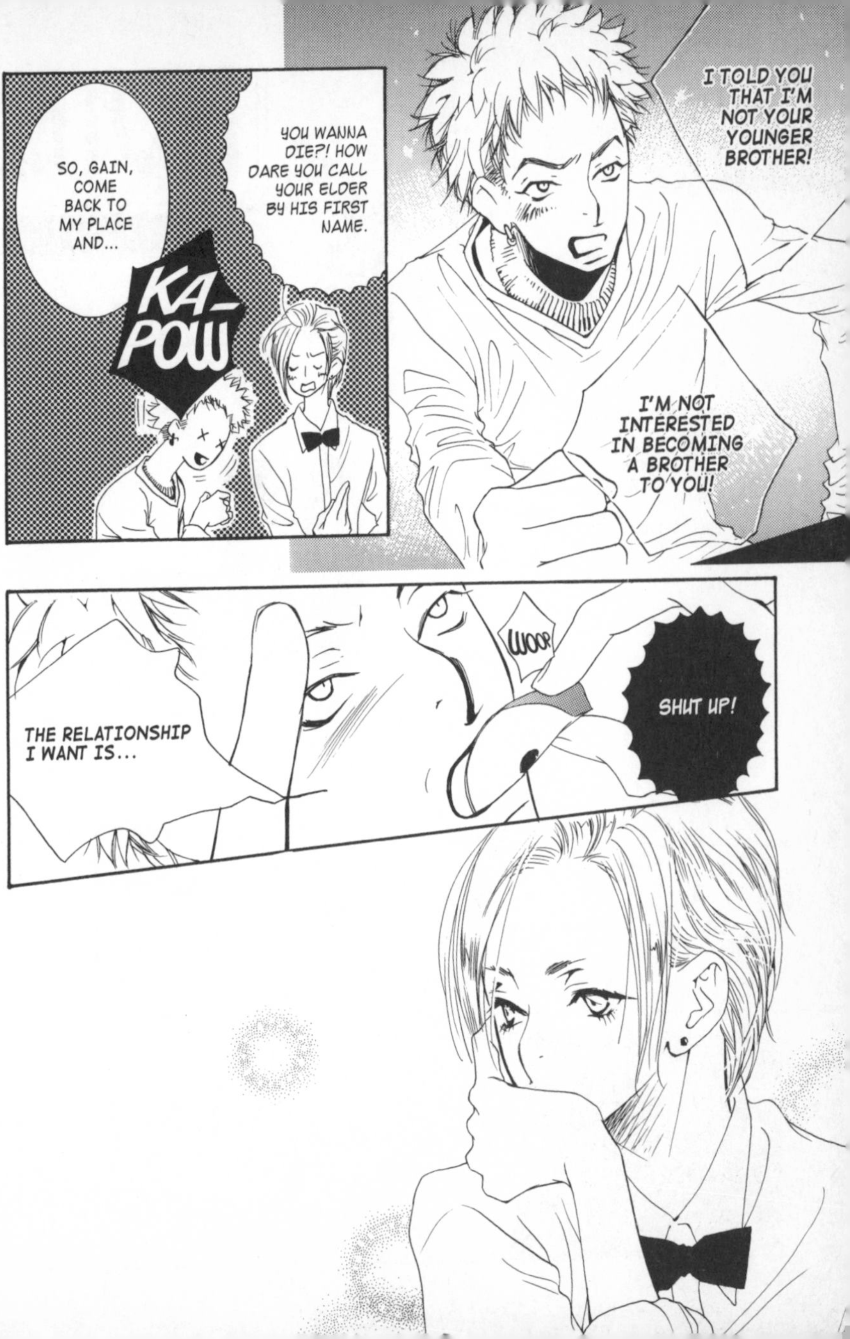
I TOLD YOU THAT I'M NOT YOUR YOUNGER BROTHER!
I'M NOT INTERESTED IN BECOMING A BROTHER TO YOU!
SO, GAIN, COME BACK TO MY PLACE AND...
KA-POW
YOU WANNA DIE?! HOW DARE YOU CALL YOUR ELDER BY HIS FIRST NAME.
SHUT UP!
WOOP
THE RELATIONSHIP I WANT IS...

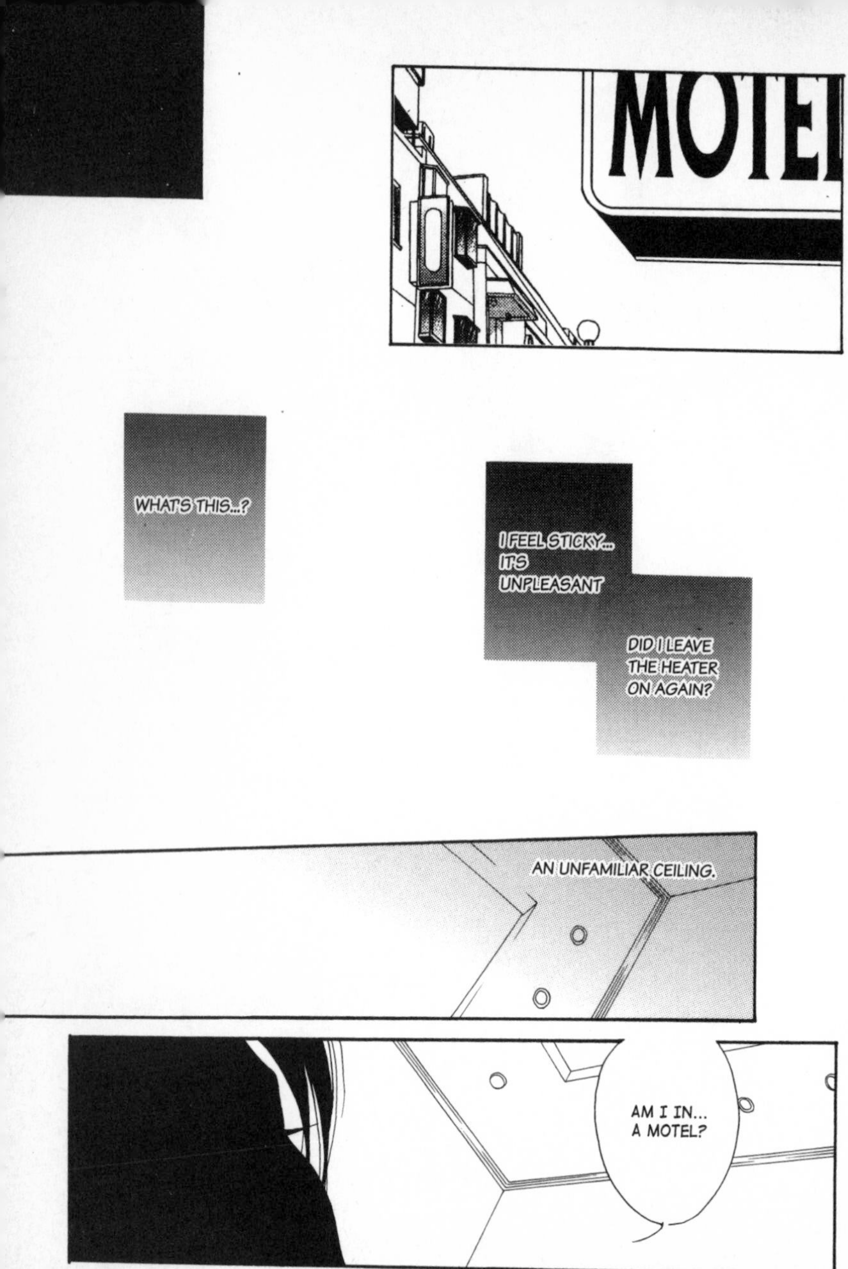
MOTEL
WHAT'S THIS...?
I FEEL STICKY... IT'S UNPLEASANT
DID I LEAVE THE HEATER ON AGAIN?
AN UNFAMILIAR CEILING.
AM I IN... A MOTEL?

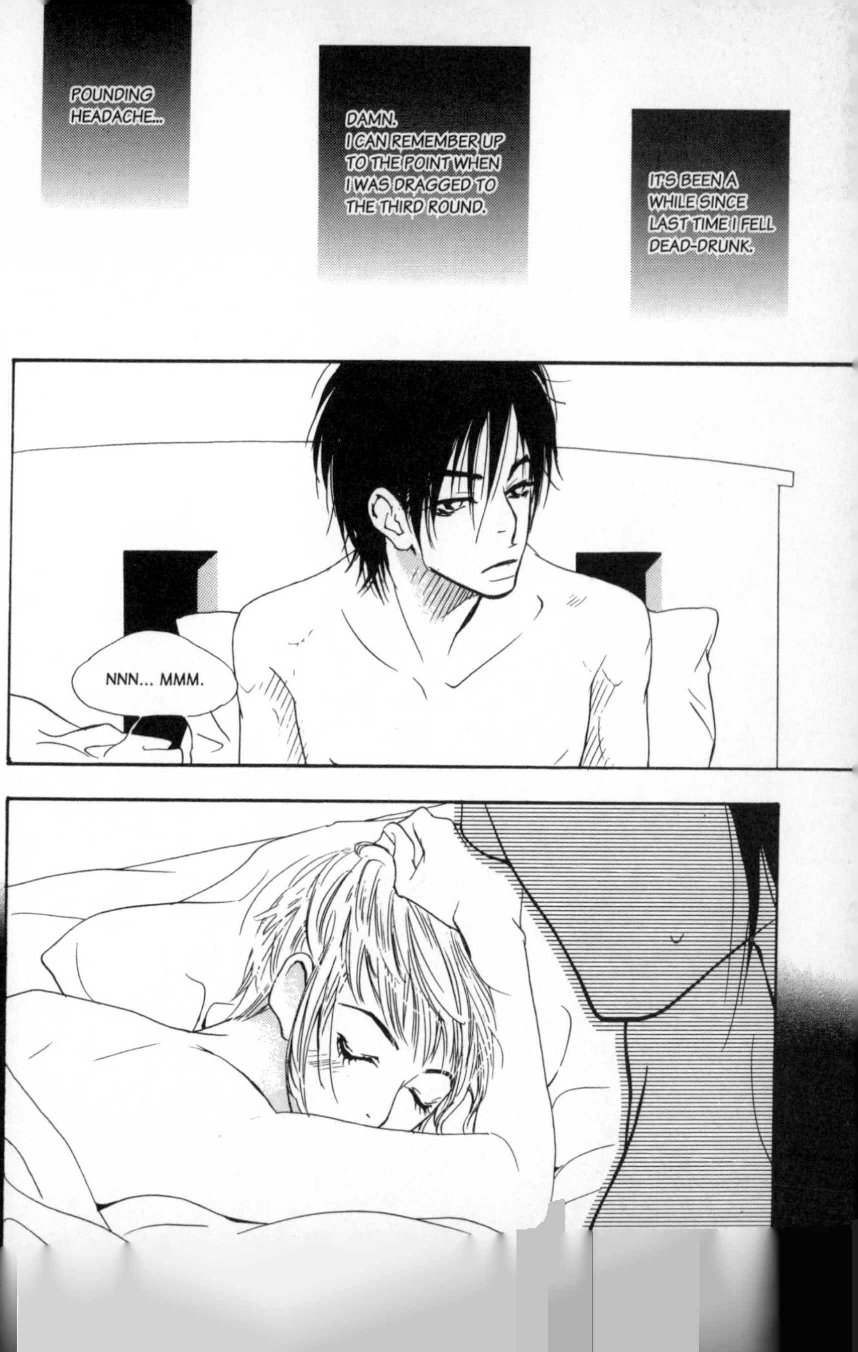
POUNDING HEADACHE...
DAMN. I CAN REMEMBER UP TO THE POINT WHEN I WAS DRAGGED TO THE THIRD ROUND.
IT'S BEEN A WHILE SINCE LAST TIME I FELL DEAD-DRUNK.
NNN... MMM.

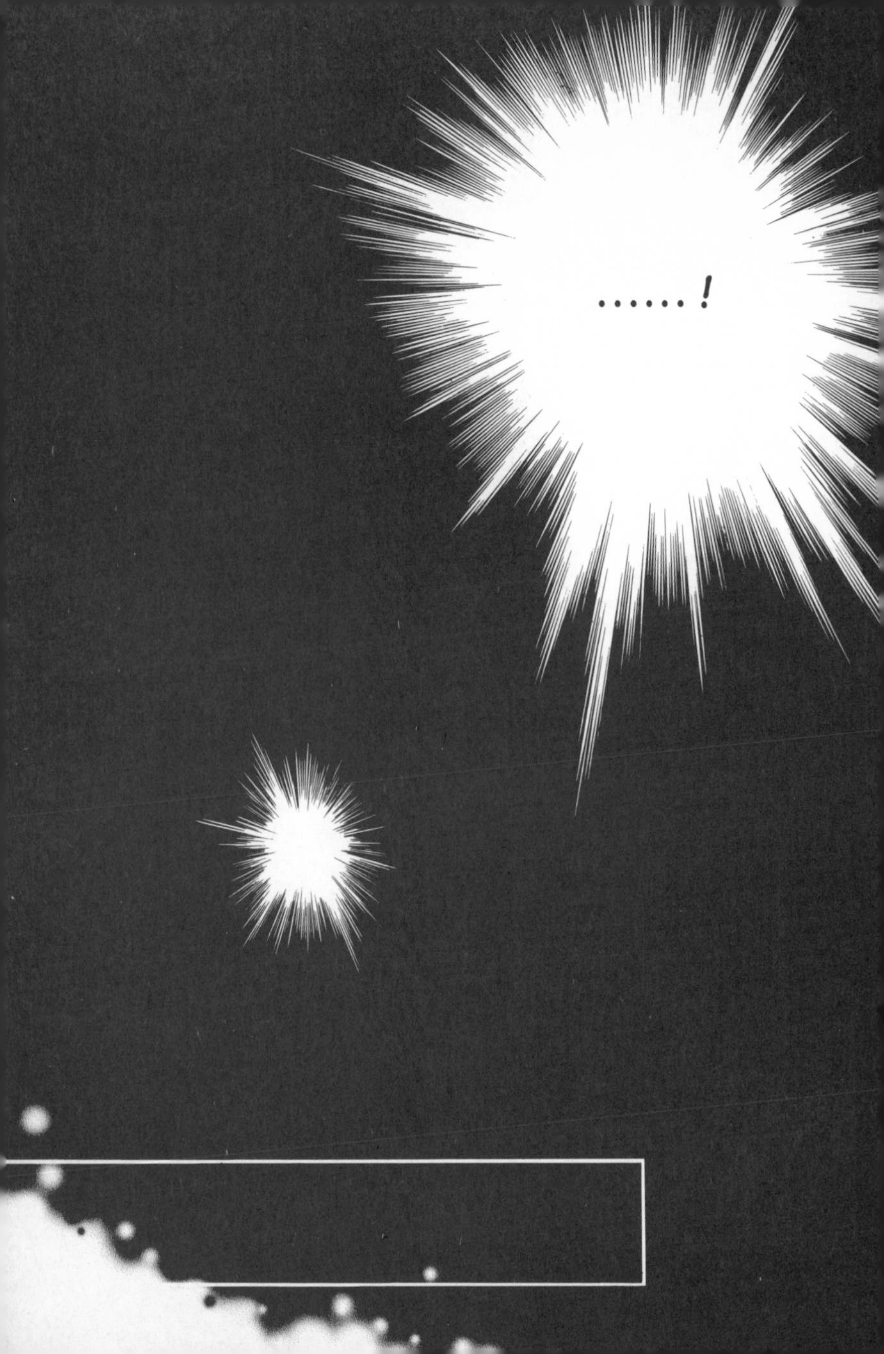
......!

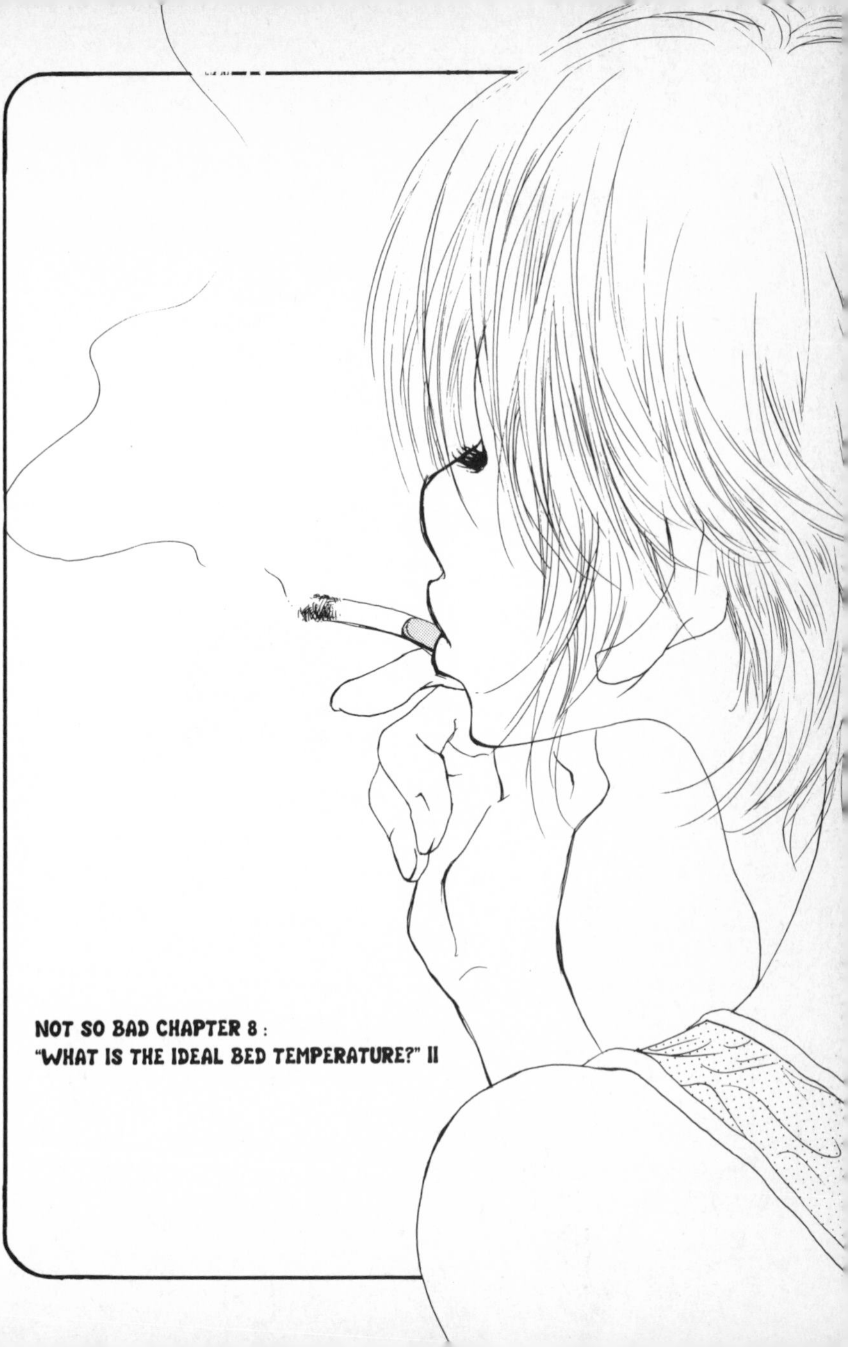
NOT SO BAD CHAPTER 8 :
"WHAT IS THE IDEAL BED TEMPERATURE?" II

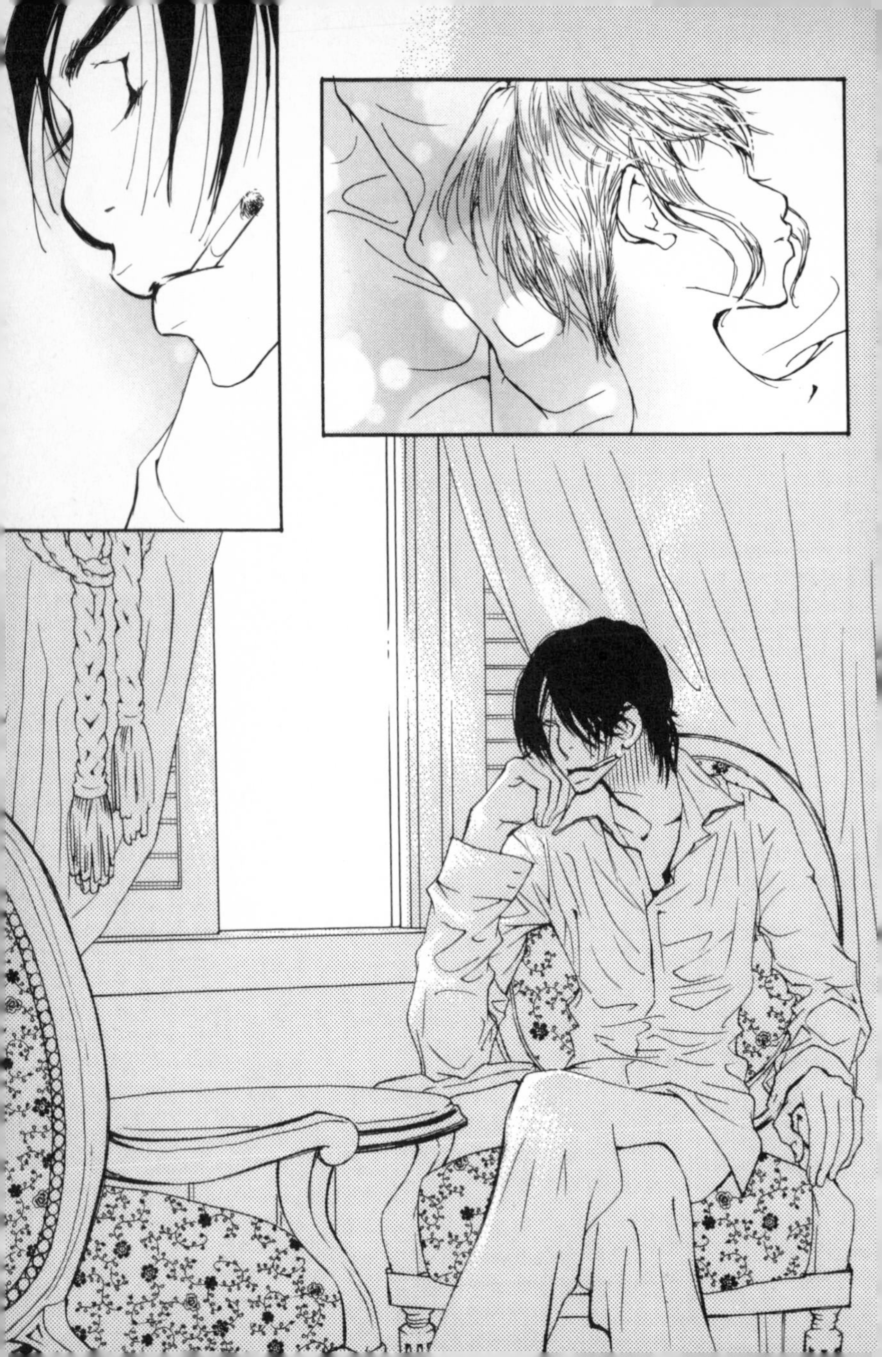

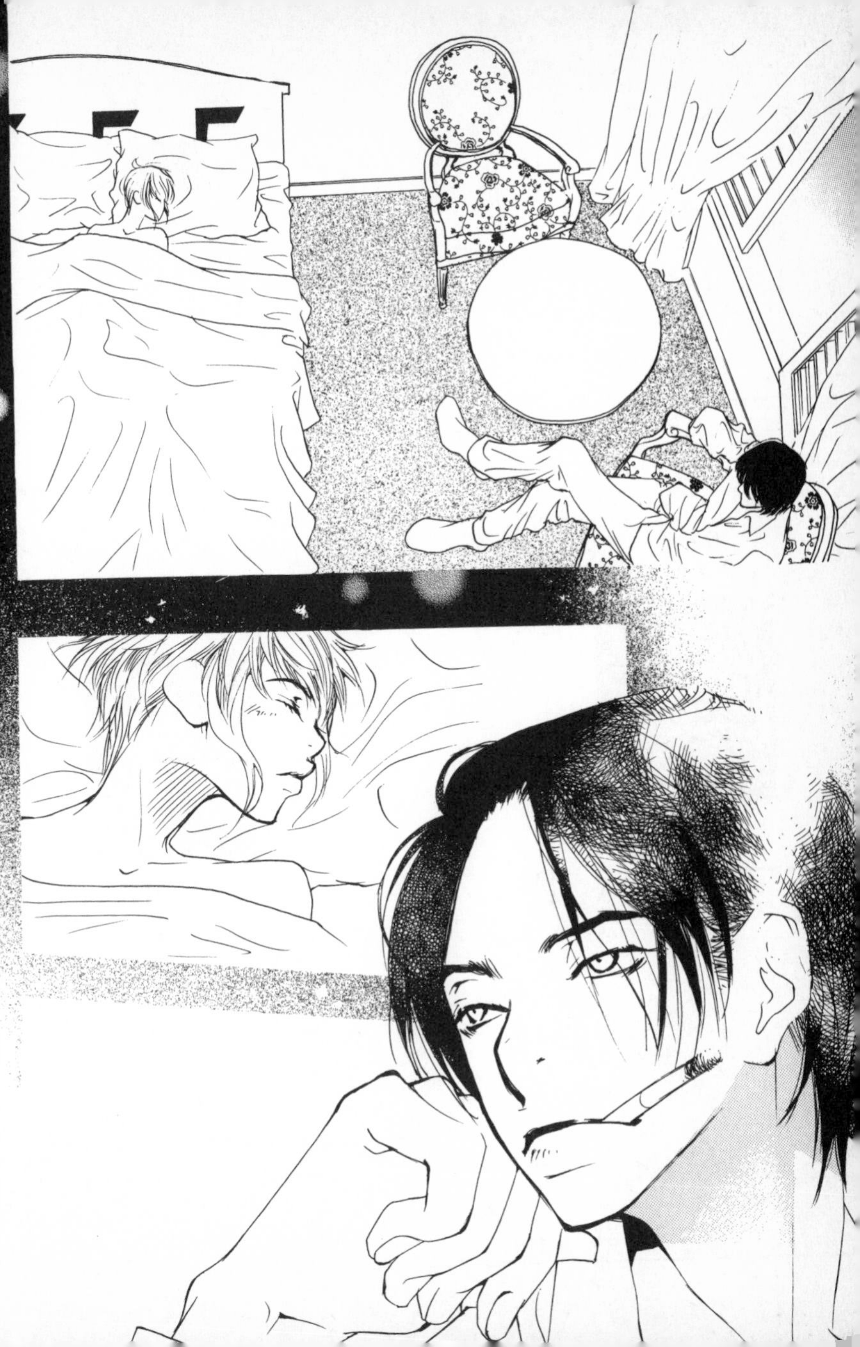

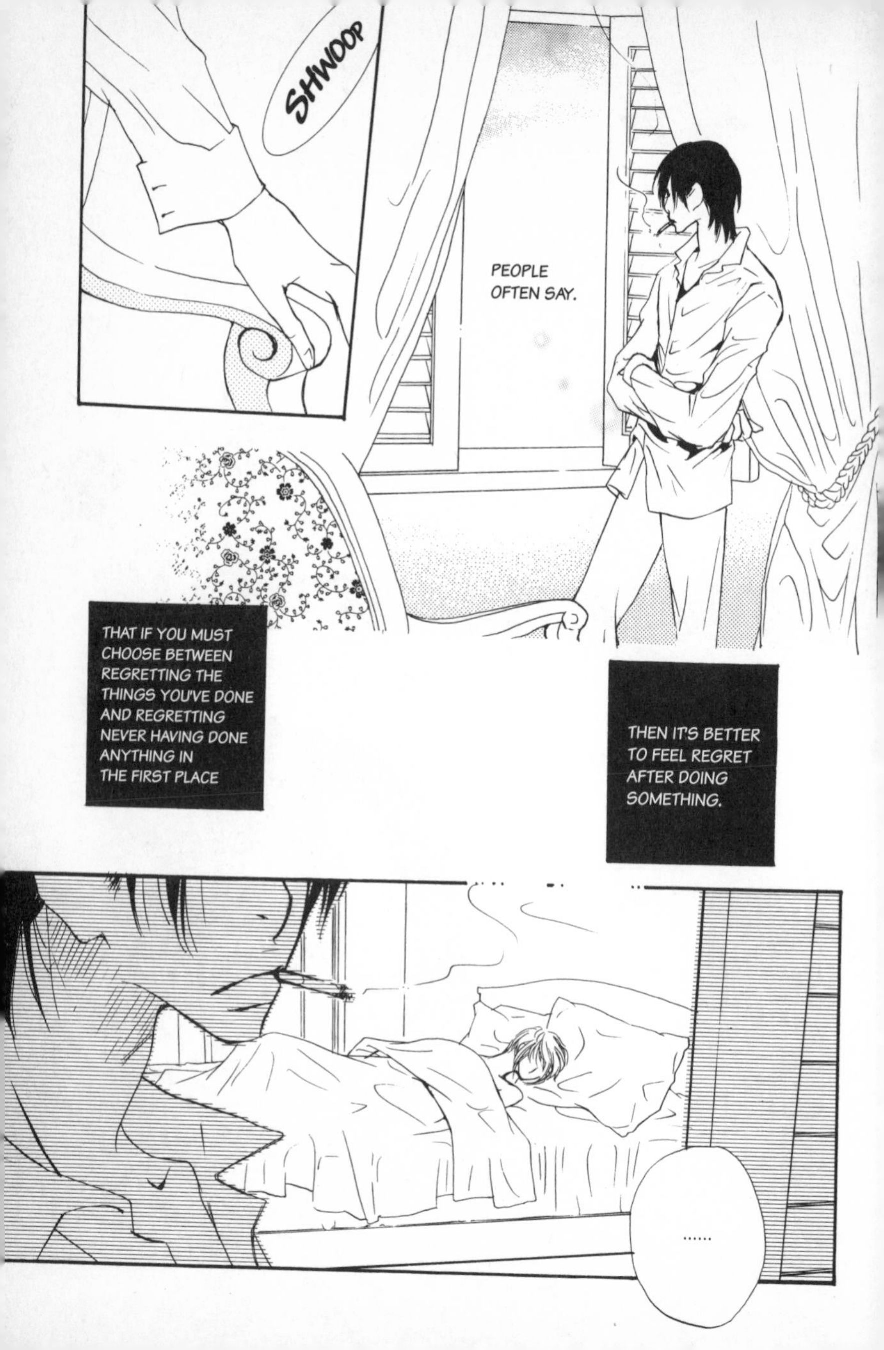
SHWOOP
PEOPLE OFTEN SAY.
THAT IF YOU MUST CHOOSE BETWEEN REGRETTING THE THINGS YOU'VE DONE AND REGRETTING NEVER HAVING DONE ANYTHING IN THE FIRST PLACE
THEN IT'S BETTER TO FEEL REGRET AFTER DOING SOMETHING.
......

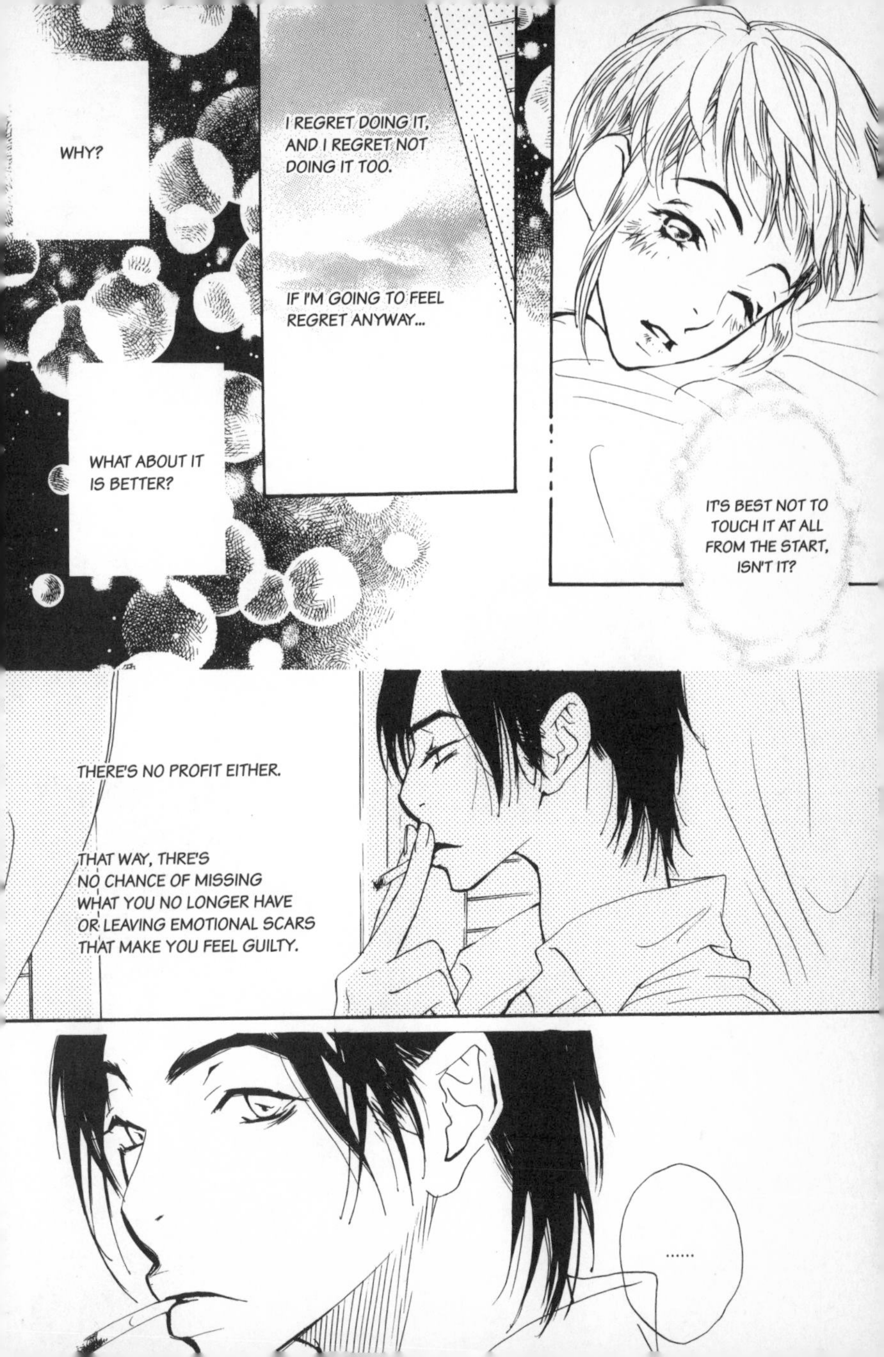
I REGRET DOING IT, AND I REGRET NOT DOING IT TOO.
IF I'M GOING TO FEEL REGRET ANYWAY...
WHY?
WHAT ABOUT IT IS BETTER?
IT'S BEST NOT TO TOUCH IT AT ALL FROM THE START, ISN'T IT?
THERE'S NO PROFIT EITHER.
THAT WAY, THRE'S NO CHANCE OF MISSING WHAT YOU NO LONGER HAVE OR LEAVING EMOTIONAL SCARS THAT MAKE YOU FEEL GUILTY.
......

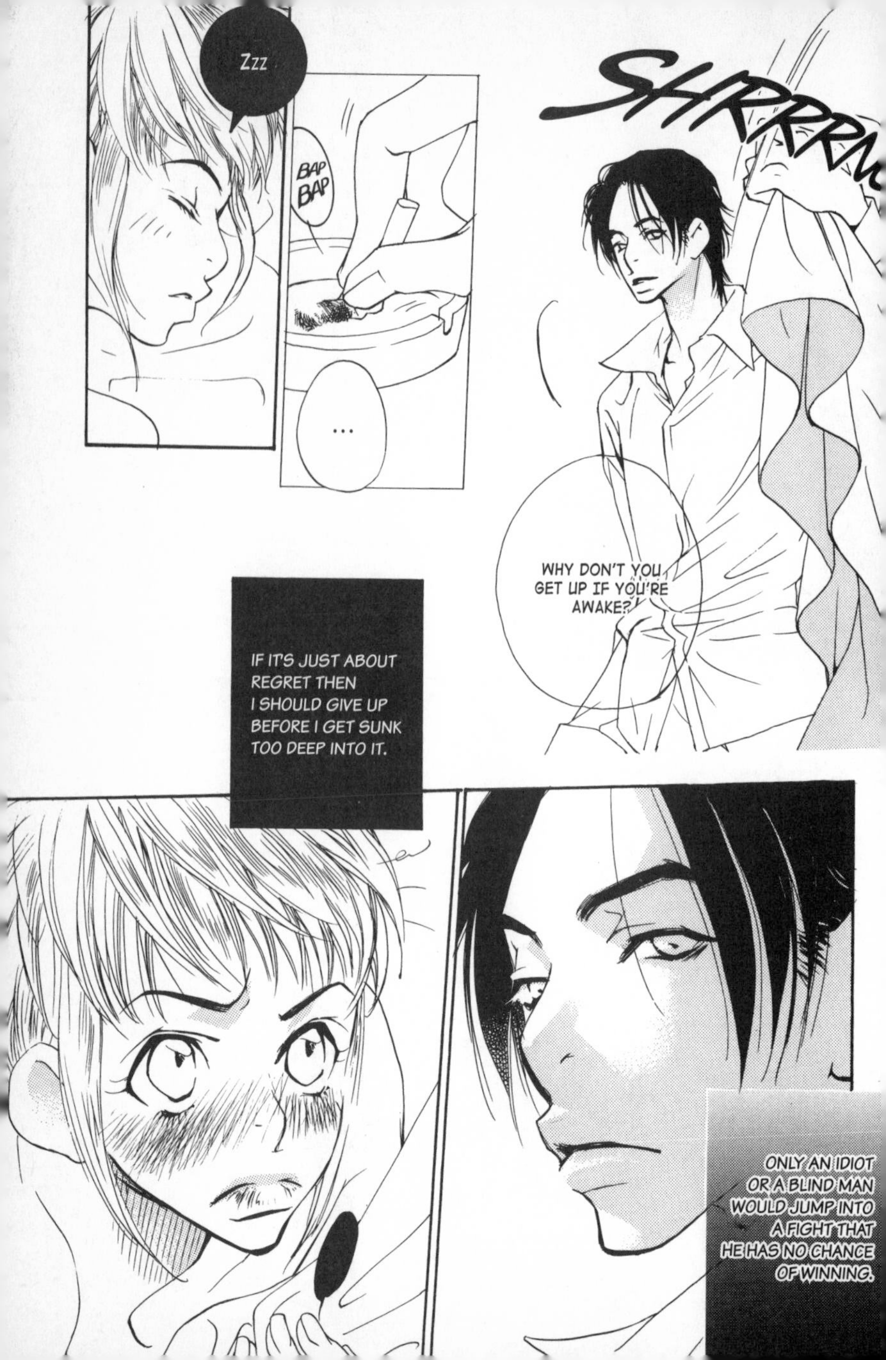

SHRRRM
Zzz
BAP BAP
...
WHY DON'T YOU GET UP IF YOU'RE AWAKE?!
IF IT'S JUST ABOUT REGRET THEN I SHOULD GIVE UP BEFORE I GET SUNK TOO DEEP INTO IT.
ONLY AN IDIOT OR A BLIND MAN WOULD JUMP INTO A FIGHT THAT HE HAS NO CHANCE OF WINNING.

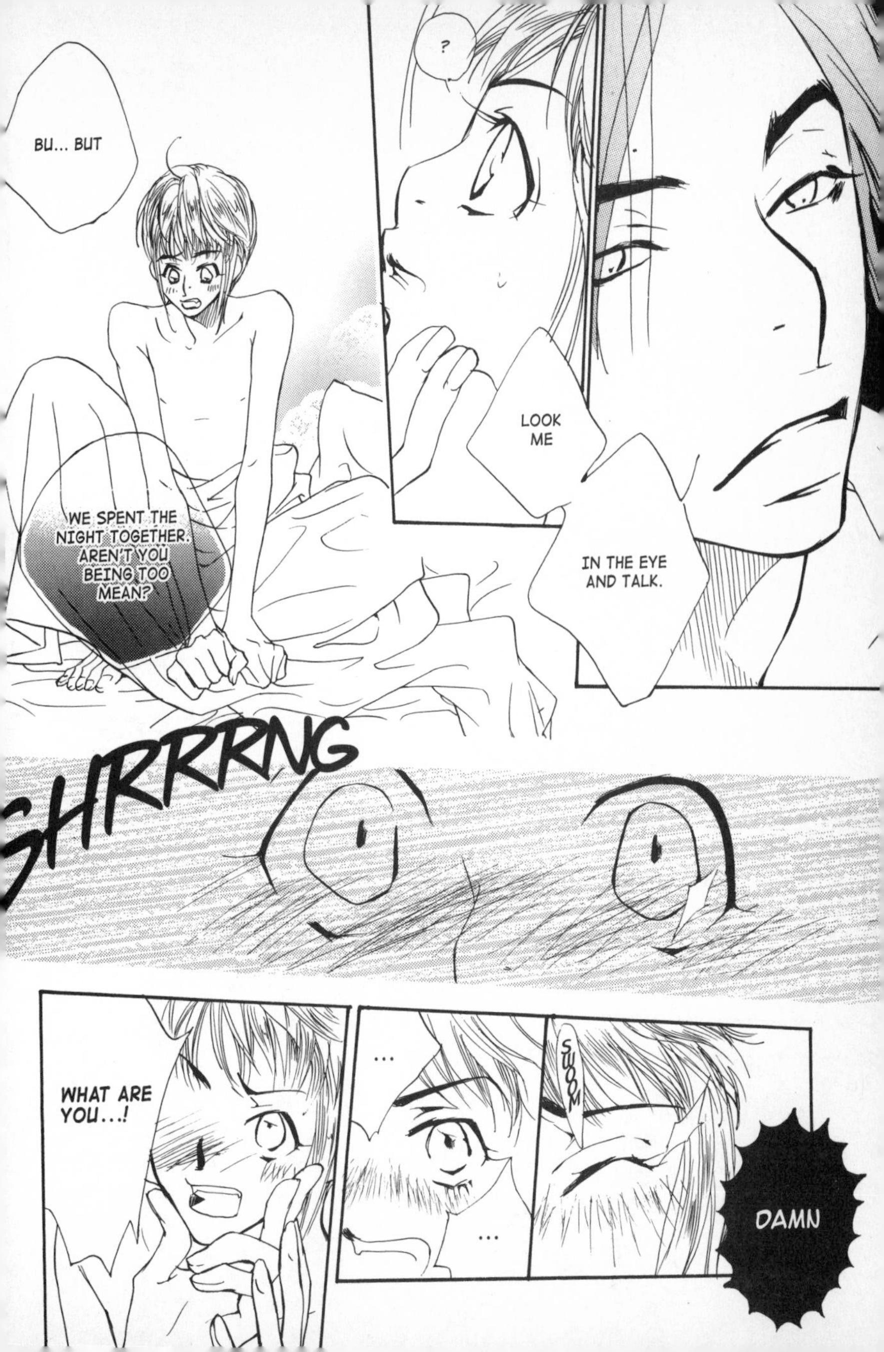
LOOK ME
IN THE EYE AND TALK.
?
BU... BUT
WE SPENT THE NIGHT TOGETHER. AREN'T YOU BEING TOO MEAN?
SHRRRNG
DAMN
SWOOM
...
...
WHAT ARE YOU...!

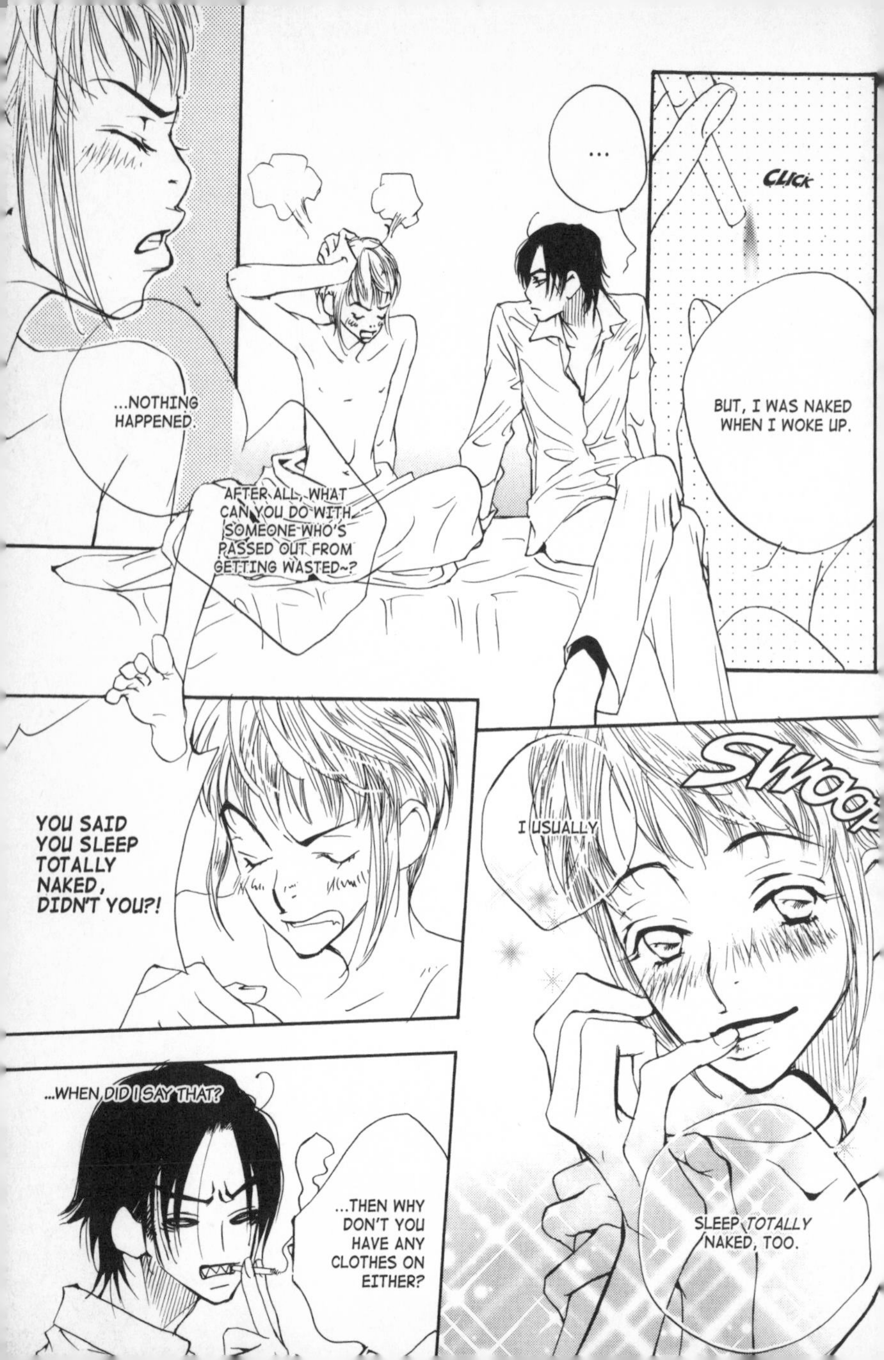
...
CLICK
BUT, I WAS NAKED WHEN I WOKE UP.
...NOTHING HAPPENED.
AFTER ALL, WHAT CAN YOU DO WITH SOMEONE WHO'S PASSED OUT FROM GETTING WASTED~?
YOU SAID YOU SLEEP TOTALLY NAKED, DIDN'T YOU?!
...WHEN DID I SAY THAT?
...THEN WHY DON'T YOU HAVE ANY CLOTHES ON EITHER?
SWOOP
I USUALLY
SLEEP *TOTALLY* NAKED, TOO.

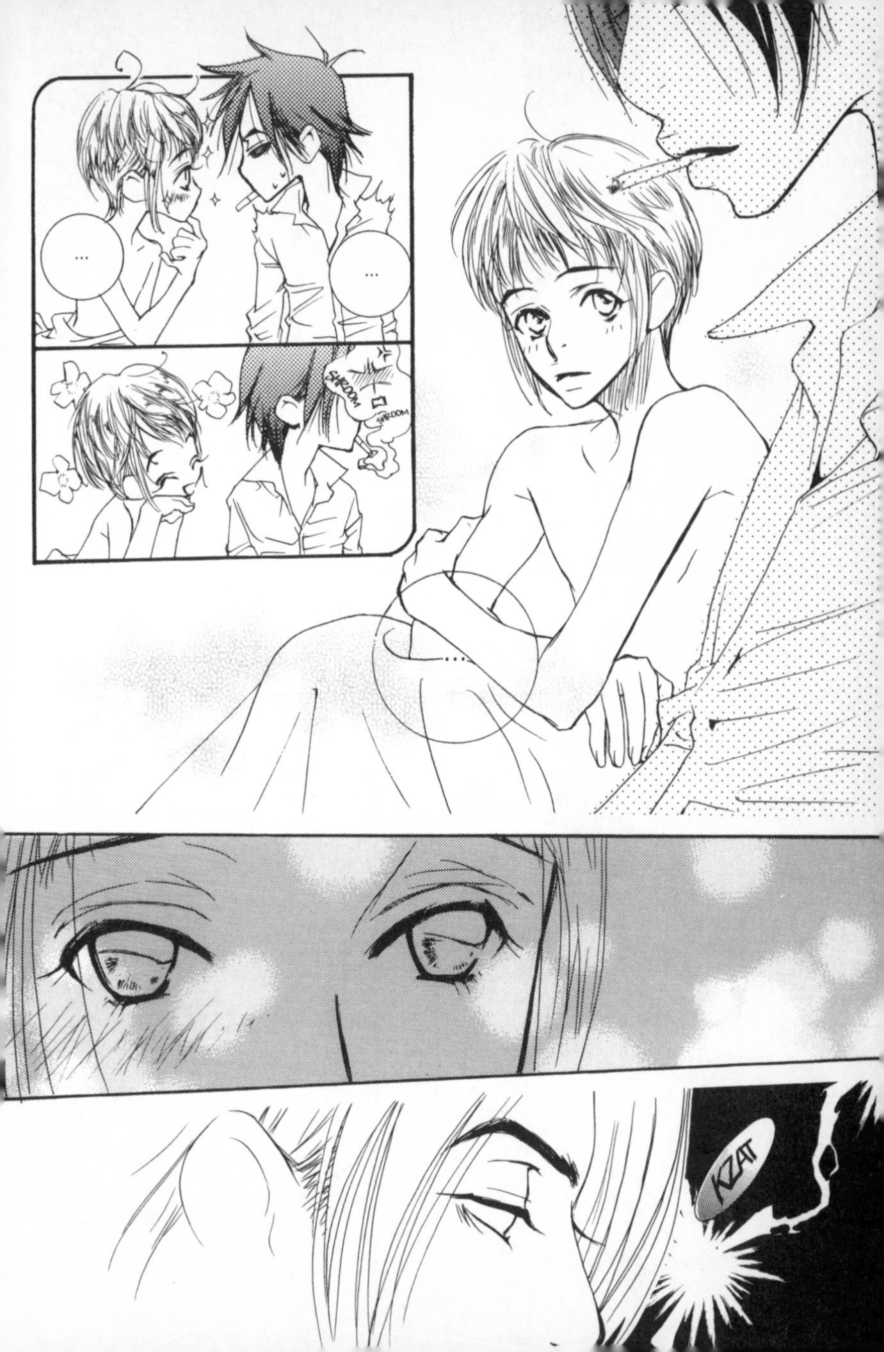
...
...
SHROOM
SHROOM
...
KZAT

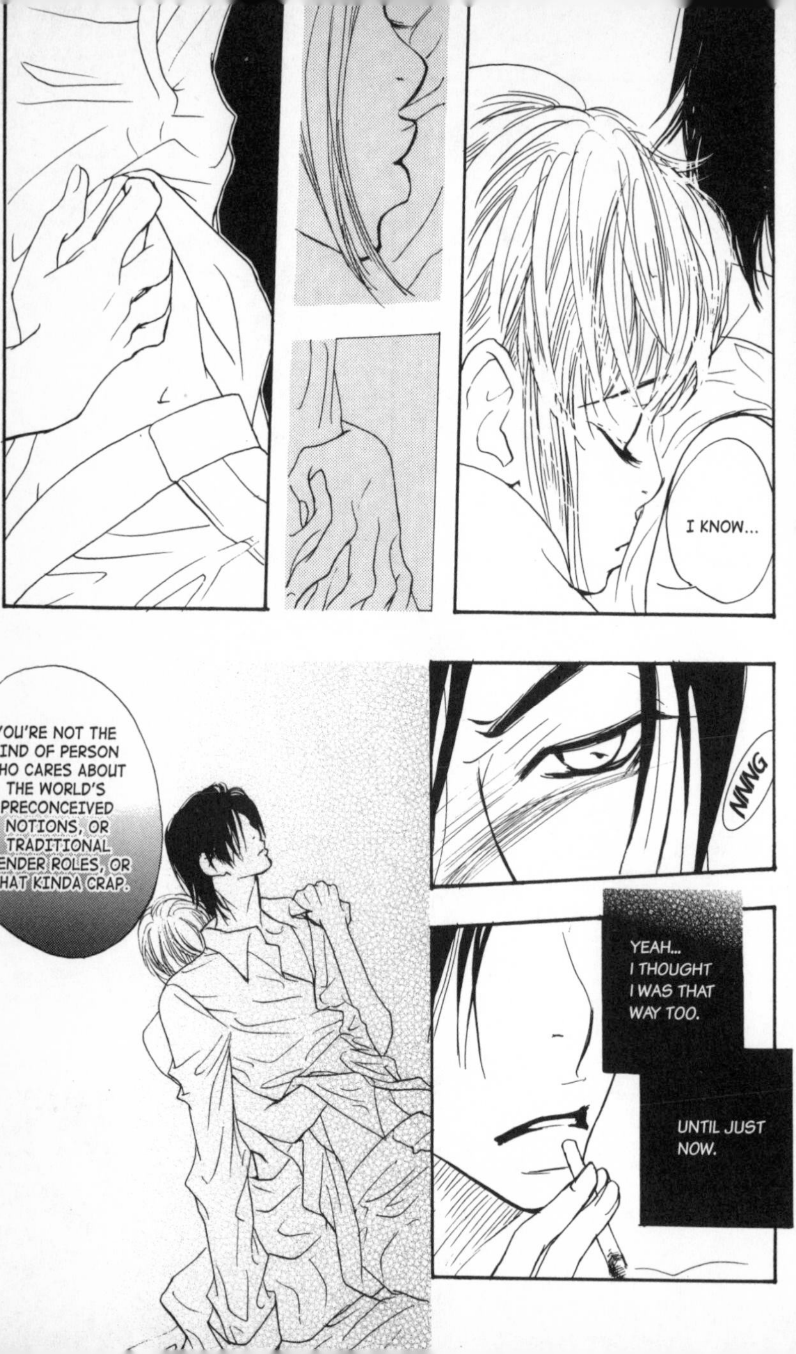
I KNOW...
NNNG
YOU'RE NOT THE KIND OF PERSON WHO CARES ABOUT THE WORLD'S PRECONCEIVED NOTIONS, OR TRADITIONAL GENDER ROLES, OR THAT KINDA CRAP.
YEAH... I THOUGHT I WAS THAT WAY TOO.
UNTIL JUST NOW.

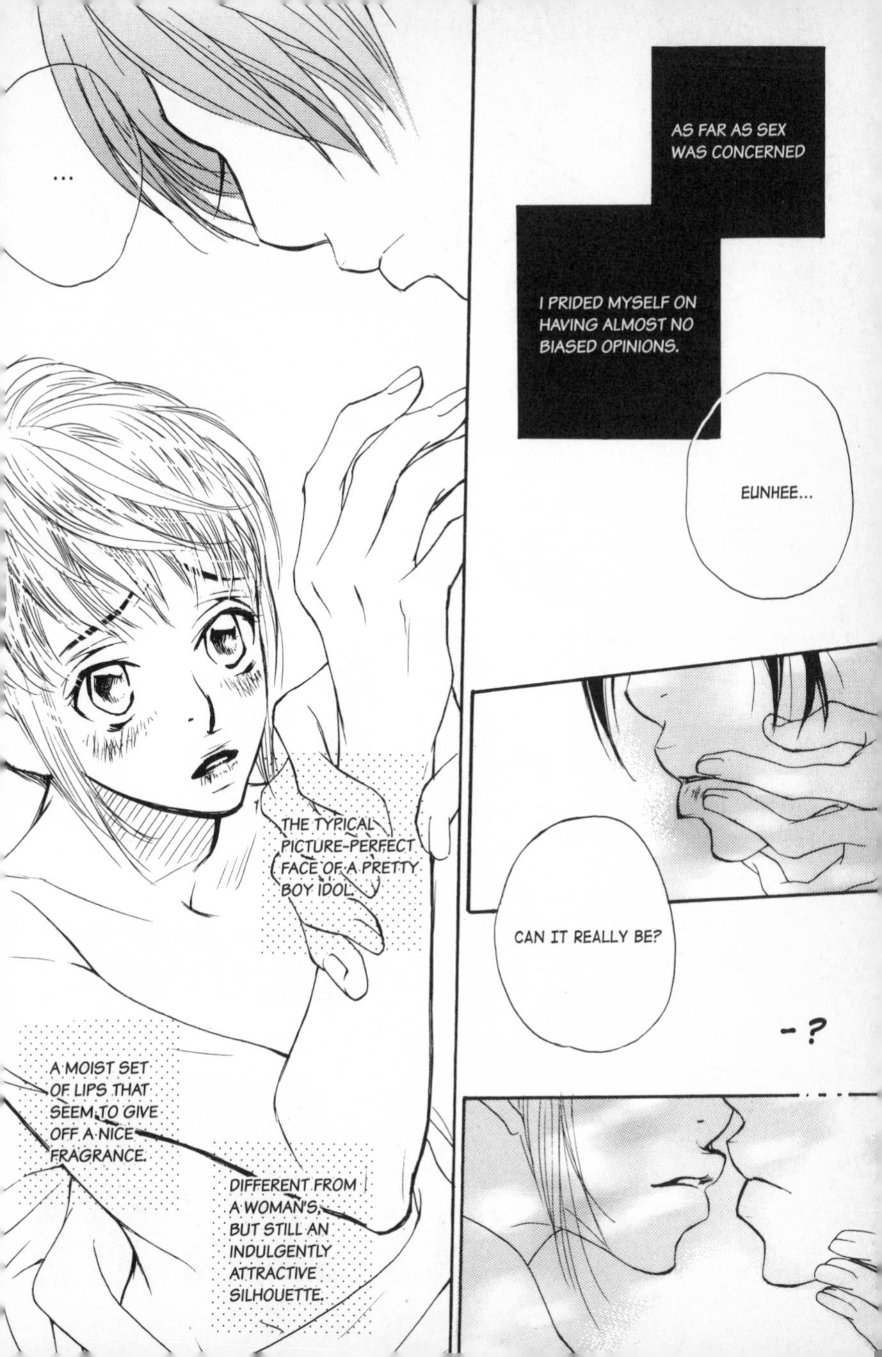
...
THE TYPICAL PICTURE-PERFECT FACE OF A PRETTY BOY IDOL.
A MOIST SET OF LIPS THAT SEEM TO GIVE OFF A NICE FRAGRANCE.
DIFFERENT FROM A WOMAN'S, BUT STILL AN INDULGENTLY ATTRACTIVE SILHOUETTE.
AS FAR AS SEX WAS CONCERNED
I PRIDED MYSELF ON HAVING ALMOST NO BIASED OPINIONS.
EUNHEE...
CAN IT REALLY BE?
-?

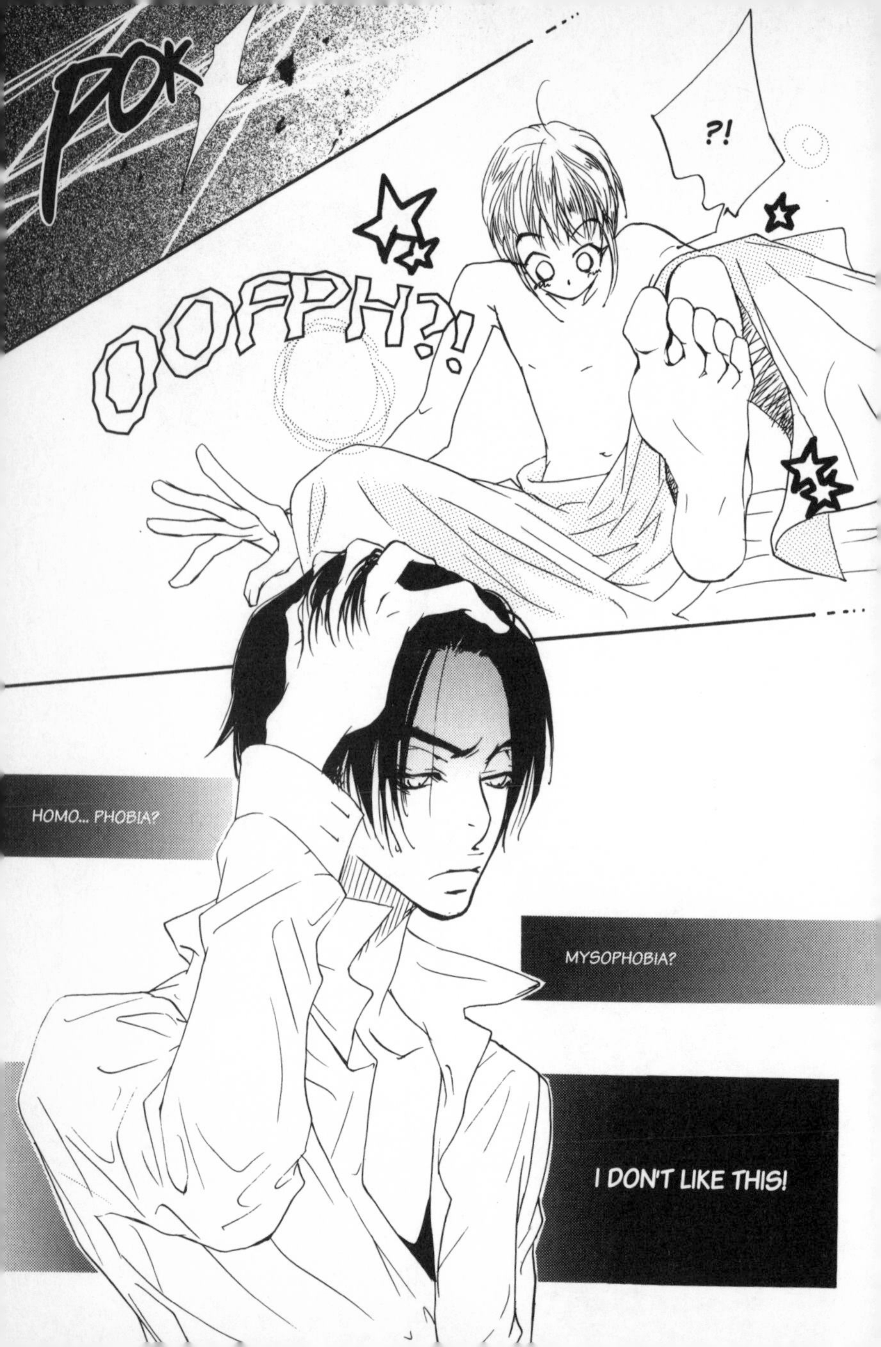
POK
?!
OOFPH?!
HOMO... PHOBIA?
MYSOPHOBIA?
I DON'T LIKE THIS!

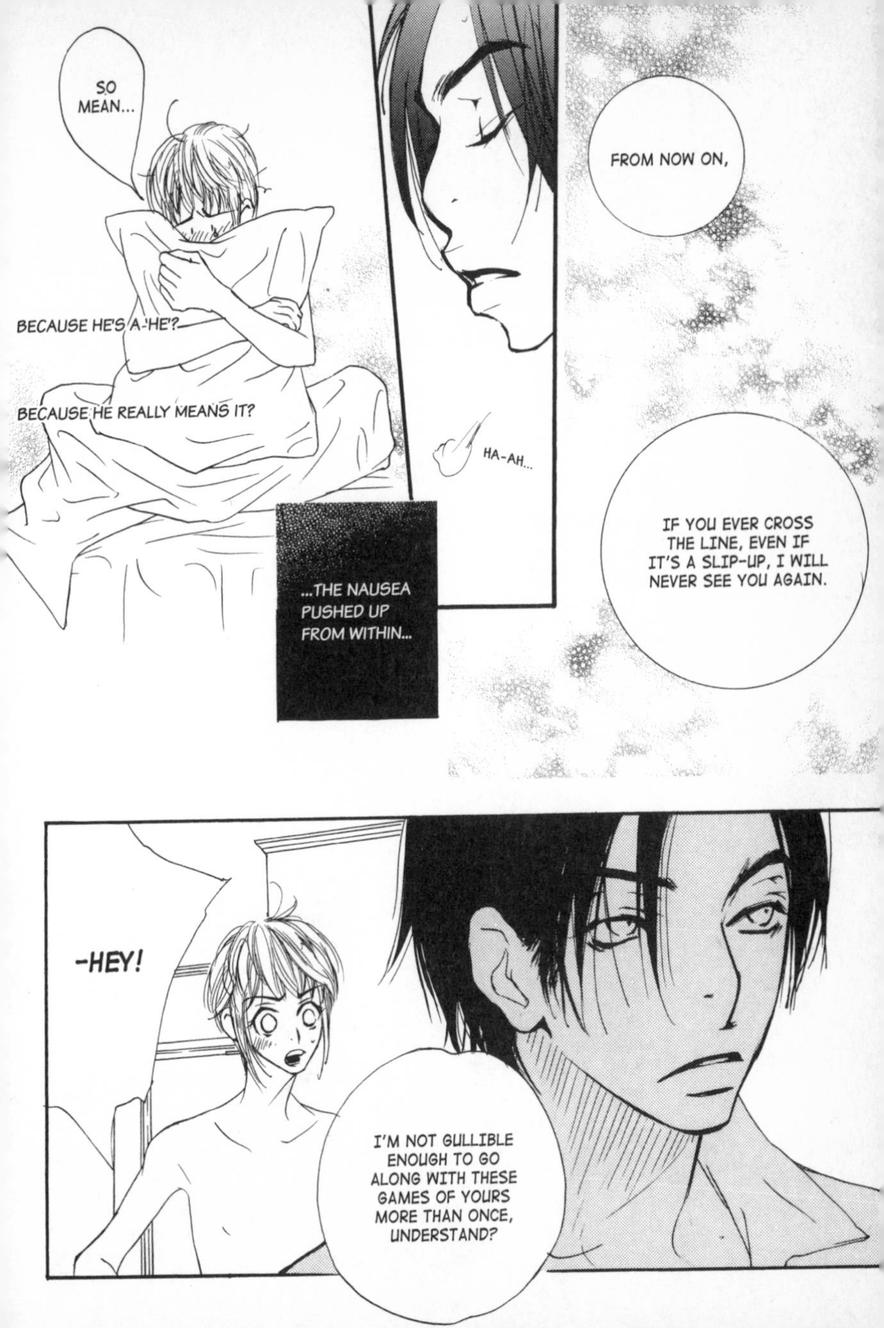
FROM NOW ON,
IF YOU EVER CROSS THE LINE, EVEN IF IT'S A SLIP-UP, I WILL NEVER SEE YOU AGAIN.
HA-AH...
SO MEAN...
BECAUSE HE'S A 'HE'?
BECAUSE HE REALLY MEANS IT?
...THE NAUSEA PUSHED UP FROM WITHIN...
I'M NOT GULLIBLE ENOUGH TO GO ALONG WITH THESE GAMES OF YOURS MORE THAN ONCE, UNDERSTAND?
-HEY!

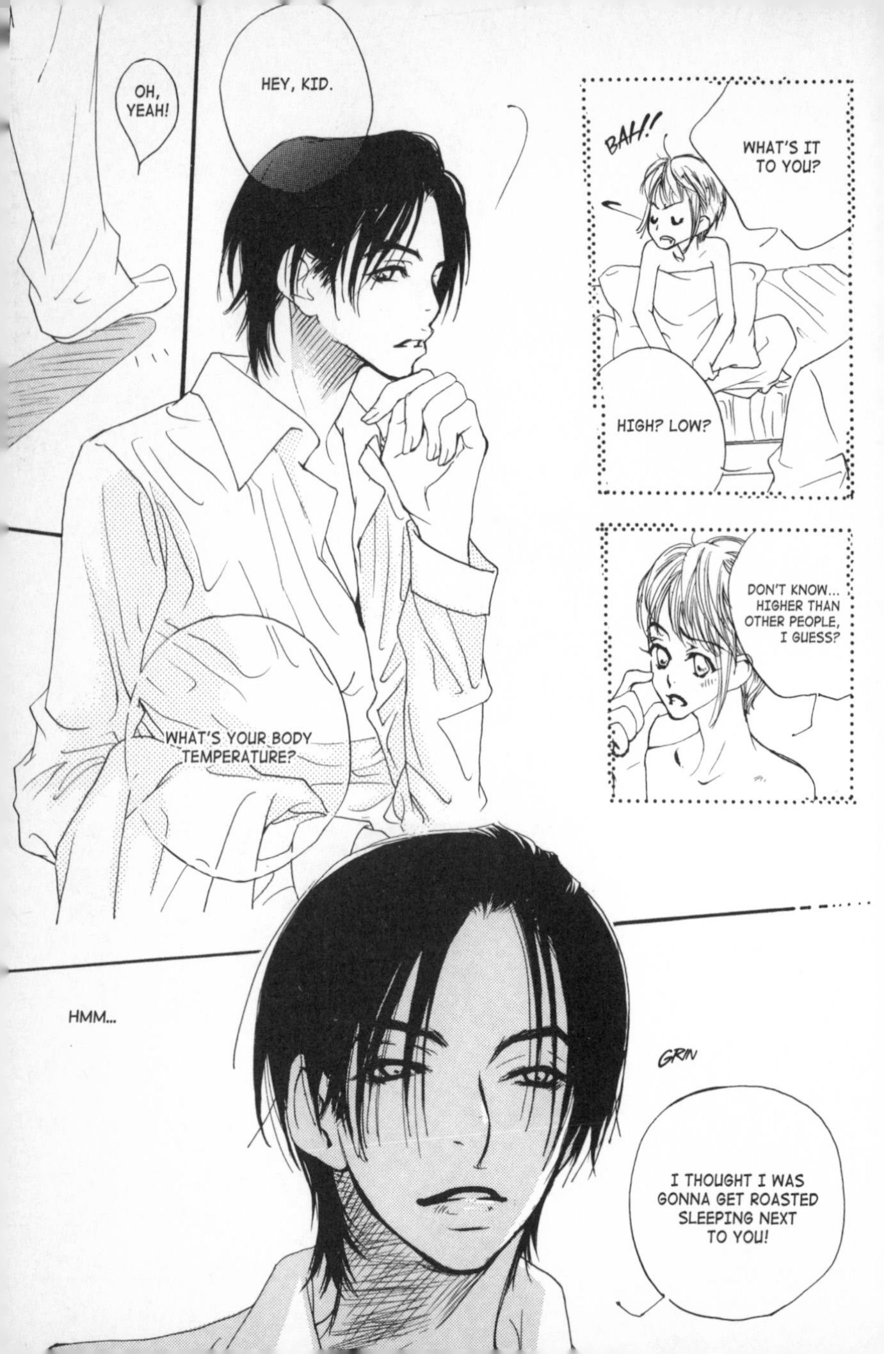
OH, YEAH!
HEY, KID.
WHAT'S YOUR BODY TEMPERATURE?
BAH!
WHAT'S IT TO YOU?
HIGH? LOW?
DON'T KNOW... HIGHER THAN OTHER PEOPLE, I GUESS?
HMM...
GRIN
I THOUGHT I WAS GONNA GET ROASTED SLEEPING NEXT TO YOU!

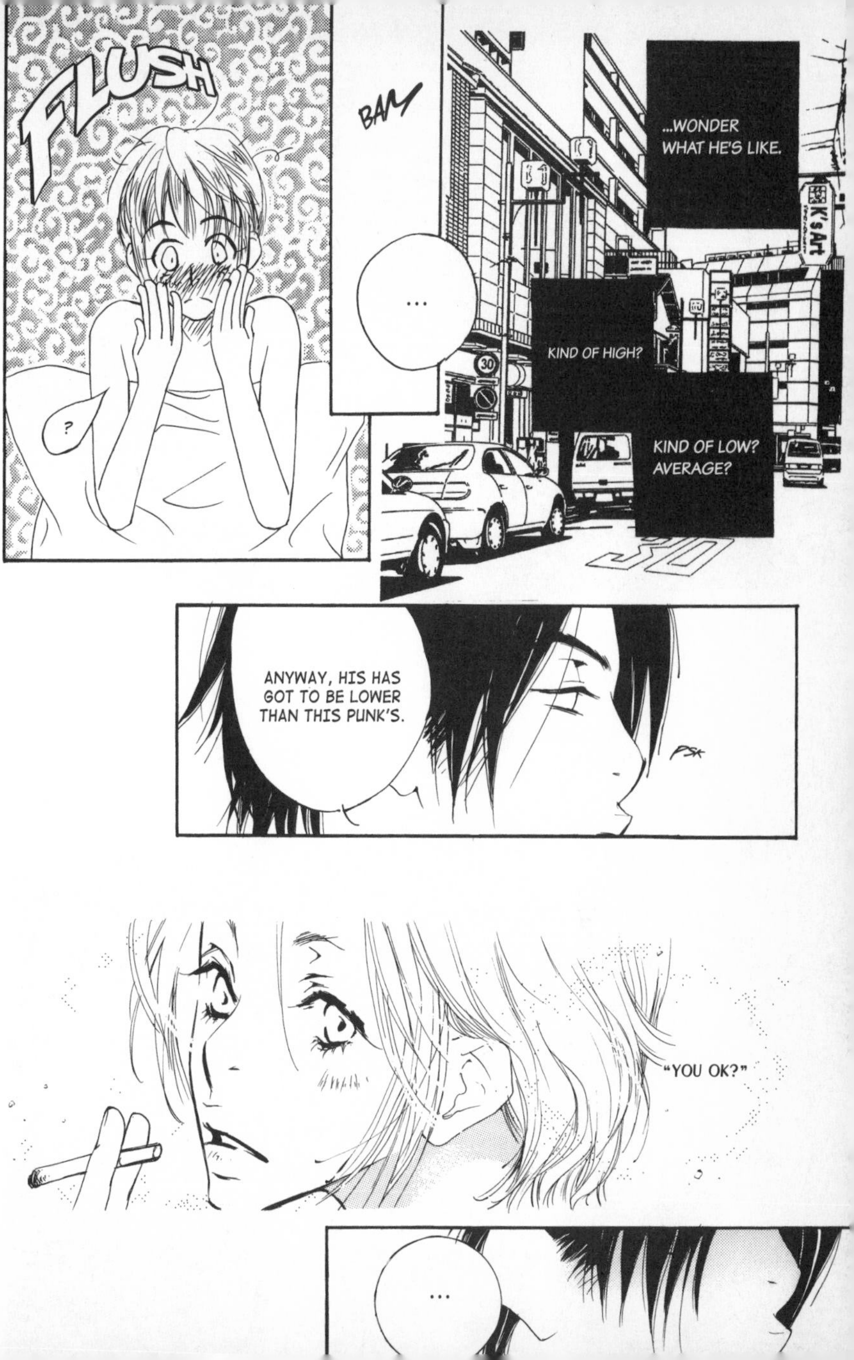
FLUSH
?
BAM
...
...WONDER
WHAT HE'S LIKE.
KIND OF HIGH?
KIND OF LOW?
AVERAGE?
ANYWAY, HIS HAS
GOT TO BE LOWER
THAN THIS PUNK'S.
PSK
"YOU OK?"
...

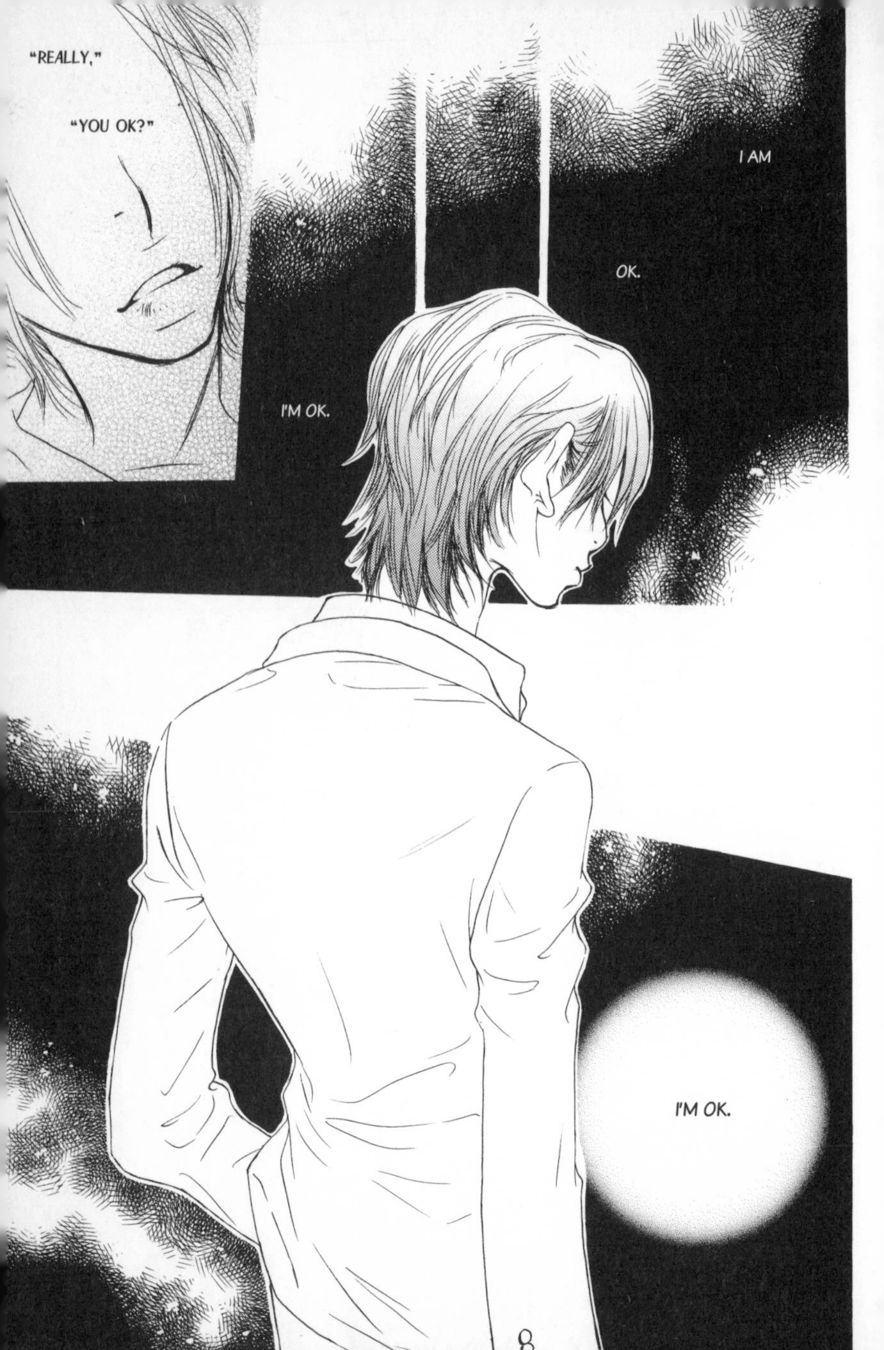
"REALLY,"
"YOU OK?"
I AM
OK.
I'M OK.
I'M OK.

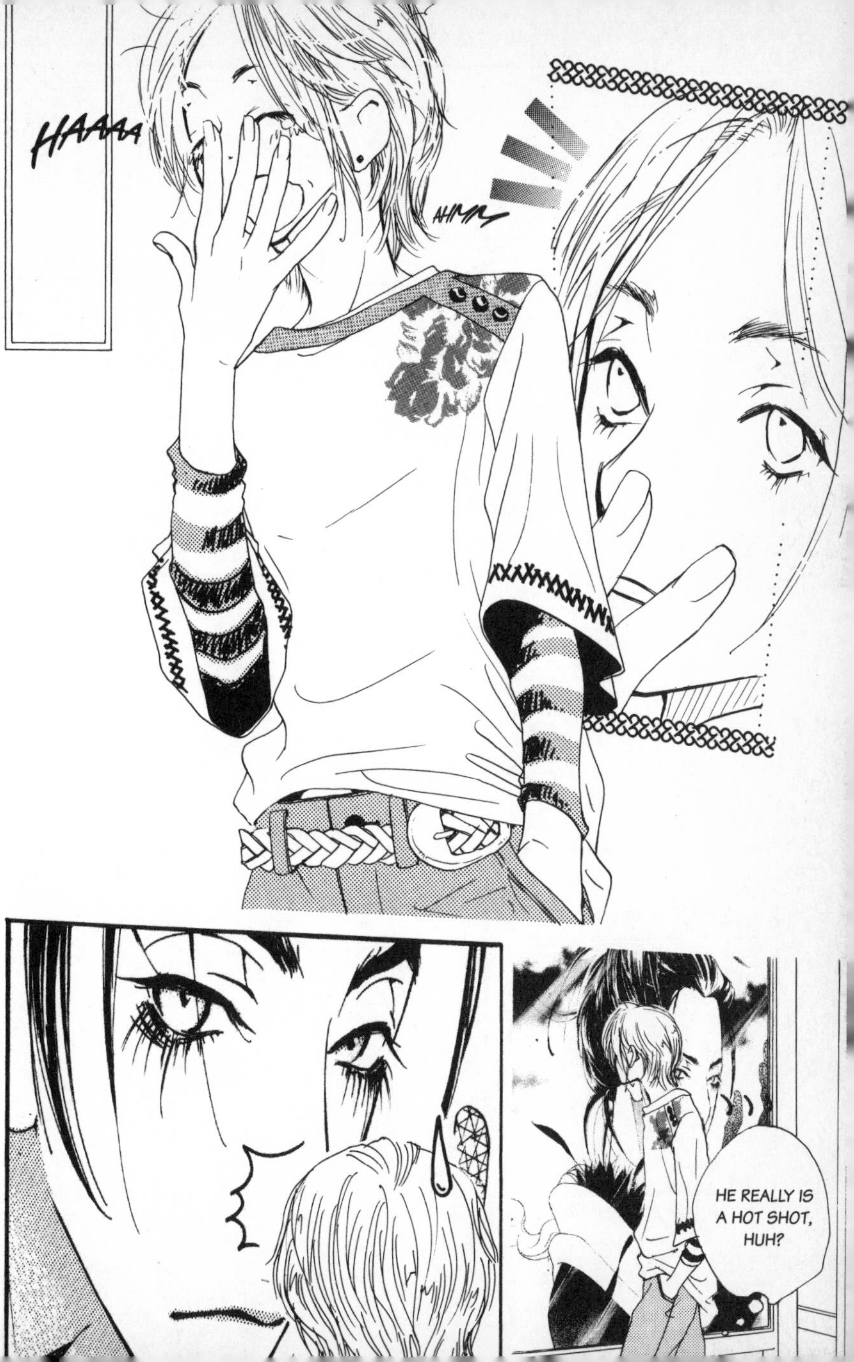
HAAAA
AHMM
HE REALLY IS A HOT SHOT, HUH?

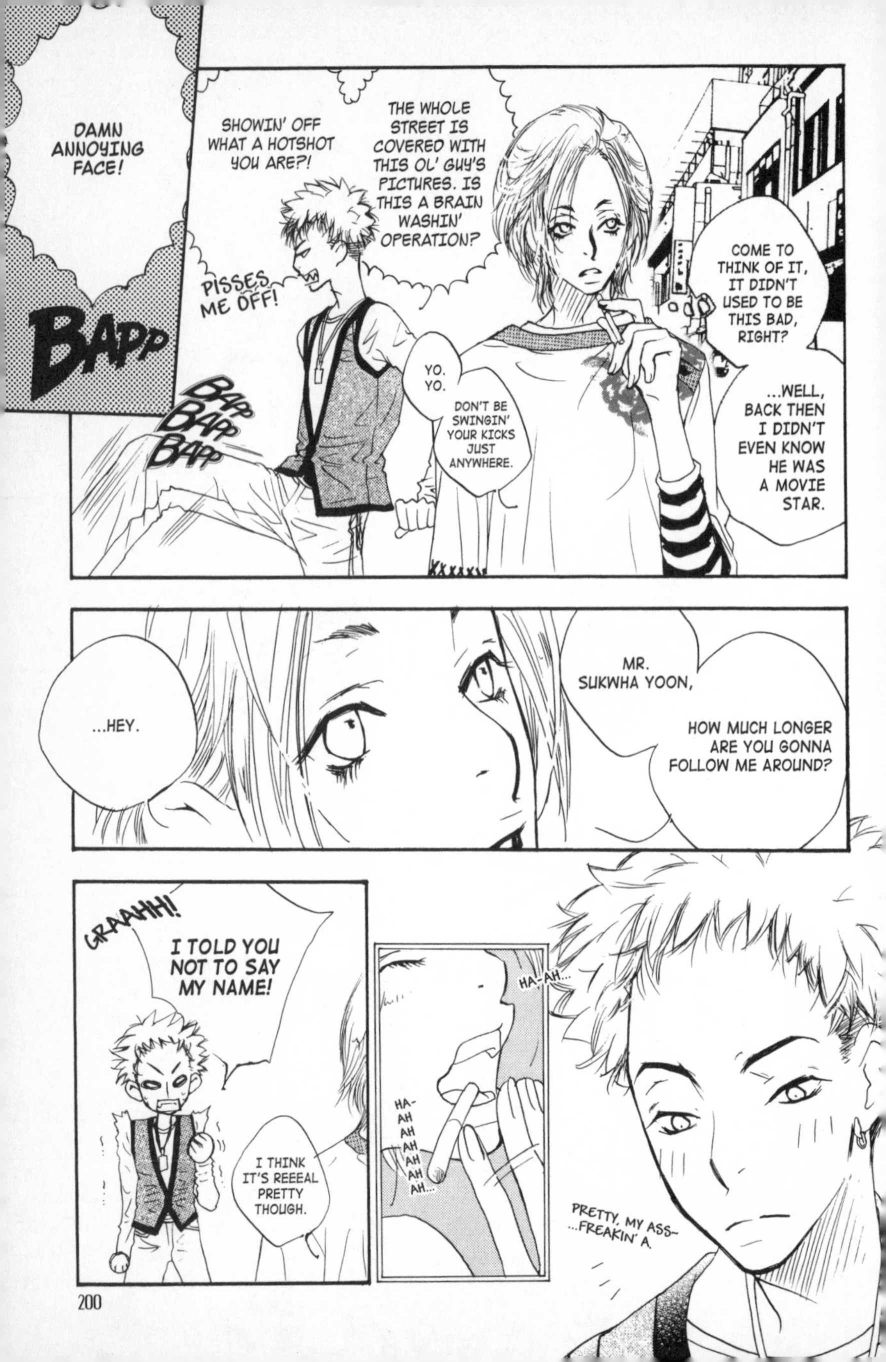
DAMN ANNOYING FACE!
SHOWIN' OFF WHAT A HOTSHOT YOU ARE?!
THE WHOLE STREET IS COVERED WITH THIS OL' GUY'S PICTURES. IS THIS A BRAIN WASHIN' OPERATION?
PISSES ME OFF!
BAPP
BAPP BAPP BAPP
YO. YO.
DON'T BE SWINGIN' YOUR KICKS JUST ANYWHERE.
COME TO THINK OF IT, IT DIDN'T USED TO BE THIS BAD, RIGHT?
...WELL, BACK THEN I DIDN'T EVEN KNOW HE WAS A MOVIE STAR.
...HEY.
MR. SUKWHA YOON,
HOW MUCH LONGER ARE YOU GONNA FOLLOW ME AROUND?
GRAAHH!
I TOLD YOU NOT TO SAY MY NAME!
I THINK IT'S REEEAL PRETTY THOUGH.
HA-AH...
HA-AH AH AH AH AH AH...
PRETTY, MY ASS-...FREAKIN' A.

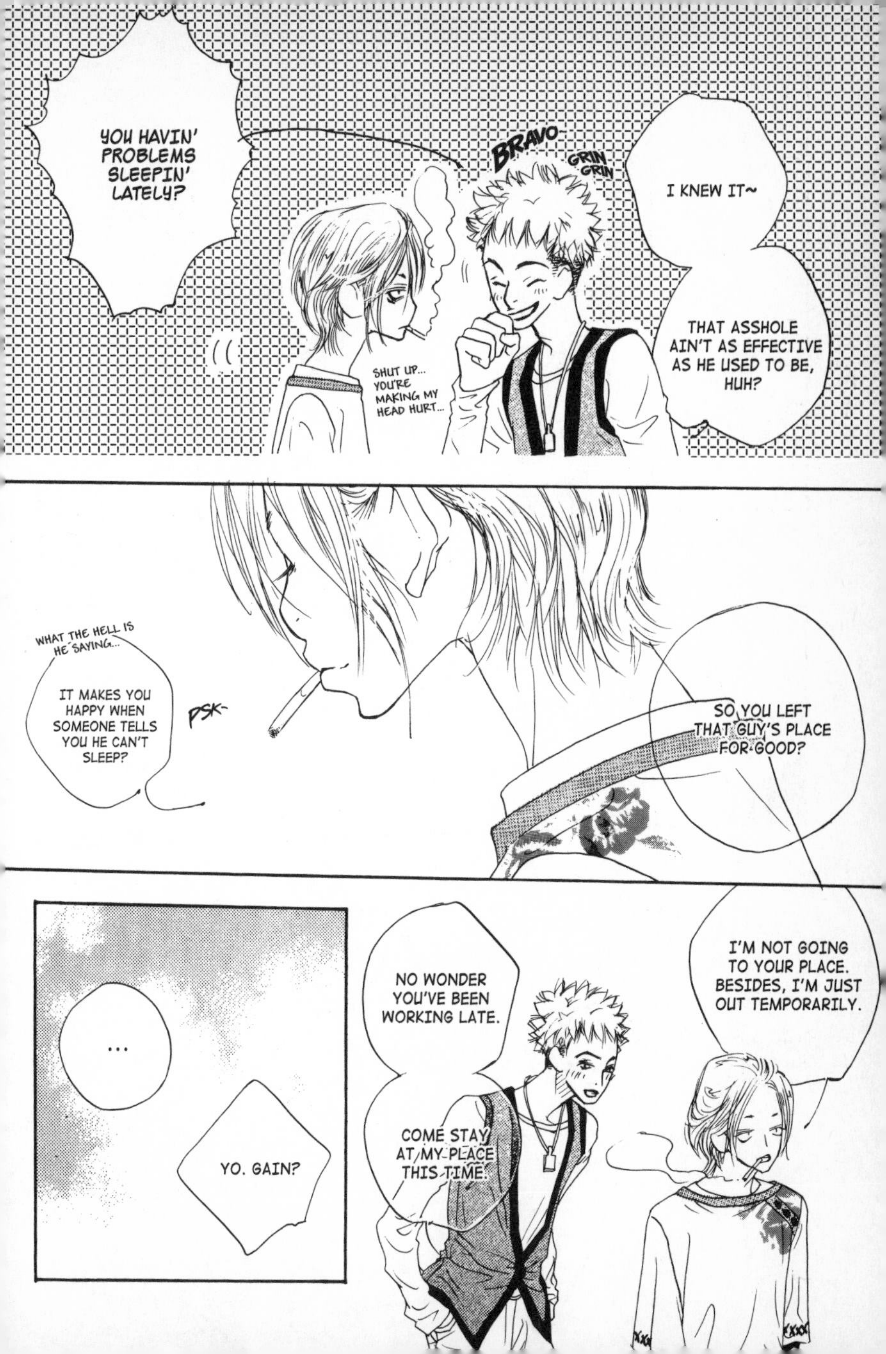

BRAVO-
GRIN GRIN
I KNEW IT~
THAT ASSHOLE AIN'T AS EFFECTIVE AS HE USED TO BE, HUH?
SHUT UP... YOU'RE MAKING MY HEAD HURT...
YOU HAVIN' PROBLEMS SLEEPIN' LATELY?
SO YOU LEFT THAT GUY'S PLACE FOR GOOD?
PSK-
IT MAKES YOU HAPPY WHEN SOMEONE TELLS YOU HE CAN'T SLEEP?
WHAT THE HELL IS HE SAYING...
I'M NOT GOING TO YOUR PLACE. BESIDES, I'M JUST OUT TEMPORARILY.
NO WONDER YOU'VE BEEN WORKING LATE.
COME STAY AT MY PLACE THIS TIME.
...
YO. GAIN?

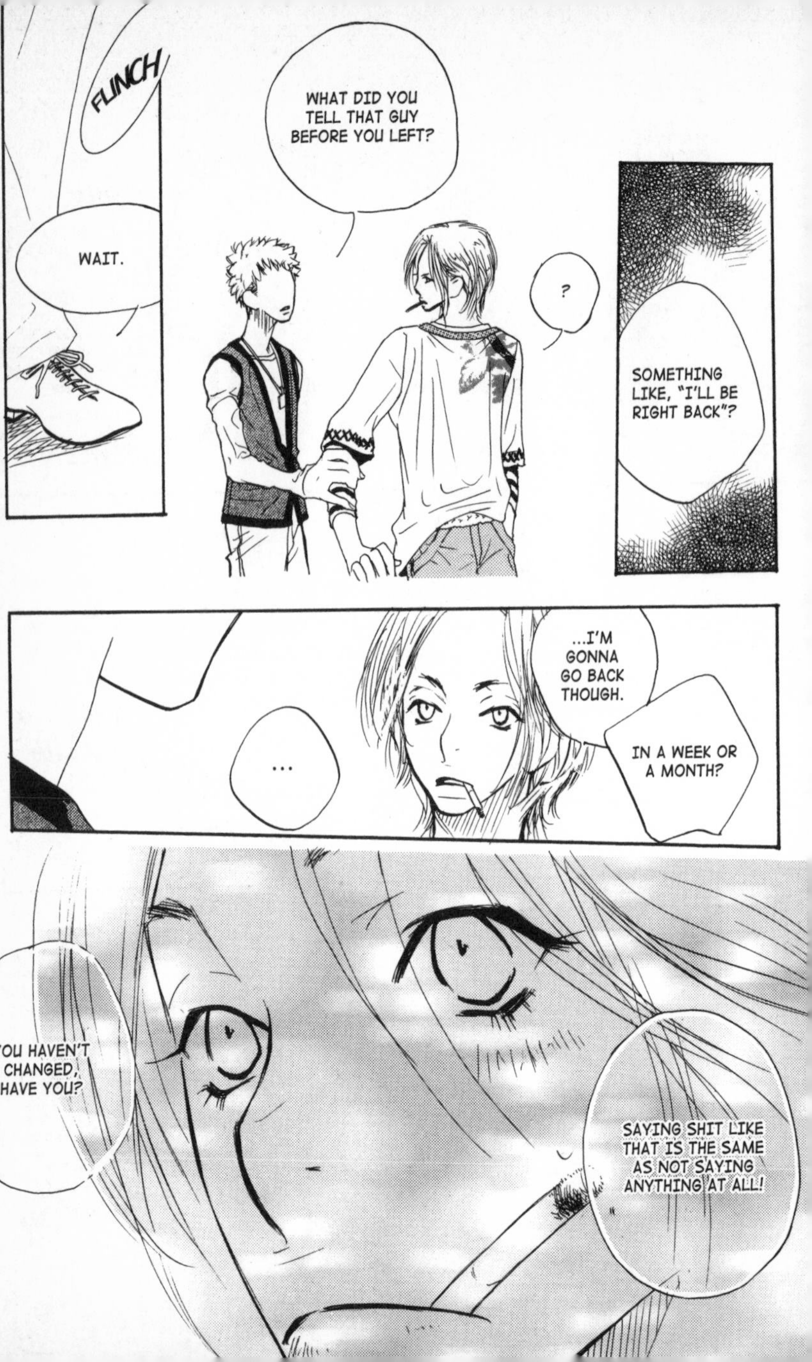
WAIT.
FLINCH
?
WHAT DID YOU TELL THAT GUY BEFORE YOU LEFT?
SOMETHING LIKE, "I'LL BE RIGHT BACK"?
...I'M GONNA GO BACK THOUGH.
IN A WEEK OR A MONTH?
...
SAYING SHIT LIKE THAT IS THE SAME AS NOT SAYING ANYTHING AT ALL!
YOU HAVEN'T CHANGED, HAVE YOU?

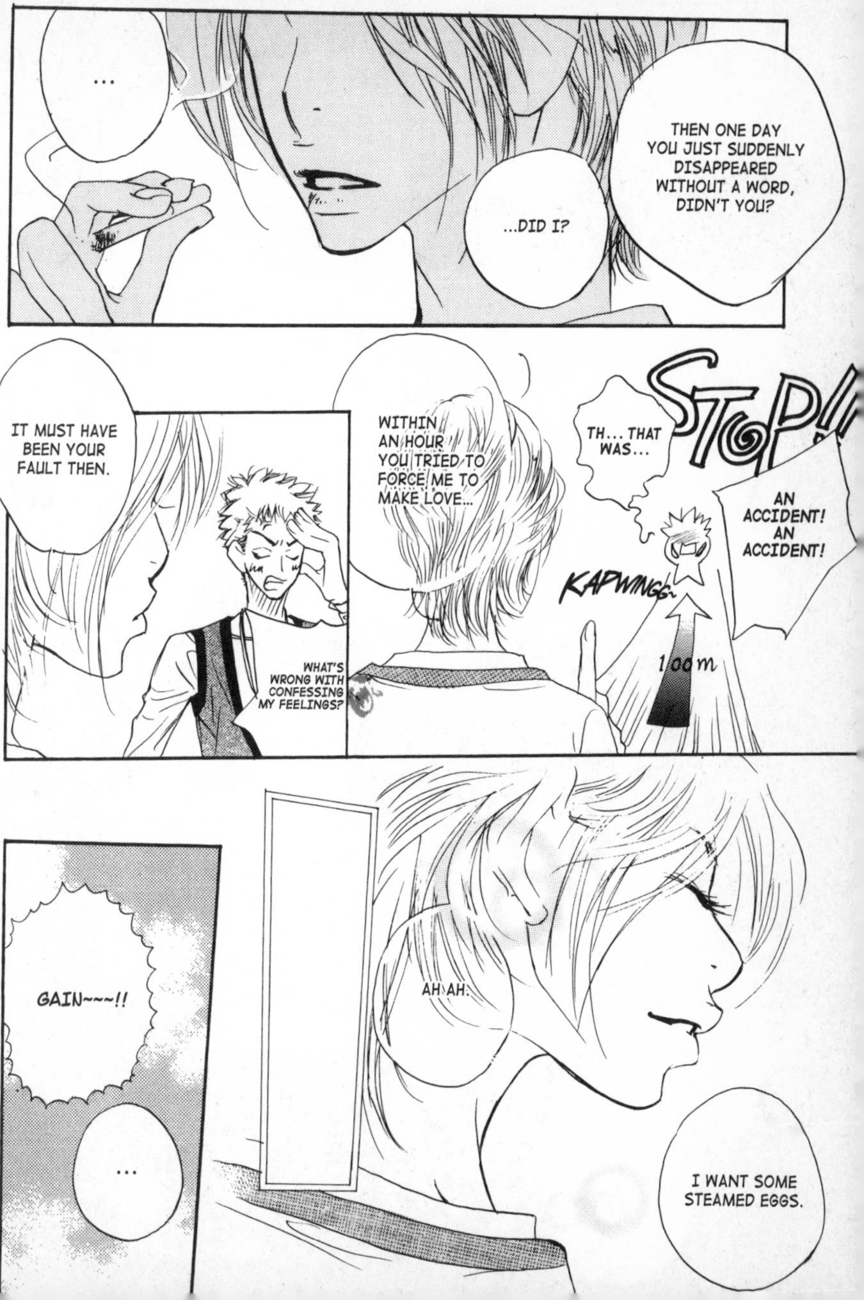
THEN ONE DAY YOU JUST SUDDENLY DISAPPEARED WITHOUT A WORD, DIDN'T YOU?
...DID I?
...
STOP!!
TH... THAT WAS...
AN ACCIDENT! AN ACCIDENT!
KAPWINGG~
100m
WITHIN AN HOUR YOU TRIED TO FORCE ME TO MAKE LOVE...
IT MUST HAVE BEEN YOUR FAULT THEN.
WHAT'S WRONG WITH CONFESSING MY FEELINGS?
AH AH.
I WANT SOME STEAMED EGGS.
GAIN~~~!!
...

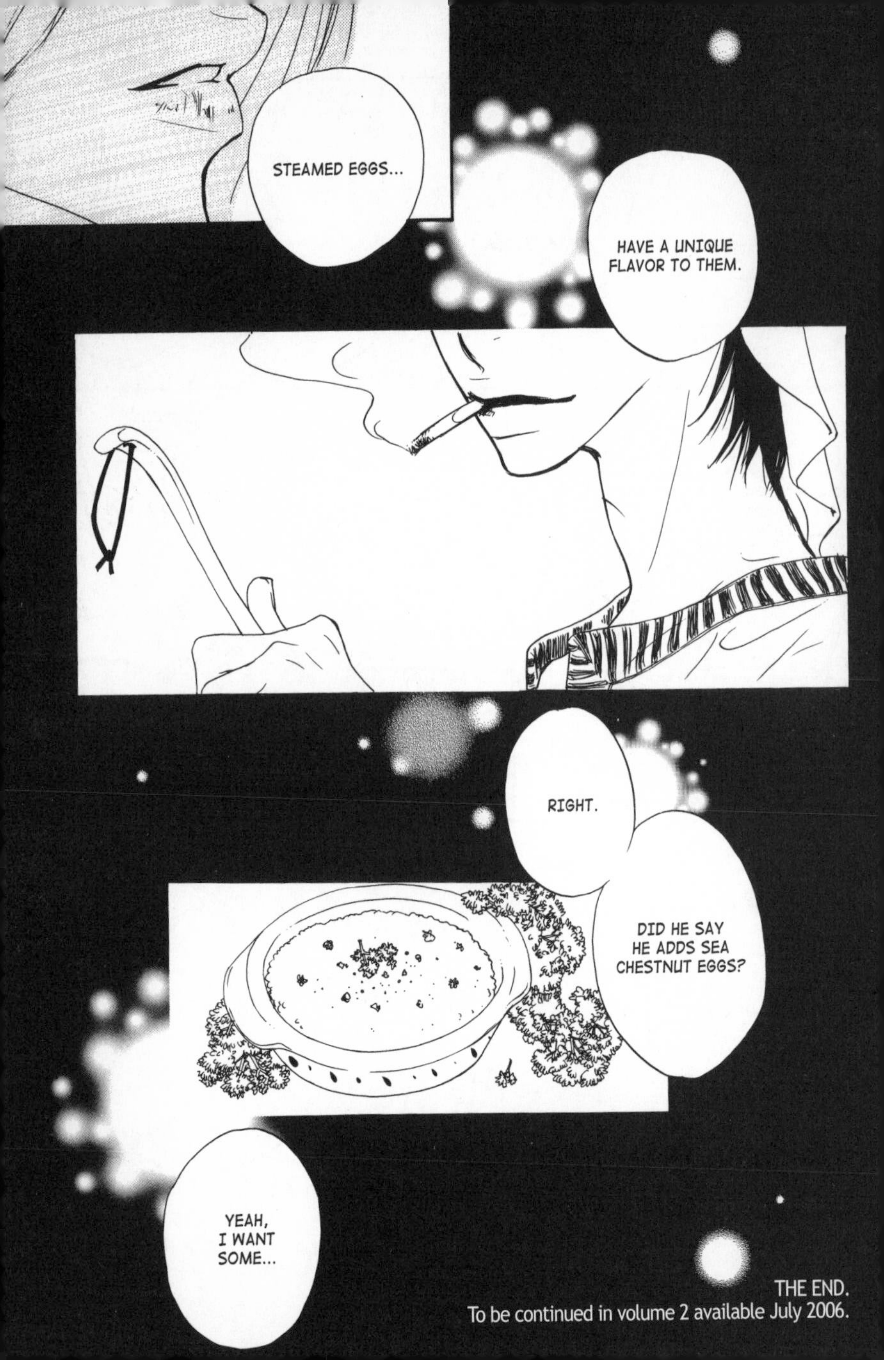
STEAMED EGGS...
HAVE A UNIQUE FLAVOR TO THEM.
RIGHT.
DID HE SAY HE ADDS SEA CHESTNUT EGGS?
YEAH, I WANT SOME...
THE END.
To be continued in volume 2 available July 2006.

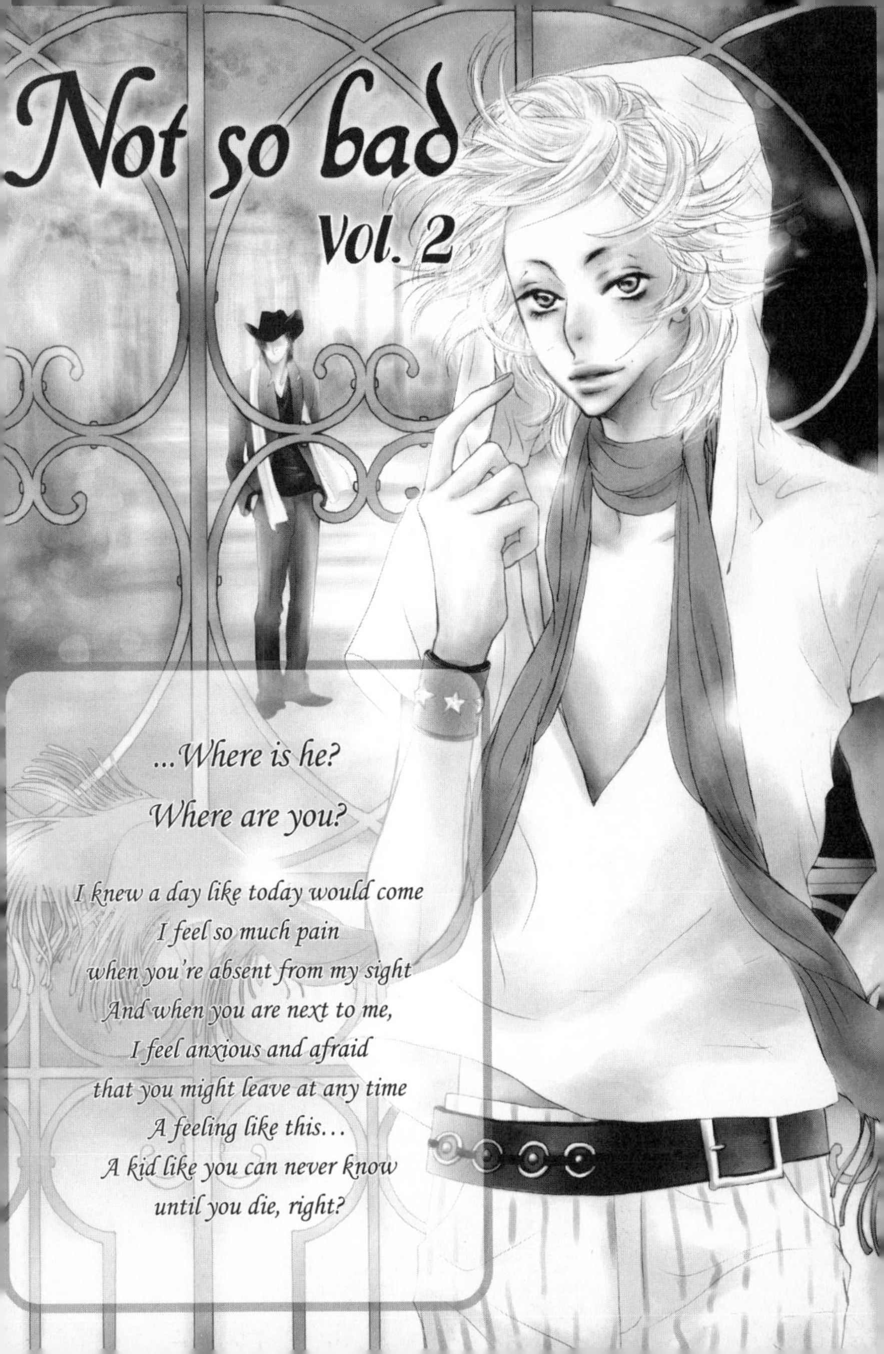
Not so bad
Vol. 2
...Where is he?
Where are you?
I knew a day like today would come
I feel so much pain
when you're absent from my sight
And when you are next to me,
I feel anxious and afraid
that you might leave at any time
A feeling like this...
A kid like you can never know
until you die, right?

HOT NETCOMICS TITLE

Scrumptious NETCOMICS Shonen-ai

Roureville

- E.HAE

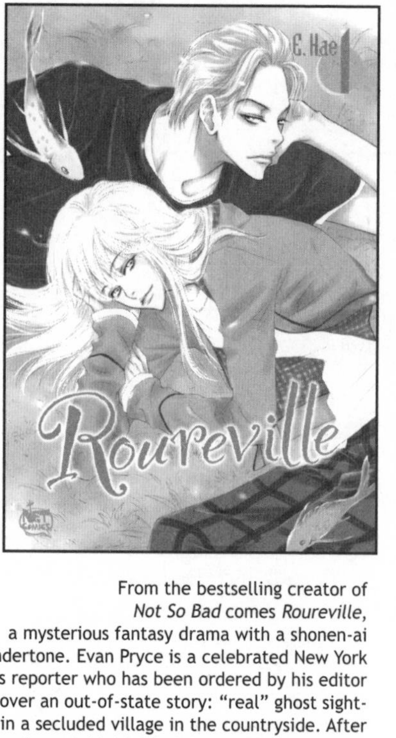

E. Hae
Roureville
NET COMICS

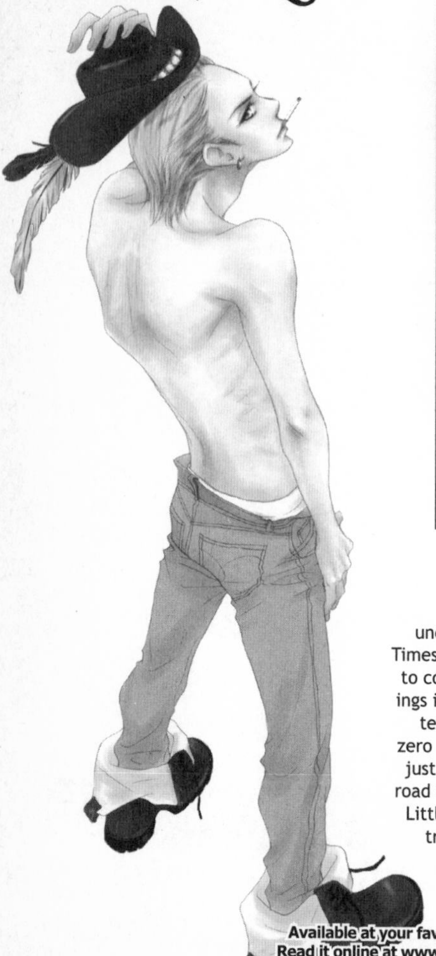

From the bestselling creator of *Not So Bad* comes *Roureville*, a mysterious fantasy drama with a shonen-ai undertone. Evan Pryce is a celebrated New York Times reporter who has been ordered by his editor to cover an out-of-state story: "real" ghost sightings in a secluded village in the countryside. After ten days of driving by sleepy rural villages with zero results, our lost and exhausted New Yorker is just about ready to give up. But then suddenly, a road sign pointing to "Roureville" catches his eye. Little does he know that the end of his long road trip is just the beginning of an incredible tale.

Available at your favorite bookstores.
Read it online at www.NETCOMICS.com!